I0815238

# SECRETS ON DISPLAY

# SECRETS ON DISPLAY

## Stories and Spycraft from the INTERNATIONAL SPY MUSEUM

Edited by Mark Stout
and Sarah-Jane Corke

First Printing

Published by the University Press of Kansas (Lawrence, Kansas 66045), which was organized by the Kansas Board of Regents and is operated and funded by Emporia State University, Fort Hays State University, Kansas State University, Pittsburg State University, the University of Kansas, and Wichita State University.

Library of Congress Cataloging-in-Publication Data

Names: Stout, Mark, 1964– editor. | Corke, Sarah-Jane, editor.
Title: Secrets on Display : Stories and Spycraft from the International Spy Museum / Mark Stout and Sarah-Jane Corke, editors.
Description: Lawrence : University Press of Kansas, [2025] | Includes bibliographical references and index.
Identifiers: LCCN 2024060647 (print) | LCCN 2024060648 (ebook) | ISBN 9780700638802 (cloth) | ISBN 9780700638819 (ebook)
Subjects: LCSH: International Spy Museum (Washington, DC) | Espionage—Museums. | Espionage—History. | BISAC: TRUE CRIME / Espionage | HISTORY / Modern / 20th Century / General
Classification: LCC UB270 .P493 2025 (print) | LCC UB270 (ebook) | DDC 327.12074/753—dc23/eng/20250408
LC record available at https://lccn.loc.gov/2024060647.
LC ebook record available at https://lccn.loc.gov/2024060648.

British Library Cataloguing-in-Publication Data is available.
Authorised Representative Details: Easy Access System Europe
Mustamäe tee 50, 10621 Tallinn, Estonia | gpsr.requests@easproject.com

Printed in the United States of America

The paper used in this publication meets the minimum requirements of the American National Standard for Permanence of Paper for Printed Library Materials Z39.48–1992.

# Contents

Color photo galleries follow pages 82, 114, and 210.

# Acknowledgments

**Mark Stout and Sarah-Jane Corke**

This project could never have been undertaken without the support of the team at the International Spy Museum. We would especially like to thank the following current and former members of the museum staff, in alphabetical order: Amanda Abrell, Dena Adams, Alexis Albion, Afua Anokwa, Tamara Christian, Joanna Church, Chris Costa, Mikaela Ferrara, Andrew Hammond, Laura Hicken, Kathryn Keane, Amanda Ohlke, Sandy Poindexter, Emily Rens, Nancy Sanders, Anna Slafer, Craig Sorvillo, Madison Strausser, Dan Treado, and Lauren vonBechmann. During this project, Alexis, Laura, Dan, and Lauren, in particular, saw a whole lot more of us than they probably wanted to, and yet they remained enthusiastic and gave more than generously of their time and seemingly boundless expertise.

In addition, we want to acknowledge H. Keith Melton and Karen Melton. Many of the best artifacts they collected are featured in this book, and Keith was immensely helpful in helping us craft captions as well as in writing an interesting foreword for this book. Similarly, we would like to acknowledge Francis Russell Dominguez and Lara Blair Dominguez as collectors of historic artifacts and friends to both of us and of the International Spy Museum.

Special thanks are also certainly due to Jonathan Best, Jack O'Connor, Sara Parsons, and Cynthia Storer for their commitment to bringing this project forward.

We would also like to express our gratitude to both Ivan Harbour and Mark Ramirez for sitting down with us to discuss the design of the museum. It was fascinating to see the ways in which "history" and "intelligence" could come alive in an architectural design. Calder Walton was of great assistance in the early phases of this project. We are also grateful for the support and important contributions and encouragement of Nada Bakos, John Fox, Aki Peritz, David Priess, Nick Reynolds, and Katie Keegin Viamari when this book was in its infancy. We would also like to acknowledge the two students at the University of New Brunswick (UNB), Henry Michael Nadeau and Bradley Garlie, who read and offered comments on the full manuscript as we endeavored to make it accessible to a vast audience. UNB also came through with the Harrison McCain Foundation Grant in aid of Scholarly Book Publishing, without which this manuscript could not have been completed.

We are also extremely grateful to Joyce Harrison of the University Press of Kansas. It is hard to imagine a better or more genial editor to work with. Many thanks are also due to Managing Editor Kelly Chrisman Jacques and freelance copy editor Jon Howard for their editorial work.

Mark Stout would like to thank his wife, Pamela Stout. She probably thinks I'm crazy for embarking on projects like this, and they certainly don't make her life any better, yet she supports me in pursuing them.

Sarah-Jane Corke would like to acknowledge the love and support of her birth mother, Mary Carol Tatar, and her husband, Andrew Tatar, who serve as an inspiration to her every day. She would also like to thank her husband, David Ian MaGee, who is excited that she is finally publishing a book with pictures in it. Dave, you are my rock, I could not do what I do without you.

To support intelligence history in North America Mark Stout and Sarah-Jane Corke have donated all royalties from this book to the Society for Intelligence History, which is a non-profit organization. If you are interested in also supporting this worthy cause, please visit https://www.intelligencehistory.org.

# Foreword

**Colonel Christopher P. Costa, United States Army, retired**
**Executive Director, International Spy Museum**

In 2018, I was fortunate to be selected as the new executive director of the International Spy Museum. I had already served 35 years as a career intelligence officer in the United States Army and in national security positions from combat zones to the White House. But like many of my former colleagues, I wanted to continue to serve, share my experiences, and give back to the community. Taking the helm as only the second director of this one-of-its-kind museum would provide me a unique platform to help educate a global audience about the mysterious world of intelligence, espionage, and national security.

I assumed this position at a busy time. After almost 17 years in its original Penn Quarter location, the museum moved in spring 2019 to its new, purpose-built facility in the L'Enfant Plaza neighborhood of Washington, DC. The reimagined exhibitions and our world-class collection of artifacts tell stories in an immersive and engaging way. They present a comprehensive look at how spying has shaped our world. And we do not shy away from the tough issues. Stories showcase the many roles individuals play in spying and intelligence work, from the agents and their handlers in the field who collect intelligence or carry out covert operations to the technical wizards who develop the critical spy gadgets that support them. From "mud to space," these stories include jaw-dropping objects, such as a section of the Berlin Tunnel and an Amber drone, a predecessor to the famous Predator. Of course, the museum's educational mission extends well beyond the experiences at our site in the nation's capital. Each year, we reach millions of people of all ages from around the world through our onsite and virtual programs, workshops, SpyCast, YouTube offerings, special exhibitions, and website materials. Our goal is to be the go-to place for all things SPY.

In 2019, the museum hosted the inaugural conference of the North American Society for Intelligence History, founded by the editors of this volume, the former museum historian Dr. Mark Stout and Dr. Sarah-Jane Corke. This volume consists primarily of versions of papers presented at that conference, allowing readers to sample a range of engaging intelligence history written by leading intelligence scholars and historians. It is also a visual record of the breadth of the International Spy Museum's collection, offering a sampling of what visitors can see on display and a rare glimpse of artifacts not on display. Readers can indulge themselves intellectually and visually in this richly rewarding book.

Intelligence is a profoundly important topic for understanding our world. Beyond that, however, it is also a topic that intrigues and captivates. I hope that you will find fascination, wonder, and a sense of discovery in this volume as it pulls back the curtain on the shadowy world of espionage and intelligence.

# Foreword

**H. Keith Melton**

This book is about passions: my own lifelong passion to find and obtain the world's most obscure and exciting espionage artifacts; the passion of historians and scholars to study these artifacts to better understand spycraft; and the passion of the International Spy Museum to preserve and display these artifacts in trust for future generations and to educate the public about the world of espionage and intelligence. All three passions came together when in 2017 I donated my personal collection of objects to the museum.

Most of the objects depicted in this book are the result of 40 years collecting, from the world's first microdot to the laptop used by Russian agent Anna Chapman. And they represent just a sample of what has now become a collection of over 5,000 artifacts, provided to the public and focusing exclusively on espionage tradecraft: artifacts used in the activities of intelligence and counterintelligence officers.

Tracking down these items and establishing provenance has presented unique challenges. Intelligence services work to maintain plausible deniability, and spy devices seldom identify the manufacturer or betray the country of origin; only decades later might they be officially acknowledged by the service that created them. To identify these objects accurately, I traveled the world meeting retired intelligence officers, honing my knowledge of espionage tradecraft, assembling a vast library of relevant books, and analyzing the function of each device. In the process, I discovered that Cold War intelligence agencies copied shamelessly from each other: an innovative microdot reader designed by the KGB, for example, might be copied almost identically by the CIA, and vice-versa. Understanding each piece's design and function allowed me to identify similar characteristics used in the tradecraft of other intelligence services.

Of the thousands of artifacts in my personal collection, the one that most eluded me was the ice-climbing axe used in the complex NKVD plot to assassinate the Russian revolutionary Leon Trotsky in Mexico City in 1940, referred to as the "murder of the century." After a decades-long pursuit, I learned that the axe was still in Mexico City. The daughter of the director of the museum of the Mexican police had the axe stowed beneath her bed. I immediately flew to Mexico and began a three-year negotiation to acquire it. It is now one of the cornerstones of the museum's collection.

When I decided to let go of my collection, I turned to the International Spy Museum. Good espionage tradecraft is not limited to any specific intelligence service or country. The museum adopts this apolitical approach, preserving artifacts regardless of country of origin and using them to tell stories that explore not only the history of intelligence but also its role in shaping history writ large.

Today, thanks to the vision and generosity of the museum's founders, Milt and Tamar Maltz, and a passionate and professional staff, the museum is a landmark in the nation's capital and a destination for the public and researchers alike. With the addition of my collection, the International Spy Museum is the world's largest espionage museum, holding some 9,000 artifacts. I am proud to have the museum be the permanent home of the Keith H. Melton and Karen Melton collection. I know this book will whet your appetite for visiting the museum and seeing these incredible artifacts firsthand.

# SECRETS ON DISPLAY

# Introduction: Designing an Open Box of Secrets

Sarah-Jane Corke and Mark Stout

Just imagine, if you will, that you are asked to design a spy museum. What is the first thing that comes to mind? With this image in your head, next imagine how to translate it into a three-dimensional building plan? This was the problem that the British architect Ivan Harbour, a senior director at Rogers Stirk Harbour + Partners (now RSHP), faced when he sat down with Milton Maltz, a philanthropist and the International Spy Museum's founder, to discuss the design of the new museum, relocated from the original location in several adjacent historic buildings elsewhere in Washington.[1] At the time, Harbour was a well-known architect with over thirty years' experience. His firm, RSHP, had twice been awarded Britain's most prestigious architectural award, the Stirling Prize, for two of their designs—Barajas Airport's Terminal 4 in Madrid in 2006, and Maggie's West London Center at Charing Cross Hospital in Hammersmith in 2009—but he had never designed anything like a spy museum. Indeed, his first thought after hearing about the project was *What on earth is a spy museum?* Yet he was immediately intrigued by the idea that such an institution would be built. He wondered, given the prominence of intelligence in popular culture, whether the museum would focus on fact or fiction.[2] Like everything else about the design, this was the first of many binaries that would be renegotiated as the museum embraced both.

Understanding what a binary is, and how it can be renegotiated, is critical to understanding the design of the International Spy Museum. A binary is nothing more than a pair of words that helps provide structure or order to the world we live in. In the modern world scholars tended to locate meaning by relying on binaries. Fact/fiction would be a perfect example. Fact and fiction are understood to be different from each other in several significant ways. Binaries of this sort also reduce complex ideas "to clear-cut, easily understandable," but "differentiated categories."[3] Some of the most frequently used binaries that we want readers to consider when thinking about the architectural design of the International Spy Museum include open/closed, visible/invisible, known/unknown, public/private, form/function, and—perhaps most important for understanding the new design—modern/postmodern.

Figure 0.1: The International Spy Museum surrounded by a number of modern buildings.

At this point it would be wonderful to provide an easily accessible definition of the terms "modernism" and "postmodernism."[4] Unfortunately, each has its own contested history, hence the "danger quotes" that frame each word. Moreover, each of the meanings change across fields and disciplines, making any simple definition virtually impossible. Therefore, we am going to avoid these debates and instead just explain how these words are used to describe architecture.[5] "Modernism" is the easiest to understand. Modernist buildings are those large, usually grey, square, or rectangular office buildings seen in most big cities. They were primarily built between the 1950s and the 1970s. They are simple, inside and out. Few frills or ornamentation. Many have flat roofs and a lot of windows. A good example are the brown and gray buildings made of concrete surrounding the International Spy Museum.

Postmodernist buildings are very different. They came into vogue in the 1980s and 1990s. The first thing you should know about them is that they are understood as a reaction to modernism. Therefore, they are very different from the square or rectangle office buildings. Many are extraordinary in their design, with nary a straight line, relying on swirls of material formed into unusual shapes. They also reflect a mixture of architectural styles. The term "pastiche" is often used to describe this mixing of styles. The same building might contain Greek columns and large modern windows. They are often ornamental and employ a variety of surfaces and

Figure 0.2: MI6 headquarters in London.

colors.[6] For lack of a better word, they're fun. Of course, intelligence aficionados would immediately point to MI6 Headquarters, Great Britain's Secret Intelligence Service, as an example of postmodernist design. This building was created by the architect Terry Farrell and opened in 1994. Its various nicknames, which include "Babylon on the Thames," the "Vauxhall Trollope," and "Legoland," are a nod to the various, and sometimes contradictory, threads of its postmodern positioning. If you have some time, you should google "postmodern architecture." I guarantee you will be amazed by what you find.[7]

Arguably, the differences between the two design trends were so great that, until recently, one could look at a building and decide very quickly if it was an example of modern or postmodern architecture, to use vernacular of the modern/postmodern binary. Lately, however, our reliance on this binary has been called into question. The problem with relying solely on binaries is that, while they can reduce complexity to "easily graspable difference," in doing so we can also "lose sight of the subtlety and even the substance of an issue. Moreover, once we have erected our structure of opposing categories, it is tempting to squeeze our analysis into it," even if it does nothing to help our understanding.[8] Therefore, we want to suggest that to understand the architectural design of the new museum we must also be aware that binaries can be renegotiated or even collapsed into each other. A literary example of a collapsed binary is the term "faction," defined as the mixing fact and fiction, in a book or article, so that the reader is left not knowing which is which.[9] Intelligence officers, former and current, have made a particularly important contribution to this genre of writing.[10] One of the best examples of faction is William Stephenson's "memoir," *A Man Called Intrepid*, which in the United States was classified as nonfiction initially, only to be reclassified as fiction.[11] In chapter 2 of this book, the historian Jonathan Nashel also explores the way fact and fiction can intermingle in the intelligence world.

Like the collapse of fact and fiction in literature, we believe that when designing the new museum Ivan Harbour collapsed several binaries in architectural design. Neither "modern" nor "postmodern" adequately captures the style of the building as it unfolded in his imagination or on the ground in L'Enfant Plaza. If you have visited the Spy Museum before reading this book, we believe you can already see the ways in which its design has undermined the dualities we outline above—open/closed, visible/invisible, known/unknown, public/private, form/function—so we are not telling you something that you did not already implicitly know—except perhaps for the last two, which you might not have thought of unless you are a student of architecture. For our purposes, the term "form" refers to what a building looks like. Postmodern architects emphasize form. As a result, they often embrace a "style that [i]s anchored in ornamentation." These buildings are designed to "upstage function."[12] The word "function" generally refers to what a building does or what it is intended for. For modern architects like Louis Sullivan, who coined the phrase "form always follows function," the purpose of the building should always be the starting point for design.[13] As we will see below, Harbour wanted the building to have both form and function, and he did not want to emphasize one style over the other.

Now that you are aware of these oppositional structures, and the problems with relying too heavily on them, let's go back to those first conversations between Maltz and Harbour. The architect recalls that it was Maltz who was the first to broach the subject of dueling images. He started by saying that when he thought about a museum about intelligence he thought of something "secretive" or "hard to get into." But then he thought of the opposite, because the craft of espionage is often "hidden in plain sight."[14] The dilemma, of course, was how one captures both principles—overt/covert—in one building. As the ideas bounced between philanthropist and architect, Harbour came up with two metaphors that captured Maltz's dilemma perfectly: a black box and a veil. With these metaphors in mind—closed/open—he immediately began to sketch what would ultimately

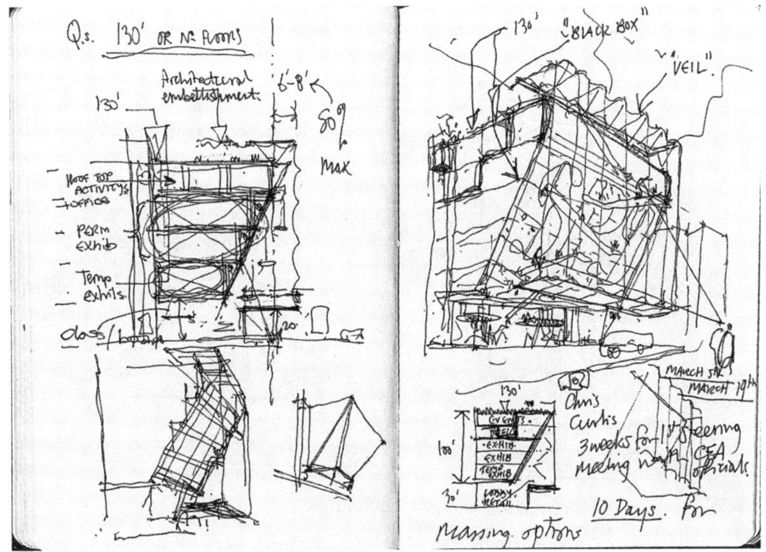


Figure 0.3: Ivan Harbour's initial sketch of the International Spy Museum drawn on February 2, 2015, during a meeting with Milton Maltz and a few of the museum's staff.

become the second iteration of the International Spy Museum.[15] His initial drawing, and the museum that you see today, are remarkably similar.

Architects need to consider several other factors when designing a building aside from its concept, however. Some of the most important include style, color, surface, content, and how the building will engage with its surroundings. There are also the needs of the client to consider. In the case of the new museum, the project had to go through the US Commission of Fine Arts, and according to Harbour there were several aspects that "were quite controversial."[16] Let's take a moment to run through each design feature, and we will show you how binaries were collapsed as the space between them was renegotiated by Harbour.

First let's return to the concept, the two metaphors around which the museum you see today was created: the black box and a veil. The core of the museum is the black box—a box of secrets if you will—where the artifacts are housed. The idea of a box would seem to fit naturally into the existing architecture surrounding Southwest DC's notable L'Enfant Plaza. But Harbour wanted his building to stand apart from its environment. Indeed, one of his goals was to disrupt the pattern of the "tough old buildings" that he believed did "nothing" for the space around them."[17] The result is the building you see today: a black box that is not really a box but an inverted pyramid, which is shrouded on one side by a glass veil and

Figure 0.4: The original International Spy Museum in four adjacent historical buildings at 9th and F Streets NW in Washington, DC. At one time, the rightmost building was the local headquarters of the Communist Party.

is topped by a glass rectangle. A museum that is, literally and figuratively, an open box of secrets.

Let me explain how all this came together. Architects, like spies, are notorious for pushing boundaries.[18] Harbour was no different. He was not content with the simple idea of a box. He decided to literally push his box over the street "as far as it could go."[19] The problem: this was not legal. There were zoning restrictions. But Harbour's design would challenge them; he just needed a loophole. After researching, he discovered that if the activity in any building extending over the property line was not stationary—if it was not exhibition space—there was legal leeway and it could be done. However, movement was critical. To get the kinetic flow that he needed, Harbour came up with the idea of the "walking circuit" whereby visitors start on the top floor and, with the help of "gravity," go downstairs to the end of the exhibitions.[20] This was a concept already established at the original museum and was seen to be successful so it was adopted for the new museum, but at a different scale. It was effective but also counterintuitive, as it complicated the traditional up/down experience. Usually when you enter a museum you start on the first floor and move up from there. Harbour reversed the process. The circuit, of course, also exposed the visitor to the veil that covers one side of the black box. It hangs over the street and connects you to the city around you. Thus, you are at once in the museum but also in the city. It was, according to Harbour, an "ephemeral

Figure 0.5: The Veil at the International Spy Museum. Arguably the largest window in Washington, DC.

sort of façade" where it is unclear "what's public, what's private, what's in, what's out . . . [what is secret] and what's hiding in plain sight."[21]

Can you see the way that Harbour was renegotiating binaries—down/up, open/closed, outside/inside, invisible/visible, unknown/known—through his use of the black box and the veil? When we asked him about the theoretical principles that were seemingly so integral to his work, the answer highlighted the complexity of his thinking. While willing to acknowledge that his "physical representation of the building" and "[our] philosophical interpretation" were "quite parallel with each other," he "would be lying" if he stated his work was informed by any theory. Then, upon reflection, he added,: "Maybe, subconsciously, in a way."[22] Whether subconscious or not, his approach was extraordinary.

That said, any student of design history might conclude as we did that given Harbour's fascination with the use of pastiche—the mixing of styles—the new building was a perfect example of postmodern architecture. Others may disagree. They could highlight the visual emphasis on horizontal and vertical lines of the box and rectangle and note its simplicity and clarity. However, neither the designer Mark Ramirez, the AIA Principal at the architectural design house Hickok Cole, who worked closely

Figure 0.6: The glass rectangle that the museum staff calls "the Ballroom."

with Harbour, nor Harbour were eager to embrace the term "postmodern." For his part, Ramirez believed that the museum was a modern representation that, above all else, privileged function above form.[23] It was a building designed to house exhibitions, and windows, which let in the sun, can play havoc with museum artifacts. Thus, the fundamental mission of the museum was to protect the integrity of the exhibitions. This was done through the creation of the black box.

Harbour was less certain. He did not see his work falling easily into either category, and as such he rejected the idea that the museum privileged function over form. In his words, "beauty is really important" and the museum "has to treat people well." When walking through, "you should feel that the building is looking after you." But at the same time, he recognized the need for a "highly practical" design with "minimal intrusions in the floors." He acknowledged Ramirez's point that the museum did not "need daylight," but he also noted that he wanted something "layered on top of that" experience because, if the museum is simply a black box, "your connection with your environment is lost." This was a nod to two of the twentieth century's most famous modern architects, Frank Lloyd Wright and Ludwig Miles van der Roche, whose buildings emphasized their connection to the outdoor spaces using windows and glass. As Harbour noted, the "veil" is perhaps the largest window in the nation's capital.[24]

The point Harbour was trying to make is that his vision cannot be easily understood by trying to fit the building into one design trend or another. Instead, his design is so compelling because it collapsed two distinct categories into something new and very different. We would like to give you a visual example of what we mean. In its earlier work RSHP had designed buildings embracing both modern and postmodern principles. The modern/postmodern binary is evident by comparing the company's two award-winning designs mentioned earlier. We would argue that while each of these works is reflective of a separate design trend—Maggie's West London Center is more representative of modern design and Terminal 4 in Barajas Airport is an excellent example of postmodern design—we believe that Harbour, in his design, collapsed the modern/postmodern binary. Look at the photos in the first color section of this book, compare the three designs, and decide what you think. Note the 90-degree angles at Maggie's. Notice the visual emphasis on horizontal and vertical lines. Notice the large square window and the way in which the garden is crucial to the building's flow. Now contrast Maggie's with the picture of Terminal 4. Notice the buildings' movement, the sweep of the roof, and the play among different, surfaces, materials, and colors. Could the two designs be more different? Now contrast these two images with the new museum: Can you see the way the three designs seem to collide?

At this point, we should probably discuss the glass rectangle that the museum staff refer to as the "Ballroom" which sits on top of, and overhangs, the black box. I hope by now you are thinking what I am thinking: visible/invisible, open/closed, known/unknown. The Ballroom also collapses the binary between public/private because Harbour recognized that while he was designing a public building it was also a privately owned museum. And like any museum it needed to raise money to keep expanding its collection. There was a very practical aspect to it. According to Harbour, it was important for Maltz to have a space that he could rent out for functions. In case you were wondering, no zoning variances were required for this extension because the land it overhangs was privately owned and permission was granted.

Another way in which the design collapses the modern/postmodern divide is in the use of color. Bold colors had been one of RSHP's trademarks since the completion in 1971 of the Centre Pompidou (officially the Centre national d'art et de culture Georges-Pompidou and, in English, the Pompidou Centre), a complex building located in Paris.[25] Yet Harbour does not believe in using color for its own sake. Instead, he argues that it is "a sort of coding" to help understand what the building is about.[26] Look at the colored pictures of the museum in the first insert and notice several bold colors: black, red, lime green, and sometimes at night royal blue. Three of those colors fit well within the modern color palette. But the royal blue does not.[27]

The red columns are one of the most prominent features of the International Spy Museum. Without the red, we would just see a black box, which, according to Harbour, could feel "quite oppressive." He believes the red columns give the museum a "certain rhythm at night." The second prominent color is the lime green of the stairs. This color runs through the museum as well. According to Harbour it is about "coding circulation."[28] In addition to the red and green, we would argue the most fascinating colors are those in the black box. If you have visited the museum after dark, you will have seen that there are lights that emanate from within the box. Although the box is made from black metal, it includes a series of louvers, which are like the grille on a car. Each grille contains lights that glow and can be changed to any color. The colors can be subtle or "very discreet" (which is how Harbour envisioned them), or they can be very sharp, like the royal blue we often see today.[29]

There is one last way in which Harbour renegotiated the design that has to do with location. The museum sits halfway between the National Mall and the Potomac River. As such the museum was designed to be a "stepping stone" between the two landmarks. However, here too Harbour was determined that his design be unique. He wanted the building to face sideways so that it was asymmetrical or at odds with the other buildings that surrounded it. Thus, he "swung the building around" so its south side became the most visible part. This ensured it had a "prime impact" on anyone approaching DC from that direction.[30] Look at the picture of the museum in the color insert. Harbour's design is truly novel.

You now know a little bit more about the International Spy Museum, than you did before you picked up the book. And that, friends, is our goal. Join us as we take you behind the scenes. The vignette above is just one of the many stories that this book contains. As will become clear, the museum is not only noteworthy because of its architecture; it is also extraordinary because of what is inside. It holds thousands of artifacts tied to some of the most exciting spy stories you never heard of. The museum also addresses some of the larger themes in intelligence history. These include intelligence analysis, covert action, counterintelligence, disinformation, and popular culture. This book will introduce you to all these subjects. The chapters that follow provide an insider's look into the exhibitions within the museum as well as other intriguing and important stories in intelligence history. However, this is not a traditional intelligence history book. Although it promises to provide an insider's glimpse into Washington's open box of secrets, it does so by combining the written with the visual. While scholarly intelligence history is seldom well-illustrated, well-illustrated intelligence history is rarely scholarly. This volume is both. It contains photographs of the exhibition spaces and the artifacts in the museum's collection, many of which are not on display. The book is also accessible, an appealing entrée into high-quality intelligence history. The stories presented are offered by some of the top intelligence historians from around the world, but they are written in a way that appeals to anyone who likes a good read.

Our book has also been produced in cooperation with the International Spy Museum, and it grows out of the inaugural conference of the North American Society for Intelligence History, now renamed the Society for Intelligence History, which was held in October 2019 at the museum. https://www.intelligencehistory.org. All but one of the contributors took part in that conference, which was attended by some 150 people and showcased the museum as a remarkable educational institution. At the time of the conference, the museum had just moved to L'Enfant Plaza from its first location at 9th and F Streets NW in Washington. Before reopening, the museum made several major acquisitions, including thousands of new artifacts from Keith Melton, the world's leading collector of intelligence and espionage artifacts. As a result, the exhibitions were completely redeveloped. Today the collection runs to more than 9,000 artifacts and includes equipment used in the conduct of espionage and intelligence operations; artifacts from the lives of numerous spies and intelligence officers; a vast array of ephemera; many reflections on the subject in popular culture such as games, toys, comic books, movie posters; and many other items.

The connection to the International Spy Museum continues throughout the book. It includes the editors, authors, and the written content. The volume's first foreword is written by the museum's executive director, Colonel Chris Costa. A second foreword is by H. Keith Melton, the leading collector of espionage-related artifacts who has given or loaned the bulk of his collection to the museum. In addition, one of the editors of this volume (Mark Stout) was historian and curator at the museum from 2010 to 2013. Three contributors were, or are, on the museum staff: Anna Slafer, former senior creative strategist; Dr. Alexis Albion, former curator for special projects and the museum's first historian and curator, left the museum to serve on the 9/11 Commission, then returned to the staff from 2012 to 2023; and Amanda Ohlke, the museum's director of adult education. Another contributor, Cynthia Storer, has done contract work for the museum and is featured in an interactive exhibition there. Several other contributors have spoken at museum events or been guests on its podcast, titled *Spycast*, which we encourage you to explore on any streaming service.

When we set out to write a book on the International Spy Museum, it was very important to us that its organization mirror the museum itself. Before diving into any exhibitions, the introduction focuses on the museum's design, and chapter 2 explains how the exhibitions in the museum came together. Alexis Albion and Anna Slafer recount how they and the rest of the International Spy Museum curatorial team approached the task of making the covert overt in a new, larger, custom-built building. Their goal was to tell deeper, richer stories while accommodating the various ways that visitors learn from museums. Furthermore, they wanted the museum to "model the intelligence process itself: asking questions, analyzing issues, weighing risks, engaging in debates, and making judgments." The chapter describes how many of the museum's exhibitions met these goals.

After that, the book unfolds in sections that broadly correspond to the organization of the exhibitions. When visitors enter the lobby, they are presented with James Bond's Aston Martin DB5 as well as a prototype of the drone that evolved into the famous Predator weapon. Thus, guests are immediately confronted with fact and fiction, side by side. Chapter 2, by the historian Jonathan Nashel, explores another binary: the life/art conundrum. He does so by focusing on the effect of James Bond on the Cold War–era Central Intelligence Agency and by allowing readers to explore the real-world analogues of this juxtaposition.[31] He accomplishes this by examining two towering figures in the history of the CIA: the agency director Allen Dulles, and the counterintelligence chief James Angleton, and he explains how their lives imitated art. He argues that "the life/art conundrum becomes a problem when real intelligence officers are taken prisoner" by fictions, thereby collapsing the fact/fiction binary.

Chapter 3 does something similar regarding spy fiction aimed at British boys of the 1950s. The historian Johnathan Best illustrates how the books by Ronald Seth, a former intelligence officer, affected the lives of young men in the early Cold War years. He argues that Seth's depiction of the qualities and skills of British spies showcased the superiority of Britain's secret service and challenged the notions of declining British national strength during the 1950s. This chapter also suggests that Seth's fiction, with all the hallmarks of the romantic spy genre, can be viewed as a means of influencing the teenage boys of the 1950s to protect British interests at home and abroad. It also reflects how Seth's writing highlights the sense of excitement and adventure that a British spy experienced when undertaking dangerous missions. These stories were appealing to the young adult readership and showcased the resilience of Britain in a time of flux.

Visitors exit the lobby by taking an elevator to the exhibition spaces, which start on the fifth floor. The first room contains exhibitions covering tools of the trade, spies and spymasters, and tradecraft, which includes specialized equipment used by spies throughout history. *Secrets on Display* illustrates this section of the museum with chapters on two of the twentieth century's first spies, both featured in the room: the infamous Mata Hari, and Dmitri Bystrolyotov, a Soviet illegal—a deep-cover intelligence officer—who worked during the interwar period. In chapter 4 Amanda Ohlke strips bare the outdated depictions of Mata Hari and paints her in a new light as a woman who would have made an excellent case officer. In chapter 5 the Russian historian Emil Draitser explores Dimitri Bystrolyotov's operations in Europe in the 1920s and 1930s. He dissects an operation in which he acted as a Romeo spy, seducing a German woman with access to Nazi secrets. Although Bystrolyotov later came to regret his involvement in such work, the tactic continues to be used today.

Visitors next enter a pair of rooms devoted to technical intelligence collection. Mirroring these themes, James Green in chapter 6 explores the use of balloons during the American Civil War in and around Washington. He argues that although the Union Army Balloon Corps served as America's first air force, its significant contributions went largely unrecognized. In chapter 7, picking up on the topic of aerial reconnaissance, Jack O'Connor, a former senior executive from the National Geospatial-Intelligence Agency, looks at the origins of geospatial intelligence. Specifically, he examines the role of the U-2 spy plane, which was a game-changer for American intelligence in the 1950s, providing, before the advent of spy satellites, the first reliable data about the Soviet military from the interior of the Soviet Union. He discusses how U-2 intelligence was gleaned by putting together an experimental team of analysts that consisted of guided-missile and nuclear engineers and physicists from American defense industries to work shoulder to shoulder with a group of photo interpreters. O'Connor argues that, although the results of the experiment were a great intelligence success, the intelligence community's hostile response to it ensured that it was never repeated.

The museum then flows into a room focusing specifically on codemaking, codebreaking, and signals intelligence (SIGINT). The chapter on the life and career of Ann Caracristi, an American SIGINTer who started her career during World War II and rose to become deputy director of the National Security Agency (NSA), and another chapter on Colossus, the computer that the British built to help their World War II codebreaking efforts, complement this room. In chapter 8 the historian David Schaefer looks at the history of one of the world's first programable computers designed to break German cryptosystems. For three decades, the story of Bletchley Park's Special Intelligence, nicknamed "Ultra," had been successfully withheld from the public. However, after its revelation in the 1970s, scholars were finally allowed to examine the documentary evidence of its use in World War II. According to Schaefer, these events were a landmark in the historical study of intelligence, encouraging a wave of new research into codebreaking and its influence over World War II in Europe. In their wake, however, the German Enigma machine came to dominate public understanding of wartime SIGINT, while Bletchley's development of pioneering computing technology and its exploitation of other sophisticated cipher devices were carefully concealed until the final decade of the twentieth century. Thus, as one avenue of Cold War scholarship opened, another shut down. Unfortunately, such is often the case with intelligence history. In chapter 9 David Sherman, a former senior executive at the NSA, provides a detailed discussion of Caracristi, who went from being one of many "code girls" in Arlington Hall Station during World War II to shattering the glass ceiling at the NSA.

After exploring SIGINT, visitors then proceed into a room about intelligence analysis, or the process of converting raw collection data into meaningful conclusions. Two chapters reflect this theme: one discussing the CIA's early days of counterterrorism analysis in the 1970s, and one that expands on the museum's interactive exhibition about the hunt for Osama bin Laden. In chapter 10, the historian Silke Zoller argues that the Central Intelligence Agency played a crucial role in defining for the US government what constituted international terrorism in the 1970s. She observes that, after the attack on the Israeli Olympic team at the 1972 Games in Munich, the CIA's analyses—notably its new *Weekly Situation Reports on International Terrorism*—systematically relabeled many nonstate violent groups as "international terrorists." Unfortunately, in the process analysts avoided important political context and nuance as they explored armed struggles around the world. This had a profound impact on how such groups were perceived and judged.

In chapter 11 Cynthia Storer and Mark Stout, both former intelligence analysts, and Sarah-Jane Corke tell the story of how the CIA located Osama bin Laden and how Storer went on to create one of the Spy Museum's most fascinating interactive exhibitions on how he was caught. We suggest that the collaborative efforts at the museum among practitioners, intelligence scholars, and museum professionals serendipitously resulted in exhibitions that reflected a major shift in how the United States Intelligence Community conceived of and practiced intelligence analysis.

Visitors next enter a room devoted to propaganda and covert action from the ancient world to today. In chapter 12, Gill Bennet, the former chief historian of the United Kingdom's Foreign and Commonwealth Office, tackles the problem of counter-disinformation. Bennett argues that history "combined with the tools of the intelligence analyst" contains "useful lessons in identifying disinformation and building resilience to it." She draws on two case studies to make this argument: the British government's mismanagement of the Zinoviev Letter in the 1920s, and the work of the Foreign Office's Information Research Department, a counter-disinformation organization of the Cold War.

At this point, visitors proceed down one floor and enter the final section of the museum, where they grapple with many of the issues that arise in the world of intelligence, particularly counterintelligence and counterterrorism. Chapters on the FBI traitor Robert Hanssen, the Canadian traitor Jeffrey Delisle, and the "enhanced interrogation" methods used by the British during the Troubles in Northern Ireland round out this section of the book. In chapter 13, the FBI's chief historian, John Fox, uses the espionage case of Robert Hanssen, the FBI special agent arrested in 2001 for spying, to argue that active counterintelligence efforts to understand and penetrate adversarial intelligence services tend to be more effective than what he terms "mirror-gazing and tightening security."

As we move from the United States to Canada, the historian Welsey Wark tells the story of Delisle, a junior officer, a sublieutenant, in the Canadian armed forces who spent his entire service career, starting in the late 1990s, in military intelligence. He was also a spy for the GRU, Russia's military intelligence agency. At the time of his arrest in January 2012, he was serving as a threat analyst for the Canadian navy, operating from HMCS Trinity, an intelligence fusion center in Halifax, Nova Scotia. Wark argues that Delisle's case illustrates the harm that can be done by an insider who is able to penetrate a sensitive national security database. The author also reflects on whether post-Delisle counterintelligence reforms have been sufficient to protect Canadian national security.

In chapter 15 the historian Tony Craig looks at British interrogation programs in Northern Ireland during the early 1970s. He suggests that Britain's Intelligence Coordinator, Sir Dick White, played a critical role in the adoption of enhanced interrogation methods against the Irish Republican Army. He points out that White's role raises important questions about the accountability of intelligence consultants. He concludes that, when those who designed the policy also write the public record, a lack of accountability can result. We need to be more careful in accepting archival documents at face value.

We believe that the fifteen stories offered in this book will provide readers with a fascinating glimpse into intelligence history, an ever-growing field of historical analysis. However, these stories, represent but a small fraction of the exhibitions found in the museum. Whether it be spies, secret operations, or code-making and codebreaking, there is something for everyone. If you have yet to visit the museum, we encourage you to do so. If you have been once, then come again—we guarantee there are more stories to discover.

## Further Reading


Cantor, Norman, and Mindy Cantor. *The American Century: Varieties of Culture in Modern Times*. New York: HarperCollins, 1997.

Gura, Judith. *Postmodern Design Complete: Design, Furniture, Graphics, Architecture, Interiors*. New York: Thames & Hudson, 2017.

Hopkins, Owen. *Postmodern Architecture: Less Is a Bore*. London: Phaidon Press, 2020.

Ward, Glenn. *Teach Yourself Postmodernism*. Columbus, OH: McGraw-Hill, 1997.


## Notes


The authors wish to thank Jonathan Nashel for reading and offering suggestions on this introduction. When one jumps fields, as we have so gleefully done here, it is wonderful to have friends and colleagues whom you respect review and discuss your work. We am also enormously grateful to Ivan Harbour and Mark Ramirez, who took time out of their busy schedules to sit down with an intelligence historian to discuss architecture.


1. Ivan Harbour is an architect and senior director at RSHP, a London-based architectural firm that was founded in 1977. The firm was originally known as the Richard Rogers Partnership. It became Rogers Stirk Harbour + Partners in 2007. In June 2022, it became RSHP.

2. Sarah-Jane Corke, personal interview with Ivan Harbour via Zoom, December 7, 2022.

3. Frank Costigliola, H-Diplo/RJISSF Roundtable Review (15–13) on Costigliola, *Kennan a Life Between Worlds*, https://issforum.org/roundtables/h-diplo-rjissf-roundtable-15-13-on-costigliola-kennan-a-life-between-worlds. For a more detailed discussion, see Frank Costigliola, "Reading for Meaning," in *Explaining the History of American Foreign Relations* (2nd ed.), ed. Michael J. Hogan and Thomas G. Paterson (New York: Cambridge University Press, 2004), 279–303.

4. Although it is not really useful in terms of this chapter, my favorite definition of "postmodernism" comes from the literary theorist Terry Eagleton. He argues postmodernism is a "contemporary movement which rejects totalities, universal values, grand historical narratives, solid foundations . . . and the possibilities of objective knowledge. Postmodernism is skeptical of truth, unity, progress, opposes what it sees as elitism in culture, tends toward cultural relativism. and celebrates pluralism, dis-

continuity, and heterogeneity." Terry Eagleton, *After Theory* (New York: Basic Books, 2004), 13.

5. For an excellent discussion of the differences, see Katherine McLaughlin, "Postmodern Architecture: Everything You Need to Know," *Architecture + Design*, August 2, 2023, www.architecturaldigest.com/story/postmodern-architecture-101.

6. Glenn Ward, *Teach Yourself Postmodernism* (McGraw-Hill, 1997), 17–27.

7. Some of my favorite postmodernist buildings are designed by the architect Frank Gehry. His buildings include the Guggenheim Museum in Bilbao, Spain; Dancing House in Prague, Czech Republic; and Walt Disney Concert Hall in Los Angeles. See Samantha Pires, "10 Influential Buildings by Postmodern Architect Frank Gehry," *My Modern Met*, May 4, 2021, https://mymodernmet.com/frank-gehry-infographic.

8. Costigliola, H-Diplo Roundtable Review.

9. Jørgen Dines Johansen and Leif Søndergaard, *Fact, Fiction and Faction* (Sønderborg, Denmark: University Press of Southern Denmark, 2010).

10. Nigel West, "Fiction, Faction and Intelligence," *Intelligence and National Security* 19, no. 2 (Summer 2004): 275–289, 276. I want to thank Mark Stout for drawing my attention to West's article. In subsequent conversations, Stout acknowledged that his favorite example of faction is Mark Henshaw's novel *Red Cell: A Novel* (New York: Gallery Books, 2012). According to Stout, much of what Henshaw, an intelligence analyst at the CIA, tells the reader about George Tenet's Red Cell is accurate even though the novel is fiction. He went on to do a podcast episode with Henshaw on *Spycast*. See "Red Cell: Fact and Fiction," *Spycast*, episode 101, August 23, 2012, http://thecyberwire.com/podcasts/spycast/101/notes. The descriptions are accurate.

11. William Stevenson, *A Man Called Intrepid* (Washington, DC: Lyons Press, 2009).

12. Brock Keeling, "The Case for Saving Postmodernism, Architecture's Wildest Buildings," *Bloomberg*, November 12, 2023, www.bloomberg.com/news/features/2023-11-12/the-case-for-saving-postmodernism-architecture-s-wildest-buildings.

13. Kanchi Modi, "Theory in Architecture: Form Follows Function," *RTF Architectural Reviews* (undated), www.re-thinkingthefuture.com/rtf-architectural-reviews/a3347-theory-in-architecture-form-follows-function.

14. The quotes come from Ivan Harbour's recollections of Milton Maltz's vision. Harbour interview.

15. Harbour interview.

16. Harbour interview.

17. Harbour interview.

18. Sarah-Jane Corke, personal interview with Mark Ramirez, AHI Principal, Hickoc Cole, via Zoom, November 28, 2022.

19. Harbour interview and Ramirez interview.

20. Harbour interview.

21. Harbour interview.

22. Harbour interview.

23. Ramirez interview.

24. It is worth noting that Harbour is less taken by the postmodern architects like Frank Gehry, especially his later work, which he believes is "too sculpted." In his words, while architecture "has to talk, it's got to make a statement about itself," and it should not do this to the determinant of "what the content is." He also believes there is a difference between an artist and an architect. His job, as he perceives it, is "to provide beautiful containers to do amazing things." In this context, he argues, without irony,

architects should not "stand out of line." Harbour interview. To get a glimpse of Frank Gehry's work see: David Sokol, Nick Mafi and Katherine McLaughlin, "33 Spectacular Buildings Designed by Frank Gehry," *Architectural Digest*, September 25, 2023, www.architecturaldigest.com/gallery/best-of-frank-gehry-slideshow.

25. Lisa de Luca, "Centre Pompidou: Eyesore or Beacon of Innovation," *The Collector* (September 2, 2021), www.thecollector.com/centre-pompidou-renowned-museum.

26. Harbour interview.

27. For a short course on how colors have changed over the last half-decade, see Francesca Valan, "The Evolution of Color in Design from the 1950s to Today," *Journal of the International Color Association* 8 (2012): 55–60, https://aic-color.org/resources/Documents/jaic_v8_06.pdf.

28. Harbour interview.

29. Harbour interview.

30. Harbour interview.

31. Capitalizing "Cold War" (or lowercasing it as "cold war") can reflect a particular historiographical position for many historians. The volume editors, in consultation with individual contributors and the publisher, will capitalize the phrase in deference to our audience's expectations and common modern usage.—Eds.

# Making the Covert Overt: Building a Modern Spy Museum

**Alexis Albion and Anna Slafer**

*The International Spy Museum is a brand recognized around the world and is one of the most popular museums in Washington, DC, a city with many first-rate museums. So when the museum moved to a new location in 2019, the curators had an unparalleled opportunity as an educational institution to teach intelligence history and a great responsibility to do it well.—The Editors*

"Have you visited the International Spy Museum in Washington, DC?"
"Sorry, I would tell you, but that's top secret."

Jokes like this come with the territory when one works on anything related to spies and spying. But there *is* something funny, or at least incongruous, about a public museum dedicated to something as clandestine as espionage. Museums, of course, have always been places to see uncommon curiosities, from George Washington's dentures to Tutankhamun's funeral mask—artifacts once private, made public. Visitors come to set eyes on these treasures from another time and place because they speak to us about human society and technology, beliefs, and cultures. So what about a rectal tool kit or the undercover activities of wartime songstress Josephine Baker? What can artifacts and stories like these from a shadow world—once covert, now made overt—tell us about human ingenuity, identity, and individual agency?

Making the covert overt is at the heart of what it means to be a modern spy museum. It has nothing to do with revealing classified information. Visiting the International Spy Museum (SPY) requires only a ticket. In contrast, the Central Intelligence Agency museum or Britain's MI5 and Russia's FSB museums (all located within headquarters) require some form of security clearance. But while those museums serve largely an internal audience, focused on instilling a sense of institutional history and culture, SPY serves the public. Like other intelligence museums open to the world at large, such as the National Security Agency's National Cryptologic Museum or the headquarters-turned-museum of the defunct Stasi in Berlin, SPY invites visitors to find connections between the secret world

Figure 1.1: French sheet music, 1928, designed by Valerio. African American entertainer Josephine Baker was a celebrity in prewar Paris. During World War II, she was also an agent for French intelligence agents who smuggled information to the Allies written in invisible ink on sheet music like this.

of intelligence and their everyday lives. That connection is important. The biggest secret about SPY is that, while visitors are drawn in by the secret world of espionage, they end up learning about things that are far less hidden: history, art, science, engineering, math, and the most interesting subject of all: themselves. For a democratic society, educating people about their government's secret intelligence capabilities—from collection to covert action—makes for a stronger citizenry. Only by understanding what intelligence agencies do (and how they do it) in the public's name (and with their money) can citizens hold governments accountable for their actions. A modern spy museum should do both: engage visitors and provide them with the tools to be better citizens. The new International Spy Museum was designed with these goals in mind.

When SPY first opened in downtown Washington, DC, in mid-2002, less than a year after the 9/11 terror attacks, the world had just entered a period of new national security concerns. For most visitors, however, popular culture rather than personal experience was their entry point into the world of spying. That is understandable. After all, James Bond is far more accessible (and entertaining) than the Worldwide Threat Assessment.[1] SPY sought to change that. The museum's mission is to educate the public about how intelligence and espionage have shaped the world we live in.

The original SPY focused almost exclusively on espionage (HUMINT, or human intelligence collection) to tell the secret history of history from biblical times to the age of terrorism. Visitors saw unique artifacts, tested their spy tradecraft skills (detecting surveillance or memorizing the details of a new identity), and heard from former intelligence officers through media pieces. In 2002, the museum's content and interactivity were novel, and innovative, and demonstrated that real espionage work was even more interesting than its fictional portrayal; only about 1 percent of total floor space touched on popular culture. And with terms such as "actionable intelligence" and "chatter" used regularly on the nightly news, the museum's content was highly relevant to the times.

Over the next dozen years, the world of intelligence and its impact on our visitors' lives changed dramatically. You did not need to work in national security to be subjected to surveillance or ID checks. You did not need to be an intelligence professional to be the unwitting target of a phishing email or doctored video from nefarious foreign sources. Visitors now came to SPY with increasingly complex questions about the scope and impact of intelligence work and the ethics of spying. At the same time, the rise of social media and breakthrough technologies such as the iPhone fueled expectations about a museum's level of engagement and interactivity. It became clear that the permanent exhibitions needed to reflect new concerns and new storytelling techniques. In 2014, with a plan to move into a brand-new building, we began developing a new, modern museum.

One of the advantages of rethinking a museum after 12 years was the visitor experience and feedback. We augmented this with longitudinal studies and analyses, all of which provided a good sense of what visitors liked, disliked, and thought was missing. Added to this, we set our own goals as museum educators and intelligence scholars. From a content perspective, we knew the new SPY needed to be more international; include more from premodern and contemporary history; be more connected to national K-12 school curricula needs especially the STEM fields (Science, Technology, Engineering, and Math); appeal to families; and be more diverse in terms of race and gender. We wanted to address intelligence writ large, going beyond espionage to address the entire intelligence cycle, how intelligence is used, and by whom. We wanted to shine spotlights on the wide range of people and skills involved in this work so visitors might find additional connections with their own lives. We also wanted to challenge visitors to think about the ethics of spying and to recognize how popular culture shapes stereotypes about spies and spying.

Importantly, we wanted to do all this using innovative interpretive techniques, telling deeper, richer stories, and integrating artifacts to make the objects and the stories come alive. The goal was multifaceted. We wanted to address the varied motivations for coming to the museum—for example, to see cool spy gadgets, to help children learn, or to gain a social experience with friends and family. We also wanted to design experiences that would make the museum accessible to a range of physical and mental abilities and address different learning styles. Decades of research shows that, in addition to preferences for learning by reading or hearing, some people absorb information best when they can make personal connections to the content; some want to hear facts and details from experts, some don't want to be told what to do but rather try it themselves, and some like to use all their senses to learn something new and speculate about the future.[2] At the same time, we wanted to model the intelligence process itself: asking questions, analyzing issues, weighing risks, engaging in debates, and making judgments. We aimed to incorporate all these approaches throughout the museum.

Ultimately, we wanted visitors to leave better able to interpret and think critically about what they were reading and hearing about intelligence. We also wanted guests to be able to better carry out their civic role in the intelligence oversight process to keep intelligence agencies accountable to the people they serve. We also hoped they might learn some skills to help navigate the twenty-first century world in general, from challenging personal cognitive biases to detecting so-called fake news. And we needed to do all this in a mere 25,000 square feet—the size of one major exhibition hall at the Smithsonian!

To meet these objectives, we spent two years developing an intellectual concept for the new SPY that involved talking to scores of people around the world and doing lots of research. We settled on a conceptual framework that took a thematic and case-study approach, structuring the galleries to follow the general process of intelligence—from gathering secrets, to analyzing information, to the role of the decision maker, to taking (or not taking) action. This would provide the museum with a kind of plug-and-play flexibility to add and remove individual stories without worrying about chronological continuity.

The new International Spy Museum opened in May 2019. It has five galleries spread over two floors and includes more than 1,000 artifacts on view, with 9,000 more in storage for future stories and preservation needs. The first three galleries (on one floor) address *what* intelligence agencies do, covering the entire intelligence cycle. First, in *Stealing Secrets*, we focus on collection—with exhibitions on human intelligence and the equipment that supports it—and on technical intelligence collection. We then move to *Making Sense of Secrets*, addressing how codebreakers and analysts transform collected information into intelligence that decision makers can use. The final gallery on this floor, *Covert Action*, looks at seven different techniques that spy agencies use to secretly influence events abroad.

On a separate floor, the museum continues with two more galleries that consider why nations and people spy. *Spying That Shaped History* explores how intelligence ideas and activities have a significant impact on the world (from the analytical failures before the 9/11 attacks to cyber operations). *An Uncertain World* looks at counterintelligence and counterterrorism—how intelligence can be used at home to ward off threats, whether real, perceived, or contrived.

All museums make hard choices about the number and type of stories they can tell within a given space. The museum's mandate—to demonstrate the richness of intelligence history around the world and across the centuries—made this especially difficult. We did not succeed in everything we tried to do, but we always kept in mind the idea of relating the secret world to our visitors' world. Here are some of the approaches we took.

As soon as visitors enter the new SPY, they encounter some main themes. In the lobby, an Amber drone exemplifies the critical role and evolution of technology in the intelligence world. An Aston Martin DB5 epitomizes the influence of popular culture in shaping views about spying, and a reproduction of the Turtle, a pedal-powered one-man submersible built during the American Revolutionary War, illustrates spying's role in history. These are some of the largest objects in the museum, and they all have human stories. Take the Turtle, which was designed for sabotage: the pilot was to secretly cross New York Harbor and attach a bomb to a British warship. The exhibition highlights technical innovation, with a short film describing the building process and the craft's surprising seaworthiness. But we also wanted visitors to put themselves in the shoes of the person who piloted this experimental craft. One of the labels for this exhibition reads: "Imagine pedaling and struggling to steer this ungainly vessel. At night. Through cold, turbulent water. Under the nose of the enemy. You have no windows to see where you're going, and just 20 minutes of air."

Throughout the museum, we try to put a human face on intelligence by featuring the people who actually do the work. Our first exhibition, *Spies and Spymasters,* for example, focuses on the human side of collection. The six stories we chose range from the sixteenth to the twenty-first centuries, from the Americas to Europe to the Middle East. They reflect the different types of people involved in intelligence collection—officers, recruits, volunteers, agents, handlers—and very different outcomes—success, failure, fame, imprisonment, exile, execution. For each individual, we highlight one human trait central to their story: risk, cunning, deceit, seduction, trust, or loyalty. To make it personal, each of our "spies" (the real person or an actor) tells their story directly to the visitor.

One striking example is Morten Storm, a Dane who became a

self-radicalized convert to Islam. After making some dangerous friends in Yemen, he had a change of heart, volunteered to work for Danish and then US and British intelligence, and ended up risking his life by going back into Yemen to betray al-Qaeda. Storm is a large, gregarious man with a big personality. We saw no better way for visitors to understand his choices than to hear from him directly. Accordingly, we flew to an undisclosed location where Storm was in hiding to film him—at the time he was under a fatwa calling for his death. Until recently at SPY, you could view Storm on a life-size screen, within an exhibition setting of a simple Yemeni home, Arab coffee pot and cups on a coffee table, and Storm's prayer rug on the floor. "You have to ask yourself, is what you're doing worth dying for?" Storm urged visitors: "If it is not, don't do it. But this is worth dying for, for me."[3]

Our other "real life spies" are equally compelling: Gonen Ben Yitzhak, a former intelligence officer in Israel's Shin Bet, who recruited Palestinian Mosab Hassan Yousef, the son of Hamas leader, as a spy. The two men talk about the uneasy relationship between handler and agent and their unique bond of trust. We hoped visitors might find it unsettling when Gonen candidly tells visitors: "You need to manipulate. . . . I needed to give him the feeling that I'm his best friend . . . while maybe I'm his biggest enemy."

Other spies needed to be brought back from the dead in order to speak to visitors. These include Sir Francis Walsingham, spymaster to Queen Elizabeth I of England; Dmitri Bystrolyotov, a pre–World War II professional Soviet intelligence officer and multilingual master of deception; James Lafayette, an enslaved African American who spied against the British during the American Revolutionary War; and Mata Hari, the self-made Dutch entertainer who had a short and unsuccessful spying career spying during World War I. Writing each of these spy's narratives, brought to life by actors, carried unique challenges: integrating historically appropriate language, using the voice from a personal memoir, interpreting events and filling in the blanks from a limited number of historical sources, and, in the case of Mata Hari, pushing back against a powerful and distorting stereotype about women spies as seducers.

Sharing space with *Spies and Spymasters* is the *Tools of the Trade* exhibition, featuring the gadgets and gizmos that help intelligence officers and agents do their work. They are organized into five tradecraft sections: covert communications; surveillance and countersurveillance; escape and evasion; disguise; and surreptitious entry. The focus here is on the artifacts: microdots and bugs, a camera concealed in a tie, a dead rat dead drop, lock picks and disguise masks, and even a rectal toolkit intended as an escape aid. Yet we also spotlight the human ingenuity behind the

Figure 1.2: Rat concealment (reproduction). During the Cold War, the CIA used gutted rats as dead drops—places to hide a message, money, and film to be passed to agents. The rats were doused with pepper sauce to deter scavenging cats and dogs.

gadgets, anchoring each of the five sections with a profile of a tech-ops officer. Once again, the goal is to remind visitors that behind each gadget and each mission is a person using personal skills to solve a problem. We hope that when visitors see a transmitter concealed in the heel of a shoe, for example, they might ask themselves *What skills do you need to come up with an idea like that?*

One of our goals for SPY was to design exhibitions that allow visitors to experience intellectually, to the extent possible, what it is like to work in the intelligence field. We wanted visitors to see spying as creative problem-solving: figuring out how to obtain information without anyone knowing. Technical collection was an ideal area to explore this idea. In the *Looking, Listening, Sensing* exhibition, our challenge was to explain complicated technical collection disciplines—SIGINT (signals intelligence), IMINT (imagery intelligence), and MASINT (measurement and signature intelligence)—in ways that are understandable and engaging. Our approach invites visitors to get inside the heads of material scientists, civil engineers, chemists, physicists, computer network operators, and others—the people who work behind the scenes and are tasked to devise technical solutions to intelligence collection. The exhibitions are themed to look like an active lab or workspace with labels written on graph paper, notes, cross-outs, and scribbled sketches to illustrate the iterative thinking process. This includes props such as slide rules and rolled-up blueprints. We frame stories as a challenge—the tasking that might have been assigned to a naval architect, an aeronautical engineer, or a forensic scientist. For example, some of the questions posed include jumping-off points such as:

HOW DO YOU RAISE A SUBMARINE FROM THE OCEAN FLOOR?
HOW DO YOU SEE INTO THE USSR WITHOUT GETTING A VISA?
HOW DO YOU USE CHEMISTRY TO FIGURE OUT WHAT OR WHODUNIT?

This approach not only allows us to explore hard-to-grasp topics such as how spectroscopy functions but also encourages visitors to view artifacts through a different lens. In our IMINT area, for instance, a full-pressure flight suit from an SR-71 reconnaissance plane becomes a solution to the challenge of keeping the pilot alive at 85,000 feet over enemy territory. In our SIGINT display, a rusty tube of metal, six and a half feet in diameter and eight feet long, illustrates the daring engineering solution to the problem of finding out what is happening behind the Iron Curtain. This tube is an original piece of the Berlin Tunnel, which was secretly burrowed into the Soviet sector of Berlin in the mid-1950s, allowing US and British intelligence to tap into Soviet military communications lines. When visitors observe this artifact, they can also hear stories told by people involved in this operation, including a US Army engineer who helped dig the tunnel and a CIA linguist who translated and transcribed intercepted conversations. Above the tunnel, a mannequin depicting an armed German guard stands on patrol atop a concrete piece of road above the tunnel, unaware of the ongoing eavesdropping beneath his nose. As visitors look and listen, a rusty piece of metal transforms into an amazing spy story.

A gallery on intelligence analysis offers one of the best opportunities to enter the mind of an intelligence professional and even think like a spy. The original Spy Museum had not tackled analysis at all, but it is one of the most important aspects of intelligence work, and we knew it was a critical topic to cover in the new SPY. Initially, however, we were stumped. What stories could we tell? An analyst sitting in a windowless office compiling statistics on Soviet military strength? What artifacts could we display? Used pencils, coffee cups, piles of books, and computer terminals? We had to tap in to what made analysts excited to go to work each day to find what excited us about this exhibition.

We found that spark when a former CIA analyst told us that analysts sort their work into three main categories: secrets, puzzles, and mysteries. Secrets need one piece of intelligence to make sense. Puzzles must be pieced together. Mysteries are problems for which no answer yet exists but on which judgments can still be made (for example: What will be the

Figure 1.3: Rectal toolkit issued to CIA operatives in the 1960s. Filled with escape tools such as drill bits, saws, and knives, it could be stashed inside the body so it would not be found during a perfunctory search. From the Collection of H. Keith and Karen Melton at the International Spy Museum.

outcome of this war?). These categories had great potential as a compelling organizing principle to which we—and our visitors—could relate. When we delved further into the topic and learned about how cognitive traps affect how analysts assess problems—and the engaging strategic techniques they use to find a way out of these traps—we knew we had struck gold.[4]

The gallery on analysis explores each analytical category through a historical case study. Our secret is the identity of Hitler's secret weapon (the V-weapons). Our puzzle is where Osama bin Laden was hiding after 2001 (which took a decade to solve). Our mystery is whether US president John F. Kennedy and Soviet premier Nikita Khrushchev were the type of leaders who would risk nuclear war over missiles placed in Cuba in 1962. In each case, we ask visitors to think through the issue as an intelligence analyst—by scrutinizing actual Royal Air Force reconnaissance photos of V-weapon sites; using starbursting (a structured analytic technique) to brainstorm key questions to help locate bin Laden guided by the CIA analyst Cindy Storer (see chapter 11); and reading excerpts from actual CIA and KGB analyses of Kennedy and Khrushchev to get into the minds of the two leaders.

In addition to these stories, the gallery offers visitors a chance to explore their own cognitive biases through a series of "Mind Games." These fun challenges use everyday examples that aim to trap participants into perceiving or processing information inaccurately or missing it completely. Such games demonstrate how our minds can trick us, revealing different biases such as misattribution, confirmation, affirmation, or inattention. Visitors then discover an actual intelligence story that was affected by that bias and the real-world consequences. By first investing participants personally in understanding what a bias is, we help them make the connection between their own experience and the spying life.

Intelligence, of course, "is only as good as the consumer's ability to believe and utilize it."[5] We knew that, for visitors to really understand what intelligence agencies do, we had to address how intelligence feeds into strategic decision-making. We wanted visitors to recognize that, unlike in the movies, the intelligence community does not make policy but informs it and that rarely, if ever, in the intelligence world is there 100 percent certainty. In our *Decision Room* interactive, visitors take part in a competitive analysis exercise called *Red Teaming*. In 2011, CIA analysts used such an exercise to challenge the assessment that bin Laden was hiding in a compound in Abbottabad, Pakistan, and to come up with alternative explanations for the intelligence gathered up to that point.

Guided by former CIA deputy director Michael Morell (who was part of the intelligence team that worked on this case), visitors are able to do the same. Just like CIA analysts, they examine physical aspects of the compound and assess whether another individual—a wealthy businessman, a local criminal, a different al-Qaeda leader—might instead be living there. As Morell suggests at one point: "Look at that balcony on the top floor . . . do you think anyone could get a good view from this one? And check out the windows facing the street . . . they're all covered. Who of our possible inhabitants might be willing to sacrifice being able to look out so that no one can see in?" Ultimately, visitors must decide how confident they are that bin Laden is at the compound and present their assessments to the president (Barack Obama in this case), who must himself decide whether to launch a raid. It is a seven-minute interactive experience—the longest in the museum—that demands deductive reasoning rather than just finding the answer, and many of our visitors know the actual outcome of the story before they even begin. Nevertheless, it holds visitors' attention throughout and is one of the more popular exhibitions.

We have always understood that one of the Spy Museum's greatest assets is the appeal of the secret-agent fantasy. Indeed, we know that many of our visitors are not only interested in finding out about espionage but also, in some sense, want to experience the life of a spy—to feel what it is like to be a spy. But how do you give people a taste of the spy experience in just a few hours? To help our visitors feel like a spy, we designed a range of experiences that focus on spy tradecraft and the physical, emotional, and mental challenges associated with doing this work—providing entry points that accommodate the diverse ways people learn. Some are simple mechanical interactives (opening a mailbox to see inside); others are complex digital experiences (designing a mission-specific gadget) or immersive physical and audiovisual experiences (entering a mirrored room that immerses visitors in the limitlessness of cyberspace). Throughout, we follow our number-one rule: never ask visitors to do something that cannot be authenticated by an intelligence professional, even if some activities, by necessity, are sped up. Thus, we have no laser maze—not a single intelligence professional told us they ever needed to navigate one—but we do have an air duct through which visitors can crawl while spying on people below (a task confirmed by former intelligence officers). We migrated this over from the original museum and increased its accessibility, and it remains our most popular interactive. Another popular experience carried over from the previous museum is *Hang Time*, which challenges visitors to hang from a bar elevated a few inches above the ground while buffeted by wind and a shaking bar. Sure, secret agents do it all the time . . . *in the movies*! (Think James Bond hanging in an elevator shaft or from a helicopter for extended periods.) Most visitors find a few seconds hard enough.

The best interactive experiences not only place visitors into the shoes of a spy but also encourage empathy. A good example is our exhibition on Noor Inayat Khan, the first female wireless operator sent to occupied France during World War II by Britain's Special Operations Executive. After her spy network was blown, she remained in Paris, lugging her 30-pound suitcase radio to different locations around the city to send and receive messages, all while evading the Gestapo. Displaying an artifact—the same model of radio Khan carried—was an option, but we wanted to help visitors connect more emotionally with Khan's experience. To do this, we created a simple replica suitcase radio, about the same size and weight, and invite visitors to pick it up. Heavy? Now imagine you are a slight woman, always on the move, whose life depends on no one suspecting what you are up to. Could *you* do it?

While individual interactives like these are valuable for depicting realistically the challenges and skills involved in spy tradecraft, they do not provide a holistic understanding of how such tasks might be integrated into a spy mission. To fully engage visitors in the challenges spies face, we created *Undercover Mission*, a highly personal and flexible secret agent fantasy experience using radio-frequency identification (RFID) and beacon technology. At the start of their visit, visitors receive an RFID-embedded badge and check in at a digital kiosk where they are assigned a cover identity

Figure 1.4: Book written in 1952 about the unexpected bravery of the author's friend, SOE radio operator Noor Inayat Khan. Captured and killed in Nazi occupied France during World War II, Khan's code name had been "Madeleine."

based on a quick personality test and a specific mission. Their challenge is to stay undercover and gather intelligence at interactives spread across the galleries where they engage in activities such as cracking codes, creating a disguise, and finding a dead drop. As they move through the museum their scores are tracked. When they check out in the "Debriefing Center" (the final exhibition), they discover the conclusion to their mission and their top two spy skills. Back home, visitors can even continue the experience by accessing a special *Undercover Mission* website portal to find their scores and hear from a real intelligence officer with similar skills. The experience has been a hit with visitors.

Since first opening in 2002, part of the museum's mission has been to provide an objective and apolitical forum for exploring intelligence. As a private, independent museum, we do not represent any government. Our role is not to be a cheerleader for any intelligence agency, or to encourage visitors to become intelligence professionals, but rather to explore the role and impact of intelligence: its successes and failures, challenges, and controversies. As such, the museum does not shy away from depicting the dark side of intelligence—the risks, loneliness, betrayals, mistakes, unintended results, questionable ethics, and oversteps. In the new museum, we wanted to explore these topics head-on and ask hard questions about the private and public consequences of spying.

We address these issues across the entire museum. In *Spies and Spymasters*, half the major spy stories we feature end up in death, imprisonment, or exile. These issues arise even more dramatically in the *Covert Action* gallery, where we include failed operations—from R. H. Lockhart and Sidney Reilly's hopeless plan to topple the Bolshevik regime in 1918 (a coup that unraveled before it even began) to France's botched attempt to sabotage the *Rainbow Warrior*, the flagship of the environmental group Greenpeace, in 1985. For the latter, the resulting blowback—the death of a passenger and a full-fledged scandal for the French government—was as much a part of the story as the operation. As visitors can see in a video, when we interviewed Jean-Luc Kister, chief of the Combat Swim Team in France's General Directorate for External Security and one of the operatives who planted bombs on the ship's hull, he told us: "It was considered as a failed operation. . . . And after that in the world we are considered as bad guys . . . we are condemned to see all our failure expressed in the media to the world."

The goal here was not just to show that stuff goes wrong in the intelligence world. We also wanted visitors to think about why operations fail or succeed and the real-world effects, both short- and long-term. To illustrate this point, we juxtapose two classic CIA paramilitary activities: Operation Zapata, the ill-fated Bay of Pigs invasion of 1961 that resulted in humiliation for President Kennedy, and Operation Cyclone, the 1980s effort to back the Afghan mujahideen in their war against Soviet invaders that is often cited by the CIA as its most successful covert operation. We break down each story into key operational components such as plausible deniability, local resistance, and political support at home, and we explore how and why these operations failed in Cuba and succeeded in Afghanistan. We also encourage visitors to look beyond the operations themselves to the unintended consequences of failure or success: How, for example, did the Bay of Pigs fiasco strengthen Fidel Castro's case to stage Soviet missiles in Cuba? And were there links between the CIA's support for mujahideen fighters in the 1980s and the 9/11 terrorist attacks?

Betrayal was another theme we wanted visitors to think about more deeply through exploring the meaning of terms such as "loyalty" and "disloyalty" or "hero" and "traitor." In our *Spies & Spycatchers* exhibition we look at individuals who turned against their government with devastating consequences to themselves and others—including the counterintelligence officers connected to these cases. We focus on four people: MI6's Kim

Figure 1.5: Tea samovar belonging to the British traitor Kim Philby. After he defected to the Soviet Union in 1963, Philby never received the hero's welcome he had expected. A pension allowed him some luxuries, however. From the Collection of H. Keith and Karen Melton at the International Spy Museum.

Philby, the Soviet Union's Adolf Tolkachev, the CIA's Aldrich Ames, and the FBI's Robert Hanssen. The exhibition brings these stories to life with extraordinary artifacts (from Philby's samovar to Hanssen's Walther PPK). The labels are fact-based, describing what these men did, why, how, and the impact of their actions—but they offer no judgment. For this reason, the exhibition has found critics (mostly former CIA officers) who object to putting Tolkachev, a man they admire for turning against an evil Soviet system, side by side with men they find contemptible for their betrayal of the values of a free society. But by including Tolkachev, we very deliberately hoped to encourage visitors to consider the meaning of disloyalty, to question their original viewpoint, and thereby to make their own judgment. Might one country's traitor be another's hero? How can an act of heroism also be seen as treason? To prompt such reflection, a question hangs from the ceiling of the exhibition in large letters: "HERO OR TRAITOR?"

Secrecy, as exercised by the state, posed a different challenge, however. Spies and spy agencies operate in secrecy in the name of national security. But how does secrecy impact society? Can there be too much secrecy? Who gets to decide? We took these conceptual questions and explored them, experientially and intellectually, in two exhibitions. In *Berlin: City of*

Figure 1.6: Forged identification card, 1970s. Soviet engineer Adolf Tolkachev photographed secret documents at his apartment for the CIA. However, to check out those documents from his organization's registry, he had to leave his identification card. Unfortunately, he also had to show his identification card to get back into his office with the documents he had just photographed. The CIA forged a second card for him to allow him to do this work. From the Collection of H. Keith and Karen Melton at the International Spy Museum.

*Spies,* we created the immersive environment of divided Cold War Berlin to give visitors a sense of what happens in a society when a government's perceived need for security overrides everything else. Visitors enter the exhibition from the West (figuratively), where there is brightly colored graffiti on the Berlin Wall and a newsstand with stories about escapes from the East. Visitors can then either slip into East Berlin through a disguised break in the Wall or cross over at a security checkpoint past an East German soldier and his barking German Shepherd (shown on a life-size screen). East Berlin is thus shown as a contrast in style and content: a realistic, colorless streetscape, a drab hotel room where every object—from the cuckoo clock on the wall to the cigarette packet on the coffee table—is a concealment device; a Stasi interrogation room where visitors discover the Stasi's methods of psychological manipulation; and an office filled with Stasi artifacts designed for audio or visual surveillance. On this side, two full-size segments of the Berlin Wall stand starkly unadorned—authentic artifacts donated to the museum from Germany—except for a question projected onto the surface: "WHO'S WATCHING YOU?" The overall intent is to convey a feeling of endemic secrecy, where anyone—the border guard, hidden cameras, spouses, fellow citizens—could be part of the surveillance state.

The *Top Secret* exhibition poses other key questions regarding secrecy: What secrets should the government keep from its citizens? Which secrets should be revealed? Who decides? And what happens when citizens take it upon themselves to reveal secrets to the public? This exhibition juxtaposes two important stories about government secrecy. One looks at the trial and 1953 execution of Julius and Ethel Rosenberg for espionage and the classified VENONA decryption project, which provided evidence that Julius, at least, was guilty but leaves open the question of what role Ethel played, if any. What was the impact of keeping that big secret from the public for over 40 years? The other follows the story of how classified US government programs were revealed, from the FBI's COINTELPRO program exposed by citizen activists in the 1970s, to National Security Agency surveillance, exposed by people such as Edward Snowden in the early 2000s. What was the impact of disclosing those secrets to the public? The centerpiece is a powerful film that features interviews with people involved in and affected by these decisions to keep or reveal secrets, challenging visitors to consider what degree of secrecy is acceptable in the name of national security.

Propaganda, as a deception technique in our *Covert Action* gallery, was a topic we knew would be engaging for visitors. Leaders and governments have long conducted influence operations, manipulating information and disinformation to shape opinions, attitudes, and actions. But as we developed SPY, we saw the subject become even more salient with the widespread use of the phrase "fake news" and the public's awareness that misleading information was being deliberately spread through social media. We thought it essential to cover history and method, with an eye to showing that so-called fake news is nothing new and that there is both an art and a science to creating effective propaganda. So, we created a wall of striking propaganda images—from a thirteenth-century BCE wall painting of the Battle of Kadesh to a 2016 Facebook ad—each printed on a two-sided panel. Flip the panel and it reveals a label that identifies the image, the story behind it, and a list of common propaganda techniques such as sparking strong emotions, targeting audience needs and values, simplifying information and ideas, and attacking opponents. The panels physically manifest the very idea of visual propaganda: overt message on one side, hidden intent on the other. Hopefully, the questions provide visitors with some basic tools that they can apply outside the museum to think critically about manipulative messages they encounter in their day-to-day lives.

Our ultimate goal for SPY has always been to make a personal connection between the world of intelligence and our visitors' lives. The final exhibition in the museum addresses this directly. In *Spying in the Marketplace,* we bring espionage right into people's homes, showcasing stories about items they probably use every day—tea, glass, silk, blue jeans, even Oreo cookies—but that, at one time, involved a secret so commercially valuable that nations tried to steal it. It is an aspect of spying—economic espionage—that has been around for millennia and remains a primary focus of counterintelligence today.

This final exhibition also underscores, in a very tangible and personal way, a theme that runs throughout the museum: spying matters. Everyone has a stake in spying: policymakers, the media, businesses, and citizens. And spying matters because it can change the world (for good or ill), protect a nation or expose it to harm, make someone a hero or a betrayer, impact our privacy and civil liberties, and help us better understand the world around us. The exhibitions at the new SPY try to address all these impacts and inspire people to think about the many ways spying affects their lives.

Have we been successful in meeting this goal? We regularly look at visitor ratings and reviews posted online as an important source of information on what is working and what is not. Overall, most visitors are finding the museum a valuable experience ("interesting, thoughtful, and fun"), with more educational content than expected ("make sure you are ready for an intellectual adventure"). But some comments clearly articulate the ways SPY is making an impact that lasts beyond their visit:

> "It's an eye-opener."
>
> "It provided a great source of inspiration for a screenplay I'm writing."
>
> "I enjoyed it immensely, but now I'm a little bit paranoid that everything is a camera or a weapon, so I don't think I'm going to sleep very well tonight."
>
> "Since going to this place I have seen a variety of stories in the news that were pertinent to what I learned at this museum."

It has always been our goal at the International Spy Museum to educate the public about intelligence, past and present. A modern museum, however, should endeavor to do more. In making the covert overt, the new SPY casts light on the shadow world but at the same time encourages people to connect that world to their own lives in diverse ways. From feeling a sense of the danger and fear involved in living a life undercover to questioning what makes someone a hero or traitor, the exhibitions we designed all encourage our visitors to consider how spying matters to them as individuals and as citizens. And that might inspire someone to take a greater interest in current events, write to their representatives in Congress, or even pen the next great spy movie. Either way, we hope that, when most visitors leave the museum, they take something with them, and not just from the gift store: a new outlook on society, their nation, and the world, and even, perhaps, how they see themselves.

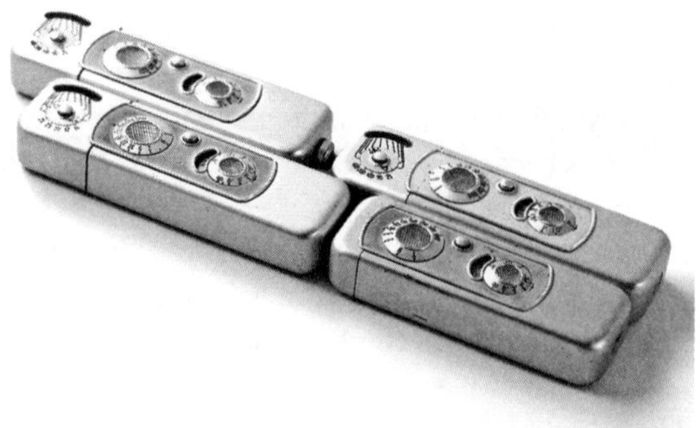

Figure 1.7: Minox cameras, a workhorse spy camera on both sides of the Iron Curtain for much of the twentieth century.

## Notes

1. The power of popular culture in shaping public views of, and expectations about, intelligence is a topic that is now being widely explored in intelligence studies. But SPY has been studying this for two decades. According to our informal polling, about 75 percent of SPY's visitors have watched a James Bond movie (a figure substantially higher than the oft-quoted estimate that "half the world's population has seen a Bond film.")

2. See, for example, David A. Kolb, *Experiential Learning: Experience as the Source of Learning and Development* (Upper Saddle River, NJ: FT Press, 2014); Bernice McCarthy and Dennis McCarthy, *Teaching Around the 4MAT® Cycle: Designing Instruction for Diverse Learners with Diverse Learning Styles* (Thousand Oaks, California: Corwin Press, 2006); Howard Gardner, *Frames of Mind: The Theory of Multiple Intelligence* (New York: Basic Books, 2011); and John Falk, *Identity and the Museum Visitor Experience* (New York: Routledge, 2009).

3. In November 2024, SPY refreshed this gallery with a new exhibit, replacing "Morten Storm" with an equally compelling story about a volunteer spy who took great risks: Virginia Hall, an American who operated in Europe behind enemy lines during World War II.

4. On cognitive traps, see, for example, Richards J. Heuer, Jr., *Psychology of Intelligence Analysis* (Washington, DC: Center for the Study of Intelligence, Central Intelligence Agency, 1999); Richards J. Heuer, Jr., and Randolph H. Pherson, *Structured Analytic Techniques for Intelligence Analysis* (Washington, DC: CQ Press, 2011).

5. Antonio Mendez and Matt Baglio, *Argo: How the CIA and Hollywood Pulled Off the Most Audacious Rescue in History* (New York: Viking, Penguin, 2012).

# The Bonding of Allen Dulles and James Jesus Angleton

**Jonathan Nashel**

*Many people's understandings of intelligence come primarily from fiction so the International Spy Museum tries to compare fiction and reality. But the two worlds don't merely contrast; they interact, as Jonathan Nashel shows us in this chapter. He demonstrates how spy fiction is important not only for what it is but also for the way it can affect even the most powerful people.—The Editors*

Art imitates life. Maybe we've got it backward. There is the curious phenomenon of individuals in the Mafia who watch, endlessly, *The Godfather* movies or *The Sopranos* series. They do so to be entertained, of course, but more important, to learn how to act like a proper wise guy.[1] And would anyone be surprised that a US senator or two learned how to do a filibuster after watching Jimmy Stewart's performance in the 1939 classic *Mr. Smith Goes to Washington*? Or there is the old story involving Alice B. Toklas and Picasso. It seems she didn't like Picasso's portrait of her partner, Gertrude Stein, complaining that it was unflattering and didn't resemble Stein. Picasso told her not to worry . . . she will come to resemble the portrait.[2] But one of the keener observers of this phenomenon was Keith Richards, cofounder of the Rolling Stones, a guitarist–songwriter responsible for the soundtrack to the lives of millions of baby boomers. While his debauched life has both an epic and fictional quality to it, he wrote an unusually good memoir. Fittingly titled *Life*, it reflects on the art/life conundrum with a tinge of regret:

> I can't untie the threads of how much I played up to the part that was written for me. . . . I think in a way your persona, your image, as it used to be known, is like a ball and chain. . . . Image is like a long shadow. Even when the sun goes down, you can see it. I think some of it is that there is so much pressure to be that person that you become it, maybe, to a certain point that you can bear. It's impossible not to end up being a parody of what you thought you were.[3]

Richards's observation has applicability far beyond the world of rock and roll. It touches, for instance, on one of the central problems faced by the Central Intelligence Agency. The Agency never learned how to deal with the "threads" of its persona because it was so complicit in its own mythmaking.

Mimesis and its inverse—life imitating art—can also be seen as a constant in the rapport between spies and the fictions that swirl around them. Tales about spies are perennial bestsellers on both the fiction and nonfiction lists. In turn, when retired spies seek out second careers, they know the potential for lucrative contracts awaits if they can create stories involving "The Agency," "The Circus," Mossad, and the KGB. Like all good authors, these former spies have followed the first commandment of writing: write what you know. Ben Macintyre, a superb nonfiction chronicler of the world of spies, noted the art-imitating-life conundrum while interviewing David Cornwell, a.k.a. John le Carré. Here, Macintyre remarked: "It's no accident that some of our greatest writers have been spooks—Greene, Somerset Maugham, Ian Fleming, Priestley and you, David."[4] From Macintyre's perspective, being a spook was the secret to understanding how these writers became writers. Many novels are filled with a cast of characters holding untold secrets and living and dying in exotic locales. But no mere civilian could replicate the dark and dangerous journeys with the veracity or nuance that these particular spy novelists brought to life on the page. Former spooks could simply touch on their own past deeds or at least extend these worlds with several degrees more substance.[5]

As readers, we think we know what the life of a spy is because we have read or seen countless examples of them prowling around on the page or up on the screen. We are swayed by these fictions, even as we acknowledge that the typical spy novel is simultaneously a peek into the shadowy world of intelligence and completely far-fetched. We recognize that Tom Cruise defying the laws of gravity in the *Mission: Impossible* film series is both entertaining and absurd. What is curious here isn't the effect these fictions have had upon a general public that apparently can't get enough of deep covers, black operations, honey traps, and sleeper cells. No, instead, the life/art conundrum becomes a problem when real intelligence officers are taken prisoner by these fictions. These spies had a Keith Richards problem. The real world of spying became their ball and chain, one they could never escape. And like Richards they probably wouldn't have been willing to trade in the notoriety and celebrity attached to their spy identity. This air of mystery that surrounded them was the source of their cultural capital and depended on public fantasies. The familiar witticism "I could tell you what happened but then I would have to kill you" plays off the power of secrecy and knowledge that only a few have access to. And these former spies deployed it in their works of art with a wink, a nod, and the knowledge that it would help pad their bank accounts. Yet they often ended up engulfed by a mystique they could no longer control.

There is no better example of life imitating art than Allen Dulles, the celebrated director of the CIA in the 1950s and early 1960s whose life became inextricably linked to the fictions that surrounded him and the CIA. Another example is James Jesus Angleton, the infamous and possibly deranged director of counterintelligence operations in the CIA from 1954 until his dismissal in 1975. What connects these men isn't that they shared the same social and cultural milieu. That is to be expected of the first generation of CIA officials. The intriguing aspect here is that they both became immersed in fiction as a way to understand their real personal and professional lives.

Fiction was a most intoxicating drug to these men and mingled very easily with the world of spying. Dulles confided to a friend that, where intelligence is concerned, "once one gets a taste for it, it's hard to drop."[6] After being forced to resign from his beloved CIA in 1961 (more on this later), Dulles spent the last years of his life comforted by spy fiction. Both he and Angleton understood their profession through the ideological lenses provided by literary traditions. Whereas Dulles viewed himself as an imperialist Romantic, Angleton went one step further: he understood his profession through a modernist lens, which viewed the very idea of certainty with a jaundiced eye. In different ways, then, they were both drawn into the web of fiction. Artists of various mediums returned the favor by using them as props in their works of art. The CIA became the perfect subject for these artists to depict their respective visions of the postwar world. The end result of all of these artistic representations of the CIA came to overwhelm what Dulles and Angleton actually did in their real lives. This in turn has overwhelmed the more dispassionate histories of the CIA. Fiction, in this sense, becomes a gateway for reconsidering the history of the CIA.

The starting point in untangling this web of fact and fiction are the classic spy novels that were read, voraciously, by so many of the men who would come into the Office of Strategic Services and later the CIA. Classics include James Fenimore Cooper's *The Spy* (1821) with its tale of intrigue during the American Revolution and his later novel *The Bravo* (1831). But of note here is *The Riddle of the Sands* (1903) by the Irish author Robert Erskine Childers. Here we see the spy novel come into its own, one involving English heroism versus German treachery. Even more impressive, the popularity of *Riddle* was such that it led the British government to develop a preparedness campaign against Germany shortly before World War I. (Childers would later be executed by the British for being a spy on behalf of Irish independence, giving the story an updated Nathan Hale quality and making it even more popular to an American audience.) Here was an instance of fictions that generated reality—a narrative of invasion that propelled fears of invasion and led to mass English military enlistments. Its popularity helped create a new genre (spy fiction) that became a staple in many publishing houses. Baroness Orczy, W. Somerset Maugham, John Buchan, Eric Ambler, and Graham Greene built on *Riddle*'s structure and produced worlds of mystery and intrigue that left indelible images in the minds of readers. These readers learned what the life of a spy was and, equally important, were imbued with a particular brand of adventurous masculinity.[7]

As good as so many of these novels were, Rudyard Kipling's *Kim* (1901) remained the quintessential spy novel to resonate, especially with young male readers. It is here that spying was linked to the Great Game of British and Russian rivalry in South Asia. Its tale of intrigue, defense of the West, orientalism, and unabashed English patriotism captivated generations of readers. Consider, for instance, a passage from the novel where Kim learned that "God causes men to be born—and thou art one of them—who have a lust to go abroad at the risk of their lives and discover news."[8] Here "news" is shorthand for intelligence: spying on behalf of the British Empire. How such a call must have resonated among its readership. A generation of English and American boys absorbed this tale and constructed images of how they, too, might live their lives according to this edict that fused spying with patriotism and excitement. And Sigmund Freud would undoubtedly chalk this up to the process of transference.

Even when these future spies turned to nonfiction, it is the fiction they had already consumed that helped shape their worldviews. Consider how many spy memoirs begin with a childhood immersed in the world of spy fiction. These proto-agents had already learned that the life of a spy was one of excitement, danger, and honor. "Honor" was a particularly important term for a profession previously considered as shameful as prostitution. It was, after all, known as the world's "second oldest profession."[9] Further, these fictions became so deeply embedded in readers' psyches that they would go on to name their children after imaginary spies. St. John Philby, the English orientalist and intelligence officer, christened his son Harold Adrian Russell Philby. The world came to know him by his nickname: Kim. The real-life Kim Philby would ultimately dishonor his fictional counterpart by becoming *the* double agent of the twentieth century. He imagined he was on the proverbial right side of history when he was working for the Soviets, but the consequences of Philby's betrayal of the British has fascinated (and appalled) historians and novelists.[10] Each writer seems compelled to examine for clues that get at Philby's interiority,

Figure 2.1: Pocket flask of the MI6 officer and KGB mole Kim Philby. Once a high flyer in British intelligence, he defected to the Soviet Union in 1963. Given little work in Moscow, he suffered from depression and drank heavily. From the Collection of H. Keith and Karen Melton at the International Spy Museum.

highlighting what the British psychoanalyst Adam Phillips has observed: "[O]ur unlived lives—the lives we live in fantasy, the wished-for lives—are often more important to us than our so-called lived lives, and that we can't (in both senses) imagine ourselves without them."[11]

For these future spies, their unlived lives are both a gateway and a form of haunting. Thirty or so years after their first taste of secrets and intrigue, many found themselves looking back at their lives and finding nothing terribly noble about their career choices. In fact, many of the felt they had been conned.[12] Instead of the world of *Kim*, they found themselves stuck in a world of bureaucratic muck in which the only constants were incessant turf battles at the office, an inability to talk about their work with anyone outside that same hated office, strained relations with spouses and children because of this code of silence, and a creeping existential angst between their professed religious beliefs and what the state apparatus was asking of them. And for many of them, this led to a losing battle with the bottle. These spies became the ultimate prisoners of fiction.

The formative power of *The Riddle of the Sands* and Kim leads in a direct narrative arc to the most famous fictional spy in the postwar era: James Bond. The story of Bond's creator, Ian Fleming, a naval intelligence officer during World War II, is so well known that to describe this history is simply to note that dozens of writers have been drawn irresistibly to the Bond flame.[13] Briefly, then, Fleming wrote the first of his novels, *Casino Royale* (1953), during his honeymoon to escape the "agony" of marriage. He called his Bond novels "straight pillow fantasies of the bang-bang, kiss-kiss variety."[14] (The fact that he wrote this to the quintessential American bang-bang, kiss-kiss crime writer Raymond Chandler is all the more entertaining). He churned out a novel per year, year after year, and this turned him into—these are his words—"the slave of a serial character."[15]

Figure 2.2: *Life* magazine with Ian Fleming on the cover in 1966, two years after his death.

The extraordinary success of the Bond novels had a tragic personal effect on Fleming and his family. His marriage went from bad to worse, and so did his health. His son was neglected by everyone and later died of a drug overdose. Fleming became an international celebrity by the early 1960s but hated what his life had become.[16]

However, there is still a great deal of history to unpack when considering Fleming and his creation, particularly how Bond touched the CIA.[17] The starting point here is the relationship between Ian Fleming and Allen Dulles. As recounted by Dulles, Jackie Kennedy introduced him to the world of James Bond in 1957 with a copy of *From Russia with Love*. She is reported to have said to him, "Here is a book *you* should have Mr. Director." (One can almost hear her deliver this phrase with a charming smile to the man who thought himself as leading the "State Department for unfriendly nations.")[18] And how could Dulles resist the novel once he dipped into this fantasy world: a dapper male spy, the renowned lover and defeater of the Soviets, a plot set largely in Turkey. Dulles might be excused for thinking this was a tale about himself given his worldwide fame as *the* Western spy. As a young man, he had been posted to the US embassy in Turkey where he was a notorious lothario. Dulles's accent even had a hint of English in it, in

Figure 2.3: President Dwight Eisenhower's new Director of Central Intelligence, Allen Dulles, on the cover of *Time*, August 3, 1953. Cover art by the famed artist Boris Artzybasheff, who was born in present-day Ukraine and fled the Bolsheviks in 1919; he perpetuated the romanticized image of the cloak and dagger. From the Collection of H. Keith and Karen Melton at the International Spy Museum.

an upper-crusty mannerism imparted by Hollywood that Americans prized at that time. This comingling of fact and fiction around the Bond novels accelerated as the novels grew ever more popular in the United States. Dulles made it a point to send President John F. Kennedy copies of the newest Bond books with "arch comments" added to them.[19] Fleming in turn sent copies of his books to the Kennedy family once he learned they were fans. Kennedy returned the favor when he told *Life* in 1961 that *From Russia With Love* was one of his favorite books. Leaving aside that this may have been a publicity stunt—JFK never wanted to appear too much of an egghead to the general public—no novelist ever received better press. And when *New Yorker* magazine published a cartoon that linked the two, Bond's entrée into the world of Camelot was sealed forever.[20]

For Allen Dulles, the process of being Bonded in Fleming's novels continued at an ever-accelerating rate. He was mentioned in *For Your Eyes Only*, *Thunderball*, and *You Only Live Twice*. These cameos clearly added to his celebrity. The man who was known within the CIA as the "Great White Case Officer" never needed to fear that he would slip into the memory hole of history; he was now a part of something so much more: Bondmania. One can guess what Dulles must have thought after reading the following passage in *From Russia with Love*: "M gestured to the chair opposite him across the red leather desk. Bond sat down and looked across into the tranquil, lined sailor's face that he loved, honoured, and obeyed."[21] One can almost see Dulles putting down the book, sighing a bit, and thinking, if only for a moment, that his own loyal agents might revere him in much the same way. Perhaps this is why Dulles told JFK that, despite all the absurdity and implausibility built into the Bond novels, he found them "professionally useful."[22] No doubt they soothed and massaged a certain CIA director's ego—and that served some point.

Dulles's greatest intelligence victory, though, was marketing himself throughout the 1950s to Eisenhower and even more to a general public that sought reassurances that communism would not triumph across the world. He seems to have convinced just about everyone that he was overseeing a razor-sharp intelligence agency, his project aided by a slew of spy-themed movies and novels. However, after the Bay of Pigs debacle in 1961 this fiction was called out, and he was asked to resign. Even after Dulles's forced retirement, the CIA realized that it was important to keep tabs on him and track his relationship with Ian Fleming's creation. On April 13, 1964, the assistant to the director for public affairs at the CIA wrote to the new Director of Central Intelligence, John McCone, about a forthcoming Bond novel: "This memorandum is *for information only*," the poor assistant wrote without irony. The memorandum goes on to explain that *Playboy* magazine would be excerpting the forthcoming Bond novel and that the CIA was monitoring this major cultural event, adding the relevant passages where Dulles was mentioned in the *Playboy* article. Happily, the assistant reported, their old boss was being discussed in a highly flattering manner. This document was, of course, heavily sanitized for security purposes and was not made available to the public until 1998.[23] Men's magazines weren't the only ones interested in the Dulles–Fleming relationship. There are multiple other articles about their relationship in CREST, the CIA Records Search Tool database. These had all been duly clipped from newspapers around the world and stamped "SECRET," only to be declassified decades later.

This Bonding of the CIA extended into the CIA building itself. For example, Walter Pforzheimer, the legendary curator of the CIA's Historical Intelligence Collection, created a display case in the main corridor of the CIA from September to November 1964. Inside it were books and ephemera to honor Ian Fleming, who had died in August 1964. As a connoisseur of all things intelligence related, Pforzheimer appreciated the good that Fleming had done on behalf of the CIA. Pforzheimer included a photograph of Fleming with Dulles. He had championed Bond and his American

Figure 2.4: A display at CIA Headquarters honoring Ian Fleming not long after his death in 1964.

sidekick, Felix Leiter. Together they all went into battle, and together they helped construct the aura surrounding the CIA.

Pforzheimer fashioned another display case honoring Dulles after his death in 1969. It was less a celebration of life, though. There is a funereal quality to it that makes plain the heartbreak Dulles (and some of his loyal aides) felt after he was fired by JFK. Pforzheimer believed that Dulles's "retirement" from the CIA in 1961 was his first step into the grave. What is also noted here was Dulles's embrace of fiction in his final years. His last book, *Great Spy Stories from Fiction*, was published in 1968, shortly before his death. It is a compendium of classic spy stories and features a host of writers including Joseph Conrad, Rebecca West, Kipling, Graham Greene, and Eric Ambler—even a section from Virgil's *Aeneid*. You can almost see Dulles drinking a nice port, seated near a roaring fire, rereading these tales with a glimmer in his eye as he recalled how they had worked their way into his imagination as a boy. He was at heart an nostalgic romantic and there was little place for him in the new bureaucratic, computer-driven, nuclear-tipped world of the 1960s.

But Dulles's turn to fiction in his later years simply mirrored what he had been doing as CIA director. When not orchestrating coups throughout the world, he was giving plot outlines for spy novels to the espionage

Figure 2.5: A display at CIA headquarters honoring former Director of Central Intelligence Allen Dulles shortly after his death in 1969.

writer Helen MacInnes.[24] Dulles also became a Cold War–era celebrity who capitalized on the fictional qualities attached to his role as CIA director. He was always in the news during moments of international tension, commenting on this or that, always puffing away on his pipe with a calm, wise demeanor. Anyone might think that a spy would prefer the shadows, but not Dulles. He sought the limelight and with it the power that came to be attached to his celebrity. This is how he became a prop in Fleming's novels. Others found Dulles a perfect vehicle to explore the men who made up Cold War America. Alfred Hitchcock was so taken with Dulles that he transformed him into The Professor in *North by Northwest* (1959). Played by the inimitable Leo Carroll, the fictional version portrayed Dulles at his grey best: ruthless, debonair, and never breaking a sweat. The Professor character in the movie was exactly as the real Dulles would have wanted to be seen outside the movie theater.

A more unsettling depiction of Dulles appeared in a series of images made of him by the photographer Arthur Fellig, better known as "Weegee." Weegee is a most curious artist who was well known to the general public and championed by critics as an artist of the first order. His "Distortions" series from the early 1950s reflects this elite/mass appeal: he was giving the public what it wanted but in sly ways. The series includes titillating and unflattering images of celebrities, with each image mutating from the celebrity's aura into a version that is almost unrecognizable yet still

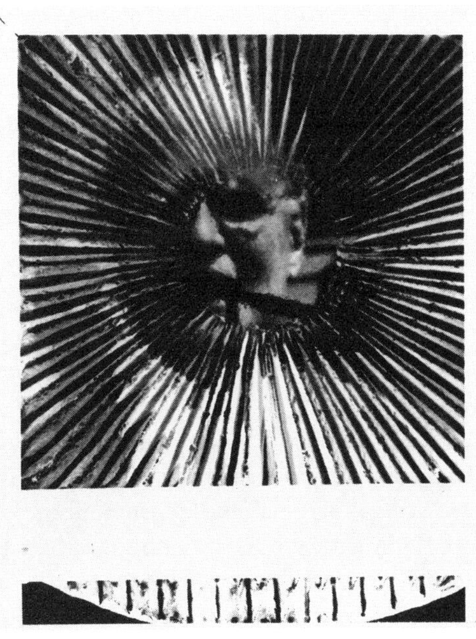

Figure 2.6: A Weegee photograph of Allen Dulles from the artist's "Distortions" series in the early 1950s.

knowable. Tucked into this series are Weegee's distortions of Dulles. Here he is commenting on Dulles's air of mystery, intrigue, and the threat of violence. Dulles's images remain instantly recognizable here, given that Weegee's art bears a knowing similarity to the *Time* cover that featured Dulles that rested on the coffee tables of millions of Americans that week. Fact and fiction merge seamlessly here as Weegee intended. After "Distortions" met with approval from Edward Steichen, the grandmaster of photography, Weegee reflected how, "feeling very much encouraged, I decided to leave the world of reality for the one of fantasy."[25] In this respect, the Bonding of Dulles, and of the CIA, occurred even before Ian Fleming took to his golden typewriter to write about the English spy.

Another notorious prisoner of fiction was James Jesus Angleton. Like Dulles, his history is well known. During World War II he worked for the OSS in London, and by the 1950s he was overseeing all counterintelligence operations in the CIA. What he did or did not do as a CIA officer has been eclipsed by the controversies that swirled around him. The CIA's own History Branch has an extended review essay about him titled, appropriately enough, "The James Angleton Phenomenon."[26] Here one can learn about a host of authors who focused on this dark, and perhaps disturbed, man. When one delves into this literature, though, an uncanny similarity binds them together: each author's appraisal of Angleton reads as if he or she is on some epic quest, á la King Arthur's knights in search of the Holy Grail.

Each writer believes that to gain entrance into the very heart of the CIA one must unlock the mystery of Angleton. The History Branch's study is a useful historiographical compendium, but it doesn't come to any conclusion about the man. When the History Branch throws up its hands and says that the Agency's most notorious employee is essentially unknowable, readers know there's a problem—or an opportunity if one is a writer or artist considering the CIA.

The fullest artistic version of Angleton is Norman Mailer's 1991 novel about the Agency, *Harlot's Ghost*. Running over a thousand pages, it is huge, and yet it ends with "TO BE CONTINUED." For Mailer, explaining American power and intrigue can never be a finished project. Hugh Tremont Montague, a.k.a. Harlot, is modeled after Angleton and sees conspiracies everywhere. He is involved in one sordid deed after another, all justified in the epic quest to defeat communism, the greatest of all conspiracies. To Harlot, communism isn't wrong or bad; it is evil itself. Communism, he tells the protagonist of the novel, Harry Hubbard, is "the entropy of Christ, the degeneration of higher spiritual forms into lower ones."[27]

Obsessing over Angleton shows no sign of ending. The journalist Jefferson Morley has written a recent biography of "Mother"—as Angleton was known within the CIA. It's titled appropriately enough, *The Ghost*, and my hunch is that Morley didn't use "Mother" as the title because it had been used in a previous novel about Angleton.[28] One does not have to be a Freud fan to see that the very word associated with Angleton here, "mother," links all too nicely back to feverish dreams and origins stories that surround the CIA. Happily, Morley's book adds new nuggets about this strange, strange man, but he can't resist pursuing the Mother of All Conspiracies: Who killed JFK? He asks a pseudo-question: "Was Angleton running Oswald as part of a plot to assassinate President Kennedy? He certainly had the knowledge and ability to do so."[29] Morley surely wants to believe it is so. Like so many before him, the idea of Angleton as a dark overlord explains the nature of the CIA. And it is the idea of Angleton controlling Lee Harvey Oswald that becomes a key to understanding the source of all the ills that have befallen the United States since that day in Dallas. While there are a number of positive reviews of the biography, it is questions like this that led to a withering review of it in the CIA's own historical journal.[30]

To be sure, Morley's question is one that has circulated in American culture since 1963. It dovetails with Don DeLillo's fictional analysis of the CIA. In his novel *The Names* (1971), DeLillo links the CIA with all of American history: "The CIA is America's myth. All the themes are there, in tiers of silence, whole bureaucracies of silence, in conspiracies and doublings and brilliant betrayals."[31] DeLillo has returned to this reading of the CIA in several novels since then, most spectacularly in *Libra* (1988), his fictional recounting of the Kennedy assassination and the CIA's (non) role in it. Again and again, DeLillo locates the CIA, or more accurately a sinister idea of a CIA, as central to understanding the history of America. His CIA is a very strange gift that needs to be unwrapped and observed with care.

Portrayals of Angleton are varied, but they tend to depict a man who cultivated an air of intrigue and fused it with a relentless quest for power within the Agency. And while he was American by birth, he was really "more English than the English," making him appear as the CIA's very own T. S. Eliot.[32] As the British writer Ben Macintyre put it, Angleton was "a little like one of the rare orchids he would later cultivate with such dedication . . . rare and remarkable, alluring to some but faintly sinister to those who preferred simpler flora."[33] By the 1960s, a combination of mental health issues and increasing dependence on alcohol led Angleton to become convinced of a Soviet plot within the CIA, one that came to be known as the "Black Hat" theory. Here the Soviets sent "defectors" to the West to provide disinformation to protect the identity of their real spies within the CIA. Angleton's embrace of this theory can be explained on many levels, with paranoia being one simple explanation. But Angleton's love for modernist fiction and literary criticism plays a part here as well. It is in this literature that nothing appears as it seems, that a coherent chronology of events is a fool's game. It also explains, for Angleton anyway, why the art of intelligence can be understood only as existing in T.S. Eliot's "wilderness of mirrors." The result of Angleton's embrace of Black Hat was more than ineffectual or tragic. Angleton's personal wilderness of mirrors hindered the CIA's efforts to understand the workings of the Soviet government well into the mid-1970s. The logical outgrowth of this wilderness led to Angleton overseeing Operation Chaos, the Agency's domestic intelligence activities targeting antiwar protestors during the Vietnam War. No one was above suspicion, and working within the confines of congressional oversight was not only foolish but also tantamount to surrendering to communism.[34]

Angleton's life story has become a cautionary tale of how one man's paranoia can cripple an intelligence agency and ruin countless lives. Yet writers tackling Angleton's story diverge at key points about his life and actions. For some biographers, he never recovered from being played or seduced by Kim Philby. These authors focus on Angleton's fevered defense when his old friend was first suspected of being a Soviet agent and how he continued to defend Philby until Philby fled to the Worker's Paradise in 1963. This helps to explain the rage, the heartbreak, and the search for excuses to explain why Angleton transformed the CIA counterintelligence office into a den of fear and loathing. In these histories, Angleton becomes the proverbial scorned lover. For others, Angleton was right in believing Philby's tale of Soviet plots within the CIA. William Safire is but one journalist who thought Angleton's Black Hat theory had merit and wrote a number of columns in the *New York Times* defending Angleton. The investigative journalist Edward Jay Epstein asks coyly in one title: *James Jesus Angleton: Was He Right?* To Epstein, Angleton was a truth-seeker, not someone in need of counsel.[35]

We now know there was no Soviet master plot, with or without a black hat. But coming to terms with Angleton remains no easy task. Any man who could say that Henry Kissinger was, "objectively, a Soviet agent" seems easy to dismiss as a crank, let alone a right-wing conspiracist.[36] And any man who could tell a Senate committee investigator that "[i]t is inconceivable that a secret intelligence arm of the government has to comply with all the overt orders of the government" can be seen as a direct threat to our democratic institutions.[37] But the fact that he wielded considerable power for decades indicates that others at the CIA thought he was worth the trouble—or feared crossing him. Artists, journalists, and historians have come to view Angleton as the CIA's very own Ahab with the white whale becoming communism writ large. The literature review of Angleton by David Robarge (see "The James Angleton Phenomenon" mentioned above) indicates the longtime fascination that so many have had. The Bonding of Angleton even includes Manuela Hoelterhoff, the Pulitzer Prize–winning art critic. She began work in the early 2000s on an opera of his life story, á la John Adams's masterpiece *Nixon in China*. It has yet to be completed, and so one can only hope.

Though Angleton carefully avoided the limelight when he was an employee of the CIA—he told the journalist Daniel Schorr that if he was photographed it "might be a death sentence"—he was shot (by a camera, at least) numerous times after his forced retirement in 1975.[38] With each image, Angleton became ever more a Cold War celebrity. Angleton understood that being in the limelight now had its pluses; it could burnish his dark star. There is a photograph, eerie as can be, of Angleton carrying the cremated body of Dulles after his funeral in 1969. There he is, splashed on the front pages of newspapers, telling the Senate that Congress couldn't be entrusted with certain state secrets. But no single image did more to explain Angleton's strange allure than when he agreed to be photographed by Richard Avedon. One can see here what one colleague recalled of the spymaster: "When Angleton spoke his mocha eyes shone, and as his lips parted, without warning a grin would irradiate his hollow face."[39] Avedon, like Weegee before him, was a renowned artist, one whose body of work illuminates postwar photography. This image was part of a series he did

Figure 2.7: James Angleton photographed in July 1976 by Richard Avedon. This was one of a series of Avedon photographs of leading figures of the American establishment that were published in *Rolling Stone* in October of that year. Photograph by Richard Avedon. © The Richard Avedon Foundation.

for *Rolling Stone* magazine in October 1976. Avedon's ghostlike portrait of Angleton has become the gateway for so many writers seeking entry into this strange man's world. It is both piercing and foggy. It highlights the WASPish qualities that defined Angleton and the gaunt, haggard look that takes hold of a man who is haunted by too many secrets (both real and imagined). These secrets had come to define him, and even gave him a life purpose, yet they were killing him at the same time. Avedon's talent is that he extracted, again like Sigmund Freud, the Eros/Thanatos quality of Angleton from this image. He has, in short, Bonded Angleton with our ideas of who and what constituted the CIA.

Another example of Angleton's bonding is in Robert DeNiro's film *The Good Shepherd* (2006), a very slow fever dream of a movie about the CIA. Matt Damon plays Edward Wilson, a mashup of Angleton and Richard Bissell, the architect of the CIA's Bay of Pigs disaster. As if that's not enough, Damon's character has pieces of other key CIA officers thrown into the mix. You can see traces of Frank Wisner, Bill Harvey, and Tracy Barnes in Damon's character.[40] Damon's acting though is a true tour de force. One sees and feels his grayness, his coldness, his persona as holder of secrets so immense that no one can be trusted with them but him and him alone. It builds on Avedon's photograph in a canny way. As one might imagine, the CIA's History Branch did not take kindly to this film. The staff there lumped

Figure 2.8: Magazine coedited by Yale undergraduate James Jesus Angleton. *Furioso* published some of the top modernist poets of the day. Angleton went on to become the controversial head of the CIA's counterintelligence staff. Courtesy of the Francis Lara Collection.

it in with the other film that historians of the CIA love to hate: *JFK*, Oliver Stone's funhouse of a movie. And during a roundtable discussion of these movies, historians of intelligence coined a word to denigrate movies like these: "propagandamentary." It's a great turn of phrase and sums up the works nicely.

But these visual Bondings of Angleton pale in comparison to what occurred on the written page and, more specifically, how the words themselves affected Angleton. He had a deep and abiding love of modernist prose, and biographers of Angleton view this as a gateway to understanding him. At Yale he was an English major (of course) and edited a poetry magazine, *Furioso*, that published E. E. Cummings, T. S. Eliot, and Ezra Pound. He would later become friends with these giants of modernist literature. Throughout his lifetime, Angleton returned to their dense, elliptical, and dense and unyielding poems to explicate the nature of the world. From this perspective Angleton can best be seen as a prisoner of modernism. He was deeply influenced by William Empson's *Seven Types of Ambiguity* (1930), a foundational text of New Criticism. They later became friends. Lionel Trilling, the preeminent literary critic of midcentury America, helps to explain the logic driving Angleton's approach to spycraft as a problem in literary analysis. Trilling believed that it was what was behind the text that should concern the critic as much as anything else, stating that "shadows are also part of reality and one would not want a world without shadows, it would not even be a 'real' world."[41] This analysis mirrors how Angleton viewed the world. It also mirrors what Adam Phillips said earlier about the importance of unlived lives. Angleton simply fused this form of literary criticism with psychoanalysis and then applied it to the world of spycraft. Angleton, in short, weaponized this form of literature. And we are all the worse for it.

On the day after Angleton's firing on Christmas Eve 1974, he granted a four-hour rambling (and probably whiskey-soaked) interview with Daniel Schorr. Schorr recorded that he had trouble following Angleton's conspiracy-laden arguments, as they seemed to link together everything and nothing. When he told Angleton that he was having difficulties connecting these issues, Angleton replied: "I am not known as a linear thinker."[42] With that one remark, one can almost see the giants of modernism smiling wry smiles of agreement upon their most devoted of students

As this trajectory makes clear, the phenomenon of bonding—of life imitating art—and its inverse is an arc that begins with a conundrum, leads to tragedy, and then becomes a fundamental problem for the CIA as an institution. The mythology of the CIA would begin to overshadow each and every thing the Agency did. The fact that the CIA could not control its image is on one level predictable. Yet its failure speaks to the uncontrollable power of celebrity when propelled by the machinery of culture. The constant efforts of the CIA and its officials to harken back to an earlier time, when Dulles and Angleton read Rudyard Kipling's *Kim*, is symptomatic of this failure.

Figure 2.9: Stamp used to classify documents for "Mongoose"—the code name for a host of activities across the US government targeting Fidel Castro's communist regime in Cuba. These included consideration of at least eight plans to assassinate Castro from 1960 to 1965. From the Collection of H. Keith and Karen Melton at the International Spy Museum.

## Further Reading

Dulles, Allen, ed. *Great True Spy Stories*. New York: Harper & Row, 1968.
Fleming, Ian. *From Russia with Love*. Thomas & Mercer, 2012.
Kinzer, Stephen. *The Brothers: John Foster Dulles, Allen Dulles, and Their Secret World War*. New York: St. Martins Press, 2014.
Macintyre, Ben. *A Spy Among Friends: Kim Philby and the Great Betrayal*. New York: Broadway Books, 2014.
Mailer, Norman. *Harlot's Ghost*. New York: Random House, 1991.
Moran, Christopher. *Company Confessions: Secrets, Memoirs, and the CIA*. New York: Martin's Press, 2015.
Morley, Jefferson. *The Ghost: The Secret Life of CIA Spymaster James Jesus Angleton*. New York: St. Martin's Press, 2017.
Talbot, David. *The Devil's Chessboard: Allen Dulles, the CIA, and the Rise of America's Secret Government*. New York: Harper Perennial, 2016.

## Notes

1. Transcript, "La Drama Nostra," *Harper's Magazine*, March 2000, 24–25.

2. Gertrude Stein, *The Autobiography of Alice B. Toklas* (New York: Vintage Reissue, 1990); Elizabeth Cowling, *Picasso: Style and Meaning* (New York: Phaidon, 2002), 153. Thanks to Micheline Nilsen for providing me with this information.

3. Keith Richards, *Life* (New York: Little, Brown & Co., 2010), 364.

4. Sarah Lyall, "Spies Like Us: A Conversation with John le Carré and Ben Macintyre," *New York Times*, August 25, 2017.

5. See, for instance, John le Carré, "The Madness of Spies," *The New Yorker*, September 29, 2008.

6. Cited in Thomas Powers, "The Underground Entrepreneur," *New York Review of Books*, May 12, 1983.

7. See Rebecca Brittenham, "Erskine Childers," in *British Writers*, Supplement XVII, ed. Jay Parini (New York: Gale Cengage, 2011), 15–27.

8. Rudyard Kipling, *Kim* (London: Penguin, 1987 [1901]), 209.

9. The phrase has biblical roots. See Philip Knightley, *The Second Oldest Profession: Spies and Spying in the Twentieth Century* (New York: Norton, 1980).

10. The fictional and nonfictional literature on Philby is immense. See, for instance, Ben Macintyre, *A Spy Among Friends: Kim Philby and the Great Betrayal* (New York: Broadway Books, 2014). John Le Carré's afterword is of note. There is, too, le Carré's masterpiece, *Tinker Tailor Soldier Spy* (Toronto: Penguin 1990 [1974]), with its Philbyesque character dueling with George Smiley.

11. Adam Phillips, *Missing Out: In Praise of the Unlived Life* (New York: Farrar, Straus and Giroux, 2012), xvi–xvii.

12. Evan Thomas, *The Very Best Men: Four Who Dared—The Early Years of the CIA* (New York: Simon & Schuster, 1995); and Scott Anderson, *The Quiet Americans: Four CIA Spies at the Dawn of the Cold War—A Tragedy in Three Acts* (New York: Doubleday, 2020). Both of these works use the lives of CIA officials to chart the rise and fall of the CIA—and the damage the CIA did to their lives.

13. Andrew Lycett, *Ian Fleming* (New York: St. Martin's Press, 2013), is the most recent full-length biography of Fleming. See also Matthew Parker, *Goldeneye: Where Bond Was Born—Ian Fleming's Jamaica* (New York: Pegasus, 2015).

14. Fergus Fleming, ed., *The Man with the Golden Typewriter: Ian Fleming's James Bond Letters* (New York: Bloomsbury, 2015), 228.

15. Fleming, ed., *The Man with the Golden Typewriter*, 127. Fleming said this in 1961.

16. This is recounted in sad detail in Parker, *Goldeneye*.

17. This convoluted history is unpacked very nicely in Christopher Moran, "Ian Fleming and the Public Profile of the CIA," *Journal of Cold War Studies* 15, no. 1 (Winter 2013): 119–146.

18. Cited in Thomas, *The Very Best Men*, 186. Dulles dutifully recounted this story after Fleming's death, in 1964, in a *Life* magazine article dated August 28, 1964. Of note is that it mirrors the time Fleming met the Kennedys for the first time. Fleming recalled: "A couple of years ago, when I was in Washington, and was driving to lunch with a friend of mine, Margaret Leiter, she spotted a young couple coming out of church, and she stopped our cab. 'You must meet them,' she said. 'They're great fans of yours.' And she introduced me to Jack and Jackie Kennedy. 'Not *the* Ian Fleming!' they said. What could be more gratifying than that? They asked me to dinner that night, with Joe Alsop and some other characters. I think the President likes my books because he enjoys the combination of physical violence, effort, and winning in the end—like his PT-boat experiences. I think James Bond may be good for him after the dry pack of the day." Geoffrey T. Hellman, "James Bond Comes to New York," *The New Yorker*, August 14, 1962.

19. Peter Grose, *Gentlemen Spy: The Life of Allen Dulles* (New York: Houghton Mifflin Harcourt), 491; Allen Dulles appreciation of Ian Fleming in *Life*, August 28, 1964. Sadly, this marked-up book cannot be located in the JFK Library.

20. The cartoon is quite clever. It shows two policemen outside the White House. It is at night and they see only two lights on in the White House. One says to the other, "Then again, it may merely be the new Ian Fleming novel." Richard Decker, *The New Yorker*, September 21, 1963.

21. Ian Fleming, *From Russia with Love* (New York: Penguin, 2003), 104. It was originally published in 1957.

22. Derek Leebaert, *Grand Improvisation: Americans Confronts the British Superpower, 1945–1957* (New York: Farrar, Straus & Giroux, 2018), 500.

23. "Mentions of DCI in New James Bond Novel," April 13, 1964 (emphasis in original). Document released December 9, 1998, www.cia.gov/library/readingroom/document/cia-rdp70-00058r000300040026-6.

24. Cited in Thomas, *The Very Best Men*, 186; Joseph Finder, "Ripping Yarns; The Spy Novel Returns," *New York Times*, November 25, 2001.

25. Christopher Bonanos, *Flash: The Making of Weegee the Famous* (New York: Henry Holt & Co.), 229.

26. David Robarge, "The James Angleton Phenomenon," *Studies in Intelligence* 53, no. 4 (December 2009): 49–61.

27. Norman Mailer, *Harlot's Ghost* (New York: Random House, 1991), 394.

28. The first paragraph in this novel describes the Angleton character very much like the real Angleton: "Mother wore black shoes, black socks, a black tie, a white shirt, and a black homburg. He was not a man who had much affinity for grays. Tall and thin with a stooped, slightly twisted body, he looked like a crooked black snake

in a garden of brightly colored orchids," Aaron Latham, *Orchids for Mother* (Boston: Little, Brown, 1977), 1.

29. Jefferson Morley, *The Ghost: The Secret Life of CIA Spymaster James Jesus Angleton* (New York: St. Martin's Press, 2017), 265.

30. David Robarge, "Review of Jefferson Morley, *The Ghost: The Secret Life of CIA Spymaster James Jesus Angleton*," *Studies in Intelligence* 61, no. 4 (December 2017): 65–69.

31. Don DeLillo, *The Names* (New York: Knopf, 1982), 317.

32. Ben Macintyre, *A Spy Among Friends: Kim Philby and the Great Betrayal* (New York: Crown, 2014), 70.

33. Macintyre, *A Spy Among Friends*, 71.

34. John Prados, *The Ghosts of Langley: Into the CIA's Heart of Darkness* (New York: The New Press, 2017), 269, 279.

35. Typical here is William Safire, "Ghost of a Spook," *New York Times*, May 13, 1991; Edward Jay Epstein, *James Jesus Angleton: Was He Right?* (New York: FastTrack Press, 2014).

36. Daniel Schorr, "Reflections on the Life of James Angleton," *All Things Considered*, NPR, May 12, 1987.

37. Quoted in Robin W. Winks, *Cloak and Gown: Scholars in the Secret War* (New York: William Morrow, 1987), 327.

38. Schorr, "Reflections on the Life of James Angleton."

39. Ben Macintyre, "Review: *The Ghost: The Secret Life of CIA Spymaster James Jesus Angleton* by Jefferson Morley," *The Times*, January 6, 2018.

40. Roundtable discussion of *The Good Shepherd*, *Studies in Intelligence* 51, no. 1 (March 2007): 1–3.

41. Lionel Trilling, *The Liberal Imagination: Essays on Literature and Society* (London: Butler & Tanner, 1951), 9.

42. Daniel Schorr, *Clearing the Air* (Boston: Houghton Mifflin, 1977), 135.

# Spying for Teenagers: Espionage Through the Eyes of Ronald Seth's Young Adult Spy Thrillers

Jonathan Best

*The large number of spy-related books, games, and action figures in the International Spy Museum's collection illustrates that children and young adults, much like their parents, are fascinated by stories about spying. In fact, spy fiction can affect children's lives in powerful ways. The Soviet Union tried to take advantage of this by promoting stories of fearless young people who denounced disguised Nazi spies and saboteurs, and even their own parents, to the secret police. But as Jonathan Best shows us in this chapter on young adult thrillers, exhortatory spy fiction also played a role on the Western side of the Iron Curtain.—The Editors*

The British public became aware of Ronald Seth, the British wartime agent who had operated for the Special Operations Executive (SOE), in 1952 when he published his memoir, *A Spy Has No Friends*. This account was among the earliest postwar memoirs by former SOE agents that dealt with the sabotage and subversive operations of this clandestine wartime British service. Seth detailed his only SOE mission, which commenced in October 1942 when he was sent to Estonia to organize sabotage operations against Nazi oil production facilities. He noted that the mission was regarded as having only a 15 percent chance of success and that he was even offered the choice of withdrawing from it. He decided, due to his "self-confidence and tinge of patriotism," to continue.[1] This sense of foreboding about the success of the mission, code-named "Operation Blunderhead," turned out to be correct: Seth, almost immediately after landing in Estonia, was captured by the Germans. In his memoir Seth detailed the failure of his mission and how he was captured and interrogated by the Gestapo. He disclosed his ingenious plot to deceive the Germans into believing he was supportive of Nazism and willing to work for them as an agent, all the while collecting vital intelligence on the inner workings of the German intelligence services that he was able to pass on to the British authorities at the conclusion of the war. Upon publication in 1952, Seth's story was well received by critics;

a review of the book in an advertisement in *The Times* stated that in "cheating the Gestapo" Ronald Seth "brought back to England one of the war's most exciting spy stories."[2]

In the years following the publication of *A Spy Has No Friends*, Seth became an established authority on the topic of espionage and penned a nonfiction book series on the history of spying. Together with his wartime memoir, these works created the image of him as a clever and heroic British spy, someone who had extensive inside knowledge of British secret service. Two of Seth's nonfiction espionage works, *The True Book About the Secret Service* (1953) and *How Spies Work* (1957), were produced for teenage audiences and dealt with the historical activities of spying. A review of *How Spies Work* noted that Seth had provided "advice for those who would like to become secret agents"; another remarked it was a "text-book for apprentice secret agents." Importantly, both these works were also regarded as giving "espionage a glamour" that was appealing to young audiences.[3]

In addition to nonfiction accounts, Seth, like many former spies and intelligence officers, turned toward writing spy fiction. What is unique about Seth's spy novels, all published during the 1950s, is that they were aimed at a young adult (YA) audience, particularly teenage boys. In total, Seth authored six spy novels published between 1953 and 1959. These novels followed the exploits of Captain Brian Grant of the British secret service.[4] Grant was depicted as a resourceful, courageous, and tenacious agent, more than capable of undertaking dangerous missions. Most of Seth's novels were set in Europe, and three novels—*Operation Retriever*, *The Spy and the Atom Gun*, and *Rockets on Moon Island*—witnessed Grant operating behind the Iron Curtain, confronting communist secret service.[5]

Seth's novels have been neglected in previous studies of twentieth-century British spy fiction. Additionally, historical accounts of Seth and his operational career, published this century, have overlooked his fiction. Instead they focused on assessing and offering different interpretations of Seth himself and his account of duping the Nazis to determine whether Seth's version of events was truthful.[6] In fact, the historian Ben Wheatley argued in a 2014 article, which was based on extensive research of declassified British intelligence records, that much of what Seth reported in his memoir was fanciful fiction, created as part of a plot to generate the impression that Seth had been a heroic spy.[7] In concluding his article, Wheatley noted that "clearly there is a chasm between the public's perception of Seth's wartime role and the reality" of his experiences.[8]

A major reason for this chasm between the public perceptions and the reality of Seth's activities was that his nonfiction and his popular YA fiction presented him as a heroic spy and an authority on the topic of espionage.

Figure 3.1: Ronald Seth, *The Spy and the Atom Gun*.

While no sales figures exist to allow us to determine how popular Seth's novels were, his works received very favorable appraisals. For example, a review in the *Western Mail* stated *Operation Retriever* was "an excitingly graphic secret service yarn for boys," and another in the *Leven Mail* noted that his novel *Operation Lama* "is a breathless story of adventure for boys."[9] Finally, a *Birmingham Daily Post* review of several 1959 Cold War spy thrillers noted that *Rockets on Moon Island* "might well go top of the list" due to its "plain excitement."[10] Additionally, the fact that Seth, in a six-year period, was able to publish six novels indicates that his spy thrillers appealed to a YA audience.

Seth's books are important because of the mirror they held up to British society at the time they were published. In the 1950s Britain was suffering from a crisis of confidence, and there was widespread talk of it being a nation in decline due to imperial decolonization. Writing in 1953, the literary critic Richard Usborne noted that "England is no longer governess of half the globe" and "there are fewer–far fewer–government houses [governors' residences] flying the Union Jack."[11] Decolonization and the Suez Crisis of 1956 shattered any ideas of Britain being a global superpower on the same scale as the United States and Soviet Union. The failed attempt by Britain,

Figure 3.2: Ronald Seth, *Rockets on Moon Island*.

along with France and Israel, to regain control of the Suez Canal after it had been nationalized by the Egyptian president, Gamal Abdel Nasser, had, as stated by the historian Jeremy Black, "revealed the limitations of British strength."[12] However, even as pessimistic views were permeating British society in the 1950s, a different picture was appearing in British spy stories that highlighted the idea of Britain's global importance. The historian David Cannadine has noted that such fiction, through the depictions of James Bond, easily the most famous and popular fictional British spy of the early Cold War period, reflected the "greatness" of Britain. Cannadine also suggested that the spy novels by Ian Fleming, the creator of James Bond, contained an "omnipresent tone of national pride and patriotic sentiment."[13]

This national pride and patriotic sentimentality were important elements that ran throughout Seth's spy fiction. In his YA novels, Grant was often aided in his missions by a teenage sidekick who displayed Grant's same tenacity and qualities and who proved to be an invaluable ally. Through Grant and his companions, Seth was demonstrating the preeminence of the British secret service. Such depictions showcased the superiority of

Britain's secret service and challenged the notions of declining British national strength during the 1950s. Seth's fiction, with all the trademarks of the romantic spy genre that glamorized spying, can be viewed as a means of influencing teenage boys in the 1950s to become future Brian Grants protecting British interests at home and abroad. Seth's glamorous spy fiction highlighted the sense of excitement and adventure that a British spy experienced when undertaking dangerous missions. These stories were appealing to the young adult readership and showcased the resilience of Britain amid a period of flux.

The presence of Grant's teenage companions was important, as it allowed the young readers of Seth's fiction to more closely associate with the British secret service, thereby developing their own interpretations about the role of the British secret service and Britain's standing on the global stage in the post-1945 period. Studies have noted that a key theme in YA fiction in the 1950s was the idea of coming-of-age stories, which allowed adolescents to transform into adults and make sense of their own identities. These stories often allowed readers to shape their own views on society and contemporary issues.[14] These young adults were impressionable and could lack a clear understanding of complex ideas; this was particularly true concerning spying and geopolitics.

To date there has been no extensive examination of young adult spy fiction, either in Britain or globally. A major reason is that, while YA fiction had existed since the early 1800s, authors of the British spy genre, which emerged in the late 1890s and early twentieth century, did not start to produce fiction specifically for young adult audiences until the post-1945 period and then only infrequently.[15] Spy literature had been aimed primarily at adult audiences, though often it was consumed by teenage boys. Richard Usborne, who served as an intelligence officer during World War II, has noted that he had been brought up reading John Buchan's fiction and the heroic exploits of fictional agents such as Richard Hannay and Sandy Arbuthnot during the interwar period. For Usborne, "my boyhood heroes had lived the lives I wanted to live myself," and he hoped that he would get "a dangerous job offered to me in the British secret service." He observed that during the war "every [intelligence] officer I met . . . , at home and abroad, was like me, imagining himself as Hannay or Sandy Arbuthnot."[16] Similarly, in the Cold War period, intelligence officers had admitted to "joining British intelligence as young men partly because they had been brought up on a fictional diet of swashbuckling yarns" of British secret service heroes.[17]

Seth's first novel, *Operation Retriever,* witnessed protagonist Brian Grant being dropped by parachute into the fictional communist republic of Poznia, a stand-in for Poland. His mission was to locate Jan, the son of a Poznian scientist, Professor Vrancyk, who had defected to Britain. The communist secret police in Poznia (the PKW) had threatened to kidnap and imprison Jan in a concentration camp if Vrancyk did not return from Britain. Grant's mission was to locate and extract Jan as quickly as possible before he was captured by the PKW.[18] In the course of his mission, Grant was repeatedly aided by Jan. For example, in one instance, Grant and Jan were being pursued by PKW agents with dogs through a forest and were hoping to reach a river, where the dogs would lose their scent. The river, unfortunately, was frozen, but Jan, thinking quickly, was able to direct them toward an underground stream that was not frozen and allowed them to hide.[19] In another case, Grant and Jan were moving across Poznia toward the German border by hopping freight trains. While getting off one train at a town close to the border, they were intercepted by a policeman guarding the tracks. As he was asking who the pair were, Jan faked an injury to distract the policeman and then attacked him with a snowball, allowing Grant the opportunity to tackle him to the ground. As Grant and the guard struggled, Jan grabbed the policeman's discarded revolver and used it to knock him unconscious. Now faced with the prospect of trying to hide an unconscious police officer, Jan again came up with the idea of stopping an incoming train by switching the tracks, forcing the train driver to stop and manually rechange the switch. This presented Grant and Jan with the opportunity to place the unconscious police officer, who had been bound and gagged, into an empty railcar.[20]

During *Operation Retriever* Jan was depicted as having several qualities that made him a valuable ally for Grant. He was smart, adapted to quickly changing situations, displayed courage, and was able to think on his feet. For example, when first interacting with Jan, Grant noted that "Jan Vrancyk was certainly a boy who had all his wits about him," and if they were both to escape Poznia alive then "it would be due as much to his [Jan's] efforts as to mine."[21] While dealing with the police officer, Grant remarked that "what he [Jan] was going to do I hadn't a notion, but up to now he had always managed to make his ideas work, and I was quite willing to back him up."[22] In another instance, Grant thought that "Jan was one of the most comforting people I've ever known. Whenever things were at their blackest, he was cool, whenever things were going wrong his steady good sense made things seem not so bad."[23] These qualities of quick thinking and courageousness exactly matched the description of real-life spies that Seth had noted in his nonfiction accounts. For instance, in his 1953 book, *The True Book About the Secret Service,* Seth noted that an important attribute of any spy was temperament. According to Seth, a spy "must never get flustered, never lose his head, be able to think quickly and be able to come to quick decisions." Qualities such as resourcefulness and courage, he advised, were essential if secret agents were "to have any success at all."[24] Thus, through Seth's fictional portrayal of Jan, Seth's young readers were learning about the qualities needed to become a secret agent.

Seth also made it clear that Grant was a heroic spy, thereby highlighting the effectiveness of the British secret service. A common aspect of Seth's novels was that, even though Grant's missions were planned out effectively beforehand, as soon as the operations commenced unforeseen challenges and obstacles presented themselves that would have thwarted lesser spies. However, Grant was able to act quickly to make decisive decisions in stressful situations to ensure that the mission could continue. For example, the opening pages of *Operation Retriever* witnessed Grant being parachuted into Poznia, on the edge of a forest close to the town where Jan was living.[25] However, his landing site was located close to an undetected Poznian military guard post, and while descending by parachute Grant was faced with guards and dogs hunting for him. Grant's parachute got caught in a tree, and he was on the verge of being discovered when he quickly decided to drop from his parachute, run into the forest, and climb a different tree to avoid detection.[26] Later, as more guards hunted for Grant, he was captured, but he pretended to be a Belgian smuggler working for a fictional international gang, the Rattlesnakes. This cover story was something that Grant invented on the spot, and in an inner monologue he noted that "I was thinking hard, but even as I spoke, the story fitted itself together so well that I might have believed it myself."[27] The story was so convincing that Grant was even able to persuade the local army commander, Colonel Vosnin, who had captured him, not to transfer him to the PKW, as Grant stated that he was willing to give up information that would lead to the breakup of a major criminal enterprise. As Grant noted, Vosnin would be "directly responsible for unmasking the notorious international Rattlesnake gang of smugglers and black marketers" and would receive "high honors."[28] By delaying his transfer to the PKW, Grant was able to gain an opportunity to escape and continue his mission.

Seth's spy fiction and many of his nonfiction accounts of espionage created the impression that Britain possessed the best secret agents. For example, in the nonfiction *How Spies Work* Seth noted that "the British secret service is as active as any other country's intelligence. Of them all, the British is the most skillful and the most feared."[29] To Seth, this reputation was due to "British temperament" and the recruitment and training of outstanding individuals as spies.[30] These quotes by Seth about the superiority of British spies are another case of how his fiction was challenging the notion of British decline. Britain was depicted as possessing the best secret service, which contributed to the projection of the country's importance in world events. Through secret agents, Britain had influence and sway on matters of international security. To emphasize the superior nature of Britain's secret service, Seth highlighted the ineffectiveness of foreign spies. He used the case of Karel Richter, a German agent who had dropped into Britain in May 1941 but was caught because he raised the suspicions after a lost lorry driver asked Richter for directions.[31] Seth argued that Richter failed in his mission because he was not prepared to react to something unexpected—in this case being asked for directions by a lost driver. In Seth's opinion, a "British spy would certainly not have been caught in such a situation." Agents like himself were "quick-witted" and would have been more than capable of thinking up an acceptable response without raising any suspicions.[32] Additionally, the skills and qualities displayed by Grant, which highlighted the effectiveness of British spies, also reinforced the image of Seth as a heroic spy who was able to successfully dupe the Germans into believing he was sympathetic to Nazism. This duplicity allegedly allowed him to work for German intelligence while, in fact, he was a double agent collecting valuable information on the German secret service.[33]

Studies of British spy fiction published during the Cold War era have noted that Fleming's novels were an apex in the romantic spy genre, with clearly defined good characters, dastardly villains, and exciting events in which Bond worked to protect Britain from aggressive foreign nations and nefarious actors. These novels were also a vanguard of the developing affluence of the 1950s due to Fleming's emphasis on luxury, sex, and violence.[34] Seth's fiction had many similarities with Fleming's, including excitement, adventure, glamor, and the heroism of Grant. Nonetheless, there are remarkable differences between the two series. In Seth's fiction, there is no mention of sex, and female characters who act as love interests are lacking. This difference can be attributed to Seth's younger audience compared to Fleming's novels. The emphasis of Seth's fiction was on themes of adventure and heroism demonstrated through the exploits of Grant and his young sidekicks. Importantly, in contrast to Bond, Grant would rather use ingenuity and cunning to outsmart opponents and resorted to violence only when it was required, usually leading to nonfatal injuries to his foes. Such resourcefulness is important for two reasons. First, it projected the view of British secret service as being highly efficient. British spies did not require the use of violence to defeat enemies, as they had the qualities and ingenuity to outsmart them. Second, such a depiction contributed to

Seth's persona as a spy who outsmarted the Gestapo during World War II and created the impression that Seth was the epitome of the audacious and adaptable British secret agent.

In the foreword to the nonfiction *How Spies Work*, Seth noted that in all stories concerning spies "courage and audacity" always come to the forefront. Reading about the activities of heroic and fearless spies created a sense of excitement and suspense that appealed to all ages.[35] The actions of real-life British spies have long remained shrouded in secrecy and kept classified by the government. Nonetheless, there has been great public interest in the secret actions of British spies. Popular culture, particularly spy fiction, has been a catalyst for this increased public interest and profoundly impacted how the public understood and interpreted the world of secret intelligence. By glorifying British prowess in spy fiction, Seth countered the narrative of British decline.

An important aspect of this public image of spying was the idea that British secret intelligence was a glamorous world filled with adventure and excitement. In this world, secret agents purportedly engaged in perilous missions that could affect the future of national and international security. British spy fiction in the early Cold War period often created the impression that spying was an alluring subject that fascinated the public's interest and was enthralling to read about. This glamorization of espionage is often noted in studies of spy fiction in relation to Fleming's novels. His novels, along with the establishment of the bestselling Bond film series, established many of the trademark glamorous aspects of espionage, such as high-tech gadgets, licenses to kill, exotic locations, luxury, and beautiful women.[36]

Yet in his nonfiction accounts Seth stressed that he did not view spying as exciting given his own wartime experiences. To him, the glamorization of spying came from popular culture or, as he put it, "from the safety of an armchair in the sitting-room." In the opening pages of *How Spies Work*, Seth wrote that "the excitement, when translated from the armchair to actual life, loses all of its glamour in the constant and awful struggle which the spy must endure."[37] Seth's spy novels were markedly different on this question. His fiction highlighted the secret agents' excitement and adventures, and often Grant remarked about his growing excitement and feverish eagerness to undertake dangerous missions for his country. Importantly, there was a difference in Seth's glamorization of spying compared to that in other spy fiction of the 1950s, including Fleming's Bond novels. Seth's fiction was aimed at young adult audiences, and as such it was not excessively violent. There was a lack of special equipment, which in turn allowed him to highlight the personal qualities and skills of the

British spies. It can be said that Seth's glamorization of espionage can be seen in the themes of adventure, excitement, and suspense, whereby he created alluring and enthralling stories showcasing the heroic exploits of Grant and his young helpers.

An important aspect of Seth's glamorization, which created the impression of superior tradecraft, was Grant's use of disguises, something that appeared in many of the novels. Grant made use of disguises to mask his identity while undertaking secret missions. Often these disguises allowed Grant to operate near enemy guards and secret agents. For example, in *Operation Lama*, Grant was sent on a mission to Tibet to extract an important religious leader from Lhasa, the Forbidden City. Communist Chinese agents were also trying to capture the same religious leader so they could create a puppet government, with him as spiritual leader, to control the local population. At the beginning of the novel, Grant was informed how a previous mission, undertaken by two experienced agents who had extensive knowledge of the region, had failed and that now Grant was being deployed. He did not know local languages such as Hindustani, Urdu, Tibetan, or Chinese and had a limited understanding of local culture and costumes. Nevertheless, he was tasked with infiltrating Tibet via Darjeeling, the most northern Indian city in Bengal.[38] Upon discovering that Chinese communist agents were hunting for him in Darjeeling, Grant quickly realized that an Englishman would be easily identified in this region and remarked: "I must cover my tracks as early as possible." Thus, he decided a disguise was the best way to escape the city.[39] Grant darkened his skin, dressed in an oriental robe, and wore a headdress; he noted that after doing this "I certainly did not look like an Englishman."[40] To aid his infiltration into Tibet, he disguised himself as an elderly Tibetan trader. He stained his face and hair and shaved off his beard. He also drew up the corners of his eyes "until they were of an almond shape of the oriental"; he fixed them in place with a special gum substance that in the process altered his face. Together with dressing in the traditional robes of a wealthy trader, such measures allowed him to transform himself from an Englishman into a Tibetan and avoid detection by Chinese military patrols.[41] This transformation into an exotic individual would have been very appealing to the young readers and created the impression that spying was indeed a glamorous career.

Similarly, Grant made effective use of disguises in *Rockets on Moon Island* when he was tasked with gathering intelligence on new Soviet rocket installations on the Estonian islands of Hiiumaa, Muhumaa, and Saaremaa. After infiltrating Estonia by working with a group of anticommunist exiles in Finland, Grant discovered that the islands were under strict

Figure 3.3: *Planet of the Apes* mask created by Hollywood makeup legend John Chambers. Tony Mendez, the CIA's chief of disguise in the 1970s, was a friend and protégé of Chambers and incorporated many of his innovations, including mask technology, into the agency's clandestine operations.

military lockdowns, and no civilians were allowed to enter. Grant was aided by the courageous Tönis Tönisson, the fifteen-year-old son of one of the leading Estonian exiles, who had accompanied Grant on his mission behind the Iron Curtain. They were forced to find a means of entering the secret military bases, and after reaching Tallinn, the Estonian capital, they collected intelligence revealing that a new garrison detachment of Soviet soldiers was passing through the city. They decided to steal military uniforms from a local bathhouse and disguise themselves as Soviet soldiers. Importantly, they also obtained identification documents and crucial information about two soldiers by eavesdropping on conversations; this allowed them to successfully impersonate the Soviet troops so they could secretly enter the base. As they prepared for this disguise, they cut their hair to look like soldiers, and Grant "spoke in Russian" and started "thinking in Russian" to perfect his disguise. During this preparation, Grant was "conscious of mounting excitement" about his upcoming infiltration into a top-secret military base and the means he was employing to carry out his mission. To the readers, this use of disguises was portrayed as an elaborate and exciting means of fooling the enemy.

Likewise, in *Operation Retriever* Grant had to disguise himself so that he could secretly take Jan Vrancyk out of his school before the PKW could seize him. After meeting his contacts in Poznia, Grant learned that a local 70-year-old man, Rikard Metzner, a school inspector who had the authority to remove Jan without raising the suspicions of the boy's teachers, had recently died. Acting with initiative—a hallmark of any successful spy—Grant dressed in Metzner's clothes, used makeup to alter his appearance, and applied ash and water to dye his hair. Showing great diligence in perfecting his disguise, he also asked about Metzner's "little mannerisms . . . phrases that people remember, little habits." As he prepared to get into character, he went around "walking as I imagined he [Metzner] must have walked, talking as he would have done, playing with the tails of my coat."[42] Not so coincidentally (from the point of view of the readers), and in a nod to the skills and qualities of British secret agents, Grant had been asked before the mission if he could successfully impersonate a 70-year-old man; he responded "certainly. . . . in my job you have to be everything."[43] This use of disguise was employed as a means to create suspense, and not long after donning the disguise Grant accidentally ran into two PKW agents on their way to collect Jan. Grant, confident in his abilities, was easily able to fool the enemy agents and misdirect them and thus get to Jan first.[44]

Again, Seth's spy fiction, with his exciting tales of Grant's derring-do and use of disguises, presented spying as glamorous and exciting, and again such representations were in marked contrast to his view that the world of spying was decidedly unglamorous. While he claimed such a view of spying was gained from reading fiction in the safety of one's armchair, he was, through his fiction, contributing to this vision of spying. Additionally, Grant's employment of disguises closely mirrored the description of spying that Seth presented in *How Spies Work*. In that book, Seth made a point of highlighting the use of disguises and how secret agents employed such means to carry out their missions successfully.[45] He noted that spies operating in enemy territory often had to use disguises and cover identities to keep their spying activities secret. At one point, Seth commented that a successful spy "will sink his own personality and take on his new personality," which might include adopting new mannerisms, changing handwriting, and wearing different clothes. Such techniques are exactly what Grant adopted during his fictional missions. According to Seth, a spy who successfully employed these techniques could "quite naturally fit into his background" and therefore carry out his mission successfully.[46]

While Seth's spy novels were largely lost to history in the decades following their publication in the 1950s, his depiction of British effectiveness and dominance in the espionage world was a long-running theme in the genre of British spy fiction. Seth's fiction, like numerous British authors from the start of the twentieth century, excelled at highlighting British superiority in the espionage world. For example, novels published before and during World War I by the prolific spy author William Le Queux depicted British secret agents operating across Europe as the elite spies on the continent. They possessed the necessary skills and abilities to access secrets that would protect British national and imperial security and were adept at

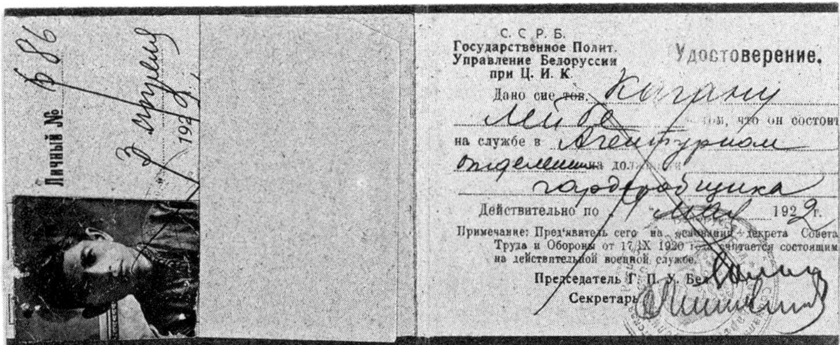
Личный №

С. С. Р. Б.
Государственное Полит.
Управление Белоруссии
при Ц. И. К.

Удостоверение.

Дано сие
что он состоит
на службе в
Действительно по 192 г.
Примечание: Пред'явитель сего на декрета Совета Труда и Обороны от 17/IX 1920 считается состоящим на действительной военной службе.
Председатель Г. П. У. Бе
Секретарь

Figure 3.4: Identification document for a member of the Belorussian branch of the GPU, 1922. Young people sometimes do play a role in espionage and intelligence. The photo suggests that this member of the revolutionary Russian secret police was scarcely out of boyhood. Courtesy of the Francis Lara Collection.

acting decisively and courageously to protect themselves.[47] This image of Britain as having the best spies continued through to the 1950s. Spy stories from authors such as John Creasey, Alexander Wilson, and Sydney Horler all depicted British agents working effectively to protect Britain. For example, one of Creasey's most successful spy series followed the exploits of agents working for Department Z, a clandestine secret service tasked with protecting British national security from domestic and foreign enemies. One of the agents was James Quinion, who was described as possessing a "dogged tenacity in the face of difficulty and a flair for probing intricate problems with a keenness" and as "an extremely resourceful young man."[48] It was implied that with agents like Quinion Department Z had developed into the best secret service in Europe.[49] The post-1945 period had seen a continuation of this theme, which was best expressed in the image of Bond. In this century Alan Judd, a former Foreign Office official and a spy novelist, has noted that Bond, with his heroic actions confronting villains from SMERSH and SPECTRE, became a "calling card" for British intelligence.[50] Similarly, the journalist Andrew Marr noted that "James Bond promoted the idea that our secret service was the best in the world."[51]

Seth's YA spy fiction of the 1950s can and should be regarded as important because it was a continuation of the established aspects of the British spy genre. However, it also reflected an evolution of the spy genre by focusing stories on young adults. His fiction was some of the earliest known British spy novels specifically aimed at, and marked for, a younger audience. Teenage boys had long been accustomed to reading adult spy fiction, but Seth's fiction was now specifically available to them. Crucially, through

Grant's young companions, the readership of Seth's fiction was presented with characters who clearly possessed the skills and qualities of a successful spy but who was also near their own age. Given that real-life British spies, active in the 1940s and 1950s, were influenced in their decision to join the secret service due to their reading of spy fiction as teenagers during the interwar period, it is likely that the spies of the 1960s and 1970s were influenced by Seth and the messages contained in his YA fiction.

In his description of the qualities and skills of Grant, Seth also demonstrated the superiority of British intelligence over other nations' secret services. Such portrayals tied into broader trends in the spy genre by highlighting Britain's greatness in the world of secret intelligence. Importantly, Seth's fiction can also be interpreted as a challenge to the notion of British decline in the post-1945 period. His novels can be regarded as a form of popular culture that highlighted Britain's importance in an era of uncertainty about the nation's future. Notably, while Seth in his nonfiction attempted to highlight the fact that spying was not glamorous, his spy fiction did the opposite by presenting spying to young and impressionable audiences as an exciting and alluring activity, thereby contributing to it being considered glamorous. Thus, Seth's fiction, specifically aimed at young adult audiences and featuring teenage protagonists, can be seen as a means of influencing the next generation's beliefs and values about both the superiority and allure of Britain's secret services as well as the nation's continuing central position on the global stage at a time of uncertainty.

Figure 3.5: Street Scene-G Man Patrol Game, circa 1930s–1940s. In the 1930s, FBI Director J. Edgar Hoover promoted the image of FBI special agents as intrepid gun-toting crime fighters. The result was a flurry of toys, comic books, books, movies, and other items such as this shooting game.

## Further Reading

Kirby, David Gordon. *Operation Blunderhead: The Incredible Adventures of a Double Agent in Nazi-occupied Europe*. Stroud: The History Press, 2015.

Seth, Ronald. *How Spies Work*. London: Geoffrey Bles, 1957.

Seth, Ronald. *A Spy Has No Friends: To Save His Country, He Became the Enemy*. London: Headline Review, 2008.

Wheatley, Ben. "MI5's Investigation of Ronald Sydney Seth, SOE's Agent Blunderhead and the SD's Agent 22D: Loyal British Agent or Nazi Double Agent?" *Journal of Intelligence History* 13, no. 1 (2014): 41–61.

## Notes

1. Ronald Seth, *A Spy Has No Friends: To Save His Country, He Became the Enemy* (London: Headline Review, 2008), 11–12.

2. Anon., "Book Reviews," *The Times*, October 13, 1952, 8.

3. J. H. C. Laker, "Spies in Kent," *East Kent Times and Mail*, May 10, 1957, 8; Ronald Seth, *The Spy and the Atom Gun* (London: Geoffrey Bles, 1957), dustcover.

4. Ronald Seth, *Operation Retriever* (London: Brockhampton Press, n.d. [1953]); Ronald Seth, *Operation Lama* (London: Frederick Muller Ltd., n.d. [1953]); Ronald Seth, *Operation Ormer* (London: Geoffrey Bles, 1956); Seth, *The Spy and the Atom Gun*; Ronald Seth, *Rockets on Moon Island* (London: Geoffrey Bles, n.d. [1959]); Ronald Seth, *Smoke Without Fire* (London: Geoffrey Bles, 1959).

5. Operation Lama dealt with Grant operating in Tibet during the Chinese invasion. Operation Ormer was set in Guernsey and witnessed Grant coming up against a secret Nazi group attempting to gain access to a stash of munitions hidden during the German occupation. *Smoke Without Fire* witnessed Grant aiding a former wartime ally who had become a leader of a small Balkan nation that was under threat from a group of monarchists who wanted to overthrow this new republic.

6. David Gordon Kirby, *Operation Blunderhead: The Incredible Adventure of a Double Agent in Nazi-Occupied Europe* (London: Military Press, 2015).

7. Ben Wheatley, "MI5's Investigation of Ronald Sydney Seth, SOE's Agent Blunderhead and the SD's Agent 22D: Loyal British Agent or Nazi Double Agent?" *Journal of Intelligence History* 13, no. 1 (2014): 41–61.

8. Wheatley, "MI5's Investigation," 60.

9. Anonymous, "Operation Retriever," *Western Mail*, May 6, 1953, 3; J. H.C. Laker, "For the Children," *Leven Mail*, January 20, 1954, 6.

10. T. W. Hutton, "Among the Satellites," *Birmingham Daily Post*, February 17, 1959, 31.

11. Richard Usborne, *Clubland Heroes: A Nostalgic Study of Some Recurrent Characters in the Romantic Fiction of Donford Yates, John Buchan, and Sapper* (London: Barrie and Jenkins Limited, 1953), 2.

12. Jeremy Black, *The Politics of James Bond: From Fleming's Novels to the Big Screen* (Lincoln and London: University of Nebraska Press, 2005), 4.

13. David Cannadine, *In Churchill's Shadow: Confronting the Past in Modern Britain* (Oxford: Oxford University Press), 203, 290–291.

14. Teri S. Lesesne, "Meeting the Standards: Criteria for Great YA literature," *Voices from the Middle* 10, no. 1 (2002): 66–69; Mary Owen, "Developing a Love of Reading: Why Young Adult Literature is Important," *Orana* 39, no. 1 (2003): 11–16; Michael Cart, *Young Adult Literature: from Romance to Realism* (Chicago: American Library Association, 2010); Michael Cart, "From Insider to Outsider: The Evolution of Young Adult Literature," *Voices from the Middle* 9, no. 2 (2001): 95–97; Linda Bachelder et al., "Young Adult Literature: Looking Backward: Trying to Find the Classic Young Adult Novel," *English Journal* 69, no. 6 (1980): 86–89; James Hardy, "Fantasy to Reality: The History of Young Adult Literature," *History Cooperative*, January 16, 2015, https://historycooperative.org/history-of-young-adult-literature.

15. Only since the start of the twenty-first century can it be said that spy fiction truly established itself as a young adult fiction genre in Britain with the appearance of popular spy series by British authors such as A. J. Butcher, Charlie Higson, and Anthony Horowitz.

16. Usborne, *Clubland Heroes*, 1–2.

17. Christopher R. Moran, "The Pursuit of Intelligence History: Methods, Sources, and Trajectories in the United Kingdom," *Studies in Intelligence* 55, no. 2 (2011): 20.

18. Seth, *Operation Retriever*, 8–9.

19. Seth, *Operation Retriever*, 138–149.

20. Seth, *Operation Retriever*, 153–158.

21. Seth, *Operation Retriever*, 103.

22. Seth, *Operation Retriever*, 157.

23. Seth, *Operation Retriever*, 174.

24. Ronald Seth, *The True Book About the Secret Service* (London: Frederick Muller Ltd, n.d. [1953]), 61.

25. This landing was almost identical to Seth's account of his landing as a SOE agent in Estonia during World War II that had been portrayed in his memoir, *A Spy Has No Friends*.

26. Seth, *Operation Retriever*, 8–14.

27. Seth, *Operation Retriever*, 34.

28. Seth, *Operation Retriever*, 38.

29. Ronald Seth, *How Spies Work* (London: Geoffrey Bles, 1957), 53.

30. Seth, *How Spies Work*, 53.

31. The case of Richter is largely factually correct but is based on evidence obtained from reports in the British media. Anonymous, "German Parachute Spy Executed," *The Times*, December 11, 1941, 2.

32. Seth, *How Spies Work*, 62–63.

33. Seth, *A Spy Has No Friends*.

34. Alan Burton, *The Historical Dictionary of British Spy Fiction* (Lanham, MD: Rowman & Littlefield, 2016), 8.

35. Seth, *How Spies Work*, 7–8.

36. James Chapman, *License to Thrill: A Cultural History of James Bond Films* (London: Tauris, 2008).

37. Seth, *How Spies Work*, 8.

38. Seth, *Operation Lama*, 8–15, 121.

39. Seth, *Operation Lama*, 15.

40. Seth, *Operation Lama*, 27.

41. Seth, *Operation Lama*, 35–36.

42. Seth, *Operation Retriever*, 83–87.

43. Seth, *Operation Retriever*, 84.

44. Seth, *Operation Retriever*, 88–91.

45. Seth, *Rockets on Moon Island*, dustcover.

46. Seth, *How Spies Work*, 73–79.

47. William Le Queux, *Spies of the Foreign Office* (London: Hutchinson & Co., 1903).

48. John Creasey, *The Death Miser* (London: Andrew Melrose Ltd., n.d. [1933]), 44.

49. John Creasey, *Thunder in Europe* (London: Andrew Melrose, n.d. [1936]), 11–14; John Creasey, *Death by Night* (London: John Long, n.d. [1940]), 35.

50. *Great Spy Books Fact or Fiction*, Peter Hennessey, BBC Radio 4Extra, August 14, 2016.

51. *Sleuths, Spies, and Sorcerers: Andrew Marr's Paperback Heroes: Spies*, Andrew Marr, BBC Four, May 29, 2020.

# Ripe for Recruitment: Mata Hari as a Plausible Intelligence Asset

**Amanda A. Ohlke**

*Perhaps the most famous spy in history was Mata Hari, and she is among the first characters a visitor meets at the International Spy Museum. However, among intelligence scholars she is perhaps the most ridiculed spy of all time. Her fame, it is said, far outstrips her actual activities. Moreover, scholars and intelligence professionals resent the way in which the legend of Mata Hari sexualized the perception of female intelligence officers. Nevertheless, Mata Hari is overdue for a reappraisal.*
*—The Editors*

Mata Hari: the seductive spy, lurking in the boudoir, ready to trade favors for secrets is a character that is easy to imagine. She's a pop culture legend with many guises: dangerous woman, femme fatale, tragic heroine, jumped-up courtesan, feminist forerunner—the list goes on. "When Mata Hari died at Vincennes in 1917 the ground was already well prepared to receive a new version of the *femme fatale* legend," and she provided rich material.[1] But before she became a myth, she was a Dutch woman named Margaretha Zelle who had created a new identity for herself, a persona that had enabled her to rise from poverty to a life of luxury. This very real woman documented her life carefully in leather-bound scrapbooks containing articles about her dance performances, magazine covers, theater programs, and photographs of her in a variety of dress and undress. It is a long way from the life captured in these glamorous images to a dramatic death by a French firing squad in 1917. How did this happen? Who recruited her to spy? And why? Although she is sometimes treated as a joke for thinking she could gather intelligence, if we clear away the mythology and legend surrounding her, I believe the spymasters who sought her out as an intelligence asset were basing their pursuit of Mata Hari on characteristics and attributes that continue to be valuable in the world of intelligence today.

Who was Mata Hari really? Zelle was born in the Netherlands in 1876. Her family was comfortable, but her father's financial losses in 1889 and her parents' separation changed her life dramatically.[2] After their divorce, her mother died, and her beloved father, who had treated her as

Figure 4.1: Mata Hari, 1905. From the Collection of H. Keith and Karen Melton at the International Spy Museum.

his favorite, chose to have the younger children live with him, but not her. Her uncle took her in. He and his wife sent her to a boarding school to learn to be a kindergarten teacher. Instead, she left school in 1893 under a cloud—there were rumors that she had had an inappropriate relationship with the much older school headmaster. At loose ends with little money, she answered a newspaper ad placed by Rudolf MacLeod in 1895. A Dutch officer serving in the Dutch East Indies, he was seeking a wife while home on leave. They had a passionate courtship and were soon married. She was 19, he was 39. In 1897, they sailed to the Dutch East Indies with their first child. The following years were harrowing. Jealousy and ugliness plagued the relationship. MacLeod had a terrible temper and probably gave Zelle syphilis. They had a daughter, but the older child, two-year-old Norman, died in 1899. There were allegations that his nurse may have poisoned him, or perhaps he died of mercury poisoning—a treatment for syphilis, which he may have inherited.[3] Sadness, jealousy, anger, financial issues, and violence made the marriage untenable. They returned to the Netherlands and separated in 1902.

Without financial support from MacLeod, who was both unwilling and unable to offer it, Zelle left the Netherlands for Paris. There she modeled, tried acting, became an equestrian performer, and took lovers to support herself. But lightning struck when Ernst Molier, the master of the Cirque Molier, suggested she pursue dance. This is when Zelle created Mata Hari, a mysterious and seductive dancer named for a Malay phrase that translated to "sunrise" or "eye of the day."[4] She danced in private society homes and then teamed with the art collector Emile Étienne Guimet to offer a truly unique performance on March 13, 1905. His home (still a museum of Asian art today) became the setting for Mata Hari's Temple Dance debut. She drew on some of the gestures of Javanese court dancers she had seen in the Indies, but the movements were her own. And she was also clever enough to know that if her dance embodied the artistry of the "East," she could show enough of her gorgeous figure to be titillating, but cloaked in the veils of culture, her partial nudity would also be socially acceptable. She became a sensation. She performed in other major European cities and was well-received by critics. She lived lavishly and was a fine figure of fashion, seen at the popular spots. She filled multiple scrapbooks with her clippings and reviews. In 1914, at the start of World War I, she was in Berlin preparing to perform. However, by this point her dancing was not as well-regarded as it had been—she had performed some comic turns inside larger shows at the Folies Bergère, and she was now a very expensive courtesan. She was at this point a well-known and charming woman who was comfortable taking lovers. Her life as a spy was about to begin.

How did this dancer become "perhaps the greatest woman spy of the century"?[5] It all began with her recruitment. In 1915, Mata Hari caught the eye of a spotter. A recent Central Intelligence Agency memoir explains: "Spotting is spy speak for noticing people with interesting access."[6] Mata Hari as a good candidate for espionage work, however, flies in the face of the common opinion about her as a spy: Pat Shipman, author of *Femme Fatale: Love, Lies, and the Unknown Life of Mata Hari*, calls her "a ridiculous candidate for a job that required clandestine behavior."[7] A scathing comment from a review of Paul Coelho's novel *Spy*, based on Mata Hari's life, calls her "a self-created exotic dancer and courtesan who, under the unique transboundary pressures of World War I, became 'Earth's least effectual double agent.'"[8] In an article in which she is christened a "spook hoofer," the author concludes that "[t]here is scant evidence she was really an important spy."[9] Douglas Porch in his history of the French secret service deems her "completely out of her depth" and "stupid rather than dangerous" and suggests that the Germans who paid her for spying "got little return of their money."[10]

However, as I began working on the Spy Museum exhibition about her, I took a fresh look at why this woman, who was held in such low esteem as an intelligence operative, was sought after as an asset by several intelligence services during World War I. During World War II, the Office of Strategic Services, the precursor of the CIA, created a series of steps for recruiting agents. The second step was to "consider the types of spies needed—insiders, specialists, cutouts, accommodation addresses, couriers, collectors of imported material, stores of material, headquarters, women."[11] Her gender alone would have qualified Mata Hari based on this rubric, and as I read more and looked at the historical record detached from the "embellished story of Mata Hari's life," I concluded that, when the miserable finale of her story is set aside, there are a number of valid reasons beyond her gender that made her a logical choice for recruitment during World War I.[12] Her would-be handlers saw an attractive set of skills and assets that made her ripe for recruitment.

The Germans were the first to spot her. In his book *Spies of the Kaiser*, Thomas Boghardt describes the backgrounds and motivations of Germany's spies in Britain during World War I.[13] Although these spies operated in England, his findings indicate ways in which Mata Hari would have appealed to German recruiters. Boghardt found that of 120 German naval agents "the largest number . . . were Germans, but Dutch citizens enlisted almost as eagerly." This reflected the "vigorous recruiting efforts of German naval intelligence in the Netherlands." Boghardt also notes that the director of naval intelligence asked the "German naval attaché in Washington to find 'some suitable dashing [schneidige] people who would enjoy espionage.'"[14] In addition to being Dutch, Mata Hari certainly fell into the dashing category. During her interrogation by the French Captain Pierre Bouchardon after her arrest in Paris in 1917, Mata Hari recalled being asked to spy for Germany in May 1916. However, her memory was faulty: it was actually in the autumn of 1915.[15] She was visited at her home in The Hague by Karl Kroemer, the honorary German consul in Amsterdam. Kroemer, she recalled, said, "I know you are going to France; would you like to do us a favour? The idea is that you collect information that may be of interest to us."[16] The French were next in line. While in France in August 1916, Mata Hari met Georges Ladoux. He was the head of the Deuxième Bureau, the intelligence component of Army Headquarters. She had gone to his offices to get a permit that would allow her to visit the resort of Vittel in the military zone. (She hoped to go there to meet with her younger lover, Vladimir de Masloff.) Mata Hari remembered that during the interview Ladoux said: "If you love all of France, you could render us a great service. Have you thought of it?"[17] And later, when she was traveling on the western coast of Spain, a third contact was made. Martial Cazeaux, a diplomat, asked her to spy for the Russians in December 1916. Of this incident she recalled:

> When I was in Vigo, I met the French Consul from the Dutch Legation. He came to me and said: "You love a Russian officer. You would give him the pleasure of sending a telegram to see if he is wounded and work a little with me. Will you do something for the Russians?' I did not tell them about the French. He said 'Can you go to Austria?" He said he wanted to know what Reserves they had, to fight. He said, "[D]o you know Austria?" I said, "Yes, I have danced in Vienna." [He said] go home and await his instructions.[18]

When Mata Hari was traveling to Amsterdam by steamer in November 1916, her ship called at Falmouth in Cornwall in the United Kingdom. Mata Hari had been under suspicion by MI5 and thus was subject to questioning during this stop. Based on her comments about the many countries who had approached her to gather intelligence, Mata Hari interviewer Sir Basil Thomson, assistant metropolitan police commissioner at Scotland Yard and head of the Special Branch at the time, provocatively suggested to her that "it would be awkward to have a levee of all the belligerent countries in your room."[19] Despite his sarcasm, three different countries had approached her as a good potential asset.

Some of the accounts are conflicting, but when you clear away the fanciful stories about Mata Hari's espionage exploits, several factors that made her a sensible target for recruitment as a spy during World War I appear, attributes that are still pertinent in the intelligence field more than a century later.

One characteristic that Mata Hari shared with a number of successful spies was her willingness to take risks. In a video interview that a former International Spy Museum historian, Vince Houghton, and I conducted in 2018 with the former KGB sleeper agent Jack Barsky, now featured in the International Spy Museum's *Spy Next Door* gallery, Barsky discussed what the KGB was looking for in potential agents. He described "specific character traits," one of which was a "well-controlled inclination to danger"—something along the lines of a calculated risk-taker. Mata Hari filled the bill on this count, As she was no stranger to taking chances. She was the unlucky teenager with few opportunities who was willing to gamble heavily to advance her status. As noted above, she met her husband by responding to a newspaper advertisement he placed in 1895 that stated: "Officer home on leave from Dutch East Indies would like to meet a girl of pleasant character—object matrimony."[20] When that relationship proved a disaster and she became a penniless divorcée, she set off for Paris. She had never been there but later said, "I thought all women who ran away from their husbands went to Paris."[21] This gives us solid insight into the bold way she reacted when faced with a challenge. Her riskiest undertaking, before her sojourn into espionage, was her dancing career. She chanced losing all access to polite society with her performances, but she gambled that, if she cloaked her performances in the veil of artistry and education, she would win over the critics. This bet paid off handsomely, and she became internationally famous, critically praised, and able to pay for a lavish lifestyle. When it came to espionage, she believed she could win again. Her self-assurance was evident in a meeting with Georges Ladoux. He recalled discussing with Mata Hari whether she would spy for the French. He cautioned: "Be serious. You really wish to enter into our service? Take care; the profession is dangerous." She clearly understood this and replied coolly: "I don't doubt it."[22] Her bold confidence and comfort with risk enabled her to enter situations with composure—situations that her spymasters hoped would yield intelligence dividends.

Mata Hari's career choice is another indicator that she would have been a good candidate for espionage. Although she billed her performances as artistic interpretations of the exotic East, many people viewed them simply as an excuse for her to remove her clothing. She herself understood that many in the audience, while "pretending to consider my dances very artistic and full of character, thus praising my art, [really] . . . came to see nudity."[23] Spying, like appearing on stage, was not considered a noble profession at the time. Even today, the International Spy Museum advisory board member and former CIA chief of disguise Jonna Mendez confides with a sly chuckle: "Spies are not the nicest people."[24] That Mata Hari was a kept woman who would stoop to solicitation when funds were scarce suggested that she would be open to opportunities that others might turn down or find insulting. If she would dance naked and perform sexual services, then what else might she be willing to do? In the opinion of one of her biographers, Pat Shipman, it was a lot: "The attribute that she possessed that was the reason so many asked her to spy for them was her willingness to do things normally judged immoral for money. Because she was visibly a woman of the demimonde—a high-class prostitute, in ugly terms—men

Figure 4.2: Bodice that may have belonged to Mata Hari. She wore similar costumes on stage—modeled on those she had seen in the Dutch East Indies—with a confident sexuality that defied traditional feminine modesty. She countered charges of indecency by describing her dance as a "sacred poem," exploiting European fascination with orientalist clichés. From the Collection of H. Keith and Karen Melton at the International Spy Museum.

assumed she would also stoop to espionage, which had a very negative connotation at the time."[25] Her savvy potential handlers correctly inferred that Mata Hari would not be offended when they asked to spy.

Her renowned sex appeal combined with her sexual prowess was critical to Mata Hari's desirability as a spy. Her handlers understood that she would use sex to gather secrets. They were counting on her magnetic attraction for men and ease with seduction as excellent espionage tools. And she delivered. In describing her pursuit of information from a German diplomat in Spain for French consumption, she said coyly, "I did that which a woman may do in such circumstances when she wished to make a conquest of a man."[26] In a separate account of the same conquest, she said more directly, "I let him do what he wanted."[27] Using sex to gather secrets did not originate with Mata Hari, and it certainly didn't end with her. As the East German spymaster Markus Wolf once observed "since time immemorial, security services have used the mating game to gain proximity to interesting figures."[28] This practice is not limited to women enticing men. Wolf explained that, as women gained higher positions and access in the field of intelligence with the rise of feminism, it is not "surprising that the male counterpart to Mata Hari should come along, the Romeo spy."[29] He acknowledged that "the ends did not always justify the means we chose to employ . . . [but] as long as there is espionage, there will be Romeos seducing unsuspecting Juliets with access to secrets."[30] Whether the target is male or female or nonbinary, this sexual access strategy has continued. The arrests in the United States of Anna Chapman in 2010 and Maria Butina in 2018 suggest that, at least for Russia, the practice of using alluring people to gain access and exert influence is alive and well in the twenty-first century. Due to her looks, Chapman remains the most famous of the 10 Russian Illegals (deep cover officers) arrested in 2010 . A contemporary article opined that Chapman's "American activities were principally confined to forging male acquaintances."[31] Butina, who was convicted in the United States for failing to register as a foreign agent, was deported after serving nearly her full eighteen-month jail sentence. Her attempts to gain influence with high-level Republicans "caught the international media spotlight after the government accused Butina of employing feminine wiles—à la the movie *Red Sparrow*—to extract information."[32] The TV talk show host Jay Leno summed up the fascination with gorgeous red-haired Russian spies when he asked then–Vice President Joe Biden in 2012: "Do we have any spies that hot?"[33]

However, to the people who recruited her, Mata Hari's value wasn't just that she would do dirty work like performing on stage and in the bedroom; it was that her work and relationships had given her a network of contacts throughout Europe. A spy's access is her most valuable asset. Mata Hari had a wide array of acquaintances, and she was used to approaching these people for whatever she needed. She was no stranger to granting favors or asking for them. She was comfortable asking for things: money, houses, introductions. This comfort level with a favor economy is evidenced in a letter from the collection of the International Spy Museum included in the *Mata Hari* exhibition. On letterhead from the Hotel Metropole in Monte Carlo, she wrote in March 1908: "Dear Mr. Bormes, I hope you remember me when I danced two years ago at the opera in The King of Lahore. Please do me a great pleasure and let me have an opera ticket for tonight. I am very grateful to you and will come by to say hello one of these days." It is a small thing to request a ticket in exchange for a greeting, but it speaks to the ease with which she approached getting what she wanted. She was clever about how to make contact—and how to exploit a contact. A good example of using one's contacts for intelligence purposes comes from World War II when the famed Anglo-Canadian spymaster William Stephenson asked the entertainer Noel Coward to collect intelligence during a musical tour of South America. "Nazis were running all over," and Coward found that, by "being as flamboyant as possible" and by being a "perfect silly ass," people "would say all kinds of things" in front of him that he would pass along to Stephenson. In this case, it was a "merry playboy" who was exploiting his contacts.[34]

Mata Hari's fame adds an interesting factor to the consideration of her as a prospective spy. Shipman calls Mata Hari a "ridiculous candidate" to spy, arguing that, "as a famous performer and striking beauty, Mata Hari attracted attention wherever she went. It was part of her personality to seek the spotlight, and she was very good at it."[35] On the face of it, the idea of a celebrity conducting espionage seems counterintuitive, but in fact spying does not always require a low profile. The famous entertainer Josephine Baker, for instance, used her glamour to gather information and smuggle documents for the French Resistance during World War II. She actually used her star power to keep suspicion away from her traveling companion, who had "all the information that had been gathered concerning the German army in France." Her companion described how, "[a]t the Spanish frontier, nobody paid any attention to me . . . the Spanish police and the German plainclothesmen were infinitely more interested in the star Josephine Baker than in the shabby little man carrying her suitcase." She later laughed and said, "You see what good cover I am?"[36] Mata Hari's fame likewise drew people to her. When she was removed from the *Hollandia* for questioning in England in 1916, the Dutch captain complained that she should not be taken, as she "was the ship's most popular passenger."[37] If everyone wanted to meet her and talk to her, it was reasonable for her prospective handlers to assume she could use her celebrity to attract any target they wished her to entice even if she didn't already know him.

Mata Hari's fame and popularity gave her an extremely diverse set of connections to draw upon for intelligence. Her network included the banker Baron Henri de Rothschild, the industrialist and art collector Étienne Guimet, the author and salonist Natalie Barney, and members of the press. Through Guimet she appeared before guests such as the Japanese ambassador to France, Baron Kurino.[38] The people she suggested to Sir Basil Thomson of Scotland Yard in 1916 who could vouch for her were respectable and included the artist Henri Edmund Rudaux and an English couple, Mr. Albert Kayzer and his wife, of whom she said "they have

Plate 1. Photograph of the International Spy Museum highlighting the red beams and the green staircase. Note the royal blue light coming through the louvres. These lights can alternate among a number of colors.

Plate 2. Maggie's West London, a cancer care center for which Ivan Harbour was the lead designer. Its simplicity and lines reflect a modern architectural design. Notice the horizontal and vertical lines of the building, the large window, and the way in which the gardens are integral to the design.

Plate 3. Terminal 4 at Barajas Airport in Madrid, also designed by Ivan Harbour. The play between different surfaces, materials, and colors and the lack of 90-degree angles and straight lines mark it as a postmodern design.

Plate 4. The inside of Terminal 4 at Barajas Airport. Notice the play between the different surfaces, texture, and color.

Plate 5. The International Spy Museum surrounded by neighboring buildings. The image illustrates Ivan Harbour's desire to create a unique stepping stone.

Plate 6. Reproduction of the pedal-powered Turtle, America's first combat submarine. Built by the inventor David Bushnell in 1776, its purpose was covert sabotage against a British warship in New York. David Bushnell Submarine Turtle created by Rick and Laura Brown, Handshouse Studios, 2002.

Plates 7 and 8. Segment of the Berlin Tunnel, used in Operation Gold, 1954–1956. The joint US-British effort involved secretly tunneling from the American sector of Berlin and tapping into the Red Army's communication lines in the Soviet sector. The Spy Museum acquired two tunnel segments in 2015 and shipped them from Germany to Washington, DC.

Plate 9. Noor Inayat Khan exhibit in the *Spying That Shaped History* gallery at the International Spy Museum. Khan was a radio operator for Britain's Special Operations Executive in Nazi-occupied France; she was captured and killed by the Nazis.

Plate 10. *Analysis* exhibit at the International Spy Museum.

Plate 11. Air Duct interactive in the *Covert Action* gallery at the International Spy Museum. Visitors can crawl through the duct while spying on people in the *Sabotage* exhibit below.

Plate 12. Hat worn by James J. Angleton, who was chief of the CIA's counterintelligence staff from 1954 to 1974. From the Collection of H. Keith and Karen Melton at the International Spy Museum.

Plate 13. James J. Angleton's briefcase. From the Collection of H. Keith and Karen Melton at the International Spy Museum.

Plate 14. Aston Martin DB5. After it appeared in the James Bond film *Goldfinger* (1964), the DB5 became one of the most famous cars in the world. This one was used to promote the film and is outfitted with machine guns, tire-slashers, oil jets, and a rotating license plate. On Loan from Mr. M. and C. Nelson.

Plate 15. Kim Philby's funeral in Moscow, May 1988. From the Collection of H. Keith and Karen Melton at the International Spy Museum.

Plate 16. *Thunderball* board game, circa 1965. In the 1960s and 1970s, James Bond's cultural influence was pervasive. He was used to sell games, puzzles, action figures and other toys, shoes, and cologne, not to mention books and movie tickets.

Plate 17. James Bond 007 branded men's cologne, 1960s.

Plate 18. James Bond lunchbox showing a scene inspired by a car chase in the 1964 film *Goldfinger*.

Plate 19. Christmas ornament portraying Allen Dulles, Director of Central Intelligence from 1953 to 1961. Sold at the store inside CIA Headquarters. From the Collection of H. Keith and Karen Melton at the International Spy Museum.

Plate 20. Special Operations Executive camouflage jumpsuit. Ronald Seth probably wore a similar suit when he parachuted into Estonia in 1942.

Plate 21. Type A Mark I suitcase radio belonging to Major John Brown, the Royal Signals officer who developed the first such clandestine radio for the British Special Operations Executive. It is the oldest known SOE suitcase radio. Ronald Seth took a modified version of this model (a Mark II) on his mission to Estonia. From the Collection of H. Keith and Karen Melton at the International Spy Museum.

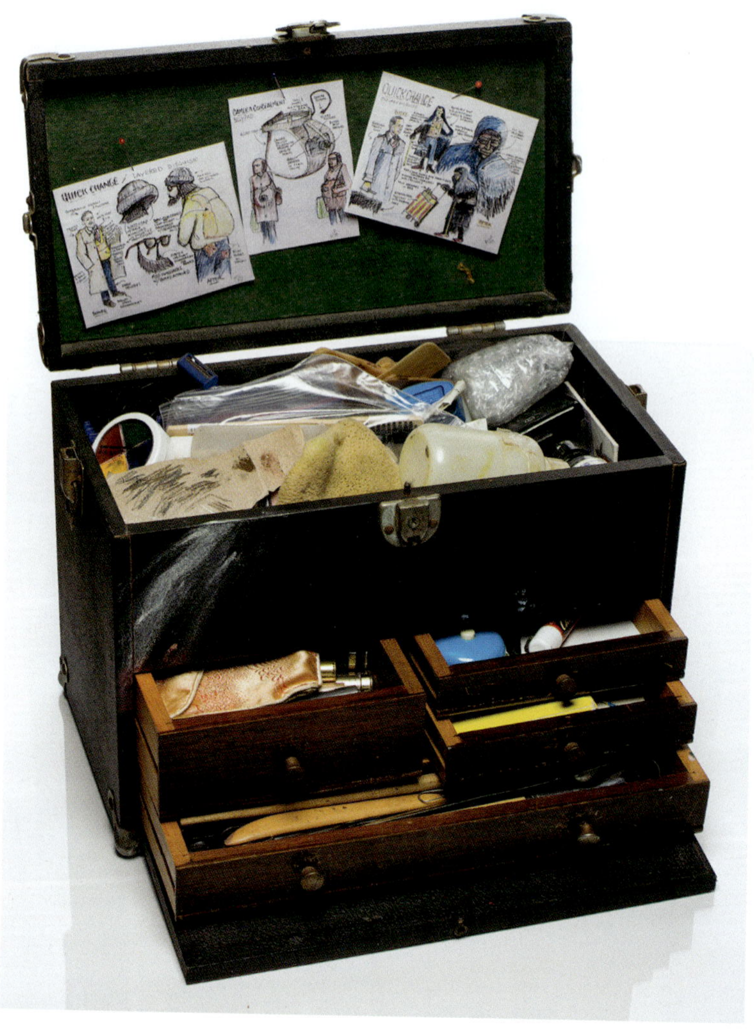


Plate 22. Disguise kit of Tony Mendez, CIA chief of disguise, who pioneered the Agency's use of Hollywood techniques. Ronald Seth's hero, Captain Brian Grant of the British secret service, frequently traveled into enemy territory in disguise. Gift of the Mendez Family.

Plate 23. Ronald Seth, *How Spies Work*. Courtesy of Jonathan Best.

Plate 24. Ronald Seth, *Operation Retriever*. Courtesy of Jonathan Best.

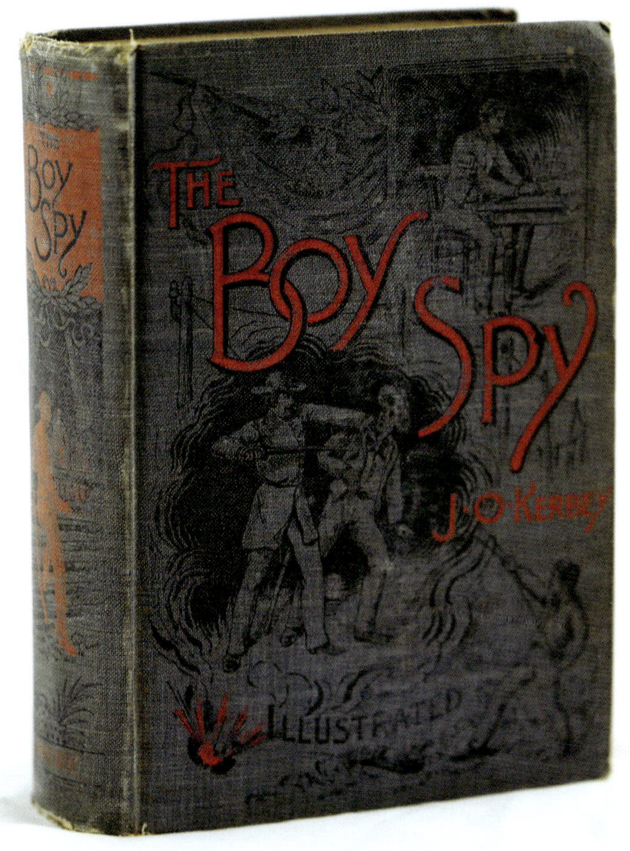


Plate 25. *The Boy Spy* by Major J. O. Kerbey, 1890 edition. American authors have written spy fiction with child protagonists since at least the nineteenth century. This one's subtitle promises "a substantially true record of secret service during the War of the Rebellion" (Civil War) as well as an account of war telegraphy and other means of signaling.

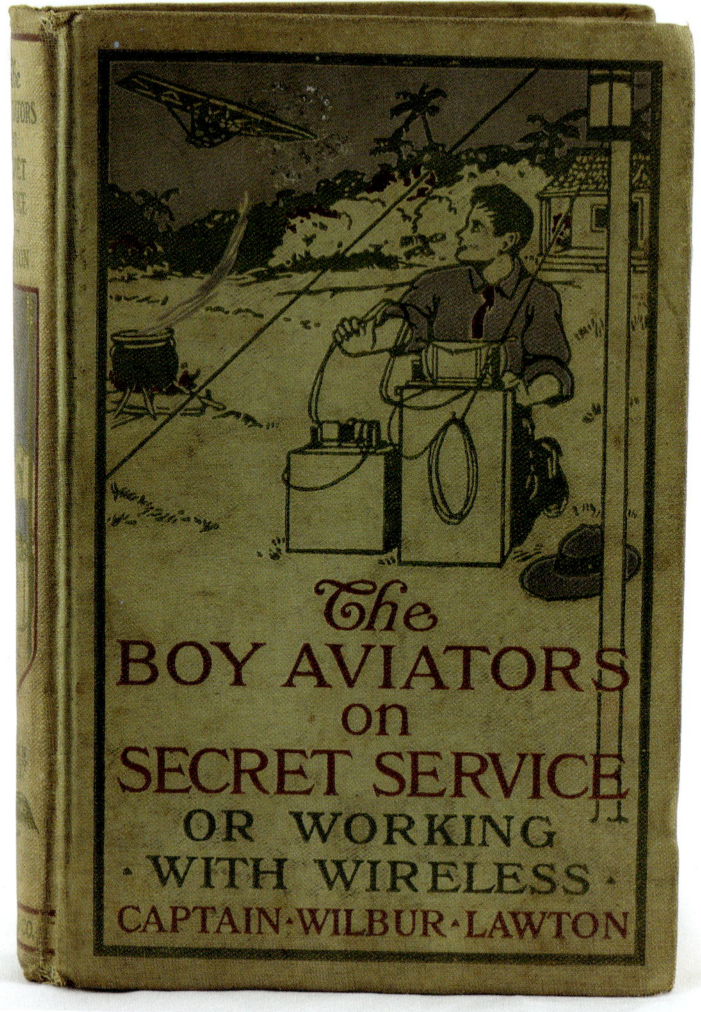


Plate 26. A volume of the popular American series *The Boy Aviators*, which ran from 1910–1915. In this book, the young heroes fly in an airship, use a "wireless telegraph" to help rescue a German inventor, and thwart the designs of Japanese spies.

Plate 27. Soviet children's book lauding the exploits of Leonid Golikov, a scout for a Soviet partisan unit during World War II, killed in 1943 at age 16. According to Soviet lore, Golikov was an expert marksman, destroyed nine bridges and large amounts of German equipment, and stole valuable documents from a German general he killed. He was made a posthumous Hero of the Soviet Union. Courtesy of the Francis Lara Collection.

Plate 28. *Spies and Spymasters* exhibit in the International Spy Museum.

Plate 29. *Mata Hari, Agent H-21* (1964) movie poster. The code name given to Mata Hari by German intelligence provided the title of this Franco-Italian film. Gift of Mark S. Zaid, Esq.

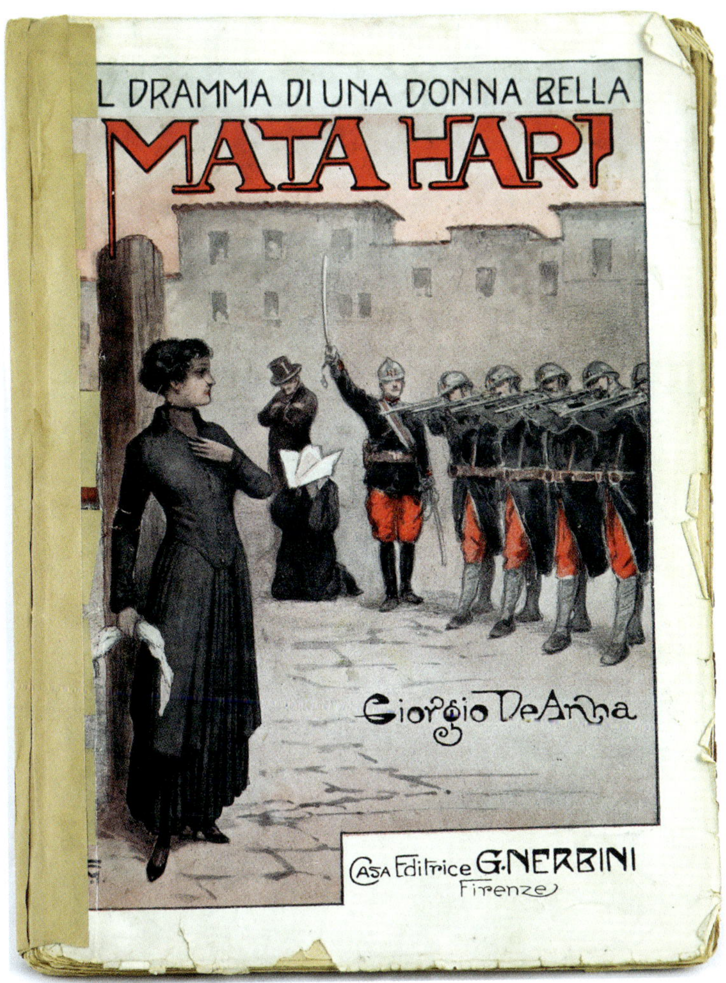


Plate 30. Romanticized image of Mata Hari's execution in October 1917. She actually died in front of a mound of earth in a wooded area at the Caserne de Vincennes outside Paris. From the Collection of H. Keith and Karen Melton at the International Spy Museum.

Plates 31 and 32. Edith Cavell commemorative figurine and memorial ribbon. Mata Hari's trial and execution by the French in 1917 painted her as a sinful, seductive spy—a useful scapegoat for French military losses. By contrast, the British nurse Edith Cavell's execution in 1915 made her a symbol of female Christian virtue—a powerful anti-German propaganda tool ("murdered by the Huns") used to recruit soldiers across the British Empire. Cavell had helped smuggle more than 200 French and British soldiers out of occupied Belgium; she may also have spied for the British. From the Collection of H. Keith and Karen Melton at the International Spy Museum.

Plates 33 and 34. Concealment earrings and bracelet crafted by the KGB's Operational Technical Directorate for use by a female KGB officer or agent. Spy gear must be appropriate to the gender, lifestyle, and work of the spy. From the Collection of H. Keith and Karen Melton at the International Spy Museum.

Plates 35 and 36. Bra camera, designed by four female East German Stasi employees to be worn under a summer dress and used for covert photography. From the Collection of H. Keith and Karen Melton at the International Spy Museum.

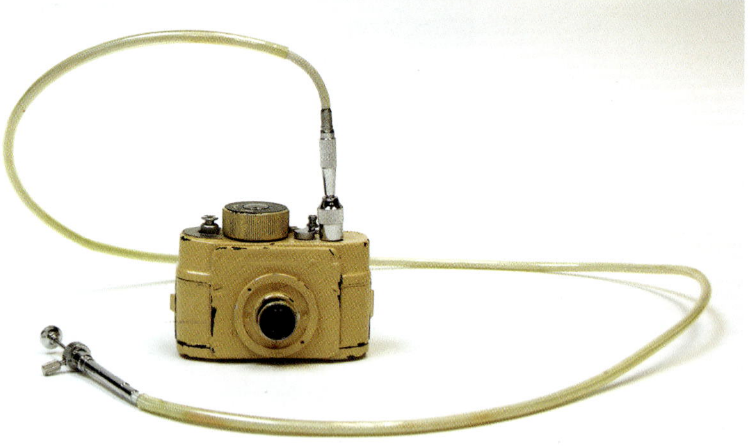

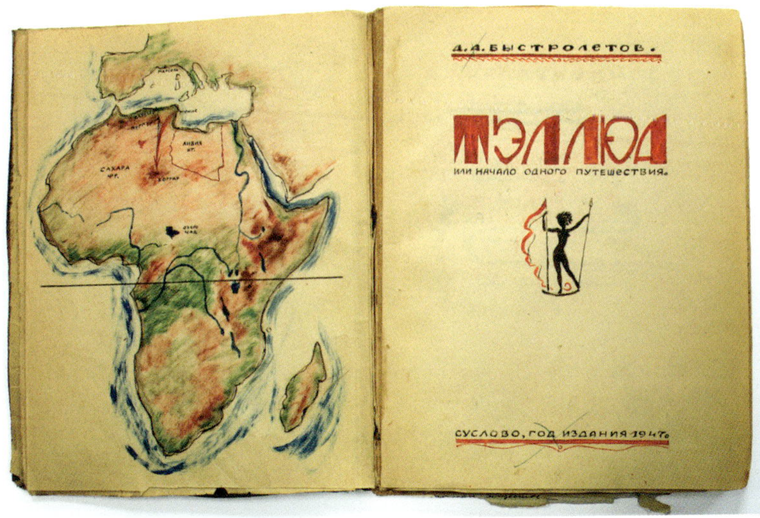


Plates 37 and 38. Handwritten and illustrated memoir of Dmitri Bystrolyotov's spy operations in Africa, written during his 16 years in the Gulag. The cover is made from a piece of his long underwear. Gift of S. S. Milashov.

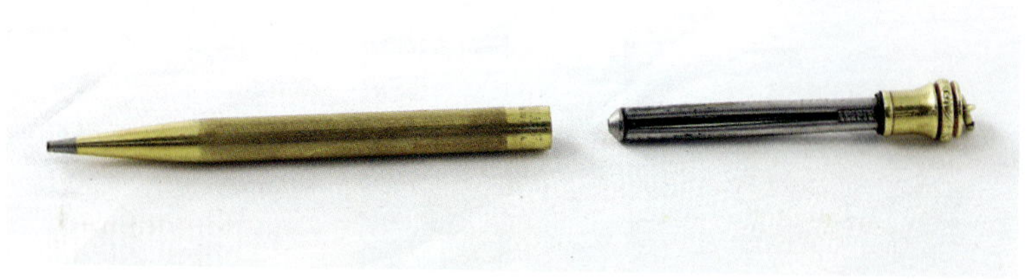

Plate 39. Pendant pencil used to hide messages by Maria Orlova, 1930s-era NKVD courier and wife of the Soviet defector Alexander Orlov. In his Berlin operations, Dmitri Bystrolyotov was aided by Soviet illegal Erica Weinstein, who might have used a similar concealment device. From the Collection of H. Keith and Karen Melton at the International Spy Museum.

Plate 40. Soviet jewelry box concealment device. To reveal the concealment cavity, the bottom spins off. From the collection of H. Keith Melton and Karen Melton at the International Spy Museum.

Plate 41. Badge issued to "honored workers" of the Soviet OGPU from 1932, the fifteenth anniversary of the founding of the Cheka. Courtesy of the Francis Lara Collection.

Пролетарии всех стран, соединяйтесь!

„ГПУ является грозой буржуазии, неусыпным стражем Революции, обнаженным мечом пролетариата"

(И. Сталин).

ВЧК ОГПУ

1917 XV 1932

СССР

# ГРАМОТА

БОЙЦУ-ЧЕКИСТУ

Тов. Кругит А.Р.

В день 15-ой годовщины существования органов пролетарской диктатуры ВЧК–ОГПУ, отмечая Вашу самоотверженную работу на боевом посту в борьбе с классовым врагом Полномочное Представительство ОГПУ по Средне-Волжскому Краю награждает Вас золотыми часами.

Полномочный Представитель
ОГПУ по С.В.К.

20-го декабря 1932 г.
г. Самара.

Plate 42. Award certificate to an exemplary chekist in the Soviet OGPU, the organization for which Dmitri Bystrolyotov worked, on the fifteenth anniversary of its progenitor, the Cheka. Chekists were to have "clean hands, a cool head, and a warm heart." Courtesy of the Francis Lara Collection.

Plate 43. Pin from Department N of the Russian SVR, which leads the operations of deep-cover illegals. Dmitri Bystrolyotov worked for its predecessor in the 1920s and 1930s. From the Collection of H. Keith and Karen Melton at the International Spy Museum.

Plate 44. *The Spy*, a US Civil War card game distributed in 1893 by the Woolson Spice Company. The general public became aware of the exploits of spies during the American Civil War. From the Collection of H. Keith and Karen Melton at the International Spy Museum.

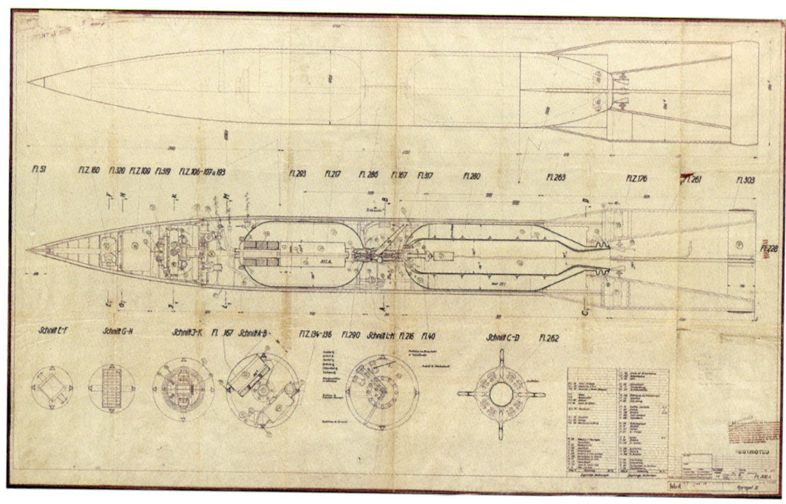

Plate 45. Much as the CIA sought to understand Soviet missile projects during the Cold War, Allied intelligence sought to understand the mysterious Nazi V-weapons during World War II. That effort involved aerial photography, signals intelligence, human reporting, and lots of technical analysis. The red stamp at the bottom-right of these technical drawings of the V-2 rocket, the first guided ballistic missile, indicate that this document eventually came into the hands of the United States War Department—probably meaning military intelligence. From the Collection of H. Keith and Karen Melton at the International Spy Museum.

Plate 46. World War I British Royal Flying Corps message streamer. Lacking radios to communicate with the ground, aerial observers wrote messages, put them in the white pouch, and dropped the streamer when above a friendly unit.

Plate 47. US Army Air Force Folmer Graflex K20 handheld aerial camera. During World War II bomber crewmembers often carried these cameras to take reconnaissance photographs. The tail gunner of the *Enola Gay* used one to photograph the nuclear mushroom cloud over Hiroshima on August 6, 1945. In the 1970s, Portugal used K20s to image Mozambican insurgents' bases.

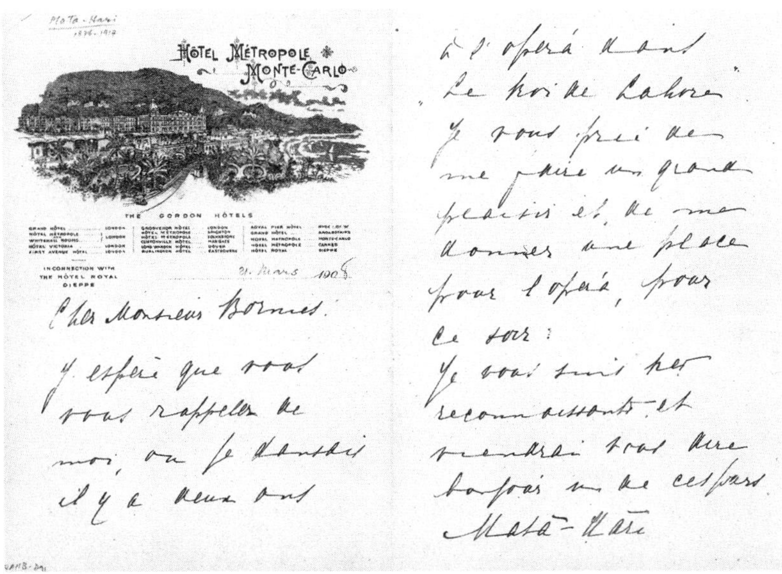
Hôtel Métropole
Monte-Carlo

The Gordon Hotels

21 Mars 1908

Cher Monsieur Bormes.

J'espère que vous vous rappellez de moi, où je dansais il y a deux ans à l'opéra dans "Le roi de Lahore". Je vous prie de me faire un grand plaisir et de me donner une place pour l'opéra, pour ce soir. Je vous suis très reconnaissante et viendrai vous dire bonjour un de ces jours.

Mata-Hari

Figure 4.3: Letter from Mata Hari to Monsieur Bormes, who had once seen her dance: "I hope you remember me." She asks for an opera ticket for that evening and says she will "come say hello one of these days."

known me for twelve years."[39] The inclusion of a married pair may seem surprising, but she was struggling to convince Thompson of her identity as a well-connected, established celebrity. An especially intriguing aspect of her contacts was her predilection for military men—and those watching her took note of this preference. Later in life she admitted "yes, I have had many lovers, but it is the beautiful soldiers, brave, always ready for battle and, while waiting, always sweet and gallant. For me, the officer forms a race apart. I have never loved any but officers."[40] Mata Hari's MI5 file includes notes about her relationships with military men. In July 1916, a message to Captain Ladoux reads: "She is a demi-mondaine who is in relation with various highly placed people and has appeared in Germany, France, and Italy. She is acquainted with many French and Belgian officers."[41] In December 1916 W. Haldane Porter, His Majesty's Inspector under the Aliens Act of the English Home Office, reported that she was "at present the mistress of a Colonel in a Dutch Hussar Regiment."[42] This was Baron E. Van der Capellan, Colonel Commandant, 2nd Regiment Hussars, Eindhoven, Dutch Army. She was also noted to be "in regular correspondence with her [] lover . . . a Russian officer on the French Front."[43] The young Vladimir de Masloff is the military man referenced here. The file further noted: "She has received letters at her home from a French and a Belgian officer."[44]

Years of gentlemen friends tallied up to a hefty little black book, but this network, which made her so appealing as a spy, became a double-edged sword by raising suspicion. The Germans had certainly noted how her liaisons with Abteilung III b, the intelligence wing of the Imperial German Army, became interested in Mata Hari because she had a relationship with General Adolphe Messimy, commander of France's Fifth Army and previously minister of war.[45] Baron von Mirbach, Nachrichtenoffizier 3, the German Third Army's intelligence officer, personally recommended that she be trained to spy.[46] At this suggestion, Abteilung III b had her assessed as to her ability "to establish personal relationships and to move in society circles."[47] This heady mix of celebrity, socialite friends, and military admirers made her seem a golden fish who would grant any wish, but Dr. Elsbeth Schragmüller, head of the intelligence section (France) of the Kriegsnachrichtenstelle Antwerpen who trained her to spy for Germany, thought that this "demi-mondaine" would bring nothing but trouble.[48] A similar dynamic existed on the French side. One of Mata Hari's French lovers, Lieutenant Jean Hallaure, in the Deuxième Bureau of the Ministry of War was warned: "My boy, in your place, I would not go around so often with this woman. You belong to the army, where the most unfortunate rumors circulate about her. She is an alien, she was [involved] with a German before the war, and I believe she is a suspect."[49]

A less problematic aspect of Mata Hari's appeal as a potential spy is still in demand in the twenty-first century. In a *Forbes* magazine article from 2014, the CIA's head of recruitment discussed what the Agency sought in applicants. He stressed that the CIA needed a candidate to have "cultural knowledge, geographical knowledge[,] and language skills—skills that allow us to do our job in that part of the world."[50] A spymaster looking for an operative in World War I would have found Mata Hari very at ease in the target area of continental Europe. Having been born in the Netherlands, Mata Hari enjoyed living in Paris and performing there, as well as in Berlin, Milan, and Monaco. She described herself as an "international woman" on more than one occasion when speaking to officials during interrogations and her trial. She felt comfortable moving through Europe and living in various cities as circumstances dictated, whether for theatrical performances or in establishments provided by wealthy men. Moreover, as she danced on stages across Europe and made new acquaintances, she picked up languages. In 1915, when she was interviewed by the British as a person of interest during a journey, it was noted that she spoke "French, English, Italian, Dutch, and probably German."[51] A 1916 report[52] stated that she spoke "French perfectly."[53] As a test during an interview by the English,

Figure 4.4: Mata Hari, 1914. From the Collection of H. Keith and Karen Melton at the International Spy Museum.

"[a]n inspector was instructed to speak to her in Dutch, and he stated that she spoke the language well, but with a Northern accent."[54] The more people she could speak with from a diverse array of countries, the better the chances that she would secure information of use to her handler—a fluency that is still of enormous value in the spy world.

Mata Hari's fluency with languages was rivaled by her mobility and lack of allegiance as convenient spy attributes. During World War I, the Netherlands remained neutral. As a Dutch citizen, she was able to cross borders that were closed to citizens of the combatant states. When she was enlisted to spy, she hoped to use this capability to pursue intelligence targets. However, her travels were not as easy as she had hoped. She described crossing borders during wartime in this way: "I have traveled a good deal during this war and judging by the inspections to which I have been subjected, I ask myself how one could pass the frontiers with secret things. One cannot even pass with a hairpin. In England, they checked the ribbons on my chemises."[55] Her Dutch passport may not have given her the mobility she expected due to the suspicions that were raised by an eye-catching woman who needed to be the center of attention and was not used to hiding her persona but rather flaunting it. As Schragmüller wrote upon first working with Mata Hari as a trainee, she was a "Grande Dame with a personality and refined elegance that attracted general attention."[56]

Another characteristic that made her willing to spy might also have made her less desirable: a lack of political allegiances. While this made her open to the offers of various countries, her lack of devotion to any cause also made her recruitment a somewhat risky proposition. An MI5 report from July 1916 states: "It seems curious that, although she is said to [advertise] pro-German feelings whilst in Holland, she has no difficulty in travelling backwards and forwards to France."[57] Less than a year later, at her trial, she avowed how "I am not French. I have the right to have friends in other countries, even those at war with France. I remain neutral."[58] Although a truthful statement and one that made her open to approach, it would not assure a spymaster that a new friend would not be as welcome as an old one.

All of this said, Mata Hari's strengths and weaknesses as a possible spy were irrelevant to her handlers if she were not open to recruitment. Any good spy handler knows that to be recruited a spy needs motivation. Intelligence agencies today carefully study psychological and social factors that lead a person to spy. The acronym "MICE" is often used to represent the most common motivations: Money, Ideology, Compromise or Coercion, and Ego. Mata Hari's primary motivation was simple: she needed money. Tales of cranky creditors swirl around her like veils from her dancing costumes. Her MI5 file, for instance, includes information about her financial position. It states: "She returned from Germany about a year ago and appeared at the French Opera in The Hague. At the time, she was known to be in straightened financial position but this soon changed and she received money from the Germans. She is said to have received 15000 frs. [francs] from the German Embassy."[59] The German consul Kroemer, who first approached her about becoming a spy, told her that, if she collected information, "I can pay you 20,000 francs." She "retorted that this was not very much." "That's right," he said, "but if you want more, you need to show us what you are capable of and then you can get everything you want."[60] Both her memories of meeting with the French officer LaDoux (and his recollection) feature the discussion of payment: "One day the Captain said to me 'You can do so many things for us if you like,' and he looked me in the eyes. I understood. I thought a long time. I said, 'I can.' He said, 'Would you?' I said, 'I would.' 'What would you ask?' I said, 'If I give you plenty of satisfaction, I ask you 1,000,000.' He said, 'Go to Holland, and you will receive my instructions.'"[61] Mata Hari said that at their first encounter, when Ladoux broached the subject of her spying for France, he stated: "You would be very expensive. According to you, what would it be worth?' She replied, 'All or nothing. If one rendered, you services as grand as you expect? Then that is worth a great deal.'"[62] According to Ladoux, when they met again in September 1916 he asked: "How much do you need?" And she replied: "You could not pay so much . . . a million!"[63] Mata Hari was facing middle age without a financial safety net. The one million francs that she sought from LaDoux would bankroll a new chapter in her life; she had hoped to settle down with her young Russian lover, Captain Masloff, who had been injured in the war. She wanted to retire, marry, and care for him. Money from spying could give her that chance. And this motivation worked in France's favor. She was more audacious in pursuit of information from Germany for France because she wanted this money so badly. She gathered and conveyed information to the French that she considered worth a million francs—intelligence gleaned from a German in Spain. Whether or not her information was as valuable as she thought, it was more detailed than anything she ever delivered to the Germans. Ironically, it was the French who not only stiffed her—they arrested and executed her.

So with a glaring need for money and the confidence and contacts to believe she could have access to remarkable information, Mata Hari began a dance with espionage that ended with her execution. Her foray into the shadowy wilderness of mirrors ended in the worst possible way for her, but her fame and the dramatic nature of her death ensured that she would be remembered. However, it is only through clearing away the century of tall tales and innuendo that we can discern that the reasons that her handlers sought to recruit her were logical and remain relevant today. Their assessment of her as a potentially useful and recruitable spy makes sense. She had desirable skills and the self-confidence to use them. But like many who choose to sell secrets, her efforts ended with her capture—caught in a web with no way out.

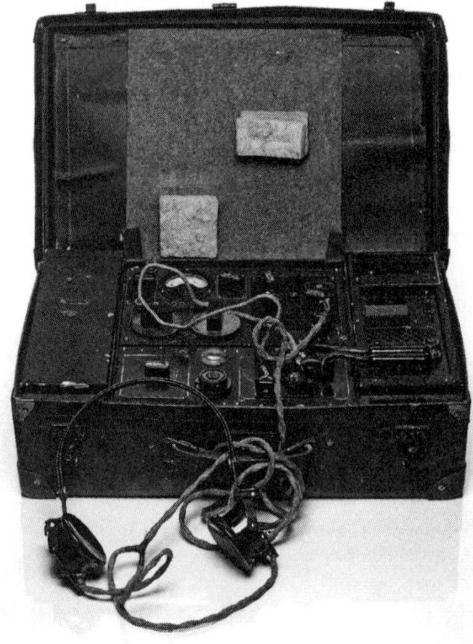

Figure 4.5: Virginia Hall's suitcase radio and headphones, circa 1944. Born to a wealthy family in Baltimore, Hall worked in occupied France during World War II, first with Britain's Special Operations Executive and later with the US Office of Strategic Services. Despite her wooden leg, she worked with resistance groups behind enemy lines, eluding the Gestapo, which labeled her "one of the most dangerous Allied agents in France." After the war she had a career with the CIA. Courtesy of Lorna Catling and John Hall.

## Further Reading


Craig, Mary W. *A Tangled Web, Mata Hari: Dancer, Courtesan, Spy*. Stroud, UK: The History Press, 2017.

Shipman, Pat. *Femme Fatale: Love, Lies, and the Unknown Life of Mata Hari*. New York: Morrow, William. 2007.

Wheelwright, Julie. *The Fatal Lover: Mata Hari and the Myth of Women in Espionage*. London: Collins & Brown, 1992.


## Notes

1. Julie Wheelwright, *The Fatal Lover: Mata Hari and the Myth of Women in Espionage* (Collins & Brown, 1992), 7.

2. Pat Shipman, *Femme Fatale: Love, Lies, and the Unknown Life of Mata Hari* (New York: William Morrow, 2007), provides an excellent account of Mata Hari's life. Unless otherwise noted, this chapter draws on that work for biographical details.

3. Shipman, *Femme Fatale*, 104.

4. Shipman, *Femme Fatale*, 148.

5. Shipman, *Femme Fatale*, 350.

6. Amaryllis Fox, *Life Undercover: Coming of Age in the CIA* (New York: Alfred A. Knopf), 108.

7. Shipman, *Femme Fatale*, 249.

8. Louis Bayard, "Paulo Coelho's 'Spy' Uncovers the Life of Mata Hari," *Washington Post*, November 15, 2016.

9. Alex von Tunzelmann, "Mata Hari: The Partially Naked Truth About the Spook Hoofer," *The Guardian*, March 20, 2014.

10. Douglas Porch, *The French Secret Services: From the Dreyfus Affair to the Gulf War* (New York: Farrar, Straus & Giroux), 98.

11. Randy Burkett, "An Alternate Framework for Agent Recruitment from MICE to RASCLS," *Studies in Intelligence* 57, no. 1 (Extracts) (March 2013).

12. Wheelwright, *The Fatal Lover*, 4.

13. Thomas Boghardt, *Spies of the Kaiser: German Covert Operations in Great Britain During the First World War* (St. Antony's College, Oxford: Palgrave Macmillan, 2004), 94.

14. Boghardt, *Spies of the Kaiser*, 95.

15. Shipman, *Femme Fatale*, 187.

16. Report of Zelle's interrogation by Captain Bouchardon, Paris, 1917, Historique de Defense, Vincennes.

17. Shipman, *Femme Fatale*, 212.

18. Scotland Yard Questioning Report, November 1916, PF2917/V1, KV 2/1, UK National Archives, London.

19. Scotland Yard Questioning Report, 61.

20. Shipman, *Femme Fatale*, 39.

21. Shipman, *Femme Fatale*, 143.

22. Shipman, *Femme Fatale*, 228.

23. Shipman, *Femme Fatale*, 149.

24. Personal interview with Jonna Mendez, International Spy Museum, Washington, DC, July 2018.

25. Shipman, *Femme Fatale*, 249.

26. Shipman, *Femme Fatale*, 254.

27. Mary W. Craig, *A Tangled Web: Mata Hari—Dancer: Courtesan, Spy* (London: History Press, 2017) 168.

28. Markus Wolf with Anne McElvoy, *Man Without a Face: The Memoirs of a Spymaster* (London: Jonathan Cape, 1997) 123.

29. Wolf and McElvoy, *Man Without a Face*, 124.

30. Wolf and McElvoy, *Man Without a Face*, 150.

31. Brett Forrest, "The Big Russian Life of Anna Chapman, ex-Spy," *Politico*, January 4, 2012.

32. Ryan Lucas, "Russian Agent Maria Butina Sentenced to 18 Months Following Guilty Plea," *NPR*, April 25, 2019.

33. Andrew Clark, "I Wouldn't Have Sent Anna Chapman Back, Jokes Joe Biden on US Television," *The Guardian*, July 11, 2010.

34. Noel Coward and Barry Day, *The Letters of Noel Coward* (New York: Vintage Books, 2006). Thanks to Henry R. Schlesinger for this suggestion.

35. Shipman, *Femme Fatale*, 249.

36. Jean-Claude Baker and Chris Chase, *Josephine: The Hungry Heart* (Lanham, MD: Cooper Square Press, 2001), 235.

37. Wheelwright, *The Fatal Lover*, 56.

38. Wheelwright, *The Fatal Lover*, 32.

39. Scotland Yard Questioning Report.

40. Shipman, *Femme Fatale*, 44.

41. Message for Captain Ladoux dated July 5, 1916, from Mata Hari's MI5 file, National Archives, London.

42. Report dated December 15, 1916, document 143727, from Mata Hari's MI5 file, National Archives London.

43. Note from Passport Office report December 18, 1916, document 145798, from Mata Hari's MI5 file, National Archives London.

44. File no. 751, document 61207, from Mata Hari Report, February 3, 1916, PF2917 /V1, KV2/1, National Archives, London.

45. Hanne Hieber, "'Mademoiselle Docteur': The Life and Service of Imperial Germany's Only Female Intelligence Officer," *Journal of Intelligence History* 5, no. 2 (Winter 2005): 105.

46. Hieber, "Mademoiselle Docteur," 104.

47. Hieber, "Mademoiselle Docteur," 105.

48. Hieber, "Mademoiselle Docteur," 92. Marianne Walle, "'Fraulein Doktor' Elsbeth Schragmüller," *Guerres Mondiales et Conflits Contemporains*, no. 232 (Octobre–Decembre 2008): 56.

49. Shipman, *Femme Fatale*, 200.

50. Maseena Ziegler, "CIA Hiring Chief Demystifies Agency's Recruitment (And Reveals Top Interview Questions)," *Forbes*, October 23, 2014.

51. File no. 751, document 61207, from Mata Hari Report, February 3, 1916, PF2917 /V1, KV2/1, National Archives, London.

52. Folkestone Questioning Secret Report, December 4, 1915, PF2917/V1, KV 2/1 UK National Archives, London.

53. File no. 751, document 61207, from Mata Hari Report, February 3, 1916, PF2917 /V1, KV2/1, National Archives, London.

54. Scotland Yard Questioning Report.

55. Shipman, *Femme Fatale*, 258.

56. Walle, "Fraulein Doktor," 56.

57. Report, July 5, 1916, from Mata Hari's MI5 file, National Archives, London.

58. Shipman, *Femme Fatale*, 352.

59. File no. 751, document 61207, from Mata Hari Report, February 3, 1916, PF2917 /V1, KV2/1, National Archives, London.

60. Report of Zelle's Interrogation by Captain Bouchardon.

61. Scotland Yard Questioning Report.

62. Shipman, *Femme Fatale*, 212.

63. Shipman, *Femme Fatale*, 225.

# The Triumph and Downfall of Dmitri Bystrolyotov, Stalin's Romeo Spy

Emil Draitser

*Another character that visitors meet in their first minutes in the International Spy Museum is Soviet intelligence officer Dmitri Bystrolyotov. He was what those in the business would call a "case officer," a person charged with recruiting people with access to secrets and inducing them to betray their country. Among other missions, he operated under deep cover in prewar Germany. Unfortunately, in 1938 Bystrolyotov was betrayed by his own country after he fell afoul of Stalin during the Great Purges. This chapter is written by Bystrolyotov's biographer and tells the tale of one of Bystrolyotov's most challenging assignments, one that required him to use all the skills of an intelligence operator.—The Editors*

After a period of less intense international hostility following the end of World War I, the early 1930s were marked by a buildup of tension among various European countries. There were several reasons for this. In October 1929, the Wall Street crash led to a worldwide economic depression. Fascists and Nazis exploited these events to promote their agendas and grew in popularity. Mussolini in Italy and then Hitler in Germany promised economic growth and pursued aggressive foreign policies, presenting them as necessary to assure their countries' prosperity. Then, there was the unresolved issue of what to do with the newly created Soviet Union. Coming to power because of the Bolshevik takeover in October 1917, the Soviet state proclaimed that its official foreign policy was to export revolution. This made the Western powers wary, especially when the policy became practice. Communist attempts to seize power in Germany, Austria, Hungary, and other European countries only strengthened the appeal to many Europeans of the new volatile political movements of Fascism and Nazism.

Fresh in the Soviet government's memory was the intervention of several European countries in the Russian Civil War to help the White forces undo the Communist takeover. The Western Allies were worried about the prospect of the Bolsheviks making good on their threats to default on Imperial Russia's massive foreign loans and the possibility that

Communist revolutionary ideas would spread. Also, on March 3, 1918, the new Bolshevik government of Russia signed a separate peace treaty (the Treaty of Brest–Litovsk) with the Central Powers (German Empire, Austria-Hungary, Bulgaria, and Ottoman Empire), ending Russia's participation in World War I. Because the British and French had supported Russia during World War I on a massive scale with war materials, they sent troops to Russian ports to prevent those war materials from falling into the hands of the Germans. By the early 1930s, Soviet leader Joseph Stalin was sure that a plot to attack the Soviet Union was in the works. However, he was frustrated at the lack of reliable information that would confirm his beliefs.

Intelligence services were key players in such a tense Europe. The Soviet Union, led by ruthless dictator Stalin, particularly prized its brutal and effective services, notably the Soviet Foreign Intelligence Department of the Joint State Political Directorate (Ob'edinennoe Gosudarstvennoe Politicheskoe Upravlenie, or OGPU, a predecessor of the KGB). Knowledge of foreign languages and the ability to blend into the upper circles of Western societies were the most desirable qualities for a Soviet spy charged with procuring diplomatic codes or stealing military documents.

These qualifications were abundantly present in Dmitri Bystrolyotov (1901–1975), a legendary Russian intelligence officer who at various times in his life worked as a sailor and painter, a medical worker, a traveler and polyglot, and a writer. But Bystrolyotov had an additional quality useful in a certain type of intelligence officer: sex appeal. While the use of sex appeal by female spies is a cultural trope (see chapter 4 in this volume, on Mata Hari), the tactic can be used by male spies as well. Accordingly, this chapter is a narrative of one of Bystrolyotov's most successful operations as a "Romeo spy." Coined in the 1960s by Markus Wolf, chief of the Stasi, East Germany's Ministry for State Security, the phrase denotes a man involved in a spy operation whose sexual attractiveness serves as an enticing tool to elicit secret information. Bystrolyotov was Stalin's first Romeo spy. He used many of the tactics and methods that decades later Wolf would make famous. As Bystrolyotov told me when we met, "I was young, good-looking, and knew several European languages. And I knew how to treat a lady."[1] Yet this story will also make clear that, while Romeo gets the most attention, he can't succeed alone. Even sexual entrapment—a seemingly very intimate, one-on-one affair—involves careful preparation and support from a team of people, all helping to maximize the chance that the target will succumb.[2]

Despite the success to be recounted here—and many others—Bystrolyotov would fall afoul of the great purges that swept the Soviet Union in the

Figure 5.1: Self-portrait of Dmitri Bystrolyotov using ink mixed with iodine from the Gulag infirmary. Gift of S. S. Milashov.

second half of the 1930s. He would be arrested and spend sixteen years as a prisoner in a Soviet gulag only to be embraced in the late Soviet period and in post-Soviet Russia as an iconic intelligence hero.

In the first years of the twentieth century, Bystrolyotov was a young Russian aristocrat believed to be an illegitimate offspring of the Tolstoy line. He was first drafted into the White Army, which opposed the Bolsheviks, but after its defeat he was recruited as a sleeper agent by the Cheka, the Soviet secret police. In the fall of 1920, the Cheka sent him to the West with the flow of Russian refugees, to be activated after he settled in Prague. Capitalizing on his knowledge of several European languages and his aristocratic upbringing, Bystrolyotov operated with ease amid the upper layers of European societies. First, he worked on the staff of the Soviet trade mission in Prague. In the 1930s, under the code names "Andrei" and then "Hans," he became a member of the "Flying Squad," a mobile group of Soviet undercover operatives capable of crossing the borders of many European countries, frequently and with ease, arousing no suspicions.

In 1925, Nikolai Samsonov (code name "Semyon"), the resident spymaster in Prague of the Cheka (by this time the name had changed to the OGPU), working as the second secretary of the Soviet trade mission using the undercover name "Comrade Holst," tutored this dashing young man in the use of seduction to make women work as Soviet agents. Putting this training to good use, Bystrolyotov obtained technological secrets of the Continental–Kern Concern in Prague and recruited a typist of the French

Figure 5.2: Pin from the Soviet Gulag system. The Cyrillic letters are "ITL," an acronym for "correctional labor camp." Courtesy of the Francis Lara Collection.

embassy in Prague (code name "Laroche") who for two years provided him with copies of the most confidential diplomatic correspondence that crossed her desk. In his future work, Bystrolyotov would use this modus operandi to recruit the wife of a British aristocrat, a German countess, and a Romanian lady from high society, who supplied the Soviets with Romanian diplomatic and military secrets. Perhaps his most famous triumph, however, came in an operation targeting a woman in the Nazi SS paramilitary force who was viewed as incorruptible.[3]

The year 1935 began with ominous developments in Germany. After the death of President Paul von Hindenburg on August 2, 1934, Adolf Hitler assumed the office of Reichspräsident and thus became commander in chief. All officers and soldiers of the Wehrmacht, the German armed forces, had to swear a personal oath of loyalty to the Führer. However, this worrisome chain of events was not unexpected. Anticipating this development, Soviet foreign intelligence had refocused its main efforts away from England and toward Germany. At the beginning of 1934, the OGPU designated the various apparatuses of Nazi Germany as targets for penetration, including the army, the police, and the Nazi Party, as well as the entourages of Hitler, Hermann Goering, and later, in 1935, War Minister Werner von Blomberg.[4]

The Treaty of Versailles that formally ended World War I had put strict limits on the German armed forces, and the manufacturing of many weapons of all sorts—such as tanks, submarines, military aircraft, and artillery—was prohibited. Then, on March 16, 1935, Hitler announced his intention to rearm Germany in violation of the treaty and to reintroduce conscription.

Of course, German rearmament was a matter of grave concern to the Soviet Union and the OGPU. Through a newly developed network of agents, the Soviet intelligence *rezidentura* in Berlin learned that Wehrmacht Headquarters had organized several safe places where they accumulated sensitive military information about future adversaries. One such intelligence center was camouflaged as the documentation department of the I. G. Farbenindustrie chemical concern, which was situated at one of the concern's branch offices, Zweighalle-5. This is where all reports came in from secret German agents dealing with military industries of foreign countries, including the Soviet Union. The department also contained exhaustive data on the placement of new Wehrmacht orders for military equipment and weaponry at various German industrial concerns including Krupp, Junkers, and Siemens.[5]

The safeguarding of this information was entrusted to one Dorothea Müller, a woman about forty years old, who held the rank of SS-Hauptscharführer (equivalent to the US rank of master sergeant). As the clerk in charge, in the mornings she would check out files to the officers working them, on the condition they sign for and later collect and lock up the files in a safe. Soviet spies learned that she preferred to be called "Doris," which, in her view, gave her name a more dignified coloring. But among themselves, the Soviet personnel assigned to find a way to break into the super-secret safe she guarded, called her "Cerberus"—in Greek mythology, a monstrous three-headed dog, with a snake for a tail and snakeheads protruding from various parts of his body, who guarded the gate to the Underworld and ensured that no living person could enter.[6]

The nickname was deliberate. Bystrolyotov describes her face, which had been disfigured by fire during a car accident in her childhood, as "astonishing in its ugliness. On the right side, her forehead, cheek, and chin were blotched by huge burn scars. The skin was stretched from her eye upward and downward and from the corner of her mouth to her ear." In addition, her right hand was blackened and gnarled.[7] In fact, her appearance was the reason why she was chosen for the job: the Nazis believed that her disfigurement left her no hope of marriage or even an affair, and thus she would not be easily recruited by a foreign intelligence service. Given her lot in life, Müller was embittered and unpleasant to deal with.[8] She was also a devoted member of the Nazi Party. In Bystrolyotov's words, she was a "chained guard dog, a mad dog, growling at anyone who approached the secrets behind the door she guarded." He was entrusted to tame this "dangerous beast," to find a way to transform this Cerberus into a "domesticated and tender puppy."[9]

To accomplish this, Bystrolyotov put back into play a legend that had worked well with an employee of the British Foreign Office, Ernest Holloway Oldham (code name "Arno"). Given that Bystrolyotov had used this alias in the past, he was well attuned to its idiosyncrasies. Specifically, he would pretend to be a Hungarian count named "Lajos József Perelly" who held a Czech passport. Bystrolyotov himself developed the backstory that the count, having been dispossessed of his considerable estates by World War I, now lived on money sent by his aunt from the United States. While he had resided there for the past several years, he had now decided to travel and see the world. This explained his presence in Germany.[10]

To get inside the head of a displaced Hungarian aristocrat, Bystrolyotov perused books on the country's history, culture, economy, and everyday life. In addition, bearing yet another passport indicating that he was a Greek merchant, Bystrolyotov went to Budapest. There he attended places frequented by the landed gentry—diplomatic receptions, opening nights at the theaters, popular horse races, important church services—making note of the aristocracy's manners and customs. To blend with that crowd, he ordered himself several suits from the best Budapest tailors and purchased a few pairs of fashionable shoes, a dozen ties, a few rings, and some other accessories. A set of his smoking pipes carried the Perelly family's coat of arms. As dictated by the Hungarian landlord's fashion of the time, he embellished one of his hats with a characteristic little brush.[11]

Then Bystrolyotov toured the country, taking pictures of himself against the background of the best-known Hungarian sites. While on the road, he seized an opportunity to solidify his legend. He learned that a Hungarian cardinal would take part in one of the forthcoming church processions. Studying the real Perelly family tree, Bystrolyotov established that the cardinal (apparently József Mindszenty) would logically be the count's uncle. Bystrolyotov feigned a fit of religious fervor and stepped out from the crowd in front of the cardinal, who smiled and blessed him. A street photographer hired for the occasion took a snapshot of the moment. The picture proved invaluable. Tucked into Bystrolyotov's fake Perelly passport, it never failed to impress customs officials at European border posts.[12]

Upon returning to Berlin, Bystrolyotov rented an apartment in one of the newly built areas of the city. As a count, he had to have a living space big enough to match his title—at least three rooms. The landlord supplied him with furniture and recommended servants. Two assistants who had worked with him previously, Joseph Leppin (code name "Peep") and Erica Weinstein (code name "Erika"), also arrived in Berlin. Leppin renewed a

Figure 5.3: Silver cigarette case for veterans of the Cheka, OGPU, and NKVD, 1935. From the Collection of H. Keith and Karen Melton at the International Spy Museum.

previous cover occupation—studying old German grammar at the university—and Weinstein found a job as a nurse in a private clinic.[13]

Of course, Bystrolyotov realized that the slightest commotion around the SS woman would attract the Gestapo's attention. Therefore, he had to be extremely careful. But how should he approach her? To feign amorous feelings toward a woman he saw as disfigured and unpleasant would not work: she would hardly believe such a crude lie. The gap between an unattractive, aging woman and a handsome young aristocrat was much too wide. Any romantic overtures toward her would only raise suspicions and alarm her; she might even find them insulting. Bystrolyotov decided to use his target's fanatical devotion to Hitler and the Nazi Party to ingratiate himself with her. But as usual, before making any moves he devoted time—about two weeks—to preparatory work learning as much as possible about his target. Leppin's and Weinstein's surveillance of Müller's everyday habits revealed little. She lived in a small room near Alexanderplatz. Her workday began at 9:00 a.m. and ended at 6:00 p.m., though sometimes she stayed in her office until ten in the evening. After work she would stop at an inexpensive café. Bystrolyotov's spotters noted that she routinely occupied the same table, third from the entrance, by a window. During the time she was followed, she twice visited a movie theater. Not surprising, and considering her political outlook, both times she chose Nazi propaganda films. Once she went to the Berlin circus. She did all of this alone. And she never smiled.[14]

From his experience, Bystrolyotov thought it would be risky to approach his target out of the blue. So he conceived of a way just to show himself to Doris without approaching her. For that purpose, he brought "Greta," a young and beautiful German lady, into the operation. He had recruited her earlier, back in 1930, soon after he moved to Berlin. On the target day, when Leppin and Weinstein reported that Doris was at her usual place in the café, Greta also went there. She knew where Fräulein Müller was sitting. After walking around the other tables, all occupied by couples, Greta stopped at Doris's table and asked whether she could join her. Doris nodded. It was raining outside. Greta looked out the window as if expecting to see someone. She ordered a black coffee with liquor, looked at her watch, and said to Doris, with the smile of a proud, yet vulnerable, young lady: "Perhaps it's a bad sign when it rains cats and dogs on your first date."[15]

The considerable age difference between Greta and Müller appeared to be a subtle call for a maternal cheering-up. Doris initially cut her off, but then she softened. When a chocolate-colored Horch sedan pulled up, a handsome, well-dressed gentleman with a foppish expression on his face exited the vehicle and scanned the café windows. Müller grinned: "It looks like it's for you." Greta left money on the table, nodded, and headed for the exit.

A week later, Greta and her "suitor" arranged a date at the same place again. This time, the fellow appeared early to pick up Greta. She sent a triumphant look to Doris, who observed the scene, inviting her to share the excitement of having such a handsome and impeccably dressed suitor. One day she introduced him to Müller. On subsequent dates, Bystrolyotov in his "Count Perelly" persona would arrive at the café before Greta and always be careful to nod politely, acknowledging the presence of the older German lady, now his girl's acquaintance. Engaging in light conversations with her, Perelly took care to project the image of a cosmopolite who wandered the world to escape boredom. One day with a vacant look in his eyes, he asked Fräulein Müller to excuse his ignorance and enlighten him about what was going on in Germany. As a foreigner who would not normally be interested in politics, he could not help but become curious about the events that were unfolding. Why so much fuss about a few people in the country? he asked. Herr Hitler . . . Herr Goebbels . . . Herr Goering . . . were they so important? Who were they? Admirals? Professors? All these gentlemen had such sound-alike names. In America, nobody could tell them apart.[16]

Fräulein Müller was horrified. She could not believe her ears! Where had this "monstrously blasphemous and ignorant" fellow grown up? The count blathered his excuses, from which emerged the portrait of a rich gentleman who led a dissipated way of life and was spoiled by his easy victories over women. Müller decided that it would benefit Germany only if she ensured that this person knew and respected the country in which he was spending his time so pleasantly.[17]

She began to ply him with books and articles on the nature and program of National Socialism, and Perelly appeared genuinely interested. Every time they met, she patiently explained to him what Nazism was all about, what a great doctrine it was, and what a genius Germany's Führer was. She eagerly engaged in talks with the count, who by that time forgot Greta, the young date who could match neither Fräulein Müller's knowledge of current politics nor her passion in imparting it to him. For Müller, educating the foreigner became a habit; then it gradually grew into an attachment. And finally, almost without noticing, she fell head over heels in love with him.[18]

Müller's feelings for Perelly were the genuine passion of a sexually awakened woman who had already given up on personal happiness. All of her unrequited need for love was now concentrated on this fake Hungarian. It seems even Bystrolyotov himself had not expected to evoke such potent emotions in her. "What a love it was!" he reminisced in his memoirs. Yet he was aware of his duplicity, writing: "[It turned out that even] bloodthirsty dogs are capable of love."[19] Though in the past Bystrolyotov himself had fallen for one of his targets, there was no danger of that sort in his dealing with Doris. Throughout his memoirs, written many years later, he avoided providing intimate details of his dealings with women. All he said of Doris in this regard was that he shuddered the first time he kissed her.[20]

After a long preparatory stage, when at last she was under his power as a lover, Perelly one day became gloomy and began acting like a man in despair. Spending time in her apartment, he suggested she get drunk with him. When she asked him what was troubling him, he replied that his income—the stream of money his American aunt was sending him—had dwindled. "Bad times are ahead of me," he confessed. "My cash flow is going down the drain."[21] He told her that as a nobleman, as a person possessing a certain level of respectability, he could not continue an illicit affair and that he wanted to marry her. The only obstacle was money. As a man of pride, he intoned that marriage had to be built on solid ground, and he needed to improve his finances.

Then Bystrolyotov sprung his trap. He told Doris about his friend and faithful assistant, another Hungarian nobleman, "Lajos Batory"—a Soviet illegal operative whose real name was Theodor Mally, one of the Soviets' most effective case officers—who managed Perelly's estate back in their home country. Batory, Perelly claimed, had offered to help with his friend's financial troubles. It seemed that the prospect of German rearmament had made the dormant stock market come back to life. Knowing the plans of the military industry, one could make good money by buying stocks of companies low, before they received government orders, and selling high after the orders were placed.[22] The key was to find out what the military intended to buy. Doris gave it some thought and concluded it would be easy to find out these things but that she would want to meet the man and see what he was all about. Bystrolyotov suggested meeting him at a popular café. Doris rejected the idea: the café was too busy a place for a confidential meeting. She proposed bringing Batory to her apartment.

Bystrolyotov arranged the encounter. Doris appeared to like the tall, well-dressed, respectful, and considerate Herr Batory.[23] He outlined his story to Doris, noting that he was thinking about getting into the promising area of stock movement in the aircraft industry. He added how, if he could just find out the government's plans for the Junkers and Messerschmitt plants, then quick money could be made. Doris asked him how the secrecy of the data would be guaranteed. He replied that the whole idea of the deal was that nobody else was to know these numbers lest too many traders jump on the bandwagon; in that case there would be little profit to be made from the buy-low, sell-high operation.

The following day, Doris took a few files from the safe to her office, studied them, and in the evening made an oral report to her beloved, who passed it to Herr Batory. After a few days, she found the procedure tiresome, so she simply brought home a piece of paper with two columns of numbers, the enciphered results of her study of the files in her care.

Soon, Doris asked Batory to tell her how to make trades herself. She had no interest in the money for her own sake but for the sake of her fiancé; after all, their marriage depended on it. Over time, Batory stepped up the pressure and told her that if she wanted to get married sooner he would borrow more money from the banks to play the stock exchange but that it would be impossible to obtain a substantial loan based on oral assurances alone. They would want to see some supporting documents, which would have to take out for an hour or two. After some hesitation, Doris brought some files home. After she left, Mally photographed them. Of course, Doris knew she had broken the rules, but she was able to rationalize it because the files she took were classified as "confidential," not "top secret."[24]

There was a risk that German counterintelligence might notice Batory's frequent visits to Doris's apartment and grow suspicious. To justify these visits, Soviet intelligence prepared backstopping documents indicating that Count Perelly had commissioned his employee Herr Batory to talk to German banks and construction and repair firms regarding the renovation of his family estate in Hungary. Perelly left copies of the papers, as if absentmindedly, on Doris's bookcase. If the Gestapo searched the apartments, finding these documents would ensure that Batory was not compromised.

Despite the success of the operation, it could not go on forever. Every day brought the risk of compromise. Already Doris had waited for over three months for her beloved count to deliver on his promise of marriage. Besides, other OGPU assignments to the illegal *rezidentura* in Berlin needed Bystrolyotov's attention. Nevertheless, Perelly could not just one day disappear into thin air without raising the suspicion of foul play. An alarmed Doris would most likely call the police to investigate her fiancé's disappearance, thereby attracting the attention of German counterintelligence, which would probably discover that information had been leaked from the secret safe.

To avoid this undesirable course of events, Boris Bazarov, an illegal OGPU chief of station in Berlin, came up with a "newspaper variant," as he called it. Following his instructions, one day Bystrolyotov told Doris that, now that some money had been made, there was no longer any reason to delay their marriage. But as a responsible man he needed to put things in order and place their future life together on a solid base. This required traveling to Hungary for a couple weeks to settle with his creditors and solidify his estate. Then he would return to plan for their wedding.

With Doris's acquiescence, Perelly left Berlin. A week later, Herr Batory paid an emergency visit to her. He was pale and could barely move his lips. He gave her a copy of a newspaper with a highlighted news item. It seemed that Count Perelly had been shot dead in a tragic hunting accident in the Hungarian provinces and his body sent to relatives in New York. Doris bought the story and went into mourning.[25]

But Bystrolyotov would see his SS lover one more time. A few months after his disappearance, another operation brought him to Berlin to meet a Soviet intelligence operative. He was about to enter a café on Leipziger Strasse for the arranged meeting when, right in front of him on the other side of the glass door, he saw his "widowed bride" staring at him in total disbelief. It happened so suddenly that they both froze, unable to tear their eyes from each other. At that very moment, a patrol of SS officers approached Bystrolyotov, who was blocking the entrance to the café, and respectfully moved him to the side. Doris produced a wild shriek, writhed in hysterical sobbing, and fainted away. The officers rushed to her and bent toward the poor woman lying on the floor. A crowd of curious onlookers gathered around the glass door. Bystrolyotov quickly fled. "One word from her," he recalled, "one slight cry or involuntary abrupt gesture [in my direction], and I would have perished."[26] Luckily, he came to his senses first, turned around, and at the nearest street corner hailed a taxi, which whisked him away from trouble.

Although there is no evidence that Bystrolyotov ever hesitated to handle his sources in whatever fashion was required for the success of the operation at hand, he was often obliged to act against his moral code—and he felt uneasy about it. He was quite aware of the inhumanity and baseness of his occupation, often referring to it as "despicable work." Undoubtedly, that was how he felt about his treatment of the women he had seduced in the course of his intelligence career. However, the time came when the tables turned, and he finally got a taste of how it felt to be sexually exploited for the sake of spying. His last operation consisted of offering his sexuality in exchange for information from Florica Titulescu, a Romanian high-society lady who was already passing Romanian diplomatic and military secrets to French intelligence.[27]

As he worked with her, Florica's demands for sex as a prerequisite for her full cooperation became tiresome for him. So to avoid her sexual demands, he replaced himself with another Soviet spy, an old collaborator named Henri Pieck. Florica was very unhappy. When Mally disciplined him for this insubordinate act, Bystrolyotov, for the first time, rebelled against being merely a tool in the callous hands of his bosses. He told Mally angrily and gloomily: "I'm a human being, Theodor, and I'm a decent man. Tell me, does an intelligence operative have the right to be decent and preserve his self-respect? I'll never become a gigolo."[28]

By that time in late 1936, Bystrolyotov had become fed up with spying. The episode with Florica made him fully realize the true essence of the Soviet regime. He determined that he wanted to quit as soon as possible and go home. So he asked for permission to return and was allowed to return to Moscow at the end of 1936—at the height of Stalin's Purges. On September 18, 1937, he was arrested and falsely accused of selling out to the enemy and engaging in terrorist activities against the Soviet Union while he was in Czechoslovakia. "Do you want to write your testimony in

Figure 5.4: The gloves that Dmitri Bystrolyotov wore in the Gulag. Gift of S. S. Milashov.

ink," the NKVD officer asked him, "or in your blood?" Initially Bystrolyotov chose the latter, and brutal torture ensued. Eventually the torture brought him to a point where he felt that he might die, and he realized that death would make it impossible for him ever to prove his innocence. The next morning, he gathered what remained of his strength and whispered that he was ready to give his testimony.[29]

Bystrolyotov was sentenced to twenty years of hard labor in the Gulag. The tragedy extended to his family. Ostracized and deprived of any means of sustenance as relatives of an "enemy of the people," both his wife and his mother took their own lives.

While serving his term in Siberian camps, Bystrolyotov experienced deep remorse concerning his actions as a spy. He came to realize the criminal nature of the regime he served, a regime that turned out to be not unlike the Nazi regime he had fought against. He eventually did what he felt would be the ultimate service to his country and humanity at large. Still in the camps, and overcoming tremendous odds—ruined health and the risk of severe punishment—he began writing his eyewitness account of Stalin's penal servitude. Because paper was at a premium in the camps, he used the backs of discarded medical records, to which he had access as an assistant to a camp doctor. Smuggled to the outside world by his fellow inmates and his second wife, whom he had met and married during his captivity, his powerful memoirs often rivals that of his famous comrade in misfortune: Alexander Solzhenitsyn, the author of *The Gulag Archipelago*.

Besides many ruminations about the senselessness of the self-sacrifices he had made during his spying career, which are scattered throughout his voluminous writings, Bystrolyotov asks himself the same rhetorical question many times: "Am I a hero or a fool?" By this time, he realized that what he had earlier considered heroic deeds for the benefit of the Motherland turned out to be nothing but "blind diligence" (*slepoe ispolnitel'stvo*). He reveals that what pushed him into espionage was his "youth and beautiful illusions," which were "dragged through the mud" on the night of his arrest. His writing shows his conscious attempts to understand himself and his motives in spying, his painful search to find an answer to what circumstances of his life, including that of his birth and his upbringing, made him susceptible to recruitment into spy work. And he clarifies that, with his life coming to a close, he considered it wasted. He sums it up in the concluding part of his multivolume memoir:

> At night, I wake up from burning grief and shame and think: for what had we [Soviet spies abroad] endured so much torment and committed so many crimes? . . . At the time, we appeased ourselves with thoughts of sacrifice for the benefit of our Motherland. Morally, it was a dubious explanation. . . . Now I burn from shame after realizing how we were fooled. Our belief in the Party and love for the Motherland have been dragged through the mud. Everything is fouled. As your life comes to a close, it's frightful to be left with zilch [*ostat'sia u razbitogo koryta*].[30]

After his release in October 1954, Bystrolyotov, as a former political prisoner, could not find regular employment, but being conversant in some twenty languages he was able to do contract work as a translator for medical research organizations in Moscow. He also continued writing. While being careful not to step on Soviet censors' toes, he published a short novel in 1974 titled *Para Bellum*, a disguised account of one of his pre–World War II foreign operations. In addition, he wrote a film script based on some of his experiences spying in Britain, but political expedience meant he moved the action to Nazi Germany. In 1973, a film titled *Chelovek v shtatskom* (A plainclothes man) based on his script was released. However, his memoirs were not published in his lifetime.

Bystrolyotov passed away on May 3, 1975. He was buried at the Khovansky cemetery in Moscow. His gray granite tombstone carries an inscription: "*Slava cheloveku v shtatskom*" (Glory to the plainclothes man). After the collapse of the Soviet Union, Bystrolyotov's official image underwent a gradual change; Moscow would reshape the real Bystrolyotov into a mythological figure to meet the political demands of the day. The FSB, a successor to the KGB, chose him to play the part of one of its heroes, a man they could be proud of, a poster boy whose exemplary life would inspire a new generation of Russian spies. Authorities transformed a complex and flawed human being—an indisputable hero in terms of accomplishments and bravery, in his later years a person tormented by self-loathing and remorse for his exploits as a spy—into a saint who did not even mind the devastation to his life caused by his employer. While an official biography mentions in passing the fact that Bystrolyotov spent years in the Gulag, the gruesome torture he endured at the hands of the notorious agency was not acknowledged. His former masters also sanitized his memoirs, deleting the most damning descriptions of the atrocities he witnessed and experienced. Of the eleven volumes he had written, they published only a small portion posthumously.

Bystrolyotov continues to be chosen as the subject of many journalism articles, a novel based on his life and dedicated to his memory, and three documentary films. In addition, the central hero of a 2003 television miniseries titled *Rodina zhdet* (The Motherland is waiting), a Russian intelligence officer fighting against terrorists, not only carries Bystrolyotov's surname but also possesses several of his personal qualities: good looks, charisma, proficiency in many languages, courage, and (of course) sex appeal.

The Russian government even used Bystrolyotov to reinforce its claim that the Crimea Peninsula—territory in neighboring Ukraine that the Russian Federation seized by military force in 2014—is an integral part of Russia. Moscow pointed to the fact that the famous spy was born in the Crimean resort town of Anapa. On October 11, 2021, in commemoration of the 120th anniversary of his birth, authorities widely publicized the unveiling of a statue of Bystrolyotov in Simferopol, the region's capital.

The real Dmitri Bystrolyotov would hardly suit the autocratic methods by which Moscow rules Russia today. The biggest and most devastating personal discovery that the famed Russian spy made at the end of his life was that all the many sacrifices he had made as a spy to serve his country's good amounted to practically nothing. A country ruled by the whim of one person (during his espionage career, it was Stalin) is bound to waste the efforts of even its most devout citizens, which Bystrolyotov was.

As for the use of sex and romance to induce people to spy, the Soviet intelligence services and their allied East European services continued employing such tactics after Bystrolyotov was sent to the Gulag and up through the end of the Soviet period. Post-Soviet Russia continues using them today.

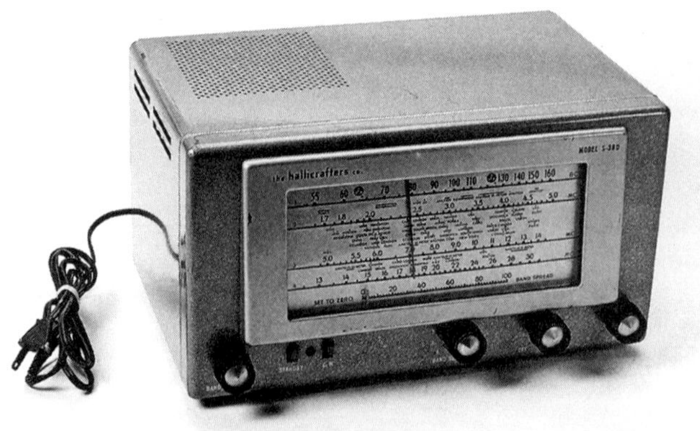


Figure 5.5: Hallicrafters Company Model C-38D shortwave radio. While living in New York City, the Soviet illegal Rudolf Abel used this radio to receive one-way voice coded messages from Moscow. He was arrested in 1957 and released in a 1962 spy swap in exchange for captured CIA U-2 pilot Francis Gary Powers. From the Collection of H. Keith and Karen Melton at the International Spy Museum.

## Further Reading

Andrew, Christopher, and Vasili Mitrokhin. *The Sword and the Shield: The Mitrokhin Archive and the Secret History of the KGB*. New York: Basic Books, 1999.

Draitser, Emil. *Stalin's Romeo Spy: The Remarkable Rise and Fall of the KGB's Most Daring Operative*. Evanston: Northwestern University Press, 2010.

Schlesinger, Henry R. *Honey Trapped: Sex, Betrayal, and Weaponized Love*. Cheltenham: The History Press, 2021.

## Notes

1. Personal interview with Dragster, n.d.

2. Emil Draitser, *Stalin's Romeo Spy: The Remarkable Rise and Fall of the KGB's Most Daring Operative* (Evanston: Northwestern University Press, 2010), 5.

3. Dmitri Bystrolyotov, *Puteshestvie na kraj nochi* [Journey to the end of night] (Moscow: Sovremennik, 1996), 585.

4. E. Primakov, ed., *Ocherki istorii rossiiskoi razvedki* [Essays on the history of Russian foreign intelligence] (Moscow, 1997), vol. 2, 327.

5. Primakov, *Ocherki istorii rossiiskoi razvedki*, 2:328.

6. Dmitri Bystrolyotov, *Pir bessmertnykh*, [Feast of the immortals] (Moscow: Granitsa, 1993), vol. 3, 377; Dmitri Bystrolyotov, *Shchedrye serdtsem* [Generous Hearts], Typescript of a screenplay ca. 1965), National Library of Russia (formerly

Slatykov-Shchedrin Library), St. Petersburg, 162. In the Mitrokhin archive, her name is spelled "Mueller," www.linearossage.it/201-248.htm.

7. Bystrolyotov, *Pir bessmertnykh*, vol 3, 377.

8. Bystrolyotov, *Pir bessmertnykh*, vol. 3, 337; Dmitri Bystrolyotov, *Para bellum* [Prepare for War], *Nash Sovremennik*, no. 3 (1974): 181.

9. Bystrolyotov, *Pir bessmertnykh*, vol. 3, 337; Bystrolyotov, *Para bellum*, 181.

10. Bystrolyotov, *Para bellum*, 174.

11. Bystrolyotov file. Record of service no. 12351. Archive no. 9529. vol. 2. "*Rukopis' Gansa*" [Hans's Manuscript]. Bystrolyotov's handwritten memo, signed October 28, 1968 [repaginated a few times], KGB archive, Moscow, Russia.

12. Bystrolyotov, *Pir bessmertnykh*, vol. 3, 371–372.

13. Primakov, *Ocherki istorii rossiiskoi razvedki*, 2:241; Bystrolyotov, *Para bellum*, 127.

14. Bystrolyotov, *Para bellum*, vol. 4, 127–28.

15. Bystrolyotov, *Para bellum*, 128.

16. Bystrolyotov, *Para bellum*, 174.

17. Bystrolyotov, *Para bellum*, 174.

18. Bystrolyotov, *Pir bessmertnykh*, vol. 3, 378.

19. Bystrolyotov, *Pir bessmertnykh*, 378.

20. Bystrolyotov, *Shchedrye serdtsem*, 175.

21. In Bystrolyotov, *Para bellum*, 132–134, and *Shchedrye serdtsem*, 169–171. The scheme Bystrolyotov prepared for Doris is rendered in three ways, slightly differently in the details. The most plausible scenario, a combination of all the elements, is reconstructed here.

22. Bystrolyotov, *Para bellum*.

23. This could be explained by Mally's background. In his youth, Theodor had studied theology in a Catholic monastic order, and was ordained as a deacon, but then chose a career in the military. He finished a military academy, served in an officer rank in the Austro-Hungarian Army during World War I, and was taken prisoner. He switched sides, joining the Red Army at the time of the Russian Civil War. Later, he joined the Soviet foreign intelligence. On Mally's background, see *Shchedrye serdtsem*, 7–8; Nigel West and Oleg Tsarev, *Crown Jewels: The British Secrets at the Heart of the KGB Archives* (New Haven: Yale University Press, 1999), 113–114.

24. Bystrolyotov, *Para bellum*, 133.

25. Bystrolyotov, *Pir bessmertnykh*, vol. 3, 379.

26. Bystrolyotov, in conversation with the author, September 11, 1973.

27. See the Mitrokhin archive, excerpt 204, www.linearossage.it/201-248.htm, accessed August 6, 2009.

28. Aleksandr Orlov, *Handbook of Intelligence and Guerrilla Warfare* (Ann Arbor: University of Michigan Press, 1963), 97; Bystrolyotov, *Shchedrye serdtsem*, 316.

29. Bystrolyotov, *Pir bessmertnykh*, vol. 1, 354.

30. Bystrolyotov, *Pir bessmertnykh*, vol. 3, 390.

# The Role of Balloons in Union Military Intelligence in the Civil War

James L. Green

*Espionage is just one method of collecting intelligence information. One section of the museum is devoted to other methods, most of which fall within technical collection. Today, one of the most important is geospatial intelligence, which involves the collection of intelligence from above. Here James L. Green tells the story of the reconnaissance balloons used during the US Civil War (1861–1865).—The Editors*

In the US Civil War (1861–1865), three key pieces of military intelligence on enemy troops were location, strength, and movement. The potential for balloons to provide this information was not lost on anyone. Indeed, at the outbreak of the war many newspapers urged the federal government to employ balloons for aerial reconnaissance. At that time, Washington, DC, was on the front lines, and local newspapers portrayed the Confederate Army as liable to cross the Potomac River at any time and invade Washington and Maryland. These news articles produced general fear throughout the region.

To calm the public and demonstrate that the nation's capital could be secured, President Abraham Lincoln brought troops in and created the first United States air force—using balloons. This organization has been designated the Aeronautics Department, Balloon Department, and the Balloon Corps (the name we will use here). Once operational, the Balloon Corps provided important aerial views of uncharted terrain for creating maps and potential battlefields. Balloons were also useful for gathering tactical and strategic military intelligence. This chapter concentrates on the types of military information that the Union's balloon observations collected and demonstrates that the power of this technological innovation for gathering intelligence from aloft went largely unrealized by the generals who could have used it the most.

In the early days of the Civil War, before the establishment of the Balloon Corps, several balloon professionals known as "aeronauts" joined infantry units. For instance, James Allen, a life long aeronaut, joined the Rhode Island Marine Artillery on May 7, 1861, which was part of the 1st Rhode Island Infantry under Ambrose Burnside, taking with him two balloons.[1]

On May 26, Burnside's regiment arrived in Washington. In early July, Allen demonstrated captive ascensions at Alexandria and Falls Church, Virginia, but he also had several failed attempts when his fragile balloons popped upon being refilled.[2] After he had satisfied his three-month military commitment, he returned to Providence, Rhode Island. In April 1862, however, Allen would be hired as a contract aeronaut in the newly established Balloon Corps.

Another example was the aeronaut John LaMountain. At the outbreak of the war, Confederates took over armories, ports, and ships in the seceded states. However, in the Hampton Roads area of Virginia, Fortress Monroe, a formidable fort on a sliver of land in the bay region, remained in Union hands. Early in June 1861, at the request of the fortress commander General Benjamin Butler, LaMountain arrived at Fortress Monroe with his balloon. LaMountain developed a strong relationship with Butler because he was able to provide detailed information about Confederate ships and troop movements over great distances that was impossible to obtain in any other way but from the vantage of a balloon. For example, on several occasions, LaMountain's inflated balloon was towed by the steamer *Fanny*. On August 10, 1861, he sketched the Confederate tents and batteries at Sewall's Point across the bay from Fortress Monroe. From a fortified Sewell's Point, Confederates could deter Union ships from coming to the aid of the fort. This proved to be important intelligence that Butler acted on by alerting all the ships in the area to skirt around the range of artillery placed at Sewall's Point.

The most important Union aeronaut, however, was Thaddeus S. C. Lowe of Philadelphia, the youngest aeronaut to come to the aid of the Union, a man whose early balloon voyages had gained public attention in the spring of 1858 in Ottawa, Canada.[3] With the urging of Joseph Henry, secretary of the Smithsonian Institution, Lowe arrived in Washington on June 5, 1861, to demonstrate to the federal government the value of tethered balloons.[4] Lowe created a national sensation when he took his balloon *Enterprise* to a height of 500 feet on the National Mall with a telegraph terminal and operator who sent the first aerial telegram to Lincoln describing the view into Virginia.[5] Lincoln invited Lowe to the White House that night for dinner for a more detailed discussion, which undoubtably fueled Lincoln's imagination for the military use of balloons. This led to Lowe being given a chance to demonstrate the practical use of making observations from balloons for the Union Army.

The establishment of the Balloon Corps can be traced to about July 1, 1861, when the government gave the famous aeronaut John Wise the first contract to build and man an observation balloon.[6] The new Balloon Corps

Figure 6.1: Thaddeus Lowe aloft with the balloon *Intrepid* during the Peninsula Campaign, May 1862.

was placed under the control of Major Albert Myer of the Signal Corps. Unfortunately, Wise's balloon burst on July 21 as it was being towed behind a wagon going down a road with trees on both sides on the way to the Battle of Bull Run.[7] Wise immediately quit and joined a Pennsylvania cavalry unit. The government then turned to Thaddeus Lowe, giving him funding on August 2 to construct a new balloon, making him the government's chief aeronaut.[8] Lowe, a master engineer, quickly developed a highly effective system of tethered balloon observation points.

With the Confederates seemingly ready to invade Washington at any moment, Lowe was kept busy making observations from tethered balloon flights from various locations in Washington, Virginia, and Maryland. Much of this work was dedicated to mapping, as the Union lacked detailed knowledge about the enemy's roads, streams, and homes even in northern Virginia across the Potomac from Washington.[9] One such location that needed to be mapped was Bailey's Cross Roads in Virginia. On August 27, 1861, Union and the Confederate forces were at a standoff when Lowe ascended in a balloon and observed Confederate fortifications being built

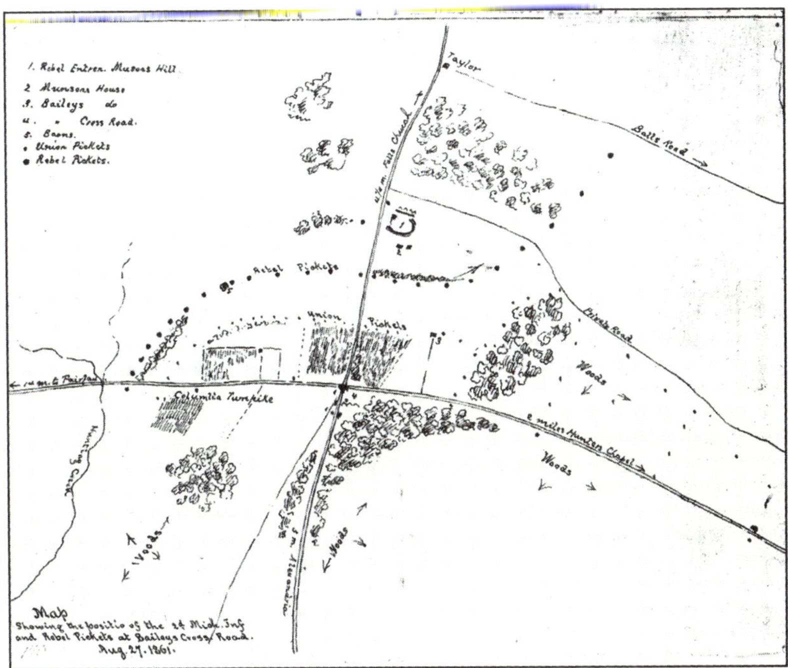


Figure 6.2: A balloon view of Bailey's Crossroads on August 27, 186,1 showing Union pickets and Rebel pickets, batteries on Munson Hill, and encampments.

on Munson Hill, a main feature of the crossroads. He reported that the fortifications were strong and well-equipped with cannons (see figure 6.2). After five weeks of holding the area the Confederates withdrew, only for the Union forces to find that the cannons Lowe had observed were merely painted logs with wagon wheels, so-called Quaker Guns.[10]

This deception discredited the balloon observations for a considerable time, since even from a balloon aloft miles away an observer couldn't distinguish between a real and a fake cannon. So to help address this problem and gain credibility, Lowe made a practice of ascending with experienced officers on as many occasions as possible. On some of these ascensions, Lowe went aloft with General Fitz John Porter, who became a major advocate of the army's use of balloons. Porter later stated:

> The value of the balloon was soon demonstrated by a few instances. Safely suspended in the air some hundreds of feet I often watched [the countryside] . . . extending from the Chain Bridge near Georgetown to Hunting Creek south of Alexandria. I soon became so familiar with the

country and the roads as to quickly recognize any changes in the landscape and to trace movements of even small bodies of friends or foes so long as within the field of vision.[11]

Lowe easily sold the potential of obtaining key intelligence through use of balloons to the commander of the Union Army of the Potomac, General George McClellan, who had him expand his efforts.[12] With government funds, Lowe constructed seven sturdy balloons with more than a dozen gas-generation systems capable of inflating them in the field with very light, but dangerous, molecular hydrogen. He also developed and employed what is commonly considered to be the first American aircraft carrier, the *George Washington Parke Custis*, a flattop balloon boat that served as a portable observing station.

Lowe's balloons were made to be tethered and withstand winds of more than 15 miles per hour. They were made with double silk in sliced orange–like sections, sewn together with double seams, coated with a special varnish, and then, once assembled into a globe, brightly painted with names on one side and decorations (eagles, faces, flags, etc.) on the other. Lowe's design called for three tethers, one thicker than the other two, which would take the main strain while the others helped keep the balloon and basket from spinning and provided stability for the observer.[13]

There were three sizes of balloons, each providing a different capability. The balloons *Union* and the *Intrepid* were 38 feet wide by 45 feet high and could lift five men. The balloons *Constitution* and the *United States* were 35 feet in diameter and could lift three men. A particular favorite of Lowe's, *Washington*, was 30 feet in diameter and could lift two men. The smallest balloons and the last to be built, in December 1861, the *Excelsior* and the *Eagle*, could lift only one man. The larger balloons required two gas generators and several hours to inflate, while the smaller *Excelsior* and *Eagle* could be inflated with only one generator in less than an hour. This rapid inflation capability would allow Lowe to move with advancing Union forces and then inflate and provide immediate intelligence. Once inflated, the balloons were designed to make continual observations for at least two weeks.

Lowe's development of portable gas generators was a perfect example of his outstanding engineering skills. Each gas generator had a fortified wooden chamber in which iron filings were immersed in diluted sulfuric acid. The chemical reaction produced hot molecular hydrogen that would flow out of the generator's tubing and into a lime solution for purification that then went through a cooling water bath so that it would flow into the balloon at a safe temperature.[14]

For a balloon operation to be set in motion, McClellan or his corps commanders would request a balloon station at a specific location. Lowe would then assign a balloon and aeronaut to support the request. Lowe's base of operations was the Columbia Armory located on the National Mall.[15] Once on site, the aeronaut in charge would be given a sergeant or lieutenant and 30–35 soldiers detailed for this service for training on the inflation, deployment, and guarding of the balloon. The aeronaut himself would typically report directly to the commanding general. Ultimately, Lowe hired nine aeronauts skilled in all aspects of balloon operations from inflation to storage and transport. He also hired his father, Clovis, to help with administrative duties.

Initially John LaMountain operated independently of the Balloon Corps, but on January 27, 1862, McClellan directed him to use only Lowe's balloons, effectively placing him under Lowe's control.[16] LaMountain objected to this arrangement, citing professional differences. He did not like tethered balloons and preferred sensational free flights at several thousand feet altitude over the Confederates before returning to the Union side by catching a counter-flowing wind. Lowe could never see the value in these flights because they risked capture and required expelling valuable inflation gas. LaMountain wanted to use Lowe's balloons, but he refused to take any orders from him. For his part, Lowe was difficult to get along with and very opinionated, which would also lead to conflicts with superiors and the eventual decline of the Balloon Corps itself. Continual quarrels between Lowe and LaMountain over the use of government balloons and Lowe's authority finally led to LaMountain's dismissal in April 1862.

After LaMountain's exit, the use of balloons played a critical role in the development of maps. Maps were a vital component of the war. Intelligence information was typically useless unless it could be plotted accurately on a map. However, both the Union and Confederate armies lacked good maps even of the eastern part of the country. So the Balloon Corps was soon placed under the control of the War Department's Topographical Bureau, responsible for surveying, creating, and printing accurate maps of the military front. Balloon observations provided a perfect vantage point for mapmakers to rapidly provide accurate information on the location of most everything including roads, farm buildings, forests, and fields. Over the course of the war Union aeronauts made approximately 3,000 balloon ascensions from more than 30 locations.

Once inflated, Lowe's tethered balloons could operate at up to 1,000 feet with three rope lines holding a basket containing observers and equipment such as a telegraph. Aside from gathering data to produce maps, the fundamental intelligence gathered from balloons was the location, strength, and movement of enemy troops. Daytime observations for these purposes typically involved counting tents or the number of troops passing a specific point or watching the dust rising from a distant road, which allowed observers to distinguish between infantry and cavalry, as the dust from cavalry typically rose higher in the air. Nighttime flights allowed the aeronaut to count campfires, providing troop locations and size estimates. On many occasions, observers would easily see many important military developments all at once, such as the building of new batteries, troop movements, and the movement of ships. Particularly urgent information could be sent to the ground by means of the telegraph. But the normal mode of communication was for the aeronaut to write out his message wrapped in a bullet for weight placed within a container attached to a wire to guide the dropped message to a waiting courier.

Other major military advantages of the balloon observations included artillery spotting and intimidation. The intimidating effect of Union balloons, an early panopticon effect, has largely been ignored, but there is plenty of evidence that Lowe's balloons unnerved the Confederates on many occasions. For instance, it was widely reported in the newspapers that Lowe's balloon at Mechanicsville enabled the aeronaut to peer into the house windows of the citizens of Richmond and watch them walk to church.[17] The locals of Richmond were mortified. In addition, because Lowe's balloons were brightly painted, they could easily be seen for miles. The concept that if you could see the balloon then the pilot must be able to see you induced caution in Confederate commanders who wanted to maneuver unobserved. In the face of the balloon threat, Confederate units sometimes hid in forested areas waiting for the balloonist to come down.[18]

Another important use of the Union's balloons was their role in breaking the Confederate blockade of the Potomac River. From September 1861 to March 1862 the Confederates maintained batteries on the Virginia side of the Potomac. The main cannon batteries extended from Freestone Point just below Neabsco Creek to Shipping Point just below Quantico Creek. These batteries, supported by converted transport steamers fitted with cannons stationed in Quantico Creek, fired on nearly every vessel going to or from Washington. This blockade impeded traffic, although no ships were sunk or even badly damaged.[19] To break the blockade, on October 24, 1861, General McClellan sent General Joseph Hooker's division to lower Maryland on the opposite side of the main Confederate blockade at a place called Budds Ferry. By mid-November, McClellan added one of Lowe's balloons.

After traveling south down the Potomac on the *George Washington Park Custis* flattop balloon boat, making observations along the way, Lowe

Plate 48. Pigeon fitted with a camera, circa 1915. Before World War I, the Germany military experimented with using pigeons to collect intelligence, releasing them over European military sites where they could snap photos of weapons, troops, and terrain. Technicians at the birds' destination developed the film. The miniature cameras were activated by a timing mechanism. From the Collection of H. Keith and Karen Melton at the International Spy Museum.

Plate 49. Escape boots designed by Britain's MI9 during World War II for use by special operators or aircrews who might be shot down over enemy-occupied territory. Unzipped, they transform into civilian leather shoes. From the Collection of H. Keith and Karen Melton at the International Spy Museum.

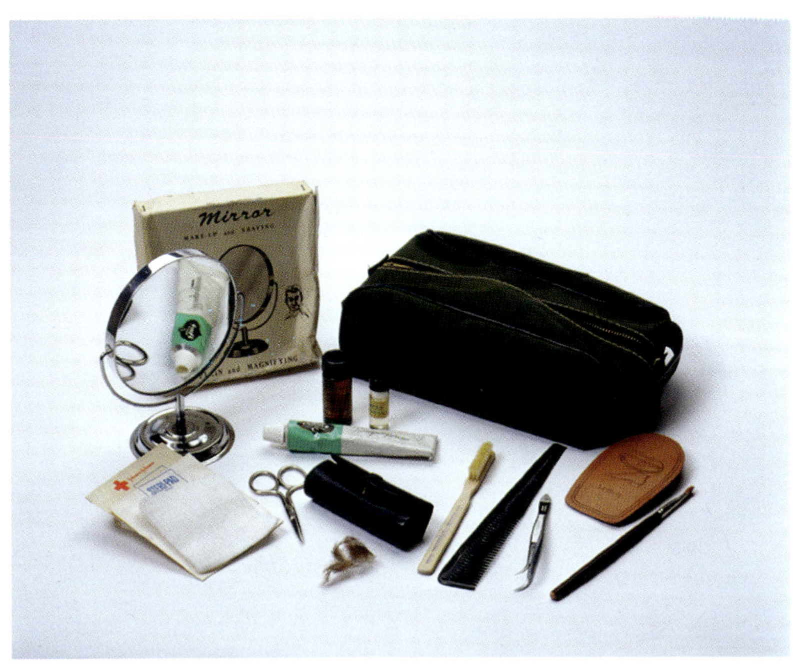

Plates 50 and 51. Disguise kit and dentures. The CIA travel kit contains disguise basics, including a dye brush and mixing dishes, spirit gum and moustache materials, as well as a heel insert to change one's gait. From the Collection of H. Keith and Karen Melton at the International Spy Museum.

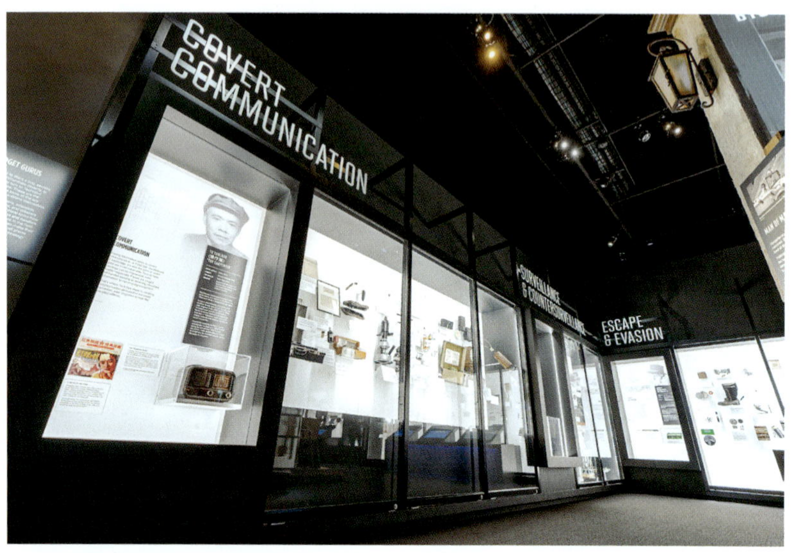


Plate 52. The *Tools of the Trade* exhibition in the International Spy Museum.

Plate 53. Russia's foreign intelligence services made this model of a 1970s CIA Insectothopter, a mini drone designed to resemble a dragonfly. The original version proved unstable in crosswinds and too small to carry surveillance equipment or be remote-controlled. That is not the case for such devices today. From the Collection of H. Keith and Karen Melton at the International Spy Museum.

Plate 54. Glass eye concealment device worn by a World War I–era Russian spy. From the Collection of H. Keith and Karen Melton at the International Spy Museum.

Plate 55. KGB lipstick pistol, circa 1960s. The 4.5mm single-shot weapon fires by pressing the barrel into the victim. From the Collection of H. Keith and Karen Melton at the International Spy Museum.

Plate 56. KGB-issued hollow coin that might have been used to conceal a ciphered message or microfilm in the 1960s or 1970s. To open, one inserted a needle into a tiny hole on the coin's face. From the Collection of H. Keith and Karen Melton at the International Spy Museum.

Plate 57. CIA key pattern device used to copy keys for warded locks, 1960s. Thumbscrews hold the key in position while the feelers are adjusted to conform precisely to the pattern of the teeth. From the Collection of H. Keith and Karen Melton at the International Spy Museum.

Plate 58. The *Looking, Listening, Sensing* exhibit at the International Spy Museum.

Plate 59. *Codes* exhibit at the International Spy Museum.

Plate 60. Early in Fidel Castro's rule of Cuba, the CIA put together a plan to overthrow him. They trained anticommunist Cuban exiles to form Assault Brigade 2506. When President John F. Kennedy came into office, he allowed the plan to proceed. The brigade assaulted Cuba at the Bay of Pigs on April 17, 1961, and was badly defeated. This is the brigade's flag. From the Collection of H. Keith and Karen Melton at the International Spy Museum.

Plate 61. Shoe heel transmitter, 1960s. When an American diplomat in an East European country sent his shoes out for repair, the local counterintelligence service secretly outfitted them with a hidden microphone and transmitter. From the Collection of H. Keith and Karen Melton at the International Spy Museum.

Plate 62. KGB Model F-21 surveillance camera concealed behind a coat button (top middle), circa 1970. To snap a picture, the wearer squeezes a shutter release in their pocket that opens the fake button, revealing the camera lens. From the Collection of H. Keith and Karen Melton at the International Spy Museum.

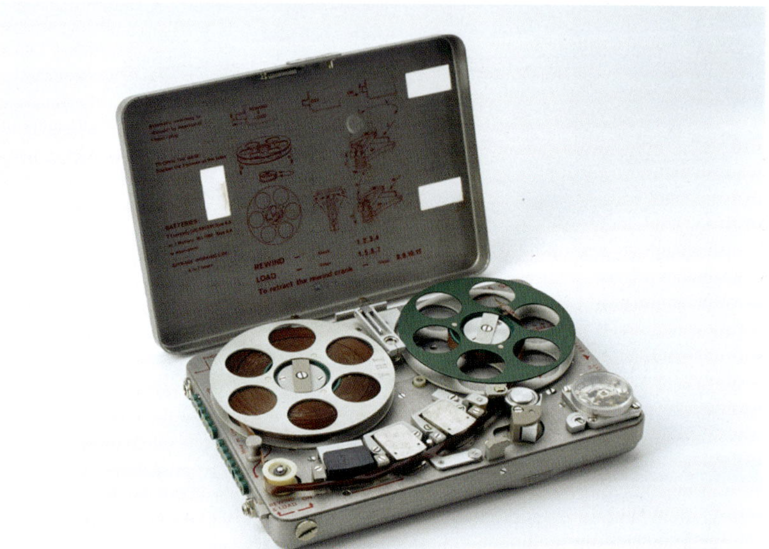

Plates 63 and 64. Portable, lightweight, self-contained audio tape recorders such as the Nagra SN (bottom) and Fi-Cord 101 (top) were used by intelligence services on both sides during the Cold War. These high-quality, Swiss-made devices could be concealed under clothing for surveillance purposes. The Stasi used this Nagra machine in the 1980s. The Fi-Cord was standard CIA equipment in 1962. From the Collection of H. Keith and Karen Melton at the International Spy Museum.

Plate 65. “G-Man” toy cars, circa 1930s. As the FBI fought back against mob violence, G-Men became all the rage. With the support of FBI Director J. Edgar Hoover, comics, radio plays, movies, and lots of toys supported the image of government men as popular heroes.

Plate 66. Silver cigar box given by the legendary British spy Sidney Reilly to the Scottish diplomat Robert Bruce Lockhart in 1919 "in remembrance of events in Moscow" the previous year. It is the only physical evidence connecting these two men and their aborted attempt to topple the Bolshevik regime in Russia.

Plate 67. Ice axe used to assassinate Leon Trotsky on August 20, 1940. The trained Soviet NKVD assassin Ramón Mercader hid the axe under his suit jacket when he visited Trotsky in his compound outside Mexico City. The axe still retains a rust mark from the assassin's bloody fingerprint. From the Collection of H. Keith and Karen Melton at the International Spy Museum.

Plate 68. The *Cyber Infinity* room at the International Spy Museum.

Plate 69. A CT scan of this fountain pen reveals a rare Tropel document camera concealed inside. These tiny handmade cameras are mechanical and optical marvels, used by the CIA inside everyday objects such as lighters and keychains. To take a photo, the user unscrews and removes the end of the pen to expose the lens. From the Collection of H. Keith and Karen Melton at the International Spy Museum.

Plate 70. "Sleeping Beauty" motorized submersible canoe from World War II and associated British diver's head piece (Plate 71) displayed in the *Covert Action* gallery in the International Spy Museum. The American Office of Strategic Services bought this craft, designed for underwater sabotage, from the British Special Operations Executive and painted it in North American camouflage colors. From the Collection of H. Keith and Karen Melton at the International Spy Museum.

Plate 71. British diver's head piece to be used when riding the "Sleeping Beauty" canoe (Plate 70). From the Collection of H. Keith and Karen Melton at the International Spy Museum."

Plate 72. World War II Welbike, issued by Britain's Special Operations Executive. This mini motorcycle was airdropped in a special container along with airborne units. After hitting the ground and unfolding the bike, an officer could be on the road within 11 seconds. From the Collection of H. Keith and Karen Melton at the International Spy Museum.

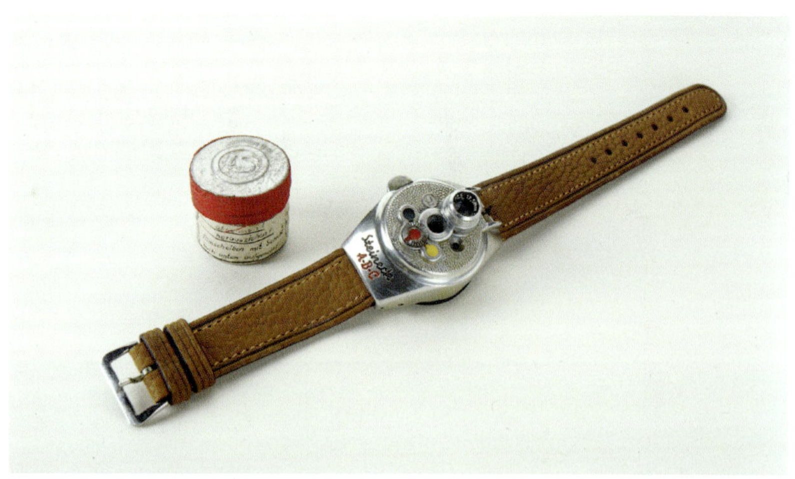


Plate 73. Steineck ABC camera, circa 1949. This commercially made German camera was worn like a wristwatch, with the lens at the 12 o'clock position, and shoots eight exposures on a film disk cut from 35mm film (special punch included with the camera). It was designed by the Austrian engineer Dr. Rudolph Steineck, who later invented the subminiature Tessina camera, used by intelligence agencies on both sides during the Cold War.

Plate 74. Brush concealing a Model III Minox camera, circa 1960s. Used by East Germany's Hauptverwaltung Aufklärung, the Stasi's foreign intelligence branch. From the Collection of H. Keith and Karen Melton at the International Spy Museum.

Plate 75. The rotunda of the International Spy Museum.

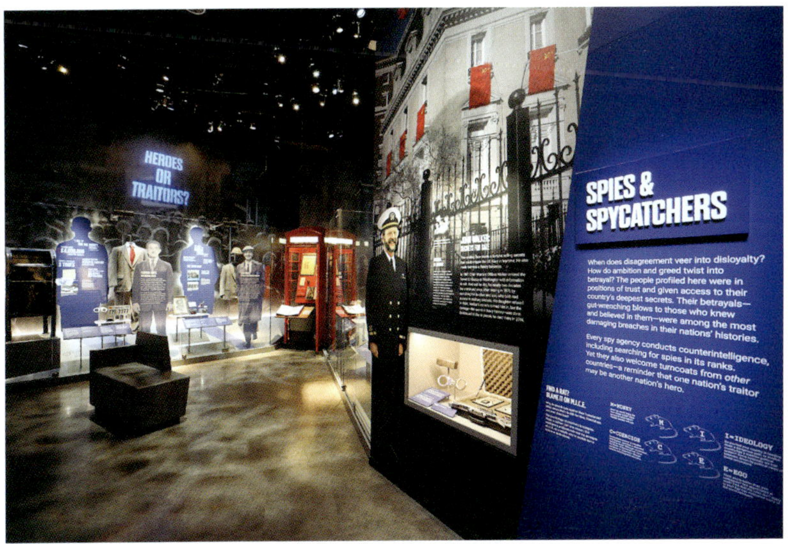


Plate 76. *Spies & Spycatchers* exhibit at the International Spy Museum.

Plate 77. Cylinder from the pneumatic tube system installed in the CIA's original headquarters building in the early 1960s. The system was used to rapidly convey documents from one part of the building to another. From the Collection of H. Keith and Karen Melton at the International Spy Museum.

Plates 78 and 79. Concealed KGB surveillance camera, 1970s. An agent might casually hold his glasses case in one hand while pressing the side to activate a lever and take a photo. Inside the mechanism, half a pair of glasses makes space for a tiny Tochka camera. Note the mesh on the left side of the case, which hides the camera lens. From the Collection of H. Keith and Karen Melton at the International Spy Museum.

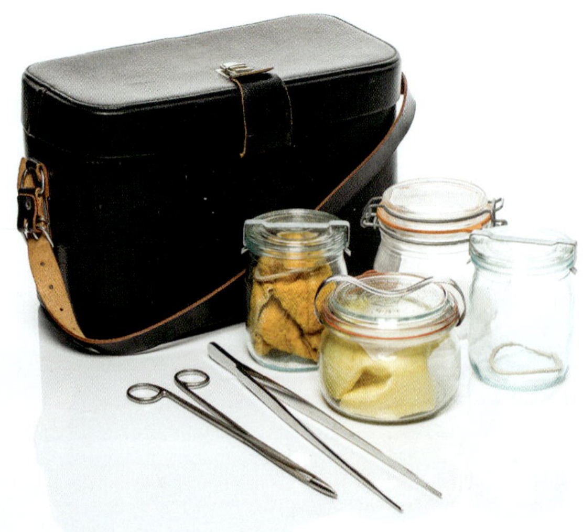

Plate 80. East German Stasi scent jars, each containing a piece of cloth with the scent of a citizen considered potentially suspicious. Dogs could use these scents to track down suspects. In the 1970s and 1980s, Stasi offices in East Berlin kept thousands of these scent jars. From the Collection of H. Keith and Karen Melton at the International Spy Museum.

Plate 81. A Stasi agent used this walnut shell to conceal one-time pads—sheets of random numbers used to encrypt or decrypt communications with a handler who holds an identical set of the pads. Each sheet is destroyed after use, making it a mathematically unbreakable cipher system. From the Collection of H. Keith and Karen Melton at the International Spy Museum.

Plate 82. Lantern made for the Marquis de Lafayette's grand tour of the United States, 1824. France's Lafayette had been one of the heroes of the American Revolutionary War. But he had help from another hero: James, an enslaved man who had been one of his most accomplished spies. During a parade, a local newspaper reported that James was "recognized by Lafayette in a crowd . . . and taken into his embrace."

Plate 83. The *Hang Time* interactive exhibit in the *Covert Action* gallery challenges visitors to compare fiction to fact by hanging from a bar elevated a few inches above the ground.

Plate 84. *An Uncertain World* gallery in the International Spy Museum.

Plate 85. East Berlin checkpoint in the International Spy Museum.

Plates 86 and 87. In the 1950s and 1960s, Civil Air Transport was an airline based in Taiwan that did contract and charter work for a variety of clients. In 1953, it was even hired by the government of Indonesia to carry Muslims to Mecca, Saudi Arabia, for the annual Hajj. It also ran scheduled passenger flights in East Asia. The airline gave passengers lovely gifts such as these. The passengers did not know, however, that the airline was owned by the CIA, which used it to support Agency stations and covert actions in the region. From the Collection of H. Keith and Karen Melton at the International Spy Museum.

Plate 88. During World War II, saboteurs used this camouflage kit, which was made by the American OSS to match the color of a large chunk of coal. It was actually a hollow shell. Then they slipped the explosive-filled shell into a coal bin. When an unsuspecting foe shoveled the phony coal into a factory boiler or train furnace, the heat detonated the charge.

Plate 89. This glove pistol, or "fist gun," was made by US naval intelligence during World War II. When the gloved hand makes a first, the trigger protrudes from the front of the device. The plunger cocks the weapon when it is pushed against an assailant, and the device fires a single .38-calibre bullet. From the Collection of H. Keith and Karen Melton at the International Spy Museum.

Plates 90 and 91. KGB-made diorama of the office of its *rezident* (head of station) in London, located within the Soviet trade mission, circa 1970s. The model shows methods used by Britain's MI5 to eavesdrop on the office, including surveillance devices embedded in the walls of the building. From the Collection of H. Keith and Karen Melton at the International Spy Museum.

Plate 92. Amber drone unit number 006. A reconnaissance drone developed in the 1980s by Abraham Karam, an immigrant from Israel, it evolved into the Gnat, which the CIA used over Bosnia in the 1990s, and then the Predator.

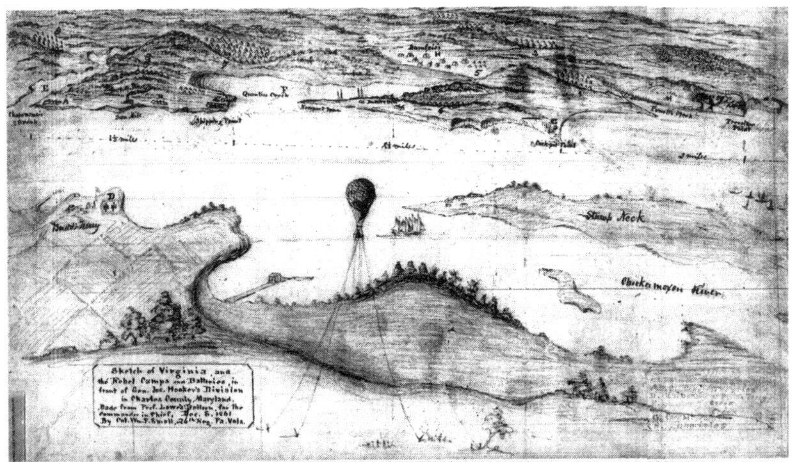


Figure 6.3: Sketch of the Confederate positions across from Budds Ferry, December 18, 1861. Colonel William F. Small of the 26th Pennsylvania Infantry made this detailed sketch from Thaddeus Lowe's balloon.

established his permanent balloon station at Budds Ferry directly opposite the main Confederate batteries at Shipping Point. The aeronaut Lowe assigned to this station had a fine view of the enemy's morning mess campfires and evening campfires and saw the Rebels constructing new batteries at Freestone Point. These observations were critically important because the Potomac River separated the two armies, inhibiting deserters from whom intelligence could often otherwise be obtained. Figure 6.4 is one of the Civil War's most famous balloon sketches, created by Colonel William F. Small of the 26th Pennsylvania Infantry from the Budds Ferry balloon. This remarkable sketch map shows the batteries, camps, and other important details across the Potomac River into Virginia. It blends a planimetric cartographic map (the ground near the balloon) with a multi-perspective view of Virginia, where distances are given in miles. From the Shipping Point batteries to the Cockpit Point batteries on the map is given as two and a third miles. The main features on the map are annotated with numbers and letters used as reference points, allowing succinct reporting of enemy troop movements in a coded fashion. This map was later sent to General McClellan back in Washington upon his request.[20]

Arguably the most famous operation conducted by the Balloon Corps contributed to Union efforts in the Peninsula Campaign. In early March 1862, a Union aeronaut across from Budds Ferry observed Confederate forces beginning to fall back toward Richmond. Rumors that McClellan was planning a massive invasion deeper into Virginia and on to Richmond

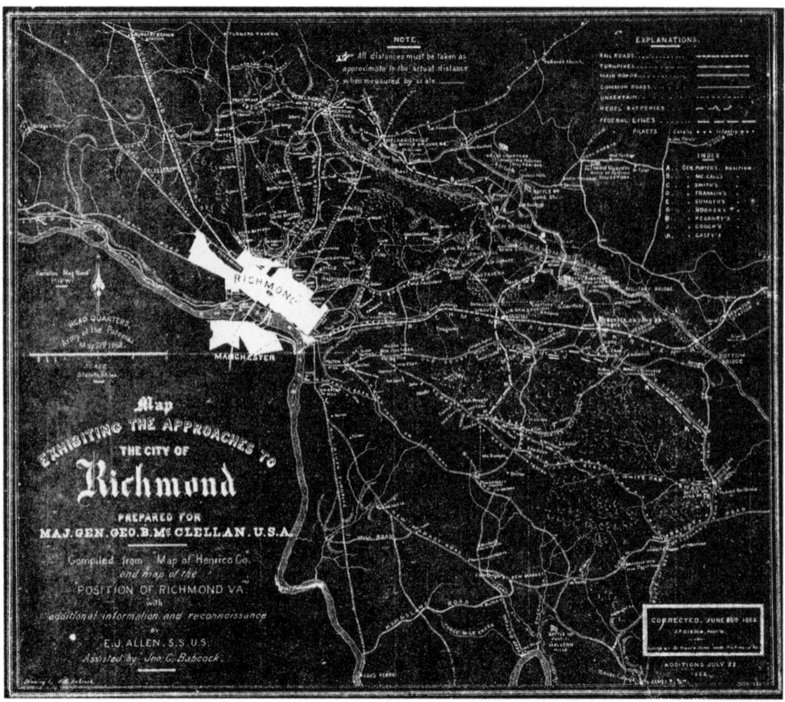


Figure 6.4: Map of Richmond annotated with observations of Confederate positions made by Thaddeus Lowe.

had persisted for some time. The Confederate retreat ended the blockade and facilitated McClellan's move down the Potomac River to the Fortress Monroe area. McClellan moved more than 100,000 Union troops that arrived at the fortress by the end of the month. McClellan's plan was to move up the Peninsula from Fortress Monroe and capture Richmond. However, the Peninsula—the area extending from Fortress Monroe all the way to Richmond bordered by the York and James Rivers—was mostly unmapped, putting Union forces at a tremendous disadvantage compared to the Confederate Army, which probably did not have good maps either but did include a few Virginia units raised in that area.[21]

By this time the aeronauts were experienced military observers, so they were able to make a significant contribution. Officers frequently went up with the aeronauts, and all the advantages of an aerial platform's ability to produce a range of intelligence became a reality. Engineers and draftsmen also made frequent ascents, sketching the roads and terrain and even making corrections on maps carried aloft. From these they created hundreds of products ranging from crude sketches to highly detailed and elaborate

Figure 6.5: *Harper's Weekly*, October 1863, imagining the exciting life and grim death of a spy. There were many ways of collecting intelligence during the US Civil War, but the public was most fascinated by espionage.

maps. In his autobiography, McClellan gave credit to Lowe, whom he referred to as "the intelligent and enterprising aeronaut, who had the management of the Balloons." He went on to note: "I was indebted for [the] information obtained during his ascensions. In a clear atmosphere, and in a country not too much obstructed by woods, balloon reconnoissances [*sic*] made by intelligent officers are often of considerable value."[22]

Helped by Lowe's work, McClellan's forces moved rapidly northwest from their landing point until they reached Yorktown on April 6, 1862. The Confederates firmly held Yorktown and had created a series of earthworks across the Peninsula. Instead of immediately breaking through these earthworks, McClellan chose to stay put and besiege the city while spending weeks bringing up large mortars and cannons that were to be used to pummel Confederate positions. During the ensuing siege, McClellan had Lowe establish a balloon station near Yorktown and the York River and another at Warwick Court House near the James River. With Lowe in charge of the York River balloon station, he hired the Rhode Island aeronaut James Allen and placed him in control of the second station at the Courthouse. Second Lieutenant George Armstrong Custer was assigned to work with the topographical engineers on the staff of Brigadier General William F. "Baldy" Smith, the commanding general of the forces assigned to the area around the Warwick Court House. Allen trained Custer in balloon observation, and Custer was soon making daily ascensions. By observing the cooking fires just before daybreak, he could identify changes in the Confederate strength and location. In the early morning hours of May 4, 1862, Custer observed the Confederates abandoning the stronghold city of Yorktown. Since Yorktown fed the defensive line across the Peninsula with soldiers, once it was abandoned the whole defensive position was lost. That message, with actionable intelligence, was relayed to McClellan's headquarters and immediately confirmed by Lowe at his balloon station near the York River. This was a golden opportunity for McClellan to act quickly, but it took him hours to ready his troops. Unfortunately, by the time he was ready to attack the Confederates had completely evacuated Yorktown, abandoning the defensive line across the Peninsula, and escaped up the road to Williamsburg.[23] A day later, McClellan's forces finally ran into the new Confederate defensive line outside Williamsburg and a battle ensued in which McClellan dislodged the Confederates.

With the Confederates retreating after the Battle of Williamsburg, additional troops raced up the Peninsula until McClellan halted about a dozen miles outside Richmond. In the meantime, on May 15, McClellan had sent Lowe with General William B. Franklin's corps by boat up the York and Pamunkey Rivers, reaching White House Landing at the location where the Richmond railroad crossed the river. At McClellan's request, Lowe set up several balloon stations at the Gaines' Farm, Mechanicsville, and the Trent House. These locations formed a crescent shape near the front lines of the Union Army, pinning down the Confederate troops with Richmond behind them. McClellan was then able to receive balloon reports on a regular basis. More than any other time in the history of the Balloon Corps, Lowe's operations became well integrated into the army's operations.

The Balloon Corps also played a significant role in the use of the telegraph. Park Spring, a telegraph operator from the Signal Corps, set up a new telegraph station in the large, five-man wicker basket used by Lowe's largest balloons. Once established, McClellan received immediate telegram reports from 1,000 feet up.[24] As more and more Rebel troops were observed and reported to mass in strength within sight of the balloons, McClellan's response was to "hold ourselves in readiness for an attack."[25] He did not have long to wait. On May 31 Confederates under General Joe Johnston slammed into McClellan's troops at the Battle of Fair Oaks (Seven Pines). During the battle, Lowe and Park Spring were in the balloon *Intrepid* sending McClellan real-time messages while another balloon operated not far away. Meanwhile, the Confederates also fielded a balloon named the *Gazelle* by its creator, though many of the Rebel troops called it

Figure 6.6: Lineman's pocket test set, a compact telegraph key that would have been appropriate for use in an observation balloon or to tap telegraph lines during the US Civil War.

the *Lady Davis* or the *Silk Dress Balloon* because the silks used in its making were from bolts of various dress-patterned materials. The *Gazelle* was tethered and reached no more than 500 feet in altitude. It was filled with illumination gas from the Richmond Gas Works and run down the Peninsula on a flattop railroad car. Although the battle was tactically inconclusive, General Johnston was injured and was replaced by Robert E. Lee. Although to date there is no archival material available on how McClennan used what had to be tremendously valuable real-time balloon intelligence, his position remained the same.

John Babcock, a member of Allan Pinkerton's US Secret Service group that reported to McClellan, was particularly talented in using many different sources of military intelligence to develop large maps of the area in front of the Union Army. Babcock made a map of special significance and beginning in June 1862 reproduced it using treated paper that, when exposed to sunlight, produced a blue and white sun print. Multiple sun prints were then made and passed out to commanders and others who needed them. Babcock would repeatedly go up in balloons to verify and add to his map. Lowe used one of Babcock's sun prints to mark enemy fortifications and enemy camp locations. Several of these maps survive today. He wrote on the map: "Balloon Camp, June 14th, 1862. The red lines represent some of the most important earth works seen this morning & are located as near as possible, as is also the camps in black ink. As soon as I can get an observation from the Mechanicsville Balloon, I can make many additions to this map."[26] Here Lowe literally watched the building of fortifications around Richmond. Detailed maps were continually improved over time, with permanent features gathered from many sources of intelligence based on the length of time the Union Army was in that area.

On June 26, 1862, General Lee initiated a series of battles, the Seven Days Battles, which pushed McClellan from the York River side to the James River side of the Peninsula. By the beginning of August, McClellan gave up on taking Richmond; the Army of the Potomac retreated to Washington. Once again, balloons had played an important role. Lowe's balloon boat, with a balloon carrying James Allen aloft, was towed by a United States Navy gunboat down the James River and gave the "all-clear" initiating the Union Army's retreat. The Union armada that used the James River route largely carried equipment, supplies, and wounded back to Washington.[27]

After the end of the Peninsula Campaign, the Balloon Corps returned to the Columbia Armory in Washington, where it stayed until after the Battle of Antietam near Sharpsburg, Maryland, in late September 1862. It was up to the commanding general to request the support of the Balloon Corps, and McClellan finally got around to it. McClellan had the balloons deployed near Harpers Ferry, West Virginia, making almost daily ascensions when the weather permitted. Lowe, along with the aeronauts James Allen and John Steiner, provided General McClellan status reports on Confederate movements until they were directed to return to Washington on November 1.[28]

McClellan, meanwhile, was frustrating President Lincoln with his disinclination to act decisively. For example, his failure to attack the Confederates while they were retreating, or at vulnerable locations that could be determined from balloon observations, disappointed the president. So Lincoln replaced him with General Ambrose Burnside on November 7, 1862. On November 20, Lowe wrote a letter to Burnside and his staff informing them of the Balloon Corps' capabilities.[29] Within days Lowe was ordered to immediately join the army at Falmouth, Virginia, and began making regular observations by early December. During the Battle of Fredericksburg on December 13 Burnside had Lieutenant Colonel William Teall, a member of his staff, go up in the balloon *Washington*. From there Teall had a bird's-eye view of the entire battlefield, but there is no evidence that he provided any significant intelligence, although he wrote extensively to his wife about what he saw.[30] Burnside lost the Battle of Fredericksburg and settled down for the winter in Falmouth on the opposite side of the river, keeping the balloon in operation during this time. During the battle, Burnside had squandered the advantages of real-time balloon observations, but after it ended the general went back to using them to monitor the enemy's strength and position.

However, Lincoln once again became dissatisfied with his commander and soon replaced Burnside with General Joseph Hooker. In late January 1863, Hooker found that the Secret Service, which McClellan had established, was in shambles. Allan Pinkerton resigned after McClellan was relieved. As a result, he could find no document telling him of the disposition and strength of the enemy in front of him. For General Hooker,

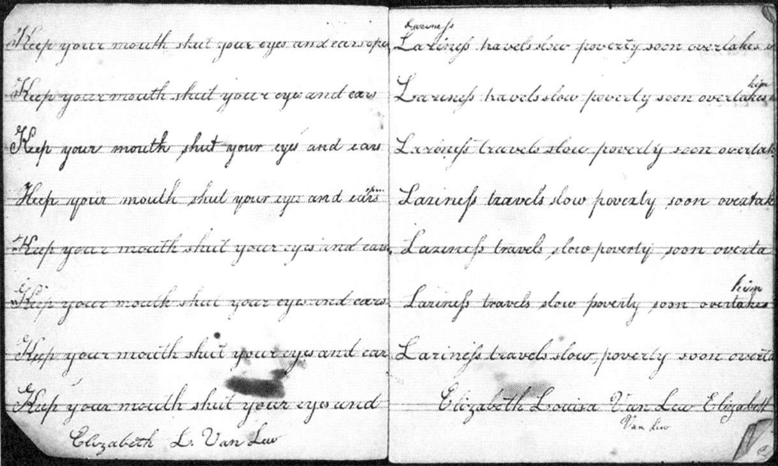


Figure 6.7: Elizabeth Van Lew's copybook. During the US Civil War, Van Lew ran a major Union spy ring out of Richmond, Virginia, the Confederate capital. When General Ulysses S. Grant visited the city after the war, he sought her out to thank her. As a girl in the 1830s, she practiced her penmanship in this notebook, writing: "Keep your mouth shut, your eyes and ears open."

military intelligence immediately became a priority. Following the recommendation of the one remaining Secret Service agent, John C. Babcock, Hooker asked his Provost Marshal Brigadier General Marsena R. Patrick, to organize a new, all-source organization that would not only collect military intelligence but also provide analysis. Patrick brought together a few key individuals, such as Colonel George H. Sharpe, and developed a new organization, the Bureau of Military Information, which also included Babcock.[31]

Hooker's staff drew on many sources of intelligence information: cavalry reconnaissance, interrogations (of escaping slaves, deserters, and locals), information from enemy newspapers, captured enemy correspondence, signal flag intercepts, trained field agents who collected information, and balloon observations. Apart from the balloon observations and signal flag intercepts, all the other sources tended to be time-consuming or involve significant reporting lags. The observation balloon provided the most flexibility to quickly acquire many of these key observations in real time.

Soon Hooker, significant intelligence in hand, created his campaign strategy. Leaving a strong force in Fredericksburg to hold down the Confederate right, Hooker moved three Union corps west along the Rappahannock River, crossing the waterway out of sight of Lee's main army at

Chancellorsville. He also sent his cavalry south to prevent a retreat of Lee's army back to Richmond. The Battle of Chancellorsville began on May 1, 1863, and lasted three days, with two of Lowe's tethered balloons initially in the air most of the time. Unfortunately, on May 2, at a critical time, Lowe was obliged to ground his balloons due to high winds. This allowed the famous flanking march by the Confederate General Stonewall Jackson to take place unobserved. Jackson's forces attacked Hooker's rear on the morning of May 3.[32] Lee simply outmaneuvered Hooker's superior force in what has been considered to be his most brilliant achievement of the war. Hooker retreated across the Rappahannock, ending the famous battle.[33]

After the Battle of Chancellorsville, Hooker directed his army to retreat to Washington. James Allen, having his balloon towed, was in the rear guard watching for Confederate movements. Starting on June 15, 1863, Allen went up a short height at regular intervals and reported that the Rebels were following the army back to Washington.[34] Lee did not, however, launch any attacks during this time, perhaps because the obvious balloon observations would have tipped off the retreating army in time to mount an adequate repulse.

Despite the Balloon Corps' numerous successes, trouble was brewing. In December 1862 one of Lowe's former aeronauts accused him of budget mismanagement. This triggered an Inspector General investigation that cast a negative light on Lowe's management of the Balloon Corps.[35] Although no charges were ever brought against Lowe, General Hooker named the Army of the Potomac's chief engineer, Captain Cyrus B. Comstock, as his successor. He took over the Balloon Corps on April 7, 1863.

Comstock was suspicious that Lowe and his contractors operated autonomously for their own benefit, so he performed a comprehensive review of the operation. After the review was completed, he instituted several significant changes. He accused Lowe of nepotism and fired Lowe's father. He also cut the pay of all the aeronauts by a third or more and directed Lowe to return to solely aeronautic duties, relieving him of all administrative roles. In protest, Lowe refused to take a salary and resigned after the Chancellorsville campaign, leaving James Allen as chief aeronaut. Allen continued to do what he was told, but instead of the experienced aeronaut Lowe as his boss he now had to deal with inexperienced officers who didn't understand how to use the Balloon Corps effectively.

Lowe was the driving force behind keeping the Balloon Corps active and relevant. He had extensive experience dealing with individuals from many different levels of command and understood Lincoln's original vision. Once gone, that initiative was lost, and with the continual change in

Union commanding generals unfamiliar with balloon intelligence methods, the Balloon Corps quickly dissolved.

On June 8, 1863, Captain Comstock was ordered to report to General Ulysses S. Grant at Vicksburg in the western theater on the Mississippi, and on June 24, 1863, Colonel Albert Myer, chief signal officer, was given complete control over the balloons. In some ways this was a logical move; the Signal Corps also gathered intelligence by viewing the enemy through telescopes and by interpreting enemy flag communications. Although they accomplished this from signal towers, hilltops, and rooftops, they wanted to always remain hidden from view.[36] However, balloons were decidedly not hidden from view, so Myer did not value this capability even though balloons had demonstrated significant advantages as a collection platform for military intelligence. Accordingly, Myer had no real interest in the Balloon Corps and believed that the expense of running it out of the Signal Corps far exceeded its ability to gather actionable military intelligence. His opinion was perhaps largely based on his early experience with the unsuccessful aeronaut Wise.[37]

Colonel Myer quickly moved to eliminate the Balloon Corps. By the end of July 1863, its entire inventory was placed in storage in a warehouse in Washington under the control of Quartermaster General Montgomery C. Meigs. Meigs was given permission by the secretary of war to sell all the balloon property after nearly a year of storage. Meigs believed that the balloon envelopes were rotting away, so he wanted to sell them as fast as he could. Within days of getting permission for the sale, on April 18, 1864, all the balloon property was sold at auction. Thus ended the nation's first air force.[38]

Meanwhile, Lincoln's continued disappointment with the progress of the Civil War led him once again to replace the top commanding general. After Hooker and Meade, Lincoln appointed Ulysses Grant commander of all US armies in March 1864. Grant immediately went on the offensive and began pushing Lee and the Army of Northern Virginia deeper and deeper into Virginia toward Richmond and Petersburg. By April 1864 Grant began to appreciate the ability of the Bureau of Military Information to provide solid analysis and actionable intelligence. There is no record, however, that the bureau requested balloon intelligence even though they received and utilized balloon observations while Hooker was commanding the army the year before. The Siege of Petersburg, which began in June, 1864, saw both sides digging an extensive system of trenches. Without balloon observations, the Union Army was deprived of consistent artillery spotting and unique views of Confederate troop movements and rearrangements in their trenches. Significant weaknesses in Confederate defenses went unnoticed, and therefore a major tactical advantage went unrealized. However, the Union Army finally breached the trenches at Petersburg in April 1865, some ten months later.

In summary, once operational under Lowe's command, the Union's Balloon Corps was a highly effective intelligence-gathering system. Lowe developed sturdy balloons for tethering and deployed portable gas generators; he even made observations from a specially designed flattop boat towed down the Potomac, proving balloons had the flexibility to go anywhere. However, the strengths of the Balloon Corps were not fully realized. Union commanders failed to task balloon observers with strategically important and focused observations as we do with military satellites today. Although the balloons provided a quick-reaction capability when linked with the telegraph, not all balloons included a skilled telegraph operator when rapid communication was necessary. In addition, many officers distrusted aeronauts, believing that either they exaggerated what they saw, or they lacked the military expertise to make actionable observations. This attitude may have been true early in the war, but over time the aeronauts became very capable observers, and Union officers frequently joined them aloft. An even greater opportunity to obtain actional intelligence was lost during the Petersburg siege.

Nevertheless, the idea of balloons as platforms for collecting intelligence was now generally accepted, though it would be a half-century before the US Army again made substantial use of balloons, this time over the trenches in France during World War I. The French, British, and German armies were already using tethered observation balloons when the United States joined the war in 1917. Trench warfare on the Western Front was highly conducive to the use of tethered observation balloons. Positioned at heights of about 4,000 feet, they were excellent observation platforms. Observers in the balloons could utilize telephone lines incorporated into the balloons' cables to maintain voice communication with the ground to regulate artillery fire (the primary mission) and enhance their utility for real-time surveillance of enemy activities. The stationary nature of the balloons allowed continuous surveillance behind enemy lines, a significant advantage over the transient observations from airplanes, and balloons proved particularly useful for correcting friendly artillery fire.[39]

The scale of the Allies' use of tethered observation balloons used during World War I was substantial, with the US Army alone sending 35 balloon companies of approximately six balloons each to France totaling 446 officers and 6,365 men. In the one year that the United States was engaged in combat, its balloons at the front made 1,642 ascensions for a total of 3,111 hours. German airplanes attacked them on 89 occasions and destroyed 35 in the air. Another twelve were destroyed by German artillery fire, and one blew over to enemy lines. The balloon observers parachuted from the baskets 116 times, with only one casualty, a remarkable success record.[40]

During World War II, less use was made of tethered observation balloons because that war was much more fluid and mobile than the previous war. However, balloons would be used again during the Cold War and after as reconnaissance and surveillance platforms. The US Air Force, for instance, flew spy balloons over Eastern Europe, the Soviet Union, and China in the 1950s, though ultimately these efforts were not particularly successful.[41] The People's Republic of China has done similar things in the twenty-first century, including one infamous occasion in 2023 in which a spy balloon overflew Canada and the United States, arousing substantial public interest. The United States has long used tethered balloons (now called "aerostats") along the southern border to counter narcotics trafficking.[42] Similarly, in Afghanistan and Iraq the US Army used the Persistent Threat Detection System to provide security for military convoys and to watch for enemy activities.[43]

While satellites, spy planes, and drones will continue to do the lion's share of overhead reconnaissance, the special capabilities of balloons, notably their ability to remain aloft in the same location for extended periods of time, will continue for the foreseeable future to make them a useful tool for the collection of intelligence.

Figure 6.8: Cartoon from *The Balloon Section of the American Expeditionary Forces* by S. W. Ovitt, 1919. Observation balloons played a major role on the Western Front during World War I as platforms from which the adversary could be observed and friendly artillery fire could be adjusted.

## Further Reading

Crouch, Tom. *The Eagle Aloft: Two Centuries of the Balloon in America*. Washington, DC: Smithsonian Institution Press, 1983.

Fishel, Edwin C. *The Secret War for the Union: The Untold Story of Military Intelligence in the Civil War*. Boston: Houghton Mifflin Company, 1996.

Haydon, Frederick Stansbury. *Aeronautics in the Union and Confederate Armies*. Baltimore: Johns Hopkins University Press, 1941.

## Notes

1. James Allen, National Archive Pension Record Group 15, Pension Number 954,607, National Archives Records Administration (hereafter NARA), College Park, MD. Allen enlisted for only three months and did not reenlist.

2. M506, roll 85, W853, NARA. Lieutenant Henry Abbot details his frustration with making maps from Allen's balloon in a written report to Major Hartman Bache, who was in command of the Topographical Engineers. Allen used a single-rope tether system, causing the balloon to easily twist in the wind. In addition, these cotton balloons were so fragile that they would easily pop, causing more delays for repairs and expenses for refilling.

3. Tom Crouch, *The Eagle Aloft: Two Centuries of the Balloon in America* (Washington, DC: Smithsonian Institution Press, 1983), 264. Crouch provided an extensive background of many American aeronauts and the evolution of the use of balloons up to and beyond the Civil War.

4. Editor, "National Hotel," *Washington Evening Star*, June 6, 1861. Includes a list of people who checked into the National Hotel.

5. Editor, "A Successful and Important Experiment," *Washington Evening Star*, June 19, 1861. Lowe's telegraph to the Lincoln was published in dozens of newspapers.

6. Editor, "Balloon Observations," *New York Herald*, July 2, 1861. The first announcement of Wise becoming hired by the government for balloon operations.

7. Editor, "From Fortress Monroe," *Lancaster Daily Evening Express*, July 24, 1861.

8. United States War Department, *The War of the Rebellion: A Compilation of the Official Records of the Union and Confederate Armies*, Series III, 5 vols. (Washington, DC: Government Printing Office, 1899–1900), vol. 3, 259 (hereafter AOR). Significant information about the workings of the Balloon Corps can be found at pages 259–319. Lowe submitted this report to Congress after he resigned from the Balloon Corps. However, it should be noted that Lowe provided material that made him and his operations look favorable.

9. June Robinson, "The United States Balloon Corps in Action in Northern Virginia During the Civil War," *Arlington Historical Magazine* 8, no. 2 (October 1986): 12–15.

10. Because Quakers held a religious opposition to the war and refused to fight, certain deceptive tactics, such as using a black-painted wooden log on a carriage with wheels resembling a cannon, would be called a "Quaker's gun." Robinson, "The United States Balloon Corps."

11. "Fitz John Porter Papers," Library of Congress. Porter mentored Lowe for many months going aloft many times and directing Lowe to make observations at a variety of locations in and around Washington.

12. AOR, Series III, vol. 3, 264.

13. Frederick Beaumont, Lecture, Friday, February 5, 1864, "Balloon Reconnaissance," *Journal of the Royal United Service Institution* vol. 8, London, 56–65, 1865. Beaumont's observations of Lowe's operational methods are well described. Also in Frederick Beaumont, F. E., "On Balloon Reconnaissance as Practiced by the American Army," *Papers on Subjects Connected with the Duties of the Corps of Royal Engineers*, New Series [1863], vol. 12, 94–102.

14. Frederick Stansbury Haydon, *Aeronautics in the Union and Confederate Armies* (Baltimore: Johns Hopkins University Press, 1941).

15. Today the National Air and Space Museum is at the approximate location of the Columbia Armory during the Civil War.

16. NARA, RG77, E153, Letter to LaMountain, January 27, 1862.

17. Haydon, *Aeronautic*.

18. John Beauchamp Jones, 1810–1866, "Diary of John Beauchamp Jones, 1865," in *A Rebel War Clerk's Diary at the Confederate States Capital*, vol. 2 (Philadelphia: J. B. Lippincott & Co.), 128, 1866.

19. Mary Alice Wills, *The Confederate Blockade of Washington, D.C., 1861–1862* (McClain Printing Company, 1975). The most comprehensive view of the Confederate blockade of the Potomac.

20. "More Than Just a Map," National Air and Space Museum, accessed October 10, 2022, https://airandspace.si.edu/stories/editorial/more-just-map.

21. George B. McClellan, *McClellan's Own Story* (Kerkhoff Books, 1887), 135.

22. Stephen W. Sears, *To the Gates of Richmond: The Peninsula Campaign* (Ticknor & Fields 1992), appendix 1: The Armies at Yorktown, 359.

23. Lawrence A. Frost, "Balloons Over the Peninsula: Fitz John Porter and George Custer Become Reluctant Aeronauts," *Blue and Gray* 2, no. 3 (January 1985): 6–12.

24. John Emmet O'Brien, *Telegraphing in Battle—Reminiscences of the Civil War* (Scranton, PA: Forgotten Books, 1910, 2012), 82.

25. Frederick Miles Edge, *Major General McClellan and the Campaign on the Yorktown Peninsula* (London: Hanse Books, 2018, 1865), 133.

26. This map can be found in the Manuscript Division of the Library of Congress (LC Civil War Maps no. 619.5).

27. Editor, "Latest Telegraphic New," *Pittsburgh Daily Gazette and Advertiser*, Monday, August 4, 1862.

28. AOR, Series III, vol. 3, 292.

29. AOR, Series III, vol. 3, 292–293.

30. Correspondence in William W. Teall Papers, Tennessee State Library and Archive, Nashvill. Teall's wartime letters to his wife.

31. Peter Tsouras, *Major General George H. Sharpe and the Creation of American Military Intelligence in the Civil War* (Havertown, PA: Casement Publishers, 2018).

32. William W. Hassler, "Matters of Fact: The Winds of Chancellorsville," *Civil War Times Illustrated* 22, no. 10 (February 1984): 44.

33. Jay Luvaas, "The Role of Intelligence in the Chancellorsville Campaign, April–May, 1863," *Intelligence and National Security* 5, no. 2 (January 2008): 99–115.

34. Robert Westbrook, *History of the 49th Pennsylvania Volunteers* (Altoona, PA: Butternut and Blue, 1999, 1898), 150.

35. Library of Congress, American Institute of Aeronautics and Astronautics, box 83, File: November–December 1862.

36. Edwin C. Fishel, *The Secret War for the Union: The Untold Story of Military Intelligence in the Civil War* (Boston: Houghton Mifflin Company, 1996), 4.

37. Haydon, *Aeronautics*, 69–71.

38. D. H. Rucker, "Sale by the United States of Balloons and Fixtures," *Washington Evening Star*, April 15, 1864.

39. L. Kennet, *The First Air War, 1914–1918* (New York: The Free Press, 1991), 25.

40. Maurer Maurer, ed., *The U.S. Air Service in World War I: The Final Report and a Tactical History* (Washington, DC: Office of Air Force History Headquarters USAF, 1978), vol. 1, no. 17, 314. The most comprehensive report available on the US usage of tethered balloons.

41. Curtis Peebles, *The Moby Dick Project: Reconnaissance Balloons over Russia* (Washington, DC: Smithsonian Institution Press, 1991).

42. Dave Long, "CBP's Eyes in the Sky," *Frontline Magazine*, www.cbp.gov/frontline/frontline-november-aerostats, accessed November 25, 2023.

43. "Persistent Threat Detection System (74K Aerostat)," *Army Technology*, September 29, 2020, www.army-technology.com/projects/persistent-threat-detection-system-us.

# The Genome of Geospatial Intelligence

Jack O'Connor

*The International Spy Museum gives a prominent place to the story of the American pilot Francis Gary Powers, whose U-2 spy plane was shot down over the Soviet Union in 1960. This chapter explains the broader significance of the early U-2 program and how it laid the groundwork for today's modern geospatial intelligence.—The Editors*

This chapter describes one of the first experimental combinations of experts in American intelligence history. The "Jam Session" experiment, which took place in November 1957, brought substantive process experts (guided-missile and nuclear engineers and physicists) from American defense industries to work side by side with military and Central Intelligence Agency photo interpreters. Art Lundahl, then-chief of CIA's Photographic Interpretation Division, designed the experiment.[1] This chapter outlines the creation of the Jam Session, its processes, its intelligence production, the intelligence community's reaction, and the implications of its discoveries on imagery intelligence collection planning throughout the Cold War. The results of the experiment were a great intelligence success, yet the intelligence community's response meant that it was never repeated. Analysis of the reasons for that outcome brings to light how the Jam Session experiment included all the components of what later became to be called "geospatial intelligence" (GEOINT). In biology, a "genome" is defined as the whole of an organism's hereditary information encoded in its DNA. The Jam Session—with its combination of imagery, imagery intelligence, and geospatial information—can be considered the genome of American geospatial intelligence. It would take 48 years of technological developments before the promise of the Jam Session could become common practice in the American intelligence community. The reaction of other intelligence organizations and agencies that viewed and treated the Jam Session as an invasive species illustrates the potency of this combination of government and contractor, of engineering and empirical analysis, and the threat that Art Lundahl's experiment posed to the American intelligence community of the 1950s.

After World War II, the Soviet Union emerged as the global rival of the United States and other Western democracies. Its ideology seemed as threatening as its massive military. After the country tested its first atomic bomb in 1949, concerns about the Soviet threat grew all the greater. The US government clamored for intelligence to help it understand and counter the threat, especially the Soviet strategic nuclear forces. The Soviet Union, a closed society, was a very hard intelligence target. A "hard target" is a country or area that is very difficult for outsiders to gain access to. (Today, Russia is still considered a hard target.) Reliable information about what the vast Soviet interior contained was virtually impossible to obtain.

The United States knew very little about Soviet military and strategic infrastructure. It knew that the Soviet Union had possessed atom and hydrogen weapons since 1949 and 1953, respectively, but had no warning before these weapons were initially tested. At the 1954 May Day parade in Moscow, the United States learned from the public display that the Soviet Union had built at least a few long-distance jet bombers, but it had no idea how many had been built, where they were deployed, or their capabilities. The surprise discovery at the parade meant that the Soviet Union had at least one way to deliver a nuclear first strike.[2]

While the United States had been aware since the late 1940s from other sources that the Soviet Union was developing nuclear weapons and the systems to deliver them, the United States lacked enough information to know the status of the Soviet missile and nuclear efforts. The collective American ignorance was best captured by Edwin "Din" Land, inventor of the Polaroid Land Camera and a member of President Dwight Eisenhower's Technical Capabilities Panel: "We simply cannot afford to defend against all possible threats. We must know accurately where the threat is coming from and concentrate our resources in that direction. Only by doing so can we survive the Cold War."[3]

To address American ignorance about Soviet military and nuclear capabilities, President Eisenhower in November 1954 directed the CIA to build the U-2, a high-altitude unarmed strategic reconnaissance aircraft.[4] The story of how Kelly Johnson and Lockheed's Skunk Works designed, built, tested, and delivered the U-2 has been told, but new information puts its collection and operational challenges in context. While testing of the aircraft, cameras, and film was ongoing over US airspace in 1955 and early 1956, a new jointly staffed Photographic Interpretation Division (PID), organized by the CIA and led by Art Lundahl, was testing its timelines and processes with the film from these same missions, various other offices of the American intelligence community were trying to come to terms with their ignorance about Soviet strategic capabilities.

As remarkable as the U-2's capabilities were, the Soviet Union was so vast that the U-2 could never photograph all of it. Accordingly, Allen

Figure 7.1: MC-3A flightsuit used by CIA and US Air Force pilots flying high-altitude aircraft, including the U-2 spy plane. If the plane depressurized, the suit squeezed the pilot's vital organs and major muscles to compensate.

Dulles, Director of Central Intelligence, created a committee to define what the U-2 should photograph. The Ad Hoc Requirements Committee (ARC), was chaired by James Q. Reber, a University of Chicago PhD and CIA officer, who had worked at the Department of State during World War II. He presided over a committee that included representatives from the US Army, Navy, Air Force, State Department, CIA, and the National Security Agency (NSA). Previously, these organizations had agreed on which broad classes of targets would be collection priorities: Soviet offensive weapons systems and forces; weapon systems research and development programs; Soviet long-range aviation bases; major submarine bases; and key production bases for long-range bombers and submarines.[5]

In spite of agreement about the priorities, at the June 1 and 4 1956 ARC meetings, held to plan collection and flight tracks for the initial U-2 missions, the entire intelligence community could locate only 45 intelligence targets on a map of the Soviet Union. As the meeting minutes record: "In the second meeting the forty-five targets, having been plotted, discussion centered around the validity of some of the targets in terms of the relevancy to Director of Central Intelligence Directive (DCID) 4/5."[6] Even before the first overflight of the Soviet Union, the ARC could not agree on the value of individual Soviet targets even when it knew only 45 of them.

Although intelligence about Soviet capabilities was essential, the White House focused equally on the political sensitivity of U-2 overflights of a nuclear-armed rival. While the ARC proposed targets, Dulles would have to show proposed flight tracks and targets to President Eisenhower for his approval before each mission. As the president had intestinal surgery in May 1956, before the first East Europe overflight missions, the initial U-2 mission conversation took place at Walter Reed Hospital. Finally, on June 21, the president gave his approval, and the first Soviet penetration overflight took place on July 4, 1956.[7]

The first Soviet penetration missions proved the U-2's value. It also revealed a critical operational flaw in the U-2 program. While these flights showed how few strategic bombers the Soviet Union had deployed, the program discovered that Soviet radars tracked each flight from end to end and that Soviet air defenses had made repeated attempts to shoot them down. American ignorance about Soviet radar capabilities increased pilot risk and political sensitivities. After July 10, when the Soviet Union delivered a written protest to the US embassy in Moscow with a map of the U-2 flight tracks, President Eisenhower halted Soviet penetration overflights. While these first U-2 overflights revealed great numbers of unknown military and industrial targets, and significant intelligence about Soviet bomber and submarine forces, most questions about Soviet strategic missile and nuclear targets remained unanswered.[8]

In the fall of 1956 and into the spring of 1957, no U-2 flew over the Soviet Union. The U-2s had been diverted in the fall of 1956 to cover the Suez Crisis, while the nearly simultaneous Hungarian Revolution increased tensions between the West and the Soviet Union. The brutal Soviet repression in Hungary caused Eisenhower to extend his order that no U-2 fly over the Soviet Union.[9]

Throughout this interval, in the monthly ARC meetings, the intelligence community continued to request collection on potential Soviet nuclear and missile targets. In May 1957, Eisenhower agreed to resume U-2 overflights, but even more than previously he scrutinized each mission, and he frequently changed flight tracks and deleted targets.[10] During this interval, the U-2 had been modified to be less detectable by Soviet radars, but the modifications would be ineffective. These early 1957 flights were restricted to the periphery of the Soviet Union. These peripheral flights did provide

Figure 7.2: Canister of film from U-2 mission 4016 launched from Adana, Turkey, on November 20, 1956. Francis Gary Powers piloted the U-2 over the southern Soviet Union (today's Azerbaijan and Armenia) before returning due to a malfunction. From the Collection of H. Keith and Karen Melton at the International Spy Museum.

some important information about Klyuchi, on the Kamchatka Peninsula north of Japan. While much construction was ongoing, so little was known about the Soviet missile test flights that the intelligence community did not know if Klyuchi was a launch point or an impact area.[11]

The ARC memoranda from May through July 1957 demonstrate the extent of American uncertainty and ignorance about Soviet strategic missile developments. On May 9, 1957, Herbert Scoville, CIA's assistant director for scientific intelligence, wrote the chairman of the ARC about U-2 Collection guidance:

> Although we, like the other ARC members, have attempted to give the best possible guidance in our participation in the development of target lists, we feel there are certain subtleties relative to our targets which cannot be recorded in the confines of a standardized target list. I have in mind here such problems as the Novokazalinek-Kyzl Orda-Dzusaly area, also Kyluchi, and our estimate of where missile or earth satellite activities may be going on there.[12]

What Scoville termed "subtleties" referred to the imprecise locations of all other intelligence sources, classified and unclassified, on this issue. The area Scoville outlined is slightly more than 220 miles long, or the distance between Washington and New York City, which illustrates the planning difficulties for the U-2 program. From a number of sources, US intelligence had been aware of activities in that area, but none of these sources could locate the facilities or activities exactly.

The lack of US intelligence about Soviet missile and nuclear targets caused the president to approve a series of nine U-2 penetration overflights that started in August 1957. These nine missions, Operation Soft Touch, were very successful and provided the first insight into Soviet nuclear and missile issues. US knowledge grew significantly when the missile test center at Tyuratam in Kazakhstan was first seen on U-2 photographs taken on August 5, 1957. The unprecedented size of the launch stand and the extent of significant construction caused the CIA, with Eisenhower's approval, to send a second U-2 mission over Tyuratam on August 28.

On the nuclear side, the photo interpreters discovered the Soviet nuclear test area at Semipalatinsk in Kazakhstan, as well as nuclear-related facilities at Tomsk. But the discovery and rephotographing of the ICBM missile test center at Tyuratam on August 5 and 28 would begin the systematic discovery of Soviet strategic missile capabilities and would have long-lasting consequences for the American intelligence community.[13]

On the U-2 photographs of Tyuratam, even the best photo interpreters saw much that was new and incomprehensible. Art Lundahl briefed the results of these missions to the Guided Missile Intelligence Committee (GMIC). Based on the intelligence gained by Lundahl's interpreters, and the great number of questions about what had been seen in the images, the committee proposed at its September 4 meeting that a "technical assessment by a group of selected, highly qualified US guided missile developmental and test personnel was essential to fully exploit this AQUATONE [code name for the U-2 program] data."[14]

Lundahl agreed to the committee's recommendation, and on September 24, 1957, he wrote a memo that scheduled and organized the joint effort: this became the Jam Session.[15] Lundahl had designed an analytic experiment to bring American scientific and engineering experts into the Steuart Building, the covert location in Washington where the Photographic Interpretation Division analyzed U-2 film.[16] However, the entire committee was not in full accord.

Although the CIA, Army, and Navy agreed and provided guidance to Lundahl on September 20, the Air Force delayed the GMIC consideration by attempting to delay the decision for the outside experts to work with Lundahl's interpreters in Washington. On September 30, the Air Force made a counterproposal for the technical assessment to take place at the

Air Technical Intelligence Center at Wright-Patterson Air Force Base in Dayton, Ohio. Director of Central Intelligence Dulles, in agreement with Herbert Scoville's recommendation, directed on October 3 that the work should be done in the Steuart Building with the participation of Lundahl's photo interpreters from the PID Military-Scientific Branch under the observation of technical liaisons from each military service.[17]

The GMIC invited the foremost American guided missile experts to come and work with the PID photo interpreters in the Steuart Building. By September 25, Lundahl had designed the working arrangements so the scientists and engineers could work side by side in concert with the support staff, the specially trained mathematicians (called "photogrammetrists"), who could measure objects accurately from photographs, and other interpreters. A total of 26 ballistic missile and nuclear energy experts came, among them Albert "Bud" Wheelon and Carl Duckett, both of whom would go on to lead the CIA's Directorate of Science and Technology.[18]

On November 4, 1957, the day after the Soviet launch of Sputnik 2 from Tyuratam, the Jam Session began at the Steuart Building, the covert site of CIA's Photographic Interpretation Division, code-named "HTAUTOMAT." The two recent surprise Sputnik launches, on October 3 and November 3, 1957, meant that the Jam Session analysis would occur amid much publicity and debate about American national security.[19]

Prior to the Jam Session, the photo interpreters' study of the two August U-2 images showed details that indicated the pace of the Soviet construction activity at Tyuratam:

> The observations were almost unbelievable. For example, at Communications Area B on the support base, on 5 August there were one double rhombic antenna array, one two-bay fishbone antenna, and one row of three stick masts. On 28 August, there were nine double rhombics, two fishbones, one three-mast array, one four-mast array, and three single masts. In those 23 days, 92 masts had been erected, an astonishing accomplishment.
>
> The feverish pace of construction indicated a crash effort to achieve operational readiness for the Center at the earliest possible date. Through the object of all this haste, whether for military advantage or some spectacular space event, was not apparent late in the summer of 1957, the reason became clear in the next several weeks. By the uninhibited use of a military booster, the Soviets were able to launch the first earth satellite.[20]

The significance of the analysis and a rationale for the pace of activity became evident before the Jam Session convened. Sputnik 2 launched on

Figure 7.3: The Steuart Building on New York Avenue in Washington, DC, housed the CIA's Photographic Interpretation Center, which interpreted U-2 imagery. In this depiction, a bulky piece of photo interpretation equipment is being delivered circa 1959.

November 3, 1957. It differed significantly from Sputnik 1. For example, it weighed six times more. Its increased size and mass meant that the Soviet Union had solved the technical problems of launching into space an object as heavy as a nuclear weapon on an intercontinental missile.

Amid the initial American political and public outcry about the two Sputniks, the photo interpretation and technical analysis at the Jam Session began in secret. But the analysis from the intelligence community provided the underpinning for President Eisenhower's moderate public response. And within the intelligence community, the Jam Session provided three kinds of timely information. The first was locational: once the exact location of the test and launch site at Tyuratam had been learned, the discovery enabled research of open-source material and tasking of other intelligence community sources to collect information about this site. The discovery also allowed analysis of Tyuratam in relation to other recently discovered sites, particularly Kyluchi. The detailed analysis of the antenna construction and orientation at Tyuratam confirmed that Kyluchi was the impact site for test-fired intercontinental ballistic missiles.[21]

The second was analytical. The unique infrastructure discovered at

Tyuratam allowed for measurement (or, as photo interpreters called it, "mensuration") of the launch tower and a volumetric estimate of the excavated flame bucket. (A flame bucket is the deep triangular excavation at the base of a launch tower. As a missile is launched the flame bucket is dowsed with thousands of gallons of water to lower the temperature outside the rocket and dissipate the toxic gases more rapidly.) Measuring the flame bucket and comparing its volume to US facilities built for the same purpose gave the scientists a sense of the thrust created by the Soviet rocket engines. These measurements enabled the rocket scientists and engineers who came to the Steuart Building to estimate the diameter, length, and thrust of the missiles that launched Sputnik 1 and Sputnik 2. Also, the rapid construction of antennas for missile telemetry, or signals sent back from the missile indicating its position and the performance of its guidance and propulsion systems, provided a great deal of technical information for the experts and alerted analysts about what activities might be forthcoming at Tyuratam.

The third piece of significant information concerned the operational nature of the Soviet missile locations. The two U-2 photos of Tyuratam showed that the sites were connected by an unimproved road network, but the Soviets had done a great deal of construction to improve and extend the rail lines inside the facility. This indicated to the engineers and photo interpreters that the missile component transfers—movements of the payload and missile stages—at Tyuratam had to be done by rail. Soviet intercontinental missiles were so large and heavy that a railroad infrastructure was necessary for their transport.

This observation turned out to be as important as the scientific and engineering analysis of the two unique objects—the large launch tower and the flame bucket. At that time, the Soviet rail network covered only 60 percent of the Soviet landmass. The discovery of this essential dependency of Soviet missile transport on the rail network became a significant collection planning tool that bounded imagery collection for the U-2 and later the CORONA satellites, for the next 15 years.[22]

While all this new knowledge about Tyuratam was essential and valuable, it was not all well received inside the intelligence community. The Jam Session results, published in preliminary form on November 27, 1957, were not in accord with prior intelligence community assessments about Soviet missiles.[23] All-source analysts in the CIA's Directorate of Intelligence and in the Air Force Intelligence Center were not pleased that the Jam Session happened without their participation or leadership, and they were less pleased that Arthur Lundahl briefed the results of the Jam Session to the intelligence community. They were least pleased when they learned

Figure 7.4: U-2 image of the Tyuratam missile test facility at Tyuratam in present-day Kazakhstan.

that Lundahl was scheduled to brief the results abroad to close allies. Their organizational displeasure grew in proportion to the rank of the audiences, and two events happened as a consequence of this displeasure.

On October 31, 1957, Lundahl received a letter from James Reber, chairman of the ARC. Lundahl had been scheduled to brief selected American allies about the Soft Touch U-2 mission results. Reber's letter directed "that Lundahl should be instructed to provide technical facts but should avoid making estimates or drawing conclusions from the material displayed."[24] In early December, shortly after the release of the preliminary Jam Session report, Lundahl briefed the Jam Session analysis again. Eight days later, on December 20, the director of CIA's Office of Scientific Intelligence (OSI) in the Directorate of Intelligence wrote Lundahl to challenge several of the hypotheses given in the briefing. The challenges were based not on the photo interpretation findings or the Jam Session analysis but on the grounds that Lundahl, in creating this briefing, had not coordinated the findings with CIA/OSI. In his response, Lundahl stated that he had indeed qualified his statements and that he would continue to do so in future briefings.[25] Nevertheless, the CIA, backed by the Department of Defense, canceled Lundahl's overseas briefing trip.[26]

The Jam Session forced the CIA and other DOD all-source analysts to rapidly change their analysis and some of their assumptions. The combined

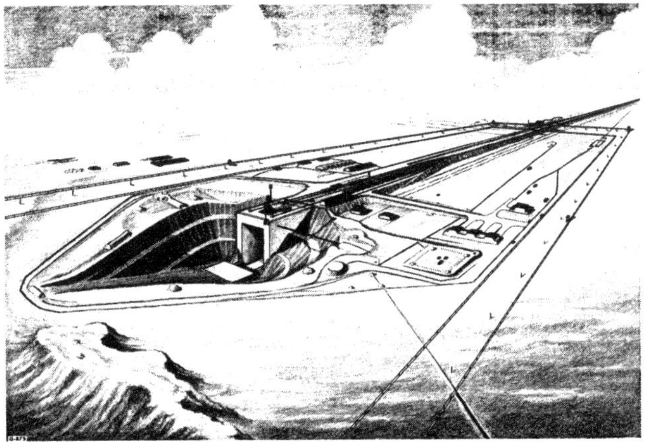

Figure 7.5: CIA artist's rendering of the flame bucket at Tyuratam.

efforts of the missile experts and the photo interpreters rendered invalid much of the previous intelligence community analysis. For the first time, the work of the photo interpreters and outside industry experts, based on only two U-2 photographs, had forced CIA and other DOD all-source analysts to rapidly revise their analysis and to recognize the amount of accurate information that could be gleaned from analysis of imagery. The consternation caused by Jam Session was not that the PID photo interpreters partnered in their analysis with the private sector technical experts; nor did it result from any serious substantive disagreement with the Jam Session analysis and findings. But the combination of the empirical evidence and measurements from the U-2 photography with the engineering and missile test analysis of the outside experts created a new kind of analysis that neither the CIA nor the Air Force could have done at that time.

While both organizations expected Lundahl's analysts and their contractor guests at the Steuart Building to obtain new information, neither expected that they would produce intelligence so compelling that it would force each organization to rethink its assumptions and as a result cause the intelligence community to issue a new Special Intelligence Estimate on the Soviet ICBM program in December 1957.[27] The Jam Session combined government capabilities to interpret aerial photography with civilian process knowledge about missile testing to produce intelligence that allowed the United States to define its strategic risks precisely, enabling the beginning of strategic mapping of the Soviet Union. It also provided the Air Force with accurate targeting information for any future strategic bombing campaign. It took only two U-2 photographs of Tyuratam to encapsulate and illustrate the potential of what, in the twenty-first century, would come to be called "geospatial intelligence." However, the all-source analysts seemed most upset at the high-level audiences who requested the Jam Session findings and who traveled to the Steuart Building to hear Art Lundahl's briefing. These visitors included Admiral Arleigh Burke, Chief of Naval Operations; General James Doolittle, Chairman of the National Advisory Committee for Aeronautics and a member of the President's Board of Consultants on Foreign Intelligence Activities; Admiral Arthur Radford, a special adviser to the president; and Air Force General Nathan Twining, Chairman of the Joint Chiefs of Staff.[28]

Art Lundahl had organized PID as a National Center (which it became four years later) to produce intelligence for all cleared parts of the US government. Yet there is no written evidence that the usually diplomatic Lundahl demonstrated any awareness of the potential effects of his lack of coordination with the CIA and Defense all-source analytic components. His concerns about Jam Session focused only on the resource and production demands on the photo interpreters, photo lab, photogrammetrists, and graphics shop.[29] The Jam Session analysis required the creation of a great number of magnified enlargements, line drawings, and photogrammetric measurements, but it was not the only HTAUTOMAT mission in November 1957. While the Jam Session was ongoing, other PID photo interpreters exploited the collection from seven other 1957 U-2 missions over the Soviet Union and China.

The Jam Session resulted in additional access to communications intelligence for the photo interpreters. The observations and azimuth mensuration of all the antennas at Tyuratam, based on the type, orientation, and locations of the antennas that collected telemetry, enabled the analysts to establish a relation between Kyluchi and Tyuratam. (All fixed antennas have an azimuth, or the orientation of the antenna to the latitude and longitude of the earth; knowing the azimuth tells the analysts which way the antenna is "pointing.") These antennas pointed toward Kyluchi. As a consequence of the Jam Session analysis, the PID Military-Scientific Branch was granted access to communications intelligence (COMINT) from the NSA.[30] The combination of locational intelligence obtainable only from overhead imagery with human intelligence and communications intelligence facilitated the beginning of the mapping of Soviet strategic missile infrastructure.[31]

The Jam Session analysis created even more pressure to schedule U-2 overflights. Moreover, following the Jam Session photo interpreters wanted even more imagery of Tyuratam. The problem was that revisiting a target greatly increased the risk that the Soviets might shoot down a U-2 and its pilot because they would be ready for the second run. But the political risk and the military likelihood of a downing grew increasingly certain.

The United States, aware that the U-2 was vulnerable, had since 1957 been busily designing and building a photographic imaging satellite.[32] By December 1957, the risk assessment of the U-2 program was sufficiently high that only six more Soviet penetration overflights were attempted: one in 1958, two in 1959, and three in 1960. On the last one, the Soviets managed to down a U-2 and capture its pilot, Francis Gary Powers. As a result, for the remainder of the U-2 program Tyuratam was photographed only three more times, in July and December 1959 and April 1960.[33] Three months after the last, failed U-2 mission, the first successful CORONA—the first American strategic reconnaissance satellite—launch and recovery occurred on August 18–20, 1960.[34]

The Jam Session had other implications for imagery collection. After the discovery of Tyuratam in August 1957, the ARC had to balance two equally important collection priorities. Target monitoring, or continuing to look at Tyuratam and other test sites, to detect any new ICBM developments, was one of these priorities. Search—the analytic process that led to the discovery of Tyuratam—was the other necessary priority to determine the size and location of the Soviet missile forces. To balance these competing priorities, Reber created a collection model that bounded the risks diminished by the new discoveries and the uncalculated risks in the unsearched areas of the Soviet Union. Reber's model introduced a new unit of measure for risk: "general accountable search." After the discovery of Tyuratam, repeated collection (monitoring the new point or specifically defined targets) would have to be scheduled in combination with searches of new areas for discovery.

These two different analytic requirements—review of the known and search for the unknown—competed against one another. Reber and the ARC had to jointly rank and schedule both kinds of collection: known targets, or facilities with defined latitudes and longitudes, commonly called "point targets," with the highest priority; and previously unsearched and unknown regions with the highest probability for discovery. The unknown regions were called "area targets" and would be defined by four sets of coordinates that formed a box-shaped area. These competing needs—to monitor point targets and to search area targets—shaped American imagery intelligence collection over the Soviet Union and Russia until 1994, when the Strategic Arms Reduction Treaty went into effect. Tyuratam became one of the first point targets. Previously unphotographed areas along the Trans-Siberian Railway would be divided into search targets. Reber's

Figure 7.6: Wreckage from Francis Gary Powers's U-2 spy plane. From the Collection of H. Keith and Karen Melton at the International Spy Museum.

contribution—general accountable search—balanced the accountability of the priority point targets—how well imagery collection satisfied the need to track the known—with a measure of accountability for previously unsearched areas of the Soviet Union.

General accountable search allowed the intelligence community to rank unknown areas initially by the probability of discovery and, after initial observation, by the interval since the last observation. The number of U-2 mission discoveries was multiplied several times after August 1960, when the first CORONA satellite mission began to return buckets of film covering much larger areas of the Soviet Union from outer space.[35]

The Jam Session, with its combination of the foremost US missile experts—with backgrounds in physics and engineering and access to COMINT and human intelligence—and Lundahl's photo interpreters—empiricists par excellence—resulted in intelligence discoveries that neither group could have achieved on its own. The Jam Session's combination of interpreting aerial photos, measuring antenna azimuths, determining the relation of Tyuratam to Kyluchi, and initial strategic mapping of Soviet Strategic infrastructure was unprecedented. For the first time in US intelligence history, all the disciplines later united under the 2005 legal definition of "geospatial intelligence" in United States Code §467: GEOINT was defined as "the exploitation and analysis of imagery and geospatial information to describe, assess, and visually depict physical features and geographically referenced activities on the earth."[36] In the 48 years between the Jam Session and the creation of this legal definition, different analytic activities took multiple organizational forms in the Central Intelligence Agency; Defense Intelligence Agency; the US Army, Navy, and Air Force military service centers; the Defense Mapping Agency; and the National Photographic Interpretation Center. However, the Jam Session was the initial event that combined all these analytic activities with extraordinary consequences. It is arguably the genome of American geospatial intelligence.

As an unintentional byproduct, these geospatial discoveries also introduced enduring tensions about which organizations can and should analyze particular intelligence topics and what reporting "belonged" to all-source analysts. The organizational reactions of the CIA and Defense Department were so significant that the successful experiment never was repeated in the photographic or imagery intelligence communities. The organizational tensions raised by the Jam Session resurfaced a number of times in the American intelligence community with the introduction of near–real-time electro-optical imagery, measurement and signals intelligence, and other new intelligence technologies. They continue today in the debates among analytic components of the American intelligence community over the relation of all-source analysts to geospatial analysts and in collection management over the competing requirements for monitoring the known and searching for the new.

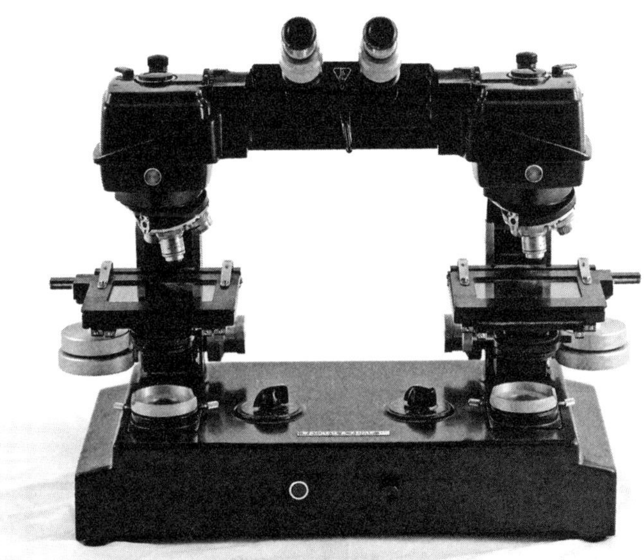

Figure 7.7: Bausch & Lomb High Power Stereoviewer for interpreting overhead imagery, 1960s–1970s. From the Collection of H. Keith and Karen Melton at the International Spy Museum.

## Further Reading

Beschloss, Michael. *Mayday: Eisenhower, Khrushchev, and the U-2 Affair*. New York: Harper and Row, 1986.

Ryan, Amy, and Gary Keeley. "Sputnik and US Intelligence: The Warning Record." *Studies in Intelligence* 61, no. 3 (September 2017): 1–16.

Thomas, Evan. *Ike's Bluff: President Eisenhower's Secret Battle to Save the World*. New York: Little, Brown, 2012.

## Notes

1. Art Lundahl was one of the five essential individuals in the creation of the U-2 reconnaissance aircraft. Edwin Land of Polaroid envisioned the capability and persuaded President Eisenhower to have CIA create the aircraft. Richard Bissell was the CIA program manager for the U-2. Land initially coordinated the efforts of Kelly Johnson of Lockheed, who designed and built the U-2. Another was James Baker of Harvard, who created the cameras for high-altitude, high-resolution aerial photography. Finally, Art Lundahl established the photographic interpretation organization that analyzed the photography.

2. Evan Thomas, *Ike's Bluff: President Eisenhower's Secret Battle to Save the World* (New York: Little, Brown, 2012), 181; Michael Beschloss, *Mayday: Eisenhower, Khrushchev, and the U-2 Affair* (New York: Harper and Row, 1986), 119.

3. Albert D. Wheelon, "Lifting the Veil on CORONA," *Space Policy* 11, no. 4 (1995): 249–250.

4. Gregory W. Pedlow and Donald E. Welzenbach, *The CIA and the U-2 Program* (Washington, DC: History Staff, Center for the Study of Intelligence, Central Intelligence Agency, 1998), 39–40; Thomas, *Ike's Bluff*, 147–151.

5. Pedlow and Welzenbach, *The CIA and the U-2 Program*, 40, 80–81; "Intelligence Vital to National Security Through AQUATONE," TB# 143488/B, CIA-RDP92B01090R002500010080-2, CIA Freedom of Information Action Electronic Reading Room, cia.gov/readingroom/ (hereafter CIAFOIARR).

6. "AD HOC REQUIREMENTS COMMITTEE ON PROJECT AQUATONE (ARC) Minutes of Meetings Held in Room 121 Administration Building, Central Intelligence Agency, at 1200, 1 June 1956 and at 1400, 4 June 1956," SAFC 678, CIA-RDP33-02415A000100010005-7, CIAFOIARR.

7. Pedlow and Welzenbach, *The CIA and the U-2 Program*, 100.

8. [Redacted], National Photographic Interpretation Center, *The Years of Project HTAUTOMAT, 1956–1958*, NPIC, vols. 1 and 2, December 1974, CIA-RDP04T00184R000400010001-1, 107–108, CIAFOIARR.

9. Pedlow and Welzenbach, *The CIA and the U-2 Program*, 123.

10. Pedlow and Welzenbach, *The CIA and the U-2 Program*, 128.

11. [Redacted], ARC and Reber memos about Kyzl Orda. 13 May 1957, Memo from Chairman Ad Hoc Requirements Committee to Director of Operations, subject, Ad Hoc Requirements Committee Requirements for the KLYUCHI Mission, CIA-RDP61S00750A000500003117-3; TCS-1411-57, ARC-M-43 Special Meeting of the Ad Hoc Requirements Committee on Project AQUATONE (ARC) 19 May 1957; 22 May 1957,

SC-03325-57 Memorandum for Ad Hoc Requirements Committee Members Subject Detailed Requirements for Penetration Flights, CIA-RDP61S00750A000200070022-7; TCS-1506-57, ARC-M-46, Ad Hoc Requirements Committee on Project AQUATONE (ARC) 27 May 1957, CIA-RDP61S00750A000200070013-7; Draft: J.Q. Reber, 10 July 1957, CIA-RDP61S00750A000200080106-3; Targets for Coverage in General Area of 4035 (no date) CIARDP61S00750A000500030098-5, CIAFOIARR.

12. [Redacted], Herbert Scoville, Jr., "Memorandum for Chairman, Ad Hoc Requirements Committee, Subject: Flight Planning for Future Aquatone Missions," 9 May 1957, CIA-RDP61S00750A000500030122-7, CIAFOIARR.

13. National Photographic Interpretation Center, *The Years of Project HTAUTOMAT, 1956–1958,* vols. 1 and 2, 159.

14. Quote taken from citation on [Redacted], 3 October 1957 Memo from Herbert Scoville, Jr., Assistant Director Scientific Intelligence for Director of Central Intelligence, Subject*: Production of Guided Missile Intelligence from Evidence Gathered by AQUATONE*, CIAFOIARR (hereafter Scoville Memo). AQUATONE was the cover name for the U-2 program. Pedlow and Welzenbach, *The CIA and the U-2 Program*, 40.

15. National Photographic Interpretation Center, *The Years of Project HTAUTOMAT, 1956–1958,* vols. 1 and 2, 186–188, CIAFOIARR.

16. This event was described by Dino Brugioni, but he had to work from memory, as much of the documentation had not been declassified when his book was published. Dina Brugioni, *Eyes in the Sky: Eisenhower, the CIA, and Cold War Aerial Espionage* (Annapolis: Naval Institute Press, 2010), 244.

17. [Redacted], Scoville Memo, 3 October 1957, CIAFOIARR.

18. [Redacted], Ed Dietel, "Charting a Technical Revolution: An Interview with Former DDS&T Albert Wheelon," *Studies in Intelligence*, January 1, 1996, C00863247, 32–34, copy at National Security Archive website, https://nsarchive2.gwu.edu/NSAEBB/NSAEBB438/docs/doc_31.PDF.

19. Amy Ryan and Gary Keeley, "Sputnik and US Intelligence: The Warning Record," *Studies in Intelligence* 61, no. 3 (September 2017): 1–16, 1–2, 9–10.

20. National Photographic Interpretation Center, *The Years of Project HTAUTOMAT, 1956–1958,* vols. 1 and 2, 213.

21. Initially, the assessment was that Tyuratam was about 40 square miles. [Redacted], Guided Missile Intelligence Committee, Report of the Special Engineering Analysis Group, 27 November 1957, Washington D.C. CIA-RDP78T05439A000300350035-6, 8; CIAFOIARR. By 1964, the United States knew that the missile test center at Tyuratam covered 1,500 square miles, an area approximately the size of Rhode Island. CIA, Scientific Intelligence Report, *New Space Facilities at the Tyuratam Missile Test Center*, 14 October 1964, CIA-RDP78T05439A000400060010-4, v, CIAFOIARR.

22. National Photographic Interpretation Center, *The Years of Project HTAUTOMAT, 1956–1958,* vols. 1 and 2, 248.

23. [Redacted], Guided Missile Intelligence Committee. *Report of the Special Engineering Analysis Group*. 27 November 1957, CIA-RDP78T05439A000300350035-6, CIAFOIARR.

24. National Photographic Interpretation Center, *The Years of Project HTAUTOMAT, 1956–1958,* vols. 1 and 2, 247–248.

25. National Photographic Interpretation Center, *The Years of Project HTAUTOMAT, 1956–1958,* vols. 1 and 2, 250.

26. [Redacted], Ad Hoc Requirements Committee on Project AQUATONE (ARC)

ARC-M-66, *Minutes of Meeting held in Room 214 Administration Building, Central Intelligence Agency at 10:00 a.m.*, 7 November 1957, CIA-RDP61S00750A000200060060-6, CIAFOIARR.

27. CIA, Special National Intelligence Estimate 11–10–57, *The Soviet ICBM Program*, 17 December 1957.

28. National Photographic Interpretation Center, *The Years of Project HTAUTOMAT, 1956–1958*, vols. 1 and 2, 243.

29. National Photographic Interpretation Center, *The Years of Project HTAUTOMAT, 1956–1958*, vols. 1 and 2, 184–188.

30. [Redacted], National Photographic Interpretation Center, *The Years of Project HTAUTOMAT, 1956–1958*, vol. 3, December 1974, CIARTP04T00184R000400030001-9, 356–357, CIAFOIARR.

31. The Jam Session segmentation of one part of Lundahl's organization from another had an unintended negative effect. After the experiment concluded, in March and April 1958, photo interpreters from the Geographic Branch began searching earlier 1956 U-2 photography of the Soviet bloc states for possible deployed missile sites. Seven months after the discoveries at Tyuratam, no deployed sites had been found on the Soviet Union Soft Touch missions, so prior 1956 U-2 coverage was reexamined.

As a result of the historical search, the Geographic Branch reported out four possible deployed missile sites, one in Ventspils in the Soviet Union and three in Poland at Kolberg Deep, at Bydgoszcz, and on the Hel Peninsula. But the Geographic Branch had not negated these targets. (Negation is the process of looking at older photographs to determine the earliest observation of new construction or an object of interest.) When the Military-Scientific Branch did negate these sites, they were identified as gun positions that had been first photographed on German World War II aerial photography. The Military-Scientific Branch did not initially participate in this search for deployed missile sites, as they judged their work on the test site at Tyuratam to be a higher priority. This analytic mistake, which required publishing a correction, mirrored the conflict in imagery collection between search and target monitoring. It resulted in the first significant correction cable in the HTAUTOMAT modern imagery era. [Redacted], Joint Photographic Intelligence Brief. Brief No. JB-10-58, 9 May 1958, *Possible Guided Missile Launch Site, Ventspils, Latvian SSR*, CIA-RDP78T04751A000300070012-3; Joint Photographic Intelligence Brief. Brief No. JB-11-58, 9 May 1958, *Probable Guided Missile Launch Site, Hel Poland*, CIA-RDP78T04751A000300070013-2; Joint Photographic Intelligence Brief, Brief No. JB-13-58, 14 May 1958, *Possible Guided Missile Launch Site, Kolberg-Deep, Poland*, CIA-RDP8T04751A000300070015-0; Joint Photographic Intelligence Brief; Brief No. JB-15-58, 29 May 1958, *Possible Guided Missile Launch Site North of Bydgoszcz, Poland*, CIA-RDP78T04751A000300070017-8, CIAFOIARR.

32. The technical challenges of building and flying that satellite, CORONA, emerged with its first failed launch on January 21, 1959, 25 months after the Jam Session ended. Kevin C. Ruffner, ed., *CORONA: America's First Satellite Program* (Washington, DC: CIA, Center for the Study of Intelligence History Staff, 1995), document 1.

33. [Redacted], Pedlow and Welzenbach, *The CIA and the U-2 Program*, 143; [Redacted] *New Launch Area and Other Developments, Missile Launching Complex Tyura Tam, USSR*, PIC/JR-17/60, July 1960, CIA-RDP78T04751A000400010038-0, 3, 7, 26, CIAFOIARR.

34. Ruffner, *CORONA*, 1.

35. An indication of what the U-2 program accomplished can be measured by comparing James Reber's August 1960 memorandum "List of Highest Priority Targets, USSR" (in Ruffner, *CORONA*, 49–59) to his May 1956 ARC committee memos. The 45 total targets in a handful of categories in May 1956 had grown to 32 categories of targets with specific coordinates for 128 point targets for monitoring and 23 area targets, mostly rail lines, to be searched. Additionally, as an indirect outcome of the U-2 penetration overflights, the locations of surface-to-air missiles were also requested, as they were valuable indicators of more important proximate targets.

36. 10 U.S.C. § 67 *US Code—Section 467: Definitions; Memorandum for Principal Director of National Intelligence, Deputy Director of National Intelligence for Collection*, from James R Clapper, Lieutenant General USAF (Ret), Director (NGA) 15 October 2005. The de jure definition of geospatial intelligence is "geospatial intelligence means the exploitation and analysis of imagery and geospatial information to describe, assess, and visually depict physical features and geographically referenced activities on the earth. Geospatial intelligence consists of imagery, imagery intelligence, and geospatial information." See https://uscode.house.gov/view.xhtml?req=granuleid:USC-prelim-title10-section467&num=0&edition=prelim, accessed September 7, 2022.

# Concealing Colossus: Britain's Wartime Computing History and Cold War SIGINT

David Schaefer

*Intelligence history overlaps with many fields, among them the history of technology. Aside from imagery, another important technical means of collection is signals intelligence, or SIGINT. This involves collecting enemy communications and then breaking the code or cipher system that protects them to reveal their secrets. The International Spy Museum tells the story about the British breaking many versions of the famous German Enigma cipher machine during World War II. However, British cryptanalysts had to break into other German cryptosystems in addition. To attack one of these, the Lorenz system, they built Colossus, the world's first digital electronic computer.—The Editors*

The study of intelligence history owes much to the availability of British wartime records, which began with the sudden release of Ultra files in the mid-1970s. Since that time academics and researchers have pored over the documentary record of Allied wartime intelligence, with the codebreaking success at Bletchley Park receiving wide public interest. This chapter explores a significant yet neglected part of the Bletchley story: the British government's campaign to suppress historical knowledge of Colossus amid the large-scale disclosure of wartime codebreaking achievements. The invention of Colossus marked a revolutionary advance in electronic computing, pioneering capabilities that continued to yield intelligence benefits into the postwar years. The omission of this technology from Britain's release of wartime records in the 1970s offers new insight into the methods of postwar secrecy and provides more context to other, high-profile exploits by Western signals intelligence in the Cold War.

The historiography of intelligence studies tends to locate the emergence of the field in the political upheavals of the Watergate era, when a variety of US intelligence operations were publicly revealed in congressional investigations. These accounts only rarely touch on the parallel experience in Britain during that same tumultuous decade, which saw the publication of two books by intelligence veterans reflecting on codebreaking and deception operations from World War II.[1] The public interest generated by these accounts was followed by the publication titled *Official History of British Intelligence in the Second World War* and the large-scale release of wartime service intelligence records to the British national archives. For three decades, the story of Bletchley Park's Special Intelligence, nicknamed "Ultra" by its military customers, had been successfully withheld from the public; after the revelations of the 1970s students of diplomacy and military history could finally examine the documentary evidence of intelligence power firsthand.

These events were a landmark in the study of intelligence, encouraging a wave of new research into codebreaking and its influence over World War II in Europe.[2] In their wake, however, the German Enigma machine came to dominate public understanding of wartime signals intelligence (SIGINT),[3] while Bletchley's development of pioneering computing technology and its exploitation of other sophisticated cipher devices were carefully concealed. This chapter examines the Cold War context to Britain's historical revelations and the importance of knowledge about wartime computing in the SIGINT contest of the 1970s. It draws on research in a related but separate publication coauthored with Michael Herman on the sudden emergence of intelligence transparency in the mid-1970s, but it explores in more detail a consequential decision by the British Joint Intelligence Committee (JIC) in October 1974 to review its wartime military intelligence records with an eye to declassifying Enigma secrets but not other aspects of Bletchley's success.[4]

A close analysis of the JIC's 1974 decision suggests that it supplied a convenient method to obscure knowledge of wartime computing, which threatened to compromise what we now know to be one of the most successful feats of Cold War SIGINT: the joint effort by the National Security Agency (NSA), Central Intelligence Agency (CIA), and West Germany's Bundesnachrichtendienst (BND), code-named "Operation Rubicon," to manipulate the production and sale of cryptographic devices on the international market. This adds a new perspective to the sudden burst of intelligence transparency during these years. As I demonstrate, the weight of evidence points to a deliberate move by British officials to "flood" their national archives with documentary material to divert attention away from more advanced cryptographic methods pioneered by Bletchley, and by extension, the vulnerability of postwar ciphers targeted in *Operation Rubicon*. As much as a principled move toward historical openness on Bletchley and Enigma, the British decision in 1974 was also an attempt to limit scholarly interest in other areas of protected SIGINT history, and one which appears to have been remarkably successful.

Figures 8.1 and 8.2: German Enigma machine designed to secure communications between the German and Japanese navies during World War II. Following the German discovery that the Allies had broken some Japanese ciphers, they prepared in 1944 to send Enigma machines with the Japanese characters to Tokyo. From the Collection of H. Keith and Karen Melton at the International Spy Museum.

## The Ultra Secret

In retrospect it seems remarkable that the story of Bletchley Park was hidden for so many years after World War II. Several participants and scholars have discussed the effort to maintain intelligence secrecy in postwar Britain, which included an immediate and indefinite extension of wartime security obligations for veterans and their rigid enforcement against aspiring writers and memoirists in the 1950s and 1960s.[5] Without repeating this story in detail, there are several aspects to Ultra as an intelligence product worth discussing in this chapter because they shaped the postwar challenge for secrecy. The first was the comprehensive nature of Bletchley's success against several Axis communications systems by the middle of World War II in Europe. Partly because the authenticity and reliability of Ultra was beyond doubt, it exercised significant influence over the calculations of Allied political leaders and the planning of military commanders. Ultra became intertwined with several areas of the war effort, notably the implementation of counterintelligence and strategic deception efforts against Germany during the reconquest of Europe. This reinforced the need for a blanket ban on all references to wartime intelligence, leaving a considerable gap in historical understanding, although with multiple avenues to discern Bletchley's role in organizational records.

The second feature of Ultra was the demographic change it prompted in Allied wartime intelligence. Communications intelligence was a specialist field during interwar Britain when a few gifted practitioners focused on the technical contest over codes and ciphers and did not presume to conduct the analytical reporting practiced by Government Communications Headquarters (GCHQ), its modern successor. The exploitation of Bletchley's output for maximum strategic effect required a substantial change in the nature and scale of recruitment, with a larger and more diverse body of personnel exposed to or assisting with the industrial-scale cryptanalytical effort. Combined with the circulation of Ultra among other military consumers, this produced a generation of practitioners who were later demobilized but maintained some working knowledge of Bletchley's wartime operations. Many of these veterans began to approach professional retirement in the 1960s, with a significant few among this diverse cohort enjoying influential careers. Unlike their World War I predecessors, some of these figures had the public standing and professional networks to lobby for recognition of their contribution to Allied victory. For insiders like Peter Calvocoressi and Donald MacLachlan, the success achieved by Bletchley was a national triumph, and they believed an official move to document the story was necessary while most of its participants remained alive.[6]

The third feature was the multinational flavor of Ultra. Collaboration between the United States and United Kingdom began tentatively before American involvement in the war but had taken on a new level of depth and integration by 1944–1945.[7] This wartime exchange of knowledge and personnel was reinforced by the intensifying espionage contest of the early Cold War. The suppression of Ultra's history therefore received full support from US authorities, who were just as keen to limit the public understanding of SIGINT cooperation for fear of the domestic political reaction against extensive peacetime arrangements for intelligence.[8] And yet the United States offered a generally more liberal media environment, where state secrets were accessible through judicial review and publishing houses presented tempting outlets to cash in on wartime memories. There was already a brief scare of this sort in late 1945 when the breaking of Japanese diplomatic ciphers was revealed during the congressional investigations into the warning surprise at Pearl Harbor, a point that was picked up and mentioned in *Time* magazine.[9] A result was that the principal British legal sanction—the "D-Notice" system, which relied on a voluntary arrangement with cooperative media outlets—could not fully restrain all the wartime personnel who had been privy to Bletchley's achievements.

All these pressures on postwar secrecy were compounded by political trends that surfaced in 1960s Britain. In 1967 the British government passed the Public Records Act, which legislated that records could be withheld only for thirty years, after which they would be transferred to the British national archives. Suddenly, the bulk of wartime records held in the Ministry of Defence (MoD) were scheduled to be released in the early 1970s. This requirement did not automatically apply to intelligence agencies, however, which could declare the need for an exemption, but there were sufficient traces of Ultra in the wartime correspondence of the military services.[10] The British government was faced with the problem that withholding files about Ultra would severely distort historical scholarship as private researchers combed through the new files released to the archives. In response, officials in Whitehall toyed with the idea of limited and controlled release of SIGINT material amid other wartime records, which would at least document Ultra while minimizing the scale and importance of codebreaking.[11] This was rejected after the MoD claimed there were few relevant Ultra documents in its possession, and it was abandoned once the government sanctioned the Official History under the editorship of Francis "Harry" Hinsley in 1969.

By the time the Official History was commissioned as a stopgap measure, the British media had also developed a more independent streak in its intelligence coverage. The immediate cause of this development was the 1967 D-Notice affair, a spat over a newspaper article that revealed the government's interception of post office cables, and the furious reaction of then–Prime Minister Harold Wilson, which damaged public trust in the government's handling of the press.[12] Furthermore, Whitehall struggled to restrain determined journalists who could interview American veterans with knowledge of Ultra. For example, the American journalist David Kahn produced a sweeping history of codebreaking in 1967, with suspected help from retired SIGINT officials.[13] When US officials approached Kahn's publisher to edit the manuscript, they also insisted on the removal of any references to Bletchley and GCHQ in the final copy.[14] Nonetheless, there was a limit to how effective these approaches could be; after working closely with the NSA to manage Kahn's impact, GCHQ was shocked when an American veteran of Bletchley reviewed the book in the *Washington Post* and criticized it for neglecting Britain's role in wartime intelligence.[15]

After the fallout over the D-Notice affair, the British government increasingly relied on personal intervention with prospective authors, but this meant it was only a matter of time until Ultra was exposed. The first detailed revelation of Bletchley's systematic victory over German communications was eventually made by Frederick Winterbotham in 1974. Winterbotham had been responsible in MI6 for the safe handling and distribution of Ultra reports during the war, and after retiring he wrote a memoir of his prewar years that was altered by the D-Notice committee secretary before publication in the late 1960s.[16] In 1972 he submitted another manuscript that drew on his experience at Bletchley and met with officials in London who encouraged him to defer publication for some time.[17] He agreed and was told that, when this security objection no longer applied, he might receive help to the correct errors in his draft. For reasons that are still not entirely clear, however, he decided to force the issue again in early 1974 after working on the manuscript with publishers in the United States and United Kingdom.[18] Facing a court fight that risked drawing unwanted public attention, and mindful of Winterbotham's resolve to publish in the United States irrespective of the problems he faced in the United Kingdom, the intelligence agency heads and senior officials represented on the JIC advised the British government not to block publication. After being informed that his manuscript did not contravene the D-Notice system, Winterbotham then published *The Ultra Secret*, a dramatic account based on his faulty memory, with extracts appearing in newspapers from July 1974.

## Releasing Wartime Files

It might seem as if this decision was a landmark event for British policy, but at the time it was not considered as such. The JIC was then chaired by Geoffrey Arthur, a Foreign Office diplomat, but the key figure in Ultra deliberations was Leonard "Joe" Hooper, the Intelligence Coordinator based in the Cabinet Office, who was responsible for overseeing the budgeting and requirements of the British intelligence community. As a former long-serving director of GCHQ, Hooper had been the key figure in efforts to persuade wartime veterans not to publish accounts of Ultra from the mid-1960s, and as coordinator from 1973 he received full support on the JIC from Arthur Bonsall, his successor at GCHQ. Before publication of Winterbotham's book, Hooper drew up revised guidelines for protecting wartime intelligence secrets, but these were modest and offered to acknowledge the existence of the Official History project—then still underway—only if it was necessary to defuse media interest.[19] The hope underlining these recommendations was that other writers could be delayed until the Official History was ready and that, once it was out, Winterbotham's book would not have much impact.[20]

Before Winterbotham's book had even been released, however, Hooper's plans encountered an unwelcome surprise in the British national archives. One reader of the *Sunday Telegraph* who had encountered Winterbotham's story replied with a letter to the editor, which explained that they had already seen documents marked "Top Secret Ultra" in the archives.[21] This letter was received by the JIC Secretariat in early September, and an investigation revealed that the national archives was the site of a major security lapse: 230 Ultra files, including decrypted German Luftwaffe and army Enigma messages, had been released by the MoD, along with more than 2,000 files from the wartime service intelligence directorates. All this material was publicly available, had been so for some time, and was known to have been accessed by several readers. It was apparently declassified in the MoD's rush to meet the deadline for transferring wartime records to the archives by 1972: some of the personnel used to "weed" these files appear to have lacked the proper security clearances and backgrounds to recognize Ultra files and appreciate their sensitivity.[22] The JIC had meticulously planned for Winterbotham's book and the possibility of some interest among reporters, but it now had an embarrassing failure on its hands. If exposed, this oversight would only draw more attention to the contents of the material that had been accidentally released.

After an emergency recall of all the files to GCHQ, the JIC held several meetings over September–October 1974 to figure out what to do. The contents and minutes of these discussions are not fully available, but a recollection by Hooper the following year indicates how they were particularly tense.[23] Astonishingly, they concluded with a recommendation not only to return the confiscated files from GCHQ to the national archives but also to expand the archival collection over time with the remainder of Ultra material in the military services records, although not those files that disclosed the specific methods and techniques of SIGINT. This decision did not extend to GCHQ's own internal archives, but the MoD service directorates, as the major customers of Ultra and supporters of the wartime interception effort through the operation of wireless and radio stations, had more than enough intelligence material of interest in their possession. As the historian Michael Herman and I have argued elsewhere, the JIC's decision was a sudden lurch toward transparency that opened the way for the mass release of Enigma-derived intelligence, spurring a wave of research into intelligence history that forever changed the practice of government secrecy.[24] Almost immediately there was a noticeable shift in official attitudes: Eddie Thomas, a coauthor of the first volume of the Official History, was soon complaining about the archival staff badgering him to return the classified files so they could be made available for the public.[25]

Beyond the obvious reversal in policy, there are several aspects of the JIC's decision that were remarkable. For one, it complicated the government's planned arrangements for the Official History, its primary vehicle for handling interest in wartime secrecy. The existence of this project was still judged too sensitive to openly acknowledge in 1974, and there was no agreement on whether the final product would even be made publicly available. In the years to come, however, the release of the service intelligence files tilted the balance, perhaps decisively, in favor of publication. As Hooper explained it to colleagues, "because World War II records of the service intelligence directorates are now being released into the public domain[,] failure to publish the Official History would probably mean that further inaccurate accounts based on incomplete material would be published by private writers."[26] Rather than draw a line under the Ultra revelations, as Whitehall had hoped, the 1974 change fundamentally altered the scope for intelligence declassification.

Another consequence was that the files supplied ready material for retired practitioners and other researchers to amplify the intelligence story. The revised guidelines developed by Hooper were aimed at discouraging other writers from following Winterbotham, and several Bletchley veterans had indeed made inquiries about the availability of wartime records shortly after Winterbotham's book was published. The national archives would not receive the service intelligence files until 1977, but once available these presented a useful avenue for those in the know to elaborate on the history of Ultra, including Peter Calvocoressi, Ralph Bennet, Patrick Beesly, and Gordon Welchman.[27] While GCHQ emphasized that wartime security obligations were still binding on retired personnel, the JIC's decision was an invitation for others to write their own accounts before government-appointed historians finished the job.

One final surprising feature of the JIC's decision is the continuing lack of insight into the committee's thinking. JIC discussions were framed by a document on the subject prepared by the JIC secretary, which is still unavailable.[28] From a later summary, it appears that Hooper himself took the initiative of recommending the change, with support from Bonsall at GCHQ, and in the face of some resistance by Arthur, the committee chairman, and likely Maurice Oldfield, the chief of MI6 who was opposed to the whole notion of intelligence history.[29] More than other members of the JIC, Hooper and Bonsall were the most knowledgeable about Ultra's sensitivity and had worked hard to limit the postwar profile of SIGINT; their conversion to a more liberal approach is a curious development that calls out for more explanation.

## Tunny and Hagelin

Based on the limited records, there is no clear explanation for why Hooper and Bonsall decided to support the release of intelligence records in late 1974 after worrying for years about Bletchley's wartime secret. There were, of course, some factors encouraging a compromise from total secrecy about wartime codebreaking. After the discovery and confiscation of the stray files at the archives, the JIC had to confront the fact that the genie was out of the bottle. Classified material had been viewed by several people, including one unnamed writer known to archival staff. One of the visitors was Aileen Clayton, a veteran of the wartime "Y" service, which operated wireless radio interception, who later lobbied her MP to restore public access.[30] Knowledge of the MoD's oversight was also circulating, with one journalist and a House of Lords peer making a reference in print to the events at the archives, although mistaking some details.[31] This likely ruled out the option of permanently withholding the files in the hope of avoiding publicity. The JIC might have opted to risk embarrassment by resisting any concession, but it also had to persuade other authors to await the release of the Official History. This task would be more difficult if Bletchley veterans discovered that some records had already been seen by others.

And yet this pressure does not explain the need to return and expand access to all the service intelligence records. In justifying this change, the JIC remarked on the advantage of bringing more consistency to historical transparency.[32] This was because most of the accidentally released Ultra records were decrypts of Luftwaffe communications, presumably held in Royal Air Force intelligence files. By returning these and extending the mandate to include British army and navy wartime intelligence records, the JIC could draw a more defensible line with other writers and journalists. Even so, it remains an unusual concession to make after 30 years of zealously guarding Bletchley's secrets amid concerns over whether to publish the Official History. The relative absence of documentary materials also suggests there were other issues at play.

Drawing on several fragments from other records, I speculate that another factor may have influenced calculations in Whitehall: the need to divert attention away from Bletchley's other codebreaking exploits, specifically its development of computing technology. For example, it is now known that Winterbotham's book obscured more of Bletchley's success than it revealed, and these omissions were a cause of some relief for British officials. As someone with little day-to-day involvement in codebreaking, Winterbotham in his account fixated on the Enigma project, but the intelligence yield from Enigma was supplemented and at times greatly surpassed by the attack against another class of German ciphers code-named "Fish" by Bletchley. The Fish machines included the Lorenz SZ40, SZ42A, and SZ42B (code-named "Tunny") and the Siemens & Halske T52 (code-named "Sturgeon"), which were advanced devices for enciphering communications on teleprinter networks. If Enigma carried a large number of operational messages among tactical commanders, Fish—and especially the Tunny machines—supplied high-level insight into the traffic between the German high command and senior army officers. More so than the cryptanalytic methods deployed against Enigma, breaking the Fish machines was a transformational moment in SIGINT history, requiring the development of a valve-operated, programmable computing machine—the world's first digital computer—that Bletchley experts named "Colossus."

Another set of British government files on computing history from the same period also reveals security concerns over the evidence of digital computing in Bletchley's history.[33] Any disclosure of Colossus's codebreaking function risked alerting rivals about the advanced state of Western SIGINT technology by the end of the war. Even 25 years later, GCHQ was worried this revelation would stimulate renewed efforts to upgrade communications security.[34] Moreover, the technical properties of Tunny as a vulnerable cryptanalytic target were closely guarded. While encryption had advanced in the postwar decades, some of the basic design principles

Figure 8.3: The teletype component of a Lorenz cipher machine. During World War II, the German high command used Lorenz machines for its most important messages. Bletchley Park codebreakers referred to this machine and its traffic as "Tunny" (tuna fish). From the Collection of H. Keith and Karen Melton at the International Spy Museum.

of Tunny as an early telecipher model were carried over into the later generation of electro-mechanical encryption devices, which were still popular in the 1960s and 1970s before the widespread adoption of digital encryption systems. It is now evident that GCHQ was exploiting vulnerabilities in some of these electro-mechanical teleciphers at the time that Winterbotham revealed the Ultra story, and it was anxious to obscure the legacy connection between these machines and Tunny. The clearest statement to this effect is a memorandum by Hooper, as director of GCHQ in August 1973 before his assumption of the coordinator role, discussing the risk of wartime histories for SIGINT operations. In this memo he cites the "now widely used Hagelin machines" as sharing similar design principles with Tunny, and he mentions how the "resemblance is close" between the Hagelin TC-55 and TY-55 models and earlier wartime machines.[35] Other correspondence in late 1974 also indicates that the modern variants of the Fish teleciphers yielded "valuable [SIGINT] at present" for GCHQ.[36]

These files—released to the public only recently—point to the likely involvement of GCHQ in the long-running campaign, later termed

"Operation Rubicon," to weaken Hagelin encryption devices for sale to unsuspecting governments during the Cold War. In 2020 a team of academic experts and investigative journalists revealed the explosive story of how CryptoAG, a world-leading developer in cryptology, was secretly used by US intelligence as a commercial front to limit the circulation of advanced cryptography and to supply suboptimal machines to target countries.[37] This arrangement arose from the close personal relationship between Boris Hagelin, owner of CryptoAG, and the NSA's William Friedman. By the 1950s a gentleman's agreement between Friedman and Hagelin limited the sale of the latter's machines, and over the 1960s this evolved, with CIA input, into a formal arrangement whereby US intelligence funded Hagelin's operations and manipulated his products so they remained vulnerable through hidden design flaws; it would later see the CIA and German intelligence jointly assume ownership of CryptoAG and recruit key staff to reassure customers about its technology.

The history of Operation Rubicon adds more context to GCHQ's position in late 1974. There are already scattered references to Britain's role in the NSA–Hagelin arrangement. Citing an internal CIA history of the program, "MINERVA: A History," Sarah Mainwaring mentions that it was GCHQ that originally persuaded senior NSA officials to back Friedman's bid for greater control of CryptoAG by stressing the advances in Hagelin's products by the mid-1950s.[38] An account of the NSA–CryptoAG relationship by the online Crypto Museum also states that GCHQ "had been briefed by the Americans, and the intelligence production was shared with them."[39] In light of this valuable arrangement, GCHQ confronted great risk from any historical revelations connecting Ultra to the predecessors of Hagelin teleciphers in the mid-1970s.[40] The references to Hagelin in GCHQ's correspondence do not specify which machines were of greatest value to SIGINT in this period; nor do they explain how this similarity in design aided exploitation—it may be that these legacy features were unrelated to NSA's manipulation of CryptoAG technology. However, what does seem clear is that British officials in 1974 were worried that publicizing Bletchley's success against wartime teleciphers could lead to greater scrutiny of CryptoAG and, presumably, its relationship with the NSA. This concern was particularly salient at a time when multiple governments were beginning to question the cryptologic strength of Hagelin's machines.[41]

There are other potential areas of connection between Operation Rubicon and British policy. In particular, the production of fully electronic Hagelin devices may also help to explain GCHQ's evolving assessment of the risk posed by declassifying the historical development of Colossus at Bletchley. Michael Herman and I have addressed elsewhere the shift in

Figure 8.4: Uniform patch of the Royal Navy's Coders (Specials), 1953–1966. The Coders (Special) were draftees trained briefly in cryptography and radio communications who undertook intensive Russian language training. They manned intercept stations in Berlin, Cyprus, Ceylon (today Sri Lanka), Singapore, and Hong Kong. Their intercepted messages were sent to GCHQ in the United Kingdom. From the Collection of H. Keith and Karen Melton at the International Spy Museum.

official thinking before Winterbotham's book once it was judged that the damage of revealing the Enigma secret had become "hypothetical."[42] However, as some in Whitehall feared, Winterbotham's book was promptly followed by other demands from well-connected experts to declassify more material about wartime codebreaking exploits. This led to pressure from political leaders for GCHQ to reconsider the possibility of revealing information about the Tunny machines and Colossus. A December 1974 GCHQ memo remarked that the head of its cryptanalytic division was leaning toward the view that "the similarities between WWII and present-day machines . . . will not be worked out by his main adversaries and are not all that important."[43] What informed this revised assessment is not available from the archival records, but it may be related to the availability of a new Hagelin device in 1973 on the market—the H-460—which substituted the remaining, World War II--vintage mechanical features of earlier ciphers with fully electronic components.[44]

## Enigma as an Opportunity

This sensitivity over Tunny and Hagelin suggests another possible explanation for the JIC's landmark decision in 1974. The JIC may have seen in the post-Winterbotham release of wartime service files an opportunity to divert attention away from Bletchley's computing efforts and its legacy connection with the targets of Operation Rubicon. As GCHQ veterans, Hooper and Bonsall likely saw in the mass release of screened Ultra records a useful way to maximize the focus on the history of Enigma, a topic of public interest that had already been stoked by Winterbotham. The outcome would capture the attention of researchers and journalists, obscuring the few threads of information about Fish that had made their way into the public domain. If so, this would have managed to use the immediate setbacks of 1974 for the long-term advantage of Western SIGINT and would explain why these two men—GCHQ leaders who were closely attuned to the liaison relationship with NSA and privy to Operation Rubicon—were more supportive of the sudden shift to transparency than their JIC colleagues.

There is no additional proof for this interpretation beyond the references Tunny and Hagelin cited above, but it would also account for the unbalanced accounts of Bletchley that developed in the following years and centered almost exclusively on Enigma. When the wartime intelligence files were eventually released in 1977, MoD screened them for any details of codebreaking methods, which had the effect of prohibiting knowledge about the Fish teleciphers or Colossus. Those Ultra files that were made available to the public offered valuable insights into military operations and kept historians engaged on these issues throughout the 1980s, but this also insulated Tunny from the boom in intelligence research. At the same time, the JIC and GCHQ continued to manage outsiders who had picked up details about Colossus as part of their Ultra research. Among these figures was David Kahn, and for a time the JIC waited anxiously when it discovered that he had been commissioned by the *New York Times* to review Winterbotham's book in December 1974. His review briefly mentioned the invention of Colossus but did not indicate what it was designed to do.[45] It would not be until 1984 that Fish, as a separate part of Ultra, was discussed in the second volume of Hinsley's Official History in a brief account listed in the appendix. At some point later in that decade the first Tunny decrypts were quietly released into the British national archives without eliciting much of a reaction.[46] The contrast with the large-scale, high-profile exposure of Enigma in the previous decade is striking.

For this approach to work, however, it required careful management of historical inquiries about wartime computing for several more years. Hooper continued to face pressure from Brian Randell, a computing academic who had picked up some vague references to early computing from Bletchley veterans in their technical writings and statements.[47] A compromise was eventually put forward by the JIC Secretariat: photos of Colossus would be released to the archives but with only the barest of accompanying information. GCHQ officials reasoned that Colossus could be revealed in the context of computing history but not intelligence or codebreaking.[48] With no details on hardware available, these photos would at least satisfy

Randell's demand for acknowledging scientific history without allowing others to deduce Colossus's function and targets by scrutinizing its hardware. This compromise was brokered in a meeting between Hooper and the academic Randell,[49] who appears to have pushed his luck by advising a computer exhibition in London, which disclosed more about Colossus than GCHQ had permitted, using the same material which Randell had found.[50] More revelations about Colossus followed in a 1978 BBC documentary, again with support from Randell and several veterans, including Winterbotham, but the details it provided about Colossus's target were incorrect, identifying the Siemens & Halske Sturgeon instead of the Tunny machines as its principal target. It was only by the early 1980s—in the age of digital encryption—when GCHQ began to allow some veterans to describe Colossus in greater detail.[51]

The events described above indicate that the secrecy surrounding Colossus was undoubtedly tied up with one of the most significant SIGINT exploits of the Cold War. It is impossible to say with certainty how this informed the JIC's thinking in September–October 1974. Taken together, however, the documentary insights into Operation Rubicon, the sensitivity of Tunny and Colossus in the mid-1970s, and the distorted understanding of Bletchley's history that developed from this time all point to another reason for the JIC's remarkable decision. At the very least this account should prompt intelligence historians to reexamine how state secrecy operates through the declassification of archival records. Postwar efforts to conceal the Ultra secret are well documented, but the efforts that followed Winterbotham's book are perhaps more sophisticated and deserving of greater scrutiny. If this account of the JIC's decision is accurate, it illustrates an effective tactic for intelligence agencies: releasing a flood of historical material designed to divert attention as much as to shine a light on past experience. While British secrecy was shaped by the rush of events in the mid-1970s, it does seem that GCHQ managed to influence this process to its benefit. The lesson should resonate with all intelligence historians, especially those of us surveying the imposing bulk of CIA and NSA records released in recent years: exceptional insights may be hidden in plain sight, buried in the details.

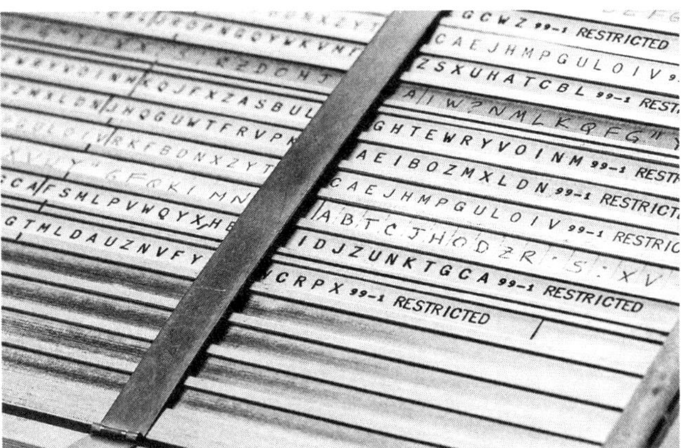


Figure 8.5: M-138-A cipher device, United States, 1940s. The US Army used this cheap and portable strip cipher system widely during World War II. It allowed soldiers to easily arrange alphabet strips to cipher and decipher medium-security messages. From the Collection of H. Keith and Karen Melton at the International Spy Museum.

## Further Reading

Copeland, Jack. "Colossus: Breaking the German 'Tunny' Code at Bletchley Park. An Illustrated History." *Rutherford Journal* 3 (2010). www.rutherfordjournal.org/article030109.html.

Crypto Museum. "Operation Rubicon: The Secret Purchase of Crypto AG by BND and CIA." www.cryptomuseum.com/intel/cia/rubicon.htm.

Moran, Chris. "The Pursuit of Intelligence History: Methods, Sources, and Trajectories in the United Kingdom." *Studies in Intelligence* 55, no. 2 (2011): 33–55. www.cia.gov/resources/csi/studies-in-intelligence/volume-55-no-2/the-pursuit-of-intelligence-history-methods-sources-and-trajectories-in-the-united-kingdom.

## Notes

1. John Cecil Masterman, *The Double Cross System in the War of 1939 to 1945* (New Haven, CT: Yale University Press, 1972); Frederick Winterbotham, *The Ultra Secret* (London: Weidenfeld and Nicolson, 1974). See also Chris Moran, "The Pursuit of Intelligence History: Methods, Sources, and Trajectories in the United Kingdom," *Studies in Intelligence* 55, no. 2 (2011): 33–55.

2. See, for example, Ronald Lewin, *Ultra Goes to War: The Secret Story* (London: Hutchinson, 1978); Ralph Bennett, *Ultra in the West: the Normandy Campaign of 1944–45* (London: Hutchinson, 1979); Peter Calvocoressi, *Top Secret Ultra* (London: Cassel, 1980).

3. In a departure from British usage, the volume editors are consistently rendering it as "SIGINT," not "Sigint."—Eds.

4. See chapter 2, "The Rush to Transparency: Releasing Wartime Codebreaking Secrets," in Michael Herman with David Schaefer, *Intelligence Power in Practice* (Edinburgh: Edinburgh University Press, 2002), 21–87.

5. Richard Aldrich, "Policing the Past: Official History, Secrecy and British Intelligence since 1945," *English Historical Review* 119, no. 483 (2004): 922–953; David Reynolds, "The Ultra Secret and Churchill's War Memoirs," *Intelligence and National Security* 20, no. 2 (2005): 209–224; Chris Moran, *Classified: Secrecy and the State in Modern Britain* (Cambridge: Cambridge University Press, 2013).

6. Both authors were eventually published. See Donald McLachlan, *Room 39: Naval Intelligence in Action 1939–45* (London: Weidenfeld & Nicolson, 1968), and Calvocoressi, *Top Secret Ultra*.

7. John Ferris, *Behind the Enigma: The Authorised History of GCHQ, Britain's Secret Cyber-Intelligence Agency* (London: Bloomsbury, 2020), 335–338.

8. Ferris, *Behind the Enigma*, 346–347.

9. "Secret Lost," *Time*, 17 December 1945.

10. JIC(66) 10th Meeting, "Disposal of Departmental Records," Confidential Annex, 10 March 1966, CAB 159/45, The National Archives UK (TNA).

11. JIC(A)(69) 23rd meeting, "The Release of Historical Intelligence Records," Confidential Annex, 12 June 1969, CAB 163/133, TNA.

12. Richard Aldrich, *GCHQ: The Uncensored Story of Britain's Most Secret Intelligence Agency* (London: Harper Press, 2010), 238–240.

13. David Kahn, *The Codebreakers: The Story of Secret Writing* (New York: Macmillan, 1967); Hooper to Richards (Secretary JIC), 13 October 1966, CAB 163/66, TNA.

14. James Bamford, *The Puzzle Palace: A Report on America's Most Secret Agency* (New York: Penguin, 1982), 127–130.

15. "Published material on the organisation of Intelligence in WWII," enclosed in Hooper to White, 27 May 1969, CAB 163/134, TNA.

16. Winterbotham to Masterman, 1 November 1971, WOR/PRO 10/1/130, Masterman Papers, Worcester College, Oxford. This first, revised book was *Secret and Personal* (London: Kimber, 1969).

17. Winterbotham to Farnhill, 2 February 1973, enclosed in INT 37 (73) 3, "Publications: Winterbotham," Annex, 26 February 1973, CAB 190/53, TNA.

18. JIC(A) (74) 12th Meeting, "Books on Intelligence: Book by Winterbotham," Confidential Annex, 21 March 1974, CAB 185/15, TNA. For a more detailed examination of Winterbotham's motives see Herman with Schaefer, "The Rush to Transparency: British Releases on Wartime Codebreaking."

19. "Proposed New Guidelines on World War II Intelligence Matters," enclosed in INT 46 (74) 5, "Note by the Intelligence Coordinator," 24 June 1974, CAB 190/74, TNA.

20. Perhaps this view reflected the limited interest in earlier publications by French cryptanalysts that revealed the earlier Allied success against the Enigma before 1940. These were Michel Garder, *La Guerre Secrète des Services Spéciaux français* (Paris: Librairie Plon, 1967), and Gustave Bertrand, *Enigma; ou, La plus grand énigme de la guerre, 1939–1945* (Paris: Librairie Plon, 1973).

21. "JIC Recommendations on Release of Intelligence Records and the Official History of Intelligence in World War II," enclosed in Hooper to White, 18 July 1975, CAB 163/255, TNA.

22. Hunt to Wilson, 5 July 1974, PREM 16/670, TNA.

23. Hooper to White, 18 July 1975, CAB 103/726, TNA.

24. Herman with Schaefer, "The Rush to Transparency."

25. "Note for the Record: The Intelligence History and the Release of Intelligence Related Records," 23 September 1976, CAB 103/726, TNA.

26. Hooper to Sykes, 23 February 1977, CAB 163/256, TNA.

27. Calvocoressi, *Top Secret Ultra*; Bennett, *Ultra in the West*; Patrick Beesly, *Very Special Intelligence: The Story of the Admiralty's Operational Intelligence Centre, 1939–1945* (London: Hamilton, 1977); and Gordon Welchman, *The Hut Six Story: Breaking the Enigma Codes* (New York: McGraw-Hill, 1982).

28. This is JIC(74) (SEC) 134, mentioned in JIC(A) (74) 45th meeting, 10 October 1974, CAB 185/15, TNA.

29. "JIC Recommendations on Release of Intelligence Records and the Official History of Intelligence in World War II," n.d., CAB 103/726, TNA.

30. Wilson to Stainton, 25 November 1975, PREM 16/1290, TNA.

31. Hunt to Wilson, 15 November 1974, PREM 16/670, TNA.

32. JIC(74) 48th meeting, 24 October 1974, CAB 185/15, TNA.

33. "Early Computers," 6 April 1976, CAB 163/247, TNA.

34. Nicoll to Chamberlain, 17 May 1972, CAB 163/230, TNA.

35. Memo by Hooper, "Unofficial Publications about Wartime Sigint," 9 August 1973, CAB 163/247, TNA.

36. "Early British Electronic Computers" enclosed in minute by A/Sec.B, 27 November 1974, CAB 163/230, TNA.

37. Greg Miller, "Intelligence Coup of the Century," *Washington Post*, 11 February 2020.

38. Sarah Mainwaring, "Division D: Operation Rubicon and the CIA's Secret SIGINT Empire," *Intelligence and National Security* 35, no. 3 (2020): 627.

39. Crypto Museum, "Operation Rubicon: The Secret Purchase of Crypto AG by BND and CIA," *Crypto Museum*, www.cryptomuseum.com/intel/cia/rubicon.htm, accessed 15 January 2021.

40. For a broad overview of Operation Rubicon's sensitivity, see Jason Dymydiuk, "Rubicon and Revelation: The Curious Robustness of the 'Secret' CIA-BND Operation with Crypto AG," *Intelligence and National Security* 35, no. 3 (2020): 641–658.

41. Crypto Museum, "Operation Rubicon."

42. Herman with Schaefer, "The Rush to Transparency."

43. Goodall to Bonsall, 4 December 1974, CAB 163/230, TNA.

44. Crypto Museum, "Operation Rubicon."

45. INT 37(75) 1, "US Press Review of Winterbotham's Book," 8 January 1975, CAB 190/84, TNA.

46. Francis Hinsley et al., *British Intelligence in the Second World War*, vol. 3, part 1 (London: HMSO, 1984), 477–482.

47. Brian Randell, "A Turing Enigma," *23rd International Conference on Concurrency Theory* (2012): 24–28.

48. Stinchcombe to Herman, 21 January 1975, CAB 163/230, TNA.

49. Hooper to Brearley, 14 May 1975, CAB 163/230, TNA.

50. Kirkland to Bonsall, 17 December 1975, CAB 163/230, TNA. At this same exhibit Tommy Flowers, the designer of Colossus, was also overheard by GCHQ officials talking about the computer and referring to some publications by his wartime colleagues on Colossus; see "Opening of Science Museum Exhibition of Computing Then and Now," 17 December 1975, CAB 162/230, TNA.

51. Tommy Flowers, "The Design of Colossus," *Annals of the History of Computing* 5 (1983): 239–252.

# Ann Caracristi: The Making of a Codebreaker

David Sherman

*The National Security Agency is the signals intelligence agency of the United States. One of the NSA's most legendary leaders was Ann Caracristi, who started her career in American codebreaking during World War II and ended it as deputy director of the agency. Here David Sherman introduces us to her life and her contributions to signals intelligence.*
*—The Editors*

In 1948, the pioneering American codebreaker William Friedman reflected on the changes he had witnessed over his three decades as a government cryptanalyst. Historically, Friedman told a group of individuals just starting out in the field that science tended to advance slowly, with knowledge accumulating in small increments. Even allowing for the overall acceleration of scientific breakthroughs during the twentieth century, however, the progress made in cryptanalysis had been exceptional. "It is rather unusual for a man to see," Friedman told his audience, "in his own short life span, so remarkable and so large an advancement as has occurred in the period from 1918 to 1948."[1] Elsewhere, Friedman spoke of codebreaking and the more general field of signals intelligence as having become "big business." The popular image of a codebreaker as a bespectacled intellectual poring over pages and pages of messages for hours until the streams of random numbers or letters made sense had yielded, Friedman observed, to a world of "electronic brains, high-speed machinery, and digital computers."[2]

Friedman's observations were based on personal experience. Throughout the 1920s, after the United States Army demobilized the relatively modest cryptanalytic organizations it had built for World War I, he had labored largely alone in his small War Department office, as did his wife and fellow codebreaker, Elizebeth, at Treasury and the Coast Guard. During the decade of the Great Depression that followed, and despite a scarcity of funding, he was able to hire a handful of apprentice codebreakers. They would be joined by thousands of raw recruits during World War II. While Friedman had overseen a transition from the manual, pencil-and-paper process for deciphering coded foreign communications to one increasingly aided by codebreaking machines, these individuals at first struggled with

Figure 9.1: Legendary codebreakers William and Elizebeth Friedman. William led the War Department's codebreaking efforts in the 1930s and continued in the business through World War II and then into the Cold War with the National Security Agency. In 1942, Ann Caracristi joined the organization he had founded. Elizebeth broke codes for the US Coast Guard and US Navy, among other agencies.

how to integrate such machines into the cryptanalytic process and then sought to harness the increasingly powerful capabilities created by the arrival of computers in the late 1940s.

One of the individuals who participated in these later developments was Ann Caracristi, who after graduating from college in mid-1942 was hired by the Signal Intelligence Service (SIS), the codebreaking organization that Friedman had created for the War Department. Over the next three years, she and what ultimately came to be 10,000 colleagues, many of them women, broke every significant code used by America's Japanese adversaries. Caracristi would stay on after World War II ended and, in 1952, joined the ranks of the newly formed National Security Agency (NSA). She would be decorated by two presidents, achieve the distinction of being one of the first women in the Department of Defense to enter the elite Senior Executive Service, and ultimately become NSA's first female deputy director, its highest-ranking civilian. After retiring in 1982 she was named to a series of blue-ribbon panels studying ways to improve America's security.

Caracristi's career thus followed an arc from a novice World War II codebreaker to a leader of all codebreaking efforts in the United States during the Cold War and a presidential adviser thereafter. Her life was emblematic of the rise of American intelligence to a position of global preeminence. Her reflections on her experiences provide us with a bird's-eye narrative and assessment of this process. Her role as the most senior of only a few women to follow such a career path during her lifetime made her perspectives in many ways unique.

For three decades after World War II, largely due to ongoing secrecy, little was written about the role of codebreaking in that conflict. Two notable exceptions were Roberta Wohlstetter's *Pearl Harbor: Warning and Decision* and several chapters in David Kahn's *The Codebreakers*, but neither book focused on the work of the individuals involved, perhaps in part because their identities remained secret.[3] Public awareness of the importance of codebreaking increased dramatically in the 1970s after the British government revealed the existence of Bletchley Park and its breaking of Germany's supposedly invulnerable Enigma machine, which was a cypher device used during World War II. Even then, however, women's role in wartime cryptanalysis remained hidden, largely because the individuals who penned memoirs or otherwise discussed their work at Bletchley and its American counterparts were almost exclusively male. Recently, with the publication of works such as Liza Mundy's *Code Girls* and Jason Fagone's *The Woman Who Smashed Codes*, the silence about the crucial role of American women in codebreaking has been broken.[4] Caracristi's story offers an opportunity to replace that silence with a more fulsome understanding. It also allows us a glimpse at how women continued to play an equally critical role in codebreaking during the Cold War, a subject where much work remains to be done.

Ann Zielinger Caracristi was born on February 1, 1921, in Bronxville, New York, a village a few dozen miles north of Midtown Manhattan. Her parents had moved there a few years earlier as part of a wave of upper-middle-class professionals seeking a suburban lifestyle. Caracristi's childhood appears to have been typical for the time and place. One of her earliest memories was of a visit to New York's Natural History Museum. She later recalled her fascination with the mummy cases displayed in a room of Egyptian antiquities. "Little could I have known," she said, "that I would spend a career involved with the modern-day equivalent of hieroglyphs."[5]

In the fall of 1938, Caracristi enrolled at Russell Sage, a women's college in upstate New York. Her arrival coincided with the European crises triggered by Adolf Hitler's ambition to bring Czechoslovakia within the Nazi orbit. By the time Caracristi began her sophomore year twelve months later, Germany's invasion of Poland had prompted Great Britain and France to declare war. Caracristi's decision to join the staff of Russell

Sage's student newspaper exposed her to discussions among students and faculty on Europe's descent into another war. During her four years with the paper, she moved from being a reporter to managing editor before being named editor-in-chief in February 1941. Caracristi also edited the campus literary journal and published four short stories in it. Graduating with honors in June 1942, she was one of only nine who received the college's Keystone Award, given "to those members of the senior class who have made outstanding contributions to their class and the College."[6] Caracristi may have seemed assured of a promising career in journalism, but world events would lead her in a different direction.

Caracristi heard the news of the December 7, 1941, Japanese attack on Pearl Harbor while listening to the radio in the common room of her dormitory that morning. Three months later, a Russell Sage administration member, Bernice Smith, attended a two-day conference in Washington, DC, on the government's need for civilians willing to support the war effort. Smith met with officers from the Signal Corps, which handled the army's communications and was the parent organization of the War Department's secret codebreaking unit, the SIS. They offered positions that could be filled by a few graduating seniors of her choosing. It is hard to say how much the Signal Corps told Smith about what these young women would be doing, but it seems unlikely that she would have learned anything about the SIS or its codebreaking effort.

Several weeks later, Russell Sage's dean, Doris Crockett, received a letter from the War Department requesting her nominees for government service. As Caracristi later recalled, Dean Crockett "nominated me and two other people, who were friends of mine."[7] The Signal Corps accepted all three without interviewing them. It also sent some training materials on codebreaking for them to review. While Caracristi later said that "being rather busy trying to graduate, I'm not sure I paid much attention to these," simply paging through them would have given her some idea of what her assignment would involve. Given the positions typically offered to young women graduating from college in midcentury America, which almost invariably were limited to teaching, nursing, or secretarial work if they did not immediately marry, Caracristi and her two classmates—Florence Woolsey and Kathryn Anderson—were probably excited by the prospect of working in Washington for a mysterious and secretive organization supporting the war effort.[8] Caracristi left for the nation's capital by train a week after graduation and reported to the SIS, located on Constitution Avenue in the Munitions Building, which then housed the War Department. One of the first things she did was sign a form swearing her to secrecy.

In June 1942, Caracristi was placed in a training course in cryptanalysis held in a borrowed classroom at George Washington University, a few blocks west of the White House. It was led by Evelyn Akeley, a former professor of mathematics from Skidmore College. Caracristi and 20 fellow classmates soon realized the amount of improvisation in the SIS's crash program to build its wartime capabilities. "We all learned," she recalled, "that she [Akeley] was exactly one lesson ahead of the rest of us. So we were all in it together."[9] The pressure on the SIS to put its new recruits to work and start cracking enemy codes meant that Caracristi had completed only half her training course when she was transferred to an operational position. There was just one difficulty. "I was assigned to the Japanese problem," she told an interviewer in 1982, "and I remember being astounded that anyone could assume that it was possible to work against these communications if you didn't know anything about Japanese." "Don't worry," she was told. "You'll learn."[10]

The woman who was Caracristi's supervisor for much of the war, Wilma Berryman, saw much of the same potential in her that her Russell Sage professors and classmates had already noted. "She was a very blond, blue-eyed, sort of pudgy little girl," Berryman recalled. "She had on bobby socks [women's ankle-length socks that were fashionable in the 1940s], and flat shoes, and a swinging skirt. She wore a pullover a lot of the time. Her hair, which was naturally curly, was all over her head." Still, Berryman noticed something else about this "bobby soxer." "She was an English major, but when she sat down and started to work, it was just obvious that she had an engineer's mind. It was the most fascinating thing."[11]

The end of Caracristi's training in July 1942 coincided with the SIS moving out of the Munitions Building. The organization's leadership had realized that its already crowded offices would become more so as recruits finished training. Accordingly, a search for a new facility began. The SIS leadership settled on Arlington Hall, a financially struggling women's college in northern Virginia. The army purchased the property in mid-June. The SIS was renamed the Signal Security Agency (SSA) and moved in a month later. Arlington Hall was a large building with offices and classrooms on its lower two floors and a dormitory on the upper two. Caracristi ended up on the top floor. It got so hot that summer that some employees suffered from dehydration. As there was no cafeteria when the SSA moved in, Caracristi and her coworkers had to bring their food from home, order a box lunch the day before, or walk across the street to a drugstore with a small lunch counter.

Despite the move, space remained so tight that intercepted Japanese communications were stored in closets and, since the water in the building had been cut off while renovations were underway, in the bathtubs on

Figure 9.2: Ann Caracristi (right) at work at Arlington Hall Station during World War II.

the dormitory floors. The SSA's codebreaking machines were so heavy that they raised concerns about the building's structural integrity. Unsurprisingly, a few weeks afterward, bulldozers began excavating a site nearby for two large office buildings. Less than two months later, the first of these was ready for Caracristi and others to move in.

Asked years later by the historian David Kahn what a camera would have seen if it had recorded Caracristi during a typical day, she replied "me, a cup of coffee, pencil and paper, and stacks of IBM runs, and [my] pencil going across the paper" as she searched for patterns in the seemingly random sets of letters and numbers in encrypted Japanese messages that might offer some clue as to how to break them. She considered herself lucky when she eventually got her own desk, as many of her coworkers sat together around long tables. At first, like virtually everyone else, she worked in one of three round-the-clock shifts. Later, Caracristi's work settled into a routine that began around 8:00 a.m. and went until 6:00 in the evening. "I found the work exhilarating," she later said. "It was like doing crossword puzzles every day and getting most of the answers."[12] Even with the inevitable humor that went with working in a large organization, Caracristi and her thousands of Arlington Hall coworkers were fully aware that there was a war on. She typically stayed until she had finished whatever she was working on, not wanting to leave it for someone on the night shift. For Wilma Berryman, one day epitomized the determination everyone in the codebreaking effort brought to the job. "I remember the day that we had a very heavy snow and the buses didn't run and nothing else ran. Everyone came to work. They walked."[13]

When Caracristi started work at Arlington Hall in July 1942, she was assigned to a section attacking the encrypted communications of the Imperial Japanese Army. Prior to Pearl Harbor, American codebreakers had paid scant attention to these codes. Instead, they focused on attacking systems used by Japan's navy and diplomats, deemed more important to understanding Tokyo's intentions with respect to peace or war.

The Japanese Army Codes Section that Caracristi joined had been in existence for only three months. It had 25 staff, all housed on the hot fourth floor of Arlington Hall's main building. That number grew to 51 military personnel and 15 civilians by the end of the year. By the end of the war in August 1945, it would be over 1,500. The number of intercepted messages flowing into Arlington Hall was rising even faster. Initially, all Japanese army intercepts were brought to Arlington Hall by couriers from American sites monitoring Japanese communications. Roughly 12,000 such messages came in every month during the first half of 1942. With the installation of a secure teletype machine at Arlington Hall and the opening of a major intercept facility in California, the number arriving rose sharply, reaching 55,000 per month by the beginning of 1943. Within a few months, that figure doubled.

At first, the most that the small staff in Caracristi's Japanese Army Codes Section generally was able to do was sort and file the hundreds of messages coming in each day. As a new recruit, Caracristi was assigned to the Traffic Handling Team for this specific purpose. She recalled her first few months as being "pretty clerical." Not surprisingly, given the number of people and papers arriving at Arlington Hall, the process was disorganized. "The wheel was probably invented at least twice and maybe more times," she recalled years later, "but it was being reinvented because we took aboard hundreds of people in a very short order and there wasn't much capability to train people. I mean, they were just plunged into doing the job. So there was certainly opportunity for ineptness." At the same time, this meant there were opportunities for creative individuals to rapidly improve the way Arlington Hall was conducting its business. As Caracristi put it: "Whoever had a smart idea was able to revolutionize the process."[14]

The individual given the task of managing the rising numbers of recruits and the increasing volumes of intercepted messages arriving daily was Solomon Kullback. Recruited by William Friedman in 1930, Kullback was one of Arlington Hall's most experienced cryptanalysts. No one else assigned to the Japanese Army Codes Section had anywhere near his level of expertise; only a handful had more than a few months on the job. None could have taken on the complex task of breaking Japanese army codes alone. Accordingly, Kullback recalled, "the job had to be broken down into simple tasks" so that new recruits like Caracristi "could just grind it out."[15]

And grind it out is exactly what Caracristi and her colleagues did. "Our assembly line routine," she said, "was sort, edit, punch." Caracristi and her colleagues first divided incoming intercepts into stacks that they thought were related in some way. They then "edited" the intercepts, or prepared them for another group—almost exclusively women—who operated machines that punched holes corresponding to the four-digit number groups in each intercept onto thick paper cards. These were fed through tabulating machines programmed to find patterns in the intercepts' streams of numbers that might offer clues on how to break them. It was tedious work. However, it also was all being done for the first time, and that offered additional opportunities to innovate.

Kullback allowed recruits who had gained some on-the-job experience to move on to more complicated tasks. Accordingly, in late 1942 Caracristi began working for Wilma Berryman in the Address Systems Section. Caracristi remained there for most of the war. As it grew in size, she became a supervisor in her own right when she was named to head its research effort. She described her job as "essentially doing the initial break-in of, and research on, some of the systems that hadn't been broken."[16] As one part of the "assembly line" process that Kullback had designed for Arlington Hall, the Address Systems Section had the task of breaking the encryption that the Japanese army used to protect the four-digit call signs that corresponded to the Japanese army units sending and receiving specific messages. Doing so provided valuable intelligence on the roles of Japanese army units throughout the Pacific. For instance, if one unit sent higher volumes of messages than others, it likely was a headquarters and the units receiving these messages probably were subordinate to that headquarters. Should the number of messages being sent back and forth between them rise suddenly, it might indicate that the Japanese were planning an offensive. Mapping these radio networks also might give American commanders an idea of where Japanese army units were located. Obtaining detailed intelligence that could be used in combat, however, required Arlington Hall to break through the more complex, multilayered encryption system protecting the actual content of Japanese messages.

In a series of offensives launched following the December 1941 attack on Pearl Harbor, Tokyo's army and navy had seized much of the Western

Pacific. Their conquests included the Dutch East Indies (modern-day Indonesia), the British colonies of Singapore, Malaya, and Burma, and the American-administered Philippines. Simultaneously, Japanese forces had occupied a series of island chains stretching from the Central Pacific to the northern approaches to Australia. The broad geographic distribution of their conquests created two vulnerabilities that Tokyo had to prevent the United States from exploiting. These were the shipping lanes north from the Dutch East Indies that carried vital supplies of oil and raw materials to the Japanese home islands, in addition to the supply routes from Japan to the troops guarding the island chains in the Central and South Pacific that served as Tokyo's first line of defense against America's rapidly expanding military might.

The arm of the Japanese military responsible for moving supplies and men across Tokyo's now far-flung empire was the army's Water Transport Command. Six weeks before the attack on Pearl Harbor, the Japanese army estimated that it would need to sustain three million tons of capacity in this supply fleet to maintain its ability to wage war. If the United States Navy was able to sink enough ships to drive available tonnage below that level, a Japanese senior logistics officer opined that "it would be questionable whether our national power could be maintained."[17] American military commanders in Hawaii soon reached the same conclusion: if they could sever Tokyo's supply lines to its forces occupying the ring of islands protecting Japan's newly conquered empire, these islands could, in the words of General Douglas MacArthur, be left to "wither on the vine," thereby sparing US troops from the need to capture them through costly amphibious assaults. Finding and sinking Japanese supply ships thus became a critical part of the American strategy—and codebreaking proved an essential element in finding them.

By the end of 1942, the long hours that Caracristi and her Arlington Hall colleagues had put in sorting traffic were enough for them to have learned how to organize Japanese army messages by the code systems used to encrypt them, as all the messages sent using a specific system had a unique four-digit number at their beginning. One of these common four-digit numbers was 2468, which Arlington Hall identified as being used for coded messages sent by the Water Transport Command. The 2468 number group, which was not encrypted but sent "in the clear," indicated which of several different codebooks the Japanese code clerk sending a message had used to encrypt it so that the receiving clerk would know which book to consult in order to decrypt it. Knowing which specific code system a set of Japanese messages used was a critical first step toward deciphering them. Having enough messages in a specific code system was the next, as by comparing them a cryptanalyst at Arlington Hall might be able to discern otherwise invisible patterns that could lead to clues in how to decode them. Once such patterns had been found, a cryptanalyst might be able to develop a solution powerful enough to decode not only a single message but also every message sent over a longer period of time, then translated from Japanese into English and sent to American commanders quickly enough to be useful in combat.

The Japanese realized that the Americans eventually would be able to reconstruct and break the 2468 codebook, containing four-digit numerical substitutes for individual words used by the Japanese army, if Arlington Hall intercepted enough messages and found four-digit groups that appeared frequently—and thus represented more commonly used words—or were repeated at the beginnings or ends of messages and represented words commonly used at the openings or closings of military orders. Accordingly, Tokyo's cryptographers added a second level of encryption known as a "substitution square," a 10-by-10 matrix whose rows and columns were designated by numbers from 0 to 9. Japanese code clerks used numbers at the intersections of the rows and columns in the square to further encipher each digit in four-digit numerical code groups drawn from the 2468 codebook, thus "superenciphering" their messages.

By the first months of 1943, Caracristi and her research team realized that the Japanese were using a substitution square to encrypt the addresses in the 2468 messages. By early April, they thought they had succeeded in breaking it. They consulted British and Australian experts in the Pacific, who confirmed their results. This achievement made the underlying code groups in 2468 messages visible. These were then quickly broken. After months of failure in their efforts to penetrate any Japanese army encryption system, the sense of triumph at Arlington Hall was palpable. Two months later, in early June 1943, it produced its first translations of decrypted Water Transport Command messages. The number of decrypts rose rapidly over the next few months as more personnel we assigned to exploit the now readable 2468 system. By the fall, Arlington Hall was providing full translations or summaries of over 6,000 messages sent by the Japanese Water Transport Command every month.

Many of the decrypted Japanese messages produced by Arlington Hall contained schedules for upcoming convoys, including their routes and the times they were expected to reach specific locations. These were forwarded to the commanders of the US Pacific Fleet in Hawaii. If a decrypt showed a Japanese convoy passing close to an American submarine, the latter was ordered to intercept it. US submarine commanders became so reliant on the decrypts to find targets that they would complain to

Hawaii if the Japanese ships did not arrive at their anticipated location on schedule.

The breakthrough into the Water Transport Code that Caracristi and her colleagues achieved had a dramatic impact on the war. The top commander of American submarines in the Pacific from 1943 to 1945, Admiral Charles Lockwood, estimated that "codebreaking stepped up our sinkings a lot—probably 1/3 more."[18] Summing up the impact of America's submarine offensive, Ronald Spector joined other historians in finding it "one of the decisive elements in ensuring the empire's [Japan's] defeat. A force comprising less than 2 percent of U.S. Navy personnel accounted for 55 percent of Japan's losses at sea."[19]

The US Navy's growing success against the Japanese merchant fleet raised morale at Arlington Hall. Following months of frustration, the codebreakers finally were providing intelligence that American forces could act on. "The product we were putting out," Caracristi said later, "was allowing the Navy to know the location of merchant marine ships and to send out submarines and aircraft to dispose of them. And it made a big difference in the winning of the war in the Pacific."[20]

Other successes followed the breaking of the Water Transport Code. Several months later, in September 1943, Arlington Hall solved the cipher used by Japanese military attachés worldwide. While this did not provide the type of tactical intelligence offered by Water Transport Code decrypts, it did offer insight into how Tokyo sized up the situation in the various war zones. Similar achievements came over the next two years. Asked in 1982 how successful Arlington Hall had been against Japanese codes during the war, Solomon Kullback gave a one-word response: "Completely."[21] Eventually, he noted, the constraint on the amount of intelligence that Arlington Hall could produce was the number of linguists fluent enough in Japanese to translate the daily flood of decrypts.

Despite these successes, advancing American forces sustained mounting casualties as they landed on one Japanese-held island after another. Then, in early August 1945, the United States dropped atomic bombs on Hiroshima and Nagasaki, leading Tokyo to sue for peace. From messages they had decrypted the day before President Harry Truman announced Japan's capitulation, Caracristi and nearly everyone else at Arlington Hall knew the war was about to end. Its commander, Brigadier General Preston Corderman, considered locking the gates and severing the phone lines to keep the news from getting out and creating the suspicion that Tokyo's codes had been compromised. In the end, such drastic steps proved unnecessary. "No word leaked out of anyone in SSA, where practically everybody knew," Kullback recalled proudly. "Nobody, nobody outside the people in the Agency had any inkling about what happened until Truman got on the radio and made the announcement."[22] Finally, Caracristi went with everyone else at Arlington Hall to downtown Washington to join in the celebrations there.

With the end of the war, virtually all of the women who had joined Arlington Hall since the start of the war—like most of the men—returned to civilian life. Some of the relatively few women who had had careers before the war resumed them; others embarked upon new ones. Many married and started families. A handful, such as Caracristi's supervisor Wilma Berryman, were asked to stay on so that America had at least some postwar codebreaking expertise. As for Caracristi, she took up her life where she had left it upon graduating from Russell Sage three years earlier. She went to New York and got an entry-level position working for a newspaper. Caracristi, however, had been permanently changed by her wartime work. Soon, she "found that working in a regular job, even though perhaps I would have thought that it would be interesting, paled by comparison to working in the cryptologic business." About a year later, with the wartime alliance between the United States and the Soviet Union fraying and the Cold War an increasing reality, Caracristi got a letter from Arlington Hall asking if she would like to come back. One suspects that she did not even have to think about it. As she said to an interviewer years later: "I took the bait."[23]

Having returned to Arlington Hall, Caracristi stayed for 36 years as it evolved into today's NSA. While most of her work during this period remains classified, the extent of her contributions can be gauged by the recognition she received. She rose rapidly through the management ranks during the 1950s. In 1965, her accomplishments received their first national recognition when she was one of six women selected to receive the Federal Woman's Award from President Lyndon Johnson in honor of their "outstanding contributions to the efficiency and quality of the career service of the Federal Government."[24] Caracristi moved into the top leadership of the NSA in the 1970s. In 1975, she became the first woman at the agency to attain the highest rank in the career Civil Service. Five years later, she was named NSA's deputy director, the top civilian at the agency, a position she held until her retirement in 1982.[25] Asked a few weeks before she retired whether she missed being a cryptanalyst, she responded: "Yes, in some ways. But there are so many bright people here, so many who are so much more capable than I am or was, that I knew the job was in very good hands."[26] Upon Caracristi's retirement, President Ronald Reagan awarded her the National Security Medal, the highest award given to a civilian working in intelligence.

Caracristi's days as a public servant did not end with her retirement.

THE NATIONAL SECURITY AGENCY

NEWSLETTER

VOLUME XIII NO. 3 FORT GEORGE G. MEADE, MARYLAND March, 1965

FEDERAL WOMAN OF THE YEAR AWARD

Ann Z. Caracristi

Figure 9.3: In-house National Security Agency newsletter for March 1965, reporting on an award given to Ann Caracristi.

In 1993, President Bill Clinton appointed her to his President's Foreign Intelligence Advisory Board (PFIAB). She remained a member for most of his administration. She also came to view her career from the standpoint of the opportunities and obstacles that existed for women in public service. World War II, she believed, allowed thousands of women to enter the workforce at a time when most professions were closed to them. Many may have been motivated, as Caracristi was, by patriotism, but the salaries offered by Arlington Hall at the time were an incentive to others accustomed to the low wages. Leaders like Solomon Kullback, moreover, "didn't hesitate to put women in charge."[27]

Caracristi proved her exceptional talent as a codebreaker in World War II and in her first decade with NSA after the war, but from her undergraduate days at Russell Sage through her tenure as NSA's deputy director in the early 1980s she demonstrated an equally formidable talent as a leader of

Figure 9.4: Belt buckle from the uniform of a crewmember of the *Hughes Glomar Explorer*. The eccentric billionaire Howard Hughes promulgated the cover story that it would mine manganese nodules off the seafloor. Actually, the CIA used it in a partially successful 1974 effort to recover a sunken Soviet submarine. The CIA hoped, among other things, to find cryptographic materials that NSA could exploit. From the Collection of H. Keith and Karen Melton at the International Spy Museum.

ever larger numbers of women and men. In terms of her gender, however, she remained a rare exception. A PFIAB report on the role of women in the intelligence community that she coauthored for President Clinton in 1995 concluded that American intelligence had failed to "take full advantage of the best available talent from the entire workforce, not just a segment of white males," and that "limitations on the progress women have made have been so apparent that it would seem they could only have resulted from discrimination or a biased environment."[28] As evidence, the report noted that, while women made up almost 40 percent of the NSA's workforce, they held only 8 percent of senior executive positions (the proportions at the Central Intelligence Agency and the Defense Intelligence Agency were similar). Elsewhere, Caracristi would wonder whether having been the first woman deputy director at NSA she also might turn out to be the last.[29] She was not; another would follow in 1997. Years later, while one might marvel at the gains made by women during the intervening years, one also might with equal justice ask whether Caracristi would note just how much more work remains to be done.

In the years immediately following the war, women at Arlington Hall could not attain the higher ranks offered to their male counterparts. After NSA was established in 1952, however, its first director, Lieutenant General

Ralph Canine, US Army, insisted they be allowed to compete for promotion to more senior grades. Caracristi admitted that she benefited from Canine's policy. "Three women—and I was one of them—seem to have been identified as the NSA 'showcase,'" she later said. "Each of us," she recalled, "in our own way tried to establish ourselves as individuals and professionals *first*—women in NSA, *second*."[30] Nevertheless, throughout the 1960s and 1970s women remained shut out of some NSA management positions, particularly more senior ones. Speaking in 1991, Caracristi noted that, "unfortunately, the world still thinks of women in the workplace in ways that set up boundaries. We are *women* executives, *women* lawyers, *women* in CIA or NSA. The emphasis on gender frequently became a subtle way to de-emphasize professional accomplishment."[31]

Ann Caracristi died on January 10, 2016. She was 94. Her obituary in the *Washington Post* said she was a woman who didn't just crack codes but cracked glass ceilings as well.[32] For all of the challenges the world has confronted since the end of World War II, what Caracristi and her Arlington Hall colleagues accomplished made it a better place. Without their work, World War II could well have ground on for longer than it did and at a time when casualty rates among combatants and civilians were rising.

The ranks of those who served at Arlington Hall have thinned to where there are only a handful of Caracristi's fellow World War II codebreakers left. She probably would have said that each should have an equal if not greater share of any praise contained in the laudatory obituaries that appeared after her death. But she might have allowed herself a brief moment of understandable pride at one point during a talk that she and Solomon Kullback gave to a group of NSA senior officials long after the war had ended. Someone in the audience asked Kullback how good a cryptanalyst Caracristi was during the war. Kullback answered the question by retelling an anecdote from during the war. At one point, he recalled, he had asked an Arlington Hall colleague: "If you were stranded on a desert island with a coded message containing instructions on how to escape and had to rely on only one person to break it, who that would be?" Kullback's fellow codebreaker responded immediately: "Ann Caracristi."[33]

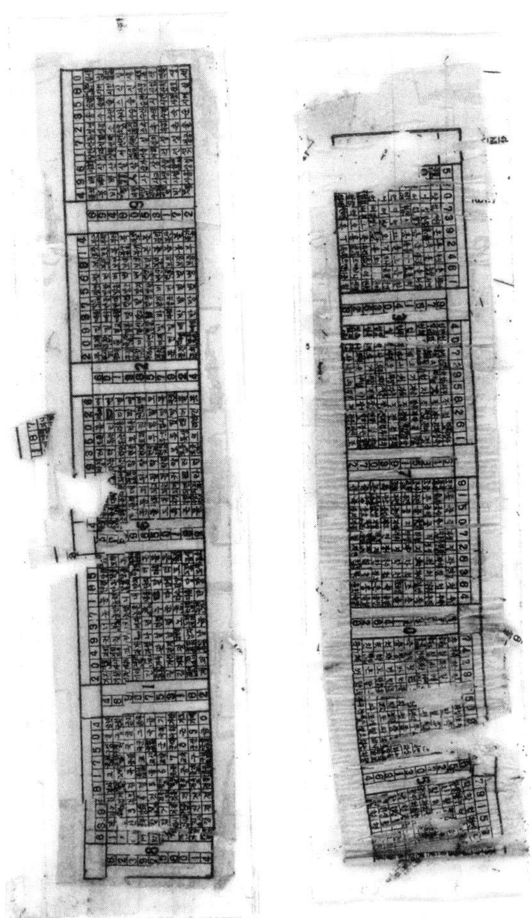

Figure 9.5: Cipher tables issued to a North Korean spy intended to be used to encrypt covert messages back to the North Korean intelligence service. South Korean authorities found and arrested the spy in 2011. Courtesy of the Embassy of the Republic of Korea.

## Further Reading

Budiansky, Stephen. *Battle of Wits: The Complete Story of Codebreaking in World War II*. New York: Free Press, 2000.

Mundy, Liza. *Code Girls: The Untold Story of the Women Code Breakers of World War II*. New York: Hachette, 2018.

Sherman, David. *Ann's War: One Woman's Journey to the Codebreaking Victory over Japan*. Fort George G. Meade, MD: National Security Agency, Center for Cryptologic History, 2019.

Smoot, Betsy Rohaly, and David Hatch. "To Command or Direct? DIRNSAs and the Historical Challenge of Leading the National Security Agency, 1952–2014." In *Intelligence Leaders in the United States and the United Kingdom*, vol. 1 of *Spy Chiefs*, ed. Christopher Moran et al., 157–182. Washington, DC: Georgetown University Press, 2018.

## Notes

1. William F. Friedman, Speech to the Army Security Agency Officer General Course, May 7, 1948. William F. Friedman Collection of Official Papers, National Security Agency, Fort George G. Mead MD, Document A41448559, www.nsa.gov/Portals/70/documents/news-features/declassified-documents/friedman-documents/lectures-speeches/FOLDER_536/41772129081121.pdf, accessed August 31, 2022.

2. William F. Friedman, Remarks on Communications Intelligence and Security to the Marine Corps School, April 2, 1960, 20. Friedman Collection/Audio Recording/Transcripts, www.nsa.gov/Portals/70/documents/resources/everyone/digital-media-center/video-audio/historical-audio/friedman-audio/Communication_Intelligence_Security_26_Apr_1960_LtCol_W_F_Friedman_Transcript.pdf, accessed August 31, 2022.

3. Roberta Wohlstetter, *Pearl Harbor: Warning and Decision* (Stanford: Stanford University Press, 1962); David Kahn, *The Codebreakers* (New York: Macmillan, 1967).

4. Liza Mundy, *Code Girls: The Untold Story of the American Women Code Breakers of World War II* (New York: Hachette, 2017); Jason Fagone, *The Woman Who Smashed Codes: A True Story of Love, Spies, and the Unlikely Heroine Who Outwitted America's Enemies* (New York: William Morrow, 2017).

5. Ann Caracrisiti, "Women in Cryptology," Ann Zeilinger Caracristi Papers, National Cryptologic Museum (hereafter AZCP/NCM), Fort George G. Meade, MD, folder 164.

6. *Russell Sage Quill*, May 29, 1942, Archives and Special Collections, The Sage Colleges (hereafter ASC/TSC), Troy, NY.

7. Oral History interview with Ann Caracristi, Veterans History Project, Library of Congress (hereafter AZC-OH/LOC), http://memory.loc.gov/diglib/vhp/story/loc.natlib.afc2001001.30844/transcript?ID=mv000, accessed August 31, 2022.

8. AZC-OH/LOC.

9. Oral History interview with Ann Caracristi, National Security Agency, July 16, 1982 (hereafter AZC-OH/NSA), 4, www.nsa.gov/Portals/70/documents/news-features/declassified-documents/oral-history-interviews/NSA-OH-15-82-caracristi.pdf, accessed August 31, 2022.

10. AZC-OH/NSA, 6.

11. Oral History interview with Wilma Davis, National Security Agency. December 3, 1982 (hereafter Davis OH), 39, www.nsa.gov/news-features/declassified-documents/oral-history-interviews/assets/files/nsa-oh-25-82-davis.pdf, accessed August 31, 2022.

12. Interview notes with Ann Caracristi, December 12, 2002, National Cryptologic Museum, David Kahn Papers (hereafter Caracristi Interview Notes, DKP), box 150, folder 6.

13. Davis OH, 43.

14. AZC-OH/NSA, 7, 23.

15. Oral History interview with Solomon Kullback, National Security Agency, August 26, 1982 (hereafter Kullback OH), 73, www.nsa.gov/Portals/70/documents/news-features/declassified-documents/oral-history-interviews/nsa-oh-17-82-kullback.pdf, accessed August 31, 2022.

16. AZC-OH/NSA, 11.

17. Emphasis in original. Nobutaka Ike, ed. and trans., *Japan's Decision for War: Records of the 1941 Policy Conferences* (Stanford: Stanford University Press, 1967), 191.

18. Letter from Lockwood to Kahn, November 25, 1964, DKP, box 62, folder 43.

19. Ronald H. Spector, *Eagle Against the Sun: The American War with Japan* (New York: The Free Press, 1984), 487.

20. AZC-OH/LOC.

21. Kullback OH, 87.

22. Kullback OH, 157.

23. AZC-OH/LOC. For Caracristi's employment with the *Daily News*, see Caracristi Interview Notes, DKP.

24. Program for the Federal Woman's Award Dinner, The Statler-Hilton Hotel, Washington, DC, March 2, 1965, AZCP/NCM, box 4.

25. See Betsy Rohaly Smoot and David Hatch, "To Command or Direct?" 175–176.

26. *National Security Agency Newsletter*, August 1982, 5, National Cryptologic Museum.

27. Caracristi, "Women in Cryptology," 6–7.

28. President Foreign Intelligence Advisory Board, "Report to the President on Improving the Role of Women in the Intelligence Community," November 1995, 1 and 5. AZCP/NCM. Box 4.

29. Caracristi, "Speech to 'Ladies of CIA,'" October 31, 1991, 1, AZCP/NCM, box 160, folder 9.

30. Caracristi, "Speech to 'Ladies of CIA,'" October 31, 1991, AZCP/NCM, Box 160, Folder 9, 3.

31. Caracristi, "Speech to 'Ladies of CIA,'" October 31, 1991, AZCP/NCM, Box 160, Folder 9, 1.

32. Martin Weil, "Ann Caracristi, Who Cracked Codes, and the Glass Ceiling, at NSA, Dies at 94," *Washington Post*, January 11, 2016.

33. AZC-OH/LOC.

# Shaping a New Threat: How the CIA Defined "International Terrorism" in the 1970s

Silke Zoller

*Modern intelligence agencies collect raw intelligence information through various human and technical means and give that mass of data to analysts who are charged with keeping policymakers informed about important developments, including discerning threats and opportunities. The International Spy Museum devotes an entire section to intelligence analysis. The work of intelligence analysts evolves constantly, and the topics about which policymakers expect to be kept informed change over time. In this chapter, Silke Zoller gives us an example of that evolution: when the CIA took on the topic of international terrorism.—The Editors*

On September 5, 1972, the Summer Olympic Games were in full swing in Munich, Germany. That morning, eight men stealthily entered the athletes' housing. They belonged to a Palestinian extremist group, the Black September Organization. The Palestinians took nine Israeli athletes and coaches as hostages and killed two other Israelis. Caught unprepared, the West German government cobbled together a rescue effort at Fürstenfeldbruck, a military airfield. It failed badly. Alerted to the rescue, the attackers turned their guns on the hostages. All the hostages and five out of the eight attackers died. The crisis was broadcast live around the world. Within days, contemporaries were describing the attackers as "international terrorists." President Richard Nixon turned to the American intelligence community to help him understand this new threat.[1] This was the turning point, at which the Central Intelligence Agency and the US government started employing the term "terrorism" in a systematic and widespread way.[2]

In the years after the Munich attack, it was the CIA that shaped the way the American government defined terrorism. The Agency collected data on potential risks and attacks that it analyzed and made available to representatives of diverse government agencies in a variety of ways, notably including the new *Weekly Situation Reports on International Terrorism*. Through this work, CIA analysts delineated which persons and events the US federal government saw through the lens of international terrorism. In the immediate aftermath of Munich, most media and government officials used the phrase "international terrorism" to apply only to Palestinians.

These CIA reports, however, systematically relabeled many nonstate violent groups around the world as "international terrorists." This move signified an important paradigm shift as the intelligence community redefined its conceptualization of anticolonial groups that included Latin American leftists and Palestinian extremists; they now fit into the same analytical basket. Also included in this new group were student radicals, European socio-revolutionary groups, nationalist movements, and a wide range of other nonstate violent actors. This recategorization not only branded these disparate groups as "terrorists" but also served to delegitimize them because suddenly the primary issue explored was their potential for violent attacks. Political context and nuance became far less relevant.

The CIA's new categorization shaped subsequent US policies against terrorism that sought to prevent attacks without substantially addressing the origins or grievances of terrorist groups. Because this conception of international terrorism did not distinguish significantly among nonstate groups, subsequent policies did not focus on resolving the nuanced political issues that drove attackers to violence. Instead, US agencies focused on strategies to harden potential targets and identify terrorism suspects, with a uniform set of assumptions about who and what they were countering. In the 1970s, federal agencies had their own counterterrorism priorities and often did not collaborate well in this field. However, all were using the same basic intelligence supplied by the CIA, which provided consistency and a common basis for agencies involved in American counterterrorism. These reports thus enabled the creation of early US counterterrorism policies geared toward preventing attacks.

Prior to 1972, the US government never clearly defined the term "terrorism," and the word's usage had changed over the decades. After World War I, it was most associated with left-leaning violent actors. State Department and Federal Bureau of Investigation officials labeled Marxists, socialists, anarchists, and leftist agitators as "terrorists."[3] After World War II, academics and bureaucrats used the term "terror" to denounce systematic state repression in the Soviet Union and other communist states. For example, the political philosopher Hannah Arendt wrote that "terror is the essence of totalitarian domination."[4] She accused the Soviet Union of using terror against its own population to prevent resistance to Soviet ideology or policies.

By the 1960s, American officials used "terror" and "terrorism" to describe state and nonstate violence against civilians, particularly in Latin America. They feared that such violence would undermine US political and economic interests there. The CIA particularly worried that Fidel Castro's revolutionary Cuban regime would inspire terrorist left-wing

Figure 10.1: Fidel Castro's calling card. Communist Cuba was a sponsor and inspiration for many of the insurgent groups of concern to CIA terrorism analysts during the 1970s. Courtesy of the Francis Lara Collection.

insurgencies throughout the region.[5] Such insurgents aimed to unseat the often authoritarian US-allied governments. At the same time, CIA analysts would also use the word "terrorism" to describe the actions of said US allies. For instance, a 1966 special National Intelligence Estimate on the Dominican Republic stated: "There is no doubt that the extreme leftists . . . have engaged in terrorist activities. Nor is there any doubt that elements of the extreme right have conducted terrorist operations in recent months."[6] These critical views of US allies aligned with critiques of the Soviet Union.

In the late 1960s and early 1970s, heightened state repression in Uruguay, Argentina, Guatemala, and elsewhere radicalized certain leftist groups and motivated them to kidnap foreign citizens for ransom or political gain.[7] In Brazil, several groups collaborated to kidnap US Ambassador Charles Elbrick in September 1969 and then traded him for fifteen prisoners. In 1968 and 1970, the Guatemalan group Fuerzas Armadas Rebeldes (FAR, or Rebel Armed Forces) kidnapped US Ambassador John Gordon Mein and West German Ambassador Karl von Spreti; neither man survived. CIA analysts framed these attacks as terrorism, continuing their use of this term to condemn leftist insurgent violence in Latin America. A 1969 *Intelligence Bulletin* stated that, in Brazil, "new terrorist attacks reportedly are planned against US personnel. Security officials in Bela Horizone expect terrorists to try to kidnap or attack US personnel there. . . . [The group] could have links to the terrorist organizations that kidnapped Ambassador Elbrick."[8]

At the same time, however, Palestinian extremists generated new forms of political violence. Radical groups like the leftist Popular Front for the

Figure 10.2: Commemorative medallion honoring George Habash, founder of the Popular Front for the Liberation of Palestine. Courtesy of the Francis Lara Collection.

Liberation of Palestine (PFLP) began attacking targets outside the state of Israel through letter bombs and hijackings. Their goal was to force the United States and other countries to take Palestinian national liberation seriously. For example, in September 1970 the PFLP hijacked several airplanes to Dawson's Field airstrip in Jordan and held hundreds of passengers hostage, half of them American citizens.

Indeed, before Munich the CIA invested substantial efforts in tracking leftist Palestinian extremist groups, especially once their repeated acts of violence threatened US interests. These attacks jeopardized a US-brokered resolution of the Arab-Israeli conflict.[9] Nevertheless, the CIA rarely referred to Palestinian extremists as "terrorists" or their attacks as "terrorism." Instead, analysts used "fedayeen," an Arabic word meaning "those who sacrifice themselves" that Palestinian extremists had chosen for themselves. So, for instance, on September 8, 1970, the CIA wrote that "[f]edayeen hijackers continue to hold two aircraft and some 180 passengers as tensions mount in the Middle East."[10] In applying the language of the Palestinians themselves, the CIA reports reminded US policymakers that Palestinians wanted to be political agents in the Arab-Israeli conflict, that they had deep stakes in its outcome, and that they would strive to affect any US-driven resolution.

The CIA kept track of additional violent actors abroad but described them with specialized terms other than "terrorist" on a case-to-case basis. In the turbulent years surrounding the 1968 global protests, for example, the CIA observed a range of foreign student protests. A 1969 survey of global student protest groups employed the term "anarchists" if the groups were inclined to violence. The survey noted that "some of the activists clearly are unwilling to participate in the political process. . . . The optimism of the anarchists is a hallmark of youth."[11] The term "anarchist" signified such protesters' opposition to established social orders and implied that they used violence for nihilist purposes. In short, before 1972 the CIA regularly called Latin American leftists and particularly violent state actions "terrorism" but generally used labels such as "fedayeen" and "anarchist" for other nonstate violent actors around the world. But the Munich attack increased the use of "terror" and "terrorism" not only within the Agency but also around the globe.

The Munich attack marked a watershed in the history and US definition of terrorism. In the days after the attack, journalists wrote of the literal terror inflicted by the Palestinian attackers and described them accordingly as "terrorists." The *Chicago Tribune* stated that "11 members of the Israeli Olympic team were massacred by Arab guerrillas in a day-long reign of terror."[12] "Eleven members of Israel's delegation to the Olympic Games were killed," reported the *Washington Post*, "two of them in a pre-dawn raid on their quarters by a band of Arab terrorists and nine others in a shootout between the terrorists and the German police."[13] The employment of the word "terrorism" emphasized the literal terror, shock, and apprehension caused by the attack around the world.

This type of attack loomed for Western officials and journalists as a new and immediate global security threat. Extremist Palestinians attacked European and other industrialized countries and ruthlessly threatened ordinary citizens.[14] Around the world, people spoke of this grave new danger. Whether in English, French, German, or Italian, 1972 was the year in which the use of the term "terrorism" reached a critical momentum and entered common usage.[15] In contrast, terms such as "guerrilla" and "fedayeen," which signified the political agency of attackers, declined commensurately.[16]

This shift in terminology affected US policy and its responses. President Nixon instituted new domestic and national security policies against violent Palestinians. Two weeks after the attack, Nixon started Operation Boulder. This secret program screened thousands of Arab citizens entering or residing in the United States.[17] Meanwhile, the president formed a new interagency working group to formulate longer-term policy options against international terrorism. The Cabinet Committee to Combat Terrorism (CCCT), founded on September 25, 1972, was a symbolic, high-level committee, but its subordinate midlevel working group met regularly and became the central location to coordinate policies against international terrorism within the federal government.

The CCCT Working Group brought together a wide range of experts from law enforcement, national security, the military, and intelligence to discuss international terrorism. Each member was responsible for policies related to international terrorism in his or her home institution and used the CCCT Working Group to collect and share experiences. To provide the group with relevant information, Nixon ordered that US intelligence collection on international terrorism increase substantially.[18] Furthermore, to disseminate this information, the CIA began to produce a weekly analytical report on international terrorism that described suspects, attacks, and potential threats.[19]

However, Nixon failed to specify the scope of what US intelligence agencies should collect. Though an informal association with Palestinians existed, Nixon did not clearly define the phrase "international terrorism." Nor did the rest of the US government have a satisfactory definition. This was evident in a State Department–hosted conference in October 1972 based on the "increasing concern of the U.S. government with the problem of terrorism" and "how to deal with it."[20] However, the conference attendees, from a variety of US agencies and academia, "arrived at no agreed definition of or a consensus around the point at which it shades into other forms of violence (such as guerilla action)."[21]

Because the US federal government writ large did not develop a uniform definition of "international terrorism," the CIA's *Weekly Situation Reports on International Terrorism* stepped into the void. Most agencies relied on the CIA's reports for operational data. These weekly reports provided a shared body of data that all agencies could use despite unclear or varying conceptions of terrorism. Despite a lack of definitional clarity, the CIA's reports also provided a de facto consistency for the federal government on what attacks were labeled "terrorism."

The first ever *Weekly Situation Report on International Terrorism*, prepared by area specialists in the CIA's Directorate of Intelligence, was published on November 1, 1972.[22] Large segments of these reports covering the period 1972–1974 have been declassified. Additionally, the full table of contents of a few reports from the late 1970s have also been released. Taken together these reveal a good composite picture of what CIA analysts considered relevant.

One major trend in the *Weekly Situation Reports* was that analysts relabeled actors with whom they were already familiar, creating a new terminology for existing threats. The bulk of 1972–1974 articles and notes discussed Palestinian extremist groups (such as Black September) and leftist Latin American insurgents (such as the Guatemalan FAR) that the CIA was already collecting intelligence on.[23] Treating these two sets of

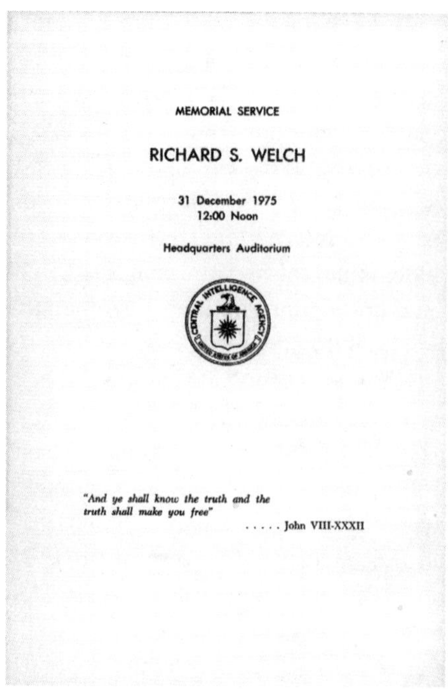
MEMORIAL SERVICE

RICHARD S. WELCH

31 December 1975
12:00 Noon

Headquarters Auditorium

"And ye shall know the truth and the truth shall make you free"
..... John VIII-XXXII

Figure 10.3: CIA's station chief in Athens, Richard S. Welch, was killed by the 17 November Group, a Greek Marxist urban guerrilla group, on December 23, 1975. The CIA officer Peter Earnest, Welch's friend and future executive director of the International Spy Museum, held this program at Welch's memorial service at CIA headquarters.

actors as one group, however, conveyed the message that these nonstate actors were a more significant threat to US interests than previously anticipated. This practice removed nuance. International terrorists threatened the United States because of their actions, no matter their political context or motivation. Thus, it was less important to analyze their claims to statehood or other aims and grievances. Rather, what was important were the attacks and dangers they posed as international terrorists.

In the *Weekly Situation Reports*, the CIA deployed the new terminology of international terrorism to analyze Palestinians such as Black September and the PFLP. In October 1972, a CIA memorandum had still referred to Palestinian groups as "fedayeen" and "guerrillas" but stressed that "[i]n recent months extremists have gained influence among the *fedayeen,* and more and more guerillas have come to see terrorist operations outside Israel as their only remaining weapon." When discussing future dangers, the memorandum homed in on the term "terrorists," emphasizing that "the terrorists are clearly going to want to continue the kind of activity which has won them this much."[24] By November 1972, the Agency's analysts almost entirely dropped "fedayeen" in favor of "terrorists" in the *Weekly Situation Reports*. For example, the first article in the inaugural issue of the *Weekly Situation Reports* began with "Palestinian terrorists hijacked a Lufthansa Boeing 727 . . . on 29 October and succeeded in obtaining the release of the three surviving Black September Organization . . . terrorists seized by West German authorities for the murder of the Israeli athletes at Munich."[25] The reports did not reserve the term "terrorists" for Black September, however; they also used it to describe other Palestinian groups that had not verifiably committed significant violence. One was Fatah, the more moderate group led by the Palestine Liberation Organization (PLO) chairman, Yasser Arafat. For example, the November 15, 1972, *Weekly Situation Report* warned that "Fatah terrorists are planning to hijack a plane from Tehran."[26]

By classifying Palestinians as terrorists, the CIA reports suggested that the Palestinians were a larger threat to US citizens and interests because they committed attacks that could easily embroil Americans. Earlier CIA analyses of the fedayeen had analyzed their influence on a US-driven resolution to the Arab-Israeli conflict. The *Weekly Situation Reports*, however, focused far more on the direct threat that Palestinians posed to Americans. Between 1972 and 1974, at least three-fourths of the articles and notes that have been declassified from the *Weekly Situation Reports* analyzed Palestinian groups, individuals, and attacks. The reports highlighted specific Palestinian extremist leaders, such as the PFLP founder George Habash, the ostensible Black September leader Salah Khalaf, and the PLO official Khalil al-Wazir.[27] All three were known planners of attacks inside and outside Israel. Other articles traced Palestinians' ideology and public stances on violence, using titles such as "Threats Reported Despite Continued Suspension of Fatah Terrorist Operations" and "PFLP Suspends Hijacking Operations."[28] Many articles also identified attacks or potential plans outside Israel that might victimize Americans. The first report, dated November 1, 1972, for instance, featured the previously mentioned Black September hijacking, the arrest of a Palestinian weapons courier, a Black September plan to assassinate King Hussein of Jordan, and the spread of letter bombs in the international mail.

In the CIA's reports, the context of the Arab-Israeli conflict and the Palestinians' struggle for their own state thus disappeared. The reports stripped out most political context and simply portrayed Palestinian extremists as a danger to US persons and interests. CIA analysts did not describe them as rational political actors in their own right. Rather, they defined them by their violent terrorist actions.

A comparable loss of nuance also occurred in the reports' coverage of Latin American leftist groups, the second most-addressed topic in the *Weekly Situation Reports*. Mirroring earlier CIA evaluations, the articles focused on the threat that such groups posed to US diplomats and businessmen, particularly highlighting kidnappings and assassination plots.

Much as had happened with the Palestinian groups, as the CIA's evaluations lumped together leftist groups in Latin America under the label "international terrorism," earlier analyses of the region's complex political dynamics and references to Cuba faded. After the Munich attack, assessments in the *Weekly Situation Reports* of Latin American terrorists focused on specific attacks and potential threats from left-leaning attackers. For example, an article about the kidnapping of Charles Agnew Lockwood, a British businessman in Argentina, specified that the kidnappers, "[i]dentifying themselves as members of the Trotskyite People's Revolutionary Army (ERP), . . . demanded a ransom of $2 million for his release . . . which is the largest ever demanded by Argentine terrorists."[29] This report described the communist associations of the kidnappers without reference to the complex political situation in Argentina during the 1970s.[30]

Because analysts focused almost exclusively on nonstate actors, a second major trend within the *Weekly Situation Reports* was to combine under the "international terrorism" label many additional violent groups, notably groups in Europe, that officials had not previously discussed in conjunction with one another or with the Palestinians or Latin Americans. This left the impression that all these groups formed one cohesive global threat against the United States, further removing nuance and political context.

The Agency's *Weekly Situation Reports* featured a chronology of recent attacks and a section on potential terrorist threats. These sections frequently featured actions by student and protest groups. Instead of focusing on such groups' political aims or opposition to the Vietnam War, they described the damage they did. For example, in December 1972, a United States Information Agency cultural center in Hamburg, Germany, "sustained over $9,000 worth of structural damage by a firebomb pushed in through a broken window."[31] Terms that signified these protest groups' political stances, such as "anarchist," vanished from reports. A similar lack of political context appeared in descriptions of radical socio-revolutionary groups that arose out of the protest movements, such as the Red Army Faction and Italy's Red Brigades. In June 1975, for example, the threats section included an article stating: "West German authorities believe the Baader-Meinhof gang may undertake further terrorist acts, in Germany or abroad, in an attempt to obtain the release of their imprisoned comrades whose trial resumed on 5 June in Stuttgart."[32] The report avoided the group's self-given name, "Red Army Faction," which would have called attention to the group's leftist political ideology. Instead, the inclusion of "gang" emphasized the criminal actions of the group and its leaders, Andreas Baader and Ulrike Meinhof.

In a similar vein, the *Weekly Situation Report on International Terrorism*

Figure 10.4: Program for Radio Rebelde, founded by Che Guevara in 1958 as a clandestine station supporting Fidel Castro's 26th of July Movement, which sought to take over Cuba. It broadcasts today as a Cuban government station. Courtesy of the Francis Lara Collection.

included many nationalist groups. Some were separatist groups such as Northern Ireland's Provisional Irish Republican Army and Spain's Euskadi Ta Askatasuna, both of which escalated violent attacks in their home countries and neighboring regions during the 1970s. Also frequently appearing in the publication were exiled right-wing nationalist actors who committed violence abroad to influence politics at home, especially Croatians, Serbians, and Cubans.[33] Such exiles were, in fact, prolific in committing violent acts around the world throughout the 1970s.[34] As with the student and leftist socio-revolutionary groups, the reports focused on the violent actions of separatist and exile groups without digging into related political contexts. While the reports usually called such actors "nationalists" or "emigrés," they did not analyze underlying nationalist struggles.[35]

By promulgating these reports, the CIA resolved in practice for the US government who and what should be handled as international terrorism when crafting antiterrorism policies. The main consumers of these reports were the members of President Nixon's interagency CCCT Working Group, which continued through President Gerald Ford's administration before being replaced with a similar group that met in the facilities of President Jimmy Carter's National Security Council.[36] From there, working group members brought the *Weekly Situation Reports* to their home agencies.

It is true that, by the late 1970s, most law enforcement, military, and intelligence institutions had their own definitions of "antiterrorism," tailored to their institution's particular needs and outlook. These different perceptions had implications for the policy creation process. Agencies developed their own counterterrorism approaches and competed for resources, often without clear lines of communication among them.[37] For example, in 1977 the State Department seized $700,000 in research funding from the Arms Control and Disarmament Agency, ending an ongoing terrorism study into which this agency had already sunk $185,000.[38]

Nevertheless, the CIA's *Weekly Situation Report on International Terrorism* provided agencies in the US government with a concrete list of international terrorists and implicit suggestions on how to handle the issue that these agencies readily adopted, thereby creating a significant degree of conceptual consistency across the government. Importantly, the CIA's specific delineation of what constituted terrorism, its inclusion of nonstate actors, and its exclusion of political context implied that US antiterrorism efforts did not have to address political issues or the root causes of terrorism. Instead, policymakers needed to find means to prevent specific attacks, for example by securing potential targets. Indeed, throughout the course of its existence, the CCCT Working Group released several major studies on terrorist tactics and how to identify and protect targets.[39] The intelligence community also released broad analyses about international terrorism. Some of these publications completely avoided defining terrorism.[40] Other studies emphasized the difficulty of defining terrorism and highlighted intelligence agencies' key role in gathering and analyzing information on the subject.[41] Overall, these studies tended to sidestep the thorny problem of defining terrorism. Instead, they discussed specific terrorist groups and practical antiterrorism countermeasures such as better security at airports. The CIA reports thus delineated what international terrorism was and, in practice, shaped related policymaking on a week-to-week basis.

CIA records on international terrorism also reached US allies, providing them with operational information on potential threats. For example,

Figure 10.5: Poison pen taken by South Korean authorities from a failed North Korean assassin in 2011. Sometimes countries mount attacks that can be called "terrorism." This assassin had been ordered to kill a North Korean defector turned high-profile activist. To release the poison inside the pen, the assassin was to twist the top to the right three or four times and then press it down. One prick from the needle that emerged would cause muscle paralysis, leading to suffocation and death. Courtesy of the Embassy of the Republic of Korea.

the West German government had no compilation of worldwide terrorist attacks in 1975. Officials in the West German Ministry of Justice requested and received lists of Palestinian and non-Palestinian terrorism incidents since 1970 from the US embassy in Bonn.[42] These lists were copied and pasted straight out of the CIA's *Weekly Situation Reports*. The phrasing, word choice, and formatting were identical.[43] Thus, the CIA helped to delineate international terrorism for intelligence consumers not only at home but also around the world.

One serious shortcoming inherent in the CIA's reports was that their content was classified and could not be disseminated to the public. By the mid-1970s, US officials and academics were interested in quantifying data about international terrorism. In that decade, the dissemination of computers, although slow, motivated government officials to gather large data sets and create computer-calculated statistics that could be the basis for policy recommendations. The CIA had its own terrorism database from intelligence that went into its reports. So did the Department of State. However, these databases could not be used without security clearances. To be able to create publicly available statements and defend policy positions, various US agencies funded the creation of new data sets and research that could be made publicly available. In fact, the US government became the main financer of terrorism research in the public sphere in the mid-1970s.[44]

Crucially, the US government financers set the parameters for what would be included in the publicly available data sets. Thus, US officials shaped indirectly what persons and events should be labeled "international terrorism" for the purpose of public research. For example, the CIA officer Edward Mickolus created the International Terrorism: Attributes of Terrorist Events data bank (ITERATE) in 1975. The CIA immediately began using ITERATE for official unclassified reports.[45] Meanwhile, from

1973 onward the Departments of State and Defense commissioned reports about terrorism from the RAND Corporation, a federally funded think tank sponsored by the Defense Department.[46] A RAND team led by Brian Jenkins compiled a database on international terrorism. Crucially, Jenkins and his team included only acts of violence committed by nonstate actors in their database, reflecting the fact that state terrorism had fallen out of the official nomenclature.[47] Both the RAND and ITERATE databases are still in use today and still influence terrorism-related research. So while the CIA's *Weekly Situation Reports* did not shape public perceptions of international terrorism directly, they had an indirect effect because their consumers structured what public research the US government would fund.[48]

The US government perceived international terrorism as a major new threat in the 1970s. In this situation, the CIA provided weekly reports to all federal agencies with a vested interest in counterterrorism. The CIA's reports shaped who and what the US government considered terrorist. Through these reports, the CIA precipitated a crucial change in language concerning terrorism. Before 1972, "terrorism" had been a rare label, and the US government applied it to political insurgents as well as instances of state repression. Afterward, the *Weekly Situation Reports* contained a new way of classifying and delegitimizing previously known violent groups. The reports connected various nonstate actors, framing them as a single interrelated problem. These reports supplied a common set of actors and attacks that were international terrorism. Consequently, they heightened US officials' awareness of international terrorism as a global danger. This practice removed nuance from the analysis. The reports labeled Palestinians and Latin American leftists as "terrorists" while reducing the use of terms that signified political agency such as "fedayeen" "guerrilla," and "insurgent." Instead, using "terrorist" prioritized that such groups committed brutal attacks of violence without broaching the larger context. International terrorists were defined by the violence that they committed. This focus, in turn, delegitimized attackers because it downplayed any subtlety or legitimate political agency on their part. Analysts paid little attention to such groups' state associations or claims to statehood. The CIA's *Weekly Situation Reports* thus framed international terrorism as a compound category of nonstate violence and simultaneously clarified that this violence was illegitimate regardless of political context. This perception of international terrorism still exists today: counterterrorism solutions and policy recommendations often concentrate on preventing actual attacks and rarely focus on addressing complex political contexts.

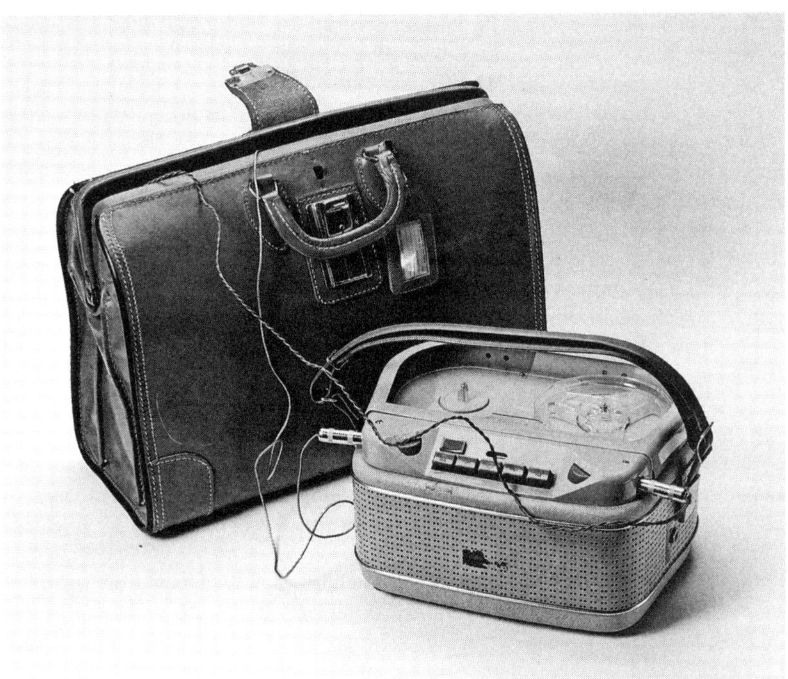

Figure 10.6: CIA-issue Butoba MT5 recorder with concealment briefcase, early 1960s. From the Collection of H. Keith and Karen Melton at the International Spy Museum.

## Further Reading


Guttmann, Aviva. "Turning Oil into Blood: Western Intelligence, Libyan Covert Action, and Palestinian Terrorism." *Journal of Strategic Studies* 45, nos. 6–7 (2022): 993–1020.

Hoffman, Bruce. *Inside Terrorism*. 3rd ed. New York: Columbia University Press, 2017.

Naftali, Timothy J. *Blind Spot: The Secret History of American Counterterrorism*. New York: Basic Books, 2005.


## Notes

1. For intelligence service's role in modern counterterrorism, see Whitney W. Gibbs, "A Question of Triumph: Effectively Measuring the Success of Intelligence Against Terrorism," *International Social Science Review* 94, no. 1 (2021): art. 4; Monica Den Boer, "Counter-Terrorism, Security and Intelligence in the EU: Governance Challenges for Collection, Exchange and Analysis," *Intelligence and National Security* 30, no. 2–3 (2015): 402–419; and Daniel Byman, "The Intelligence War on Terrorism," *Intelligence and National Security* 29, no. 6 (2014): 837–863. For historical studies, see Aviva Guttmann, "Turning Oil into Blood: Western Intelligence, Libyan Covert Action, and Palestinian Terrorism," *Journal of Strategic Studies*, nos. 6–7 (2022): 933–1020; Timothy J. Naftali, *Blind Spot: The Secret History of American Counterterrorism* (New

York: Basic Books, 2005); and Richard Immerman, *The Hidden Hand: A Brief History of the CIA* (Chichester, West Sussex: Wiley Blackwell, 2014).

2. See Peter S. Pereny, State Department, Bureau of Intelligence and Research, Office of Research and Analysis for Near East and South Asia, External Research Study "State Department Conference on Terrorism," December 29, 1972, National Archives and Records Administration, Record Group 59: Records of the Department of State, Central Foreign Policy Files 1970–73, POL 23-8, 12/1/72, 3.

3. Mary S. Barton and David Wright, "International Terrorism and the United States," *Oxford Research Encyclopedia of American History,* ed. Mark Lawrence, June 25, 2019, https://oxfordre.com/americanhistory/view/10.1093/acrefore/9780199329175.001.0001/acrefore-9780199329175-e-743.

4. Hannah Arendt, "Ideology and Terror: A Novel Form of Government," *Review of Politics* 15, no. 3 (July 1953): 303–327, 310.

5. See Naftali, *Blind Spot*, 26; and Lisa Stampnitzky, *Disciplining Terror: How Experts Invented "Terrorism"* (Cambridge: Cambridge University Press, 2013), 51–53.

6. CIA, "Prospects for Stability in the Dominican Republic," April 28, 1966, National Intelligence Estimate, 86.2-66, *Foreign Relations of the United States* (hereafter *FRUS*), 1964–1968, Volume 32, Document 171, https://history.state.gov/historicaldocuments/frus1964–68v32/d171.

7. Deputy Under Secretary of State for Administration William Macomber to Under Secretary of State for Political Affairs U. Alexis Johnson, Action Memorandum "U.S. Policy Toward Politically Motivated Kidnapping of U.S. Officials Abroad," April 2, 1970, *FRUS,* 1969–1976, Volume E-1, Document 38, https://history.state.gov/historicaldocuments/frus1969-76ve01/d38.

8. CIA Directorate of Intelligence, *Central Intelligence Bulletin*, October 3, 1969, 7, CIA Freedom of Information Act Electronic Reading Room (hereafter CIAFOIARR), General CIA Records (CIA), CIA-RDP79T00975A014700010001-7, cia.gov/readingroom.

9. CIA, NIE 30-71, "The Palestinians and the Fedayeen as Factors in the Middle East Situation," February 2, 1971, CIA-RDP00T02041R000100220001-1, cia.gov/readingroom.

10. CIA Directorate of Intelligence, Central Intelligence Bulletin, September 8, 1970, 1, CIA-RDP79T00975A017100030001-8, cia.gov/readingroom.

11. CIA, Survey 0519/70 "Restless Youth," May 1, 1970, v, 0002987248, cia.gov/readingroom.

12. Cooper Rollow and Robert Markus, "Olympic Terror: 16 Die: 11 Israelis Slain," *Chicago Tribune,* September 6, 1972, 1, 4.

13. "All Hostages Slain at Munich Airport; Games in Doubt," *Washington Post,* September 6, 1972, A1.

14. See, for example, Walter Laqueur, "The Terrorist Attacks: An Exercise in Futility: Arab Terror: More to Come," *Washington Post*, September 10, 1972, B1, B5.

15. Ngram Viewer, "Terrorism," *Google Books*, https://books.google.com/ngrams/graph?content=Terrorism&year_start=1800&year_end=2019&corpus=26&smoothing=3, accessed January 9, 2022.

16. Ngram Viewer, "Guerilla," *Google Books*, https://books.google.com/ngrams/graph?content=guerilla&year_start=1800&year_end=2019&corpus=26&smoothing=3, accessed January 9, 2022; and Ngram Viewer, "Fedayeen," *Google Books,* accessed January 9, 2022, https://books.google.com/ngrams/graph?content=fedayeen&

year_start=1800&year_end=2019&corpus=26&smoothing=3&direct_url=t1%3B%2Cfedayeen%3B%2Cc0.

17. See Salim Yaqub, *Imperfect Strangers: Americans, Arabs, and U.S.-Middle East Relations in the 1970s* (Ithaca: Cornell University Press, 2016), 96–100; and Naftali, *Blind Spot,* 57–58.

18. President Richard Nixon to Secretary of State William Rogers, Memorandum "Action to Combat Terrorism," September 25, 1972, *FRUS,* 1969–76, vol. E-1, Document 110, https://history.state.gov/historicaldocuments/frus1969-76ve01/d110.

19. William Rogers to Richard Nixon, Memorandum "Action against International Terrorism," January 8, 1973, *FRUS,* 1969–1976, vol. E-3, Document 203, https://history.state.gov/historicaldocuments/frus1969-76ve03/d203.

20. Pereny, "State Department Conference on Terrorism," 2.

21. Pereny, "State Department Conference on Terrorism," 3.

22. CIA, *Weekly Situation Report on International Terrorism* (hereafter *WSRIT*) November 1, 1972, CIA-RDP79-01209A000100010001-7, CIAFOIARR.

23. *WSRIT,* November 1, 1972, 1, 6, 8, CIA-RDP79-01209A000100010001-7, CIAFOIARR.

24. CIA, Office of National Estimates, "The Fedayeen-Politics of Spoiling," October 26, 1972, 2.8, CIA-RDP79R00967A000500030016-0, CIAFOIARR.

25. CIA, *WSRIT,* November 1, 1972, 1 CIA-RDP79-01209A000100010001-7, CIAFOIARR.

26. CIA, *WSRIT,* November 15, 1972, 25, CIA-RDP79-01209A000100010001-7, CIAFOIARR.

27. See CIA, "George Habbash—PFLP Leader," *WSRIT,* January 17, 1973, 8; CIA, *WSRIT,* "Salah Khalaf—Black September Organization Leader," January 24, 1973, 14; and CIA, "Khalil al-Wazir—Al Fatah Leader and Black September Organization Leader," *WSRIT,* January 31, 1973, 14; all found in CIA-RDP79-01209A000100030001-5, CIAFOIARR.

28. CIA, *WSRIT,* November 21, 1973, CIA Records, CIA-RDP79-01209A000300030001-3, 3; and CIA, *WSRIT,* December 10, 1974, CIA-RDP79-01209A000500050001-9, 3.

29. CIA, *WSRIT,* June 13, 1973, CREST, CIA, CIA-RDP79-01209A000200030001-4, 6.

30. See Philip W. Travis, *Reagan's War on Terrorism in Nicaragua: The Outlaw State* (Lanham, MD: Lexington Books, 2016).

31. CIA, "WSRIT," January 3, 1973, CREST, CIA, CIA-RDP79-01209A000100030001-5, A1.

32. CIA, "WSRIT," June 10, 1975, CREST, CIA, CIA-RDP79-01209A000600020001-1, C-1.

33. Good examples of the broad bandwidth of nonstate actors are CIA, "WSRIT," January 10, 1973, CREST, CIA, CIA-RDP79-01209A000100030001-5; and CIA, "WSRIT," December 13, 1972, CREST, CIA, CIA-RDP79-01209A000100020001-6.

34. See Alan McPherson, "Caribbean Taliban: Cuban American Terrorism in the 1970s," *Terrorism and Political Violence* 31, no. 2 (October 2019): 390–409, DOI:10.1080/09546553.2018.1530988.

35. CIA, "WSRIT," November 9, 1972, CREST, CIA, CIA-RDP79-01209A000100010001-7, 13; and CIA, "WSRIT," April 4, 1973, CREST, CIA, CIA-RDP79-01209A000200010001-6, 15–16.

36. National Security Advisor Zbigniew Brzezinski to Vice President Walter Mondale et al., Memorandum "Terrorism," September 21, 1977, Jimmy Carter Presidential

Library, National Security Advisor's Files, General William Odom's Files, Box 55, Terrorism SCC Working Group, 9/77–12/78.

37. Law Enforcement Assistance Administration (LEAA), *Facing Tomorrow's Terrorist Incidents Today*, by Robert Kupperman (Washington, DC, October 1977), i, Hoover Institution Archives (Hoover), Robert H. Kupperman Papers (Kupperman), box 4, folder 5.

38. Arms Control and Disarmament Agency Chief Scientist Robert Kupperman, Memorandum "Dr. Robert H. Kupperman's Activities in the Counterterrorism Field," July 14, 1977, Hoover, Kupperman, box 7, folder 2; and LEAA, *Facing Tomorrow's Terrorist Incidents Today*, ii.

39. These include the *Mass Destruction Terrorism Study* (1975), *The Near-Term Potential for Serious Acts of Terrorism* (1976), *An Overview of Counter-terrorism Technology* (1976); and *Facing Tomorrow's Terrorist Incidents Today* (1977). See LEAA, *Facing Tomorrow's Terrorist Incidents Today*, i.

40. See, for example, Cabinet Committee to Combat Terrorism/Working Group, *The Near-Term Potential for Serious Acts of Terrorism* (Washington, DC, April 1976), Gerald Ford Presidential Library (FPL), Bobbie Greene Kilberg Files (Kilberg), Box 16, Intermediate-Level Terrorism Study (I); and CIA Directorate of Intelligence, Report "International Terrorism in 1976," July 1, 1977, CREST, Argentina Declassification Project—The "Dirty War" (1976–83) (Argentina), 02064822.

41. LEAA, *Facing Tomorrow's Terrorist Incidents Today*, 3.

42. International Criminal Law Division Director Paul-Günter Pötz to West German Justice Minister Hans-Jochen Vogel, Memorandum "Innere Sicherheit: Fälle von Enführugen im Ausland," March 5, 1975, with attachments "Significant Non-Fedayeen International Terrorist Incidents: January 1970-March 1974," undated, and "Significant Fedayeen and Fedayeen-Related International Terrorism Incidents: January 1970-March 1974," undated, Federal Archives Germany (BArch), Federal Republic of Germany (B) Records of the Ministry of Justice (141)-65262, 130–194.

43. Compare for example ibid., 193, to CIA, "WSRIT," February 6, 1974, CREST, CIA, CIA-RDP79-01209A000300060001-0, A-2, A-3.

44. See Stampnitzky, *Defining Terror*, 100.

45. These include CIA, Research Study PR 76 10300 "International and Transnational Terrorism: Diagnosis and Prognosis," April 1976, by David Milbank, i, FPL, Kilberg, box 17, International and Transnational Terrorism-Diagnosis and Prognosis; and CIA Directorate of Intelligence, Report "International Terrorism in 1976," July 1, 1977, i, CREST, Argentina, 02064822.

46. RAND Corporation, Working Note WN-9006-1-DOS/ARPA "Numbered Lives: Some Statistical Observations from 77 International Hostage Situations," August 1975, by Brian Jenkins, Janera Johnson, and David Ronfeldt, iii, FPL, Kilberg, box 16, Hostage Episode Study.

47. RAND Corporation, *International Terrorism: A Chronology, 1968–1974*, by Brian Jenkins and Janera Johnson (Santa Monica, March 1975), accessed January 9, 2022, www.rand.org/content/dam/rand/pubs/reports/2007/R1597.pdf, 2.

48. Businesses such as the Pinkerton Detective Agency also established a few private databanks for insurance and risk analysis. See National Consortium for the Study of Terrorism and Responses to Terrorism (START), "Global Terrorism Database," *START*, www.start.umd.edu/gtd, accessed January 9, 2022.

# Mysteries, Secrets, and Puzzles: Designing Intelligence Analysis at the International Spy Museum

Cynthia Storer, Mark Stout, and Sarah-Jane Corke

*In 2011, US Navy SEALs killed al-Qaeda leader Osama bin Laden. Before the SEALs could do that, however, intelligence analysts had to find him. The International Spy Museum devotes substantial space to this complicated process, including an audio-visual interactive featuring the former CIA counterterrorism analyst Cynthia Storer. In this chapter she tells the interlocking stories of how analysts found bin Laden and how she conceived the museum's exhibition to bring the process to life.*
*—The Editors*

The first International Spy Museum opened on May 12, 2002, and immediately became one of Washington, DC's most popular tourist attractions. In part, this was due to the public's interest in intelligence in the aftermath of the terrorist attacks of September 11, 2001, and the buildup to the Iraq War.[1] As Americans watched the hunt for Osama bin Laden and the war in Iraq unfold, their awareness of the complexities of modern intelligence grew. The museum took note and started to think about how the museum should evolve. Although the original museum focused mostly on espionage and covert action, it soon became clear that a redesigned museum at a new location would need to portray intelligence analysis in its exhibitions. While in the public's imagination espionage is arguably the sexier subject, intelligence professionals know that the important stories often lie in the analytical realm.

When serious planning started for a new International Spy Museum around 2013, the museum's curatorial staff quickly decided that it wanted to highlight the analytic story behind the hunt for bin Laden.[2] To develop the exhibition, the museum turned to Cynthia Storer, a former Central Intelligence Agency counterterrorism analyst who did pioneering work on bin Laden's group in the 1990s. Storer left the Agency in 2007 and was not involved in the post-9/11 hunt for bin Laden, but during the intervening years she turned to teaching intelligence analysis. According to Jacqueline Eyl, a member of the SPY staff and who worked with Storer, in general it is very hard to find people who have both "lived the life" and could "extrapolate skills to teach it."[3] Storer fit both criteria, and she played a central role in the exhibition that you see at the museum today, which consists of three interwoven stories: her experience as a counterterrorism analyst, the hunt for bin Laden, and the briefing to President Barack Obama that led to his decision, in the face of uncertain intelligence, to launch the raid on the Abbottabad compound. Picking up on these threads, this chapter relies on Storer's experiences to drive the narrative that unfolds below.

In this chapter we show how the collaboration at the museum among practitioners, intelligence scholars, and museum professionals resulted in interactive exhibitions that reflected a major shift in how the United States Intelligence Community (USIC) conceived of and practiced intelligence analysis. Beginning in 2004, the USIC began the process of reevaluating the way it approached intelligence analysis. This resulted in a new set of analytical standards used in training and educating analysts. Central to these changes was the adoption of structured analytic techniques, which are intended to be ways of ensuring sound analysis. Two of these techniques became the basis for the two interactive exhibitions Storer worked on.

This chapter also highlights three stories of teamwork and critical thinking as they came together at the CIA, at the International Spy Museum, and in the writing of this article. At the CIA, "the sisterhood"—an informal group of women from various branches—played a critical role in the CIA's Counterterrorism Center (CTC), which addressed the bin Laden problem. At the International Spy Museum, collaboration among curators, historians, and outside experts played an instrumental role in the design of the exhibition you see today. Finally, this chapter is a joint effort between intelligence practitioners and historians. We believe that partnerships of this type hold great promise for those of us who are interested in working through the problems of the past and the present.

When al-Qaeda attacked the World Trade Center and the Pentagon on September 11, the world was stunned. However, many experts in the CTC were not surprised. For several months they had been warning policymakers that bin Laden—who had declared war on the United States in 1996—had set the wheels in motion for a major attack on American interests.[4] Indeed, analysts had suggested that not only was the World Trade Center a possible target but also that aircraft might be hijacked.[5] One of the experts working on al-Qaeda was Storer. In 1986, she began her career as an imagery analyst for the National Photographic Interpretation Center (NPIC), which was part of the CIA's Directorate of Science and Technology. In 1989, she arranged a temporary assignment to the Directorate of Intelligence and landed in the Office of Near East and South Asia Analysis to work on Afghanistan, where she was introduced to the problem of foreign fighters, then called "Afghan Arabs." This was a long-standing problem; analysts had been warning about the potential threat from these fighters since at least 1982.

Although Storer returned to NPIC in 1990, she went back to the Directorate of Intelligence permanently in 1992 as the senior political-military analyst on Afghanistan. In the intervening eighteen months, her colleagues had begun to study the network of foreign fighter training camps that remained in Afghanistan after the Soviet withdrawal and the threats their graduates posed to American interests. These analysts were producing all-source "finished intelligence" for decision makers from the president on down. They, along with Gina Bennett, an analyst at the State Department's Bureau of Intelligence and Research, drafted multiple warnings that these men were committed to attacking US interests abroad. One such warning was eventually included in a President's Daily Brief submitted in the weeks before the bombing of the World Trade Center in New York in 1993.[6] Meanwhile, the Federal Bureau of Investigations was working on multiple cases involving foreign fighters across the United States and abroad.[7]

In 1995, Storer was sent to the CIA's Counterterrorist Center, later renamed the "Counterterrorism Center." It was the CIA's first joint office designed to unify the efforts of the Directorate of Operations and the Directorate of Intelligence, along with representatives from several other agencies.[8] CTC reported to the Director of Central Intelligence, with a leader from the Directorate of Operations and a deputy from the Directorate of Intelligence. In the CTC, operators and analysts worked side by side to penetrate terrorist groups and thwart their efforts. However, the CTC was considered a backwater within the Agency. Women were still fighting for respect at CIA and so were overrepresented in the CTC, making up 70 percent of its staff.[9] Theirs was not an easy job. They faced discrimination on several levels. Many of the men did not want to listen to women. This was especially true in the Directorate of Operations, particularly if those women were analysts from the Directorate of Intelligence. Thus, their work was often ignored or belittled. In the words of Glen Carle, a CIA operator who served in the CTC, the women from the operations side "had to be the toughest SOBs in the universe to survive."[10]

Equally disturbing, the Islamic Extremist Branch at CTC was often referred to as the "Manson Family," a reference to a murderous cult in Southern California during the late 1960s that consisted of a male leader and mostly female followers.[11] While the trope was designed to undermine both the women in the unit and their boss, Michael Scheuer, whose intensity was often criticized, there can be little doubt that its use showed a remarkable degree of animosity toward the group. In the face of this discrimination, a bond was forged among many of these women, and by the late 1990s they were providing a network of support for each other during this difficult period. Throughout these years, this group of women referred to themselves as the "sisterhood."

At CTC, Storer worked in a small group of Directorate of Intelligence analysts who covered terrorist threats from across the world. Her account related to South Asia, the Middle East, and the global mujahideen network including bin Laden and those who followed him. These efforts led to close collaboration with the analysts in Scheuer's branch. Working together they were able to get direct insight into the workings of the bin Laden group as it morphed into a terrorist support network.

In January 1996, CTC created its first "virtual station" to track bin Laden. In the CIA, a "station" usually refers to an established Agency presence in a foreign country. This virtual station, however, was at CIA Headquarters. Though it had various names, today it is best known as "Alec Station," after the son of its first chief, Michael Scheuer. Its members often worked 16-hour days, sometimes seven days a week, many for years on end.[12] Meanwhile, Storer, who was not in Alec Station, began to see patterns emerge from the fragmentary pieces of information about the former foreign fighters who had flocked to Afghanistan during the war and then scattered around the globe after it ended. At one point, her mind went back to a graduate-school course on organizational theory, and she had a eureka moment, realizing that what she had been looking at was an organization. What had once been thought to be merely a network of fellow travelers was a bureaucracy, opening and closing offices, keeping detailed accounting records, sending paychecks, and routing issues for approval.[13]

The effort that led to identifying al-Qaeda exemplifies the different approaches to counterterrorism analysis at the time. Storer and her colleagues used social network diagrams and Microsoft Word files to sort and make sense of the information being collected about bin Laden and his colleagues. However, their work was often dismissed as nothing more than bean-counting by many Directorate of Intelligence analysts. Storer recalls being told more than once by analysts outside CTC that, given the type of work she was doing, she and her colleagues were not real political analysts. However, her theory about al-Qaeda was confirmed in 1996, when a man named Jamal al-Fadl defected after embezzling funds from the group.[14] Yet at the time she continued to receive pushback from other analysts who argued that her concept of bin Laden's group was flawed. Some insisted that his group was merely a loosely organized group of guys.

Others believed that terrorists must, out of necessity, organize in a compartmented, secret, cellular structure—not something that looked like the wiring diagram of a corporation or military unit. Undaunted, Storer continued to push her theory.

By early 1997, the information collected suggested that a major attack on US interests was being planned, possibly in Africa. On August 7, 1998, al-Qaeda bombed the US embassies in Nairobi, Kenya, and Dar es Salaam, Tanzania, killing 200 people and injuring approximately 4,000 more, mostly Africans.[15] After these bombings, George Tenet, the new Director of Central Intelligence, briefed President Bill Clinton on Storer's theory that al-Qaeda was an organization.[16] Soon after, Tenet, worried that policymakers were not understanding the implications of the analysts' conclusions, began writing letters to senior administration officials to highlight the threat.[17]

Eventually, the analysts' message gained traction in the Clinton White House. However, by this time Storer had moved on to a stint in the Near East Division in the Directorate of Operations. As her replacement, Storer recommended a former colleague from the Office of Near East and South Asia Analysis in the Directorate of Intelligence, Barbara Sude, a senior analyst with a doctorate in medieval Arabic thought from Princeton. Prior to landing at the Office of Near East and South Asia Analysis, Sude had worked in the Foreign Broadcast Information Service, an open-source intelligence component of the intelligence community, an experience that provided her with unique insights into al-Qaeda.

As the year 2000 approached, the CIA received intelligence that the group was planning multiple attacks around the turn of the millennium. Ultimately, several plots were broken up, and although none in the United States came to fruition, attacks did happen elsewhere.[18] But al-Qaeda was not done, and in the spring of 2001 it became clear that a major attack on US interests was coming. In the words of Director Tenet, "the system was blinking red."[19] CTC in particular, and the intelligence community in general, gave strategic warnings that al-Qaeda intended to mount a major attack. They also gave an operational warning that al-Qaeda had set its plan of attack in motion. The CIA published numerous articles in intelligence publications to this effect, and Tenet emphatically spread the word to the senior officials of the new George W. Bush administration. Yet it was not enough. The CIA was unable to definitively identify the tactical details of the plot: dates, means, targets.

On September 11, 2001, 19 hijackers took control of four commercial airliners and succeeded in crashing two of them into the World Trade Center and one into the Pentagon, killing 2,977 people. The passengers took away control of the fourth plane from the hijackers, and it crashed in a field in Pennsylvania. Over the next month, President Bush and his administration planned the American response. Beginning in October 2001, a US-led military coalition drove the Taliban from power in Afghanistan, where that group had been sheltering bin Laden and many of his followers, and hunted down members of al-Qaeda across the globe. Amid the fighting, bin Laden fled to a mountain hideout at Tora Bora, where coalition forces began a sustained attack to root him out.[20] However, he was able to escape, and his trail went cold. He eventually took up residence in a custom-built compound in Abbottabad, Pakistan, in 2005. From there, eschewing telephones and the internet, he continued to issue a string of long statements urging Muslims to take up arms.

Over the next four years, Storer continued her work as a strategic terrorism analyst at CTC. Then, in 2005, she took an 18-month sabbatical at the University of Maryland, where she worked in the National Consortium for the Study of Terrorism and Responses to Terrorism, a "center of excellence" funded by the Department of Homeland Security. She returned to CTC for a brief period in 2007 before deciding to leave the Agency and began her teaching career at the University of Maryland. There, another CIA analyst who had worked on bin Laden for years wrote a memo titled "Inroads." In it, she proposed four ways that he might be found: through his couriers; through his family; through his communications with other members of al-Qaeda's senior leadership; and through his outreach to the media. These four approaches became the framework that CIA analysts used to explore new information on the subject.[21]

In 2003, the 9/11 attacks and the subsequent failure to capture bin Laden was followed by incorrect assessments that Iraq had weapons of mass destruction (WMD).[22] These intelligence failures ignited calls for intelligence reform. In response, Congress passed the Intelligence Reform and Terrorism Prevention Act of 2004 (IRTPA), which created a new head of the USIC, the Director of National Intelligence (DNI), and the National Counterterrorism Center (NCTC) under the DNI's authority. The law also codified standards for intelligence analysis, mandating that it be objective, independent of political considerations, timely, and based on all sources of available intelligence. In addition, analysis was to exhibit sound tradecraft, which included the exploration of multiple hypotheses and explicit statements of likelihood and confidence.

In 2007, the Director of National Intelligence released Intelligence Community Directive 203, titled "Analytic Standards," implementing the IRTPA's requirements regarding analysis. Some of these new standards codified existing CIA practices, while others broke new ground.[23] However, they all continued a historical trend in American intelligence analysis that used social science approaches to assess and forecast human behaviors in the political, economic, and military spheres. As a self-conscious discipline, American intelligence analysis came out of World War II and the Research and Analysis Branch (R&A) of the Office of Strategic Services. R&A was largely staffed by professors and graduate students in the social sciences, including some Europeans who had fled Adolf Hitler. These men and women came from several academic fields, including history, which was then understood by some as a social science. These scholars believed that their mission was to "transform raw intelligence into concise, factual[,] and rigorously objective analyses for the use of government agencies."[24]

After the war, Sherman Kent, a history professor at Yale before he came to R&A, became the most important figure in the burgeoning field of intelligence analysis. His 1949 book, *Strategic Intelligence for American World Policy*, set out a theoretical approach largely based on social science models and logical positivism, an idea, popular at the time, that observation of the world and the application of logic could produce the truth about what was happening;[25] this truth could be presented to policymakers without being policy prescriptive, a professional no-no for analysts.[26] Over time, however, academic social science proved a poor fit with the reality of intelligence analysis, and it grew even less so as social science became more methodologically sophisticated and more quantitative.

One of the reasons for this poor fit is that social scientists often embrace a top-down, deductive approach that starts with a theory or hypothesis to be tested. This does not work well for analysts, who routinely face questions that are narrow, novel, and classified, the latter meaning that few social scientists would be in the position to develop a relevant theory. Moreover, they must frequently give answers to policymakers before their research is complete or when no good answer exists at all. In addition, the data that analysts work with is usually messy, unstructured, and incomplete. Nor is it usually collected in accordance with a uniform protocol as a scientist would want. Moreover, quantitative information is seldom available, let alone relevant, to most intelligence questions, for example, "Where will al-Qaeda attack next?" It is not possible to have control groups or run experiments. Finally, the data collected often comes from adversaries who attempt to either thwart collection efforts or to deceive intelligence officers. Given these difficulties, analysts tend to work according to an *abductive* process. This involves an endless loop of gathering data; applying an apparently relevant theory or model; identifying the gaps between the data and the model; and then either gathering more data and applying the model again to see if there is a better fit or, alternately, applying a new

Figures 11.1 and 11.2: Lanyard cards, distributed to analysts in the US intelligence community in the 2010s by the Office of the Director of National Intelligence, reminding them of the standards for good analysis.

model. This process bears some similarities to the way law enforcement investigations are conducted and has elements of the "rich description" inductive approach to social science.

Over time, this process and the associated methods of communicating findings became known to analysts as "tradecraft," a pragmatic substitute for the social science theories imagined by Kent and others. As a result, in the early 2000s the anthropologist Rob Johnston pointed out that, although many CIA analysts said they applied social science methods, this was not really true. Nevertheless, the CIA applied formal social science approaches and theory where time and resources allowed, including an increased emphasis on psychology in the years after 9/11.

This shift had its roots back in the 1970s. Stung by criticisms that its analysts were not using the new social science methods that had been developed in the 1960s, the CIA created the Analytic Methodology Research Division. In 1975, Richards Heuer, a member of this division, presented a paper on its work to the annual conference of the International Studies Association. He made what he thought would be a controversial argument: quantitative analysis was seldom useful to intelligence analysis. After his talk, Heuer was approached by Zvi Lanir, an Israeli military intelligence officer, who told him that he agreed with him, adding that "the answer is not in the numbers, it's in the head."[27] Lanir, sent by the Israeli government to Columbia University to study emerging quantitative approaches to intelligence analysis in the wake of the 1973 surprise attack by Egypt and Syria, found little of value in quantitative analysis. However, he had discovered the groundbreaking work in cognitive psychology of Daniel Kahneman and Amos Tversky.[28] Inspired by Lanir, Heuer read Kahneman and Tversky and went on to write a series of papers on the importance of psychology to intelligence analysis. He also began to lecture CIA recruits on the subject.[29]

Heuer retired from the CIA in 1979 but received a contract from the agency to continue exploring these issues. In the course of this work during the 1980s, he developed the first structured analytic techniques (SATs), the analysis of competing hypotheses (ACH).[30] This involved identifying alternative hypotheses and then systematically evaluating data that was consistent or inconsistent with each hypothesis. It challenged analysts to reject hypotheses rather than seeking to confirm them.[31] Later, the bulk of Heuer's post-retirement work was compiled in his book *The Psychology of Intelligence Analysis*.[32] In this influential work, he showed how unconscious cognitive biases and heuristics can lead astray even the most careful analysts.

In the 2000s, Heuer began working with the retired CIA officials Randolph and Katherine Pherson, the first a former analyst, the other a former counterintelligence officer. Along with Heuer, they pioneered the development and application of SATs, which essentially turned abductive processes into discrete methodologies. Some of these techniques they borrowed and adapted from other disciplines including business, law, and medicine. They called SATs "a mechanism by which internal thought processes are externalized in a systematic and transparent manner so that they can be shared, built on, and easily critiqued."[33] They hoped that SATs could stimulate out-of-the-box thinking that would encourage analysts to consider alternative outcomes. In addition, they believed that SATs could reduce surprise by identifying indicators of change together with key assumptions, uncertainties, intelligence gaps, and disagreements that might be relevant to policymakers.[34] In January 2003, the Phersons founded a company that provided training in intelligence analysis for USIC analysts.[35] Their timing could not have been better; stung by 9/11, the failure to capture bin Laden, and the Iraq WMD failure, and facing challenges from Congress in 2004 and the DNI in 2007 to improve analytic tradecraft, intelligence agencies were eager to use their insights.[36]

In 2007, Storer joined Pherson Associates and for about two years taught courses on intelligence analysis, including SATs. In 2009, she moved to South Carolina to be closer to her family. She continued to teach for Pherson for a time but soon took a job with Coastal Carolina University's undergraduate program on intelligence. Later, she began teaching courses on intelligence analysis and intelligence and counterterrorism as an adjunct in Johns Hopkins University's graduate program on intelligence. In 2011, Richards Heuer and Randolph Pherson published a book titled *Structured Analytic Techniques for Intelligence Analysis* in which they acknowledged Storer as a contributor.[37] The book gathered in one place fifty SATs. Two of them, ACH and so-called Starbursting, would make their way into the Spy Museum's exhibitions.

In contrast to ACH, which relied on identifying alternate hypotheses, Starbursting is a "form of brainstorming that focuses on generating questions rather than . . . answers." Analysts using this technique start with the classic journalists' questions of who, what, where, when, why, and how. For each query they reflect on additional questions about the topic. Later the questions are prioritized or grouped into categories.[38] The objective of this exercise is to identify the central issues at stake and the parameters of the problem.

As Pherson and Heuer were working through their ideas, President Barack Obama came into office and named Leon Panetta as CIA director. Discovering that the effort to find bin Laden had splintered across the agency, Panetta instituted an important change at the Counterterrorism Center. He put an analyst and an operator in charge of a unified effort to find the terrorist leader.[39] It appears that analysts at the CTC also employed SATs over the years to work through the problem of finding bin Laden. On August 27, 2010, Panetta was told that the Agency might have tracked bin Laden to a fortress-like residence in Abbottabad, Pakistan. A little over a month later, on September 21, 2010, Panetta and his deputy Michael Morell briefed the president on the Abbottabad compound.[40] However, lacking conclusive evidence, debate continued in the agency over whether it was in fact bin Laden.[41] Still, the possibility seemed serious enough that on December 10 President Obama directed his national security team to start thinking about "finishing options."[42]

Despite the new mandate, everyone involved knew that a raid against someone who turned out not to be bin Laden could be catastrophic. This high-risk/high-reward situation led the motivated intelligence managers to encourage dissent. According to one official, "[W]e kept explaining to our group: 'if you see something that doesn't make sense you need to raise your hand now.'"[43] John Brennan, a former CIA analyst heading the White House's counterterrorism efforts, told analysts: "I'm tired of hearing why everything you see confirms your case. What we need to look for are the things that tell us what's *not* right about our theory. So, what's not right

Plates 93 and 94. Chinese pamphlet lauding two fighter pilots for shooting down an American U-2 spy plane. No such incident is known to have occurred, though China is thought to have used surface-to-air missiles to shoot down five U-2s flown by Taiwanese pilots in the 1960s. From the Collection of H. Keith and Karen Melton at the International Spy Museum.

Plate 95. Patch of the US Air Force's 6593rd Test Squadron (Special). Corona and other early American spy satellites dropped "buckets" containing film from orbit. The 6593rd flew specially equipped aircraft to snatch those buckets out of the air over the Pacific Ocean. On loan from Carolyn Leonard.

Plate 96. Photographic Interpretation Kit, F-3, Model N-2. Used by a US military photo interpreter who served during World War II and into the Cold War.

Plate 97. Rotors for a World War II–era German Enigma cipher machine. Each Enigma had slots for three or four rotors that were interchangeable to increase the complexity of the cipher. From the Collection of H. Keith and Karen Melton at the International Spy Museum.

Plate 98. German three-rotor Enigma cipher machine, circa 1944. From the Collection of H. Keith and Karen Melton at the International Spy Museum.

Plate 99. Hagelin H-4605 cipher machine. Sold by the Swiss firm CryptoAG, this was a popular cipher machine with many intelligence agencies in the 1970s. Users were unaware, however, that the CIA and Germany's Federal Intelligence Service had acquired CryptoAG and its machines were designed with NSA assistance and had numerous backdoors. Operation RUBICON, as it was code-named, continued until 2018. From the Collection of H. Keith and Karen Melton at the International Spy Museum.

Plate 100. Soviet-made Fialka cipher machine. Similar to the Enigma but with ten rotors, it was developed in the late 1950s and would have been an important target for GCHQ codebreakers. This machine was probably used by Czechoslovakia. On loan from Roger W. Harrison.

Plate 101. Pin worn by trade union members of GCHQ, Britain's signals intelligence organization. GCHQ employees could be in unions from 1947, and there were occasional union strikes until the British government banned membership from 1984 to 1997.

Plate 102. US Navy uniform patch for a World War II–era member of the WAVES, Women Accepted for Voluntary Emergency Service. The patch indicates that its owner, Eleanor Barnhart, recruited into the navy from a small mining town in Pennsylvania, was a Specialist Q (Communication Specialist) First Class. Many Specialist Qs worked in cryptography and radio intelligence. They operated codebreaking machines, staffed intercept stations, and performed other important work for the navy's signals intelligence effort. From the Collection of H. Keith and Karen Melton at the International Spy Museum.

Umol-huun tah-tiyal

William Frederick

*yetel*

Elizebeth Smith Friedman

*Lay ca-huunil kubenbil tech same.*

This our book we entrusted you a while-ago.

*Ti manaan apaclam-tz'a lo toon*

It not-being you-return-give it us,

*Epahal ca-baat tumen ah-men.*

Is-being-sharpened our-axe by the expert.

Plate 103. Bookplate of the US codebreakers Elizebeth and William Friedman. Treating Mayan hieroglyphics as a code, it threatens dire consequences to the person who does not return a borrowed book. Elizebeth's career included work for the Coast Guard and supporting FBI investigations. William worked for the War Department—leading the team that broke the Japanese Purple cipher system—and then the National Security Agency. From the Collection of H. Keith and Karen Melton at the International Spy Museum.

Plate 104. President Ronald Reagan pinning the National Security Medal on Ann Caracristi in October 1982, the year she retired from the NSA.

Plates 105 and 106. *Album of the Cuban Revolution, 1952–1959*. Designed to be "enjoyable and appropriate for the youth," it tells the story of the Fidel Castro–led insurgency against the regime of the dictator Fulgencio Batista. One section portrays the March 13, 1957, assault on Batista's presidential palace. He survived this attack but fled Cuba on New Year's Day 1959. Courtesy of the Francis Lara Collection.

Plate 107. East German reproduction of a 1932 poster. The slogan "War on imperialist war!" was popular with European Marxist terrorist groups of the 1970s and 1980s. Courtesy of the Francis Lara Collection.

Plate 108. Puzzle interactive in the analysis exhibit at the International Spy Museum. Cindy Storer guides visitors through the structured analytic technique of starbursting to brainstorm and investigate questions that might help locate Osama bin Laden.

Plate 109. Red teaming interactive in the *Decision Room* exhibit at the International Spy Museum. Michael Morrell, former deputy director of the CIA, leads visitors through an analysis of a competing-hypotheses exercise so they can present their assessment to President Barack Obama as to whether Osama bin Laden is in the Abbottabad compound.

Plate 110. Award given to Cindy Storer for her service in the CIA's Counterterrorism Center. Gift of Cynthia Storer.

Plate 111. Cynthia Storer.

Plates 112, 113, 114, and 115. Cards advertising an in-house CIA training course offered in the 2010s encouraging creativity in intelligence analysis. Some class sessions were held at the International Spy Museum.

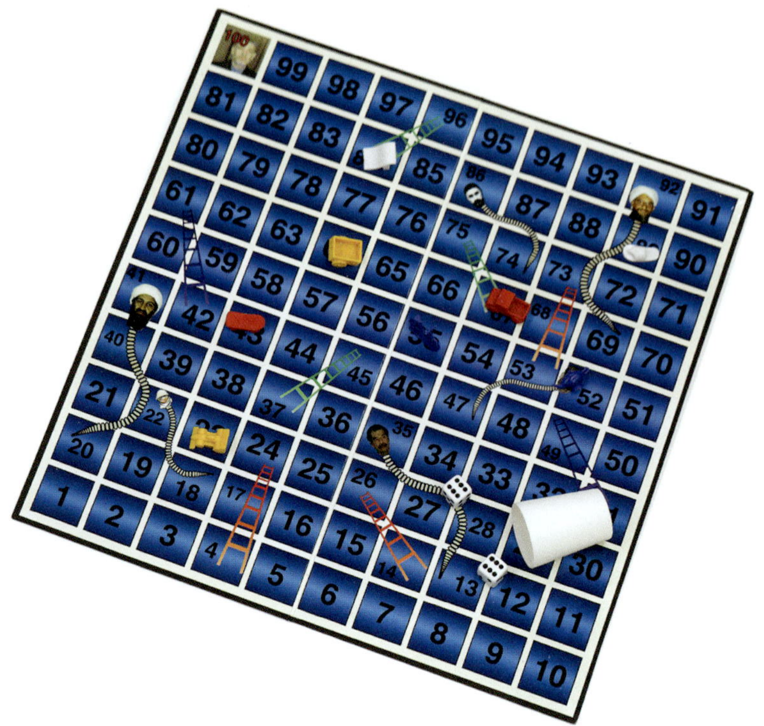

Plate 116. Prototype game based on *Chutes and Ladders* and intended to convince Arab children of the evils of al-Qaeda and Saddam Hussein, the dictator of Iraq. The al-Qaeda figures shown are Osama bin Laden; Ayman al-Zawahiri, bin Laden's deputy; and Abu Musab al-Zarqawi, the leader of al-Qaeda in Iraq, which eventually morphed into ISIS. The game was designed by Donald Levine, the inventor of the G.I. Joe action figure. Levine had previously designed, at the request of the CIA, an Osama bin Laden action figure, the skin of which would peel away to reveal a demon underneath. The Agency apparently passed on this game, however. Courtesy of Mark S. Zaid, Esq.

Plate 117. World War II German propaganda rocket. This rocket contains leaflets intended for the Soviet army, as can be seen through the windows cut in it after it was found in 2017. On loan from the Minister of the Interior of the State of Brandenburg, Federal Republic of Germany.

Plate 118. On D-Day in June 1944, the Allies dropped hundreds of dummies with cotton parachutes across France, far from where the real paratroopers were landing. Though just a third the size of a person, the fakes—nicknamed "Rupert"—would have looked larger in the air. They were designed to explode on landing, destroying evidence of the trick. From the collection of H. Keith Melton and Karen Melton at the International Spy Museum.

Plates 119, 120, and 121. Communist Vietnamese cards meant to intimidate American troops and encourage defections during the Vietnam War. Their customization indicates that communist intelligence knew precisely which units and even individuals they were facing. Courtesy of the Francis Lara Collection.

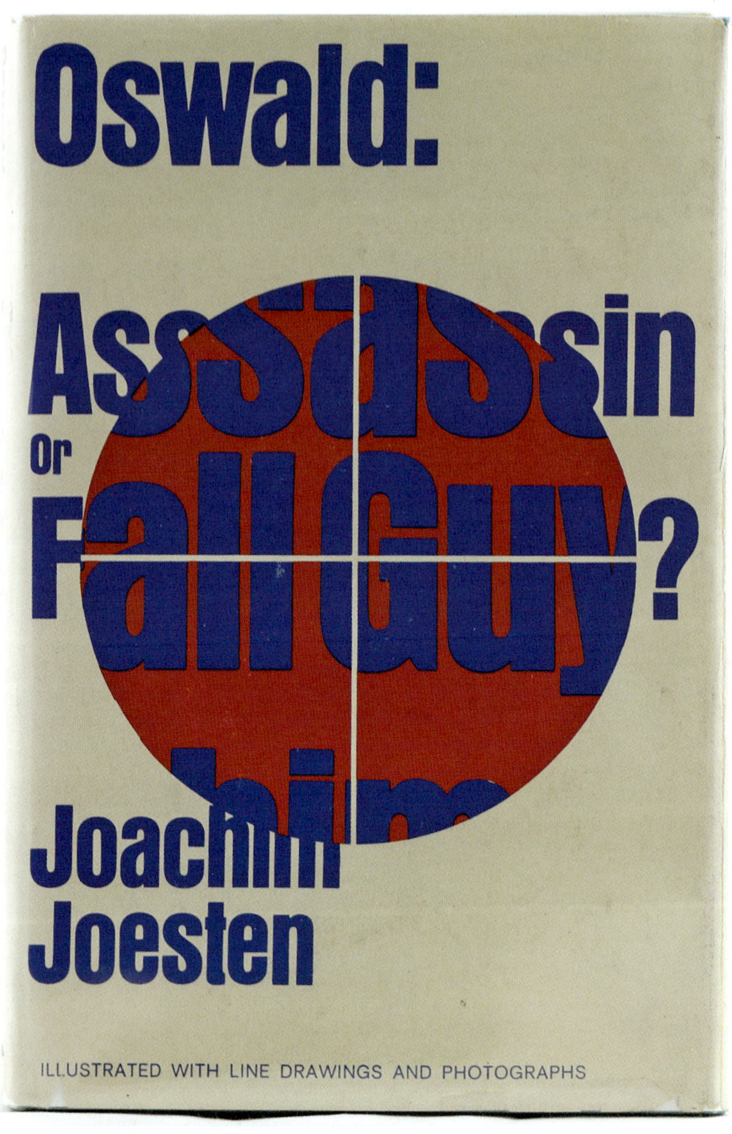


Plate 122. Book published by a KGB-funded publishing house in the United States shortly before the Warren Commission report came out in 1964. This book was the first to argue that the CIA killed President John F. Kennedy, a myth that persists to this day.

Plate 123. Metal sign made in the 1980s by the CIA to encourage Afghans to join the resistance to the Soviet military occupation. On loan from Milt Bearden.

Palte 124. Patches of fake US Army divisions from World War II. During the war, British and American deception staffs convinced German intelligence that the US Army had many more divisions than it actually did. The army's Institute of Heraldry created uniform patches for the nonexistent units in the hope that German spies might see them.

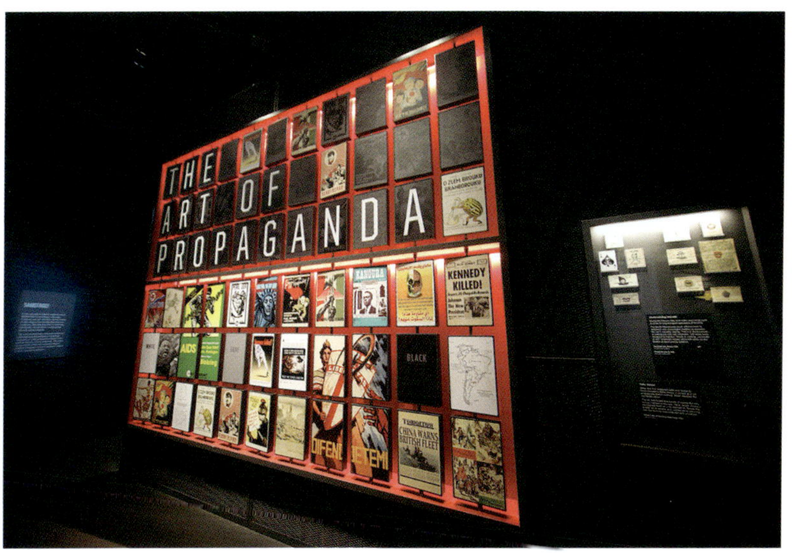


Plate 125. Propaganda exhibit in the *Covert Action* gallery, showing examples of government attempts to manipulate public opinion from ancient Egypt to the 2016 US presidential election. When governments hide their role, propaganda becomes a form of covert action. The operations outlined in this exhibit tapped into emotions ranging from patriotism and love of family to fear and hatred of others.

Plate 126. French polygraph machine, circa 1930. Popularly known as "lie detectors," polygraphs were originally used as medical diagnostic devices for cardiovascular conditions. Today, they are a counterintelligence and counterespionage tool used in many countries, including the United States, Canada, and Russia.

Plates 127 and 128. Rejected cover designs for the classified Robert Hanssen damage assessment. From the Collection of H. Keith and Karen Melton at the International Spy Museum.

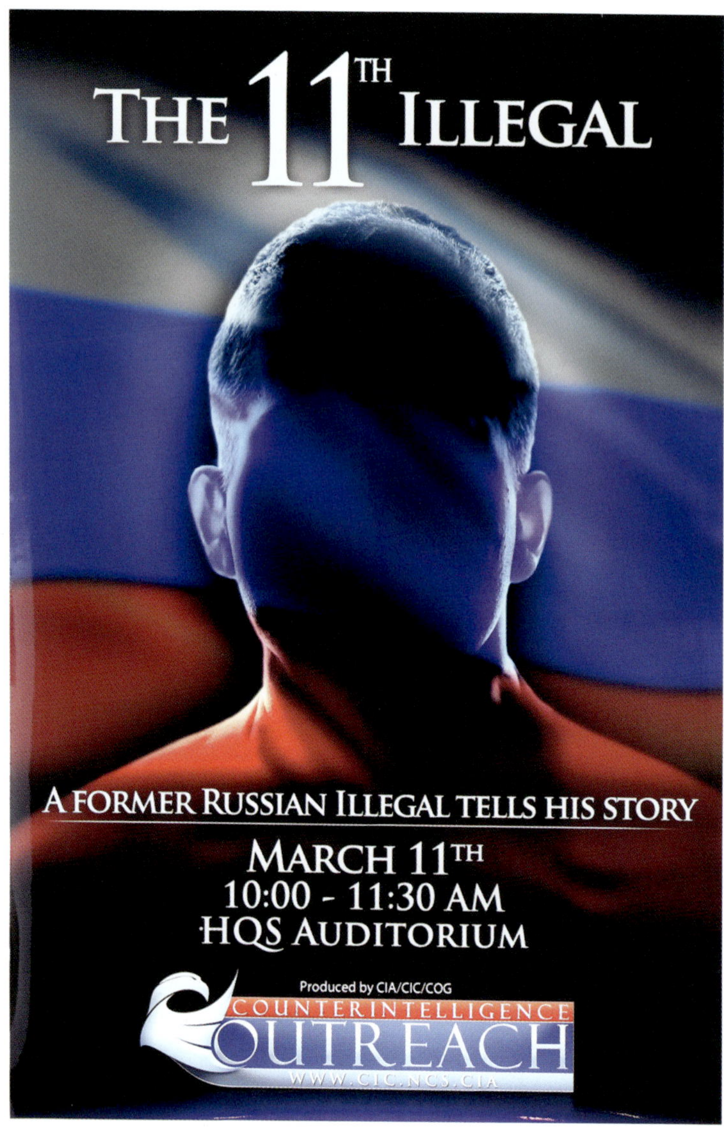


Plate 129. Poster advertising a lecture by a former deep cover Russian intelligence officer to be held in the auditorium at CIA Headquarters, 2010s. From the Collection of H. Keith and Karen Melton at the International Spy Museum.

Plate 130. Russian model illustrating a 1981 operation in which the CIA sent an officer down a manhole on the outskirts of Moscow to tap a buried telecommunications cable carrying Soviet military secrets. The tap was connected to a nearby transceiver that the CIA could interrogate from 2.5 kilometers away. The CIA defector Edward Lee Howard betrayed the operation in 1985. From the Collection of H. Keith and Karen Melton at the International Spy Museum.

Plate 131. US Defense Intelligence Agency security poster featuring Aldrich Ames. From the Collection of H. Keith and Karen Melton at the International Spy Museum.

Plate 132. Reproduction of a bug found in 1999 concealed in a chair rail at the US State Department in Washington, DC, made by the Russian intelligence officer behind the surveillance operation. Such discoveries demonstrate the well-founded nature of the Canadian government's concern about bugs hidden in buildings where Jeffrey Delisle previously worked. From the Collection of H. Keith and Karen Melton at the International Spy Museum.

Plate 133. F-67M rollover camera concealed inside an English–German dictionary, Soviet Union, GRU, 1960s. Such cameras were used to photograph documents rather like a modern-day hand scanner but using film. From the Collection of H. Keith and Karen Melton at the International Spy Museum.

Plate 134. Concealment rock used as a dead drop by the Russian GRU. From the Collection of H. Keith and Karen Melton at the International Spy Museum.

Plate 135. Interrogation glove, UK Special Air Service, 1970s. The original owner reported having used this glove while interrogating members of the IRA. From the Collection of H. Keith and Karen Melton at the International Spy Museum.

about your inferences?"[44] Both men were implicitly encouraging their analysts to use SATs

On March 14, 2011, President Obama chaired a meeting of his top advisers at the White House. At this meeting, Panetta reported that the evidence "pointed toward the possibility of [bin Laden's presence at the compound], but it was not . . . conclusive."[45] Members of the intelligence community remained divided. Michael Morell was only 60 percent confident that bin Laden was at the compound. However, the counterterrorism analysts and analytic managers directly involved with the search were more optimistic because of their repeated success over the previous years in thwarting attacks and capturing al-Qaeda members. One analyst even claimed a 95 percent probability that it was bin Laden. (A fictionalized version of this moment appears in the Hollywood thriller *Zero Dark Thirty*.) Gun-shy because of the Iraq WMD disaster, other analysts continued to offer alternative explanations in their briefings, but none of them seemed more persuasive than the bin Laden argument.[46]

In late April 2011, Michael Leiter, head of the National Counterterrorism Center, newly briefed on the Abbottabad issue, made a recommendation to Brennan. Leiter had served on the Commission on the Intelligence Capabilities of the United States Regarding Weapons of Mass Destruction investigating the Iraq WMD failure, and he wanted to make sure that all options were explored this time around. He recommended that Brennan set up the Red Team to reexamine all the intelligence analysis from an alternative perspective.[47] Brennan was persuaded and had Leiter coordinate with Morell at the CIA. They selected two NCTC analysts (a man and a woman) and two CTC analysts to conduct the experiment. None of the four had previously worked on the question.[48]

This Red Team seems to have used the analysis of competing hypotheses. Over 48 hours they examined three different explanations for the Abbottabad compound: that it was associated with bin Laden, but he was not there; that another senior al-Qaeda leader lived there; and that another unidentified criminal was staying in the compound. The Red Team's analysts found the first hypothesis to be the most likely. The second they found much less likely simply because, in Leiter's words, "we actually thought we had a pretty good handle on all the [high-value targets]." The criminal idea seemed unlikely given that a known resident of the compound, known as Abu Ahmed al-Kuwaiti, had strong ties to al-Qaeda in the past, even serving as a courier for bin Laden.[49] Overall, the analysts judged that none of these hypotheses were as compelling as the CTC's assessment that bin Laden was at the compound. This probability they estimated to be between 40 percent and 60 percent.[50] On April 28, Leiter briefed the Red

Team findings to President Obama.[51] Having now heard estimates ranging from 40 percent to 95 percent, the president made the hard call and decided to launch the raid. On May 1, 2011, a group of US Navy SEALs flew into Pakistan, raided the Abbottabad compound, and killed bin Laden.

In the period after the Abbottabad raid, the International Spy Museum ramped up its efforts to design a new museum. In November 2013, the museum asked Storer to become a consultant. She began her work for the museum's Exhibitions and Programs Department, which was led by Anna Slafer, who had held the position since before the museum opened in 2002. Slafer's department, which consisted mostly of women, was somewhat unusual in the museum world in that it combined the curatorial staff and the education staff. This setup (which mirrored the Directorate of Intelligence/Directorate of Operations mix in the CIA's Counterterrorism Center) had important implications. First and most important, the educators, who put on public programs and frequently worked with schoolteachers and students, had a strong sense of how to convey complex issues to museum visitors. Second, because the curatorial staff and the education staff both pitched in on curatorial work, the educators were able to bring their expertise to exhibition design, especially interactive features.

In December 2013, Storer got a separate contract to develop a program for schoolchildren under the supervision of Jacqueline Eyl, the museum's director of youth education. This contract called for her to design "an interactive game that engages students in the critical thinking process used by intelligence analysts when faced with unknown information."[52] The first game was to be based on the hunt for Osama bin Laden. For Storer, the central issue was how to approach the design. Outside the intelligence community, the work of counterterrorism analysts to catch terrorists or thwart attacks was often compared to connecting the dots. However, for Storer and many of her colleagues, this was not the best analogy. They preferred the metaphor of a puzzle, with a few additional twists.

According to Storer, the concept of a puzzle is embedded in the business of intelligence analysis. She believes that analysts generally face three types of problems: mysteries, secrets, and puzzles. Mysteries are not knowable, usually because they involve the future, or complex human motivations, and so are best expressed in terms of potential scenarios or even probabilities. Secrets, in contrast, are knowable, but only when one has the right source—for example, a spy who can provide the right document or a key intercepted signal. Puzzles, meanwhile, are secrets for which no single source can be found to provide the answer. For example, many people probably knew the secret of Osama bin Laden's whereabouts, but ten years of searching had not turned up a source that could or would reveal that secret. So the answer had to be put together as a puzzle: from little bits and pieces. The situation was further complicated because the types of puzzles analysts encountered were not straightforward. As Storer told *Salon* magazine in 2013, often "pieces fall from the sky and add to the pile the analyst already has." However, "there is no picture [and] no edge pieces" to guide the analyst. Furthermore, she explained, "not all of the pieces fit in the puzzle"; some belong in a different box entirely.[53]

In tasking Storer with the project, the museum staff also emphasized that she should keep the project as "close to the real facts of the case as possible."[54] Since Storer was not involved in the capture of bin Laden, she would need to use her experience to extrapolate from the public record what had happened. This required extensive research, rigorous validation, and cross-checking sources while remaining conscious of the fact that the full story was not yet available—and might never be. In addition, some of the public record might not be accurate, and she could not correct that. So her goal became to pick pieces that suggested what probably happened without including those pieces that probably never happened. The game she developed was called *Analyze This*. It involved asking questions, developing lines of inquiry, and matching those lines with the information made available at the start. Once this process was completed, the players could request additional information and match it to the new questions. In short, the game was a Starbursting exercise and an exercise in the abductive process of analysis.

In the meantime, planning for a new International Spy Museum started in earnest, and Slafer asked Eyl, who had been working with Storer on the game, to lead the development of the interactive exhibitions. Thereafter both Eyl and Storer turned their attention to the exhibition. By this time, more material on the hunt for bin Laden had come out, including Michael Morell's memoir, *The Great War of Our Time*.[55] These materials augmented and validated much of what Storer's research had found, including a strong hint that CIA analysts had used Starbursting and ACH to guide their work to locate bin Laden.

A second key to the development of the interactive exhibition was an online, collaborative mind-mapping program, which Storer used in her university courses, as it allowed collaborative work on multiple SATs. This program gave her an idea of how to visually display the hunt for bin Laden in a way that would make sense to others. Using both the program and Morell's account of the analytical process as well as the data she had put together for the game, Storer mapped the analytical process that led to locating bin Laden. She started with the intelligence questions outlined in Morell's book, then worked through what she could learn of the intelligence community's early efforts in answering those questions and homing in on the Abbottabad compound. She highlighted the distinct stages of the inquiry, as publicly revealed, and depicted some important dead ends as well as productive leads.

Something else that Storer had to keep in mind as she put together her package was time. Intelligence analyses are typically brief because policymakers have little time to engage with them. A similar issue arises in the museum world, where an interactive experience is generally limited to no more than 10 minutes. Taking this into account, Storer whittled down the diagram to what she thought were the key lines of inquiry and key leads. Upon seeing it, Eyl's response was "this is amazing." She forwarded it to Anna Slafer. Her response was "that's the [exhibition], that's it!"[56]

In the world of analysis, imagery and graphics specialists often play major roles in shaping the input. Something similar also happens in the museum world. The International Spy Museum shared Storer's mind map with Gallagher and Associates, a design company the museum had hired to work on a new museum. Specifically, Gallagher was charged with coming up with the user's experience, developing the interactive technology, and designing the physical exhibition, including its graphics.[57] The Spy Museum provided input and reviewed each phase of the work. Storer did not work directly with Gallagher, but she did continue to consult throughout the process.

Based on the input from Storer and Eyl, Gallagher put together a "choose your own adventure game," which put players in the shoes of analysts. In the exhibition each player sits at a console in front of a video wall on which a "senior officer" sets the stage and provides them with their first assignment—find Osama bin Laden—and subsequent updates. Working through a Starbursting exercise, the players view several who–what–when–where questions and decide which to pursue. Along the way, they explore new evidence or encounter specific events and must make decisions about which path to follow. Some paths lead to dead ends; others provide essential clues. These clues are then displayed on the wall for everyone to see, encouraging collaboration. Players can then backtrack if they wish. At key junctures they are directed by a "senior intelligence officer"—Storer herself—to move on to the next stage of the investigation. These stages mirror points in the real investigation where analysts stepped back to assess their progress and options. The game ends when the visitors have enough clues to lead them to the compound in Abbottabad.

With this exhibition completed, the museum staff turned to the next project. They had always wanted to have an exhibition immediately after the analysis room that would show the delivery of assessments to policymakers. The International Spy Museum also wanted to find a way to incorporate President Obama's decision to raid the Abbottabad compound. Storer saw this as an opportunity to introduce ACH, probably the mostly widely used SAT. For several reasons, she surmised that the analysts looking for bin Laden had gone through this exercise themselves. First, the requirement in Intelligence Community Directive 203 to do alternative analysis would have pushed them in this direction. Second, Morell's book said that the CIA had held Red Team exercises to assess the likelihood that bin Laden was using the compound, including assessing multiple hypotheses about who might be in the compound in Abbottabad.[58] Third, Peter Bergen had noted in his book *Manhunt* that in October 2010 the analysts had subjected the intelligence on al-Kuwaiti to a formal process of structured analytical techniques and came up with four alternative hypotheses: that he was hiding from al-Qaeda; he was working for a different al-Qaeda leader; he was working for an unassociated criminal; or that bin Laden's family but not bin Laden himself was living at the compound.[59]

So the exhibition was designed to guide visitors through an interactive display in which they would analyze four competing hypotheses about who resided at the compound: Osama bin Laden; another senior al-Qaeda figure; an organized crime leader; or a wealthy businessman. Players would be presented with pieces of information and asked to assess whether they seemed consistent with each hypothesis. These pieces included facts such as that the compound had no telephone or internet and that the balcony had a privacy wall. As this interactive exhibition came together, the question arose of who would narrate the videos and lead players through the exercise. At the last minute, Storer suggested that Morell would be ideal. Eyl thought that was a good idea, and the museum reached out to him. Eyl recalls that "it was like the stars aligned." Indeed, he "loved the concept" and was able to bring to bear his experience of being in the room with President Obama when the decision was made to raid the compound.[60]

As the two exhibitions came to fruition, and unbeknownst to Storer, Eyl also was planning to include a display focused on Storer that would immediately precede the *Hunt for bin Laden* interactive. She asked Storer to contribute personal artifacts for the museum "to bring her work and who she is as an individual to life."[61] Storer provided her "Terrorist Buster" pin, which in the 1990s was given to employees joining the Counterterrorism Center as a symbol of the person's entry into a special team. She also

Figure 11.3: Whistle/signal light issued by the CIA to employees after September 11, 2001. Designed to hang on lanyards, they could be used to summon rescuers if the wearer was buried under rubble in a terrorist attack. That was a plausible possibility: additional attacks were expected, and CIA Headquarters was known to have been in the terrorists' crosshairs. On loan from Cynthia Storer.

contributed the combination whistle and light issued to Agency employees after 9/11 so they could summon help if they were buried under rubble in an attack; a commendation medal; and a going-away card signed by her colleagues.

As we have shown throughout this chapter, several different groups, including intelligence practitioners, scholars, and museum professionals, worked together to create two exhibitions at the International Spy Museum that reflected the new set of analytical standards that were adopted by the CIA in the 2000s. Two of these techniques were used to hunt down Osama bin Laden and to tell the story of how and why it all happened. Today, because of these collaborations, the public can get a glimpse of how intelligence analysts managed to uncover one of the world's biggest puzzles. And today, because of a partnership between analysts and historians, everyone can read about how it all came together. We believe that these types of collaborative efforts—among practitioners, curators, and scholars—hold great promise for bringing hidden stories of the past into the light.

Figure 11.4: World War II escape map concealed in a deck of cards, designed by Britain's MI9, the intelligence organization created to help Allied POWs escape and downed airmen evade capture. Users peeled off the top layers of the cards to reveal numbered map sections and assembled them to form a complete map. From the Collection of H. Keith and Karen Melton at the International Spy Museum.

## Further Reading

*The 9/11 Commission Report: The Final Report of the National Commission on Terrorist Attacks Upon the United States* (Authorized Edition). W. W. Norton: New York, 2003.

Bergen, Peter L. *MANHUNT: The Ten-Year Search for Bin Laden from 9/11 to Abbottabad*. Doubleday, Canada, 2012.

Coll, Stephen. *Ghost Wars: The Secret History of the CIA, Afghanistan, and Bin Laden, from the Soviet Invasion to September 10, 2001*. New York: Penguin Press, 2004.

Heuer Jr., Richards J., and Randolph H. Pherson, *Structured Analytic Techniques for Intelligence Analysis*. 2nd ed. Washington: CQ Press, 2015.

Morell, Michael J. *The Great War of Our Time: The CIA's Fight against Terrorism from al Qa'ida to ISIS*. New York: Twelve, 2015.

## Notes

1. Glenn Kessler, "The Iraq War and WMD's: An Intelligence Failure of White House Spin," *Washington Post*, March 22, 2019. James N. Gilmore, "Zero Dark Thirty and the Writing of Post-9/11 History," *Intelligence and National Security* 34, no. 3 (2017): 275–294.

2. Bin Laden's name has been spelled several ways, as it has been transliterated from the original Arabic. The authors choose to use "bin Laden" in this article because

it is the most common version in English. Researchers should be aware that the CIA's original spelling was "Bin Ladin."

3. Jacqueline Eyl (Director of Youth Education, International Spy Museum) in discussion with Mark Stout and Sarah-Jane Corke, August 12, 2022.

4. A list of some of these warnings is in Peter L. Bergen, *Manhunt: The Ten-Year Search for Bin Laden from 9/11 to Abbottabad* (Canada: Doubleday, 2012), 104–105.

5. National Commission on Terrorist Attacks Upon the United States, *The 9/11 Commission Report: The Final Report of The National Commission on Terrorist Attacks Upon the United States* (New York: W. W. Norton, 2004), 260–262.

6. There were more than 40 intelligence articles in the President's Daily Briefs from January 20 to September 10, 2011, that related to bin Laden. *9/11 Commission Report*, 254.

7. *9/11 Commission Report*, 74–76.

8. *9/11 Commission Report*, 92.

9. Steve Coll, *Ghost Wars: The Secret History of the CIA, Afghanistan, and Bin Laden, from the Soviet Invasion to September 10, 2001* (New York: Penguin Press, 2004), 453.

10. Bergen, *Manhunt*, 78.

11. Coll, *Ghost Wars*, 453, 511, 518.

12. Mark Stout, "American Intelligence Assessments of the Jihadists, 1989–2011," in *The Image of the Enemy: Perception of Foes since 1945*, ed. Paul Maddrell (Washington, DC: Georgetown University Press, 2015), 255.

13. Bergen, *Manhunt* 55.

14. Jane Mayer, "Junior: The Clandestine Life of America's Top Al Qaeda Source," *The New Yorker*, September 11, 2006, www.newyorker.com/magazine/2006/09/11/junior.

15. *9/11 Commission Report*, 70.

16. Central Intelligence Agency, "Bombings in Nairobi and Dar es Salaam-An Update," August 14, 1998, *National Security Archive*, June 19, 2012.

17. George Tenet, *At the Center of the Storm: My Years at the CIA* (New York: HarperCollins, 2007), 122–123.

18. Tenet, *At the Center of the Storm*, 124–126.

19. *9/11 Commission Report*, 259.

20. Bergen, *Manhunt*, 74.

21. Bergen, *Manhunt*, 90.

22. Stephen J. Cimbala, "CIA Must Explain Its Failure on WMD," *Baltimore Sun*, February 3, 2004, www.baltimoresun.com/news/bs-xpm-2004-02-03-0402030073-story.html.

23. Office of the Director of National Intelligence, "Analytic Standards (Effective June 21, 2007)," Intelligence Community Directive Number 203, www.dni.gov/files/documents/ICD/ICD%20203%20Analytic%20Standards%20pdf-unclassified.pdf. Conversation with Pamela Stout, August 17, 2022.

24. Barry M. Katz, *Foreign Intelligence: Research and Analysis in the Office of Strategic Services, 1942–1945* (Cambridge, MA: Harvard University Press, 1989), 5–14.

25. Sherman Kent, *Strategic Intelligence for American World Policy* (Princeton: Princeton University Press, 1949).

26. Kent, *Strategic Intelligence*, 182.

27. Richards J. Heuer, Jr., "The Evolution of Structured Analytic Techniques," presentation to the National Academy of Science, National Research Council Commit-

tee on Behavioral and Social Science Research to Improve Intelligence Analysis for National Security, Washington, DC, December 8, 2009, www.e-education.psu.edu/geog885/sites/www.e-education.psu.edu.geog885/files/file/Evolution_SAT_Heuer.pdf, 1.

28. Heuer, "Structured Analytic Techniques."

29. Heuer, "Structured Analytic Techniques," 2.

30. Heuer, "Structured Analytic Techniques."

31. Richards J. Heuer and Randolph H. Pherson, *Structured Analytic Techniques for Intelligence Analysis*, 2nd ed. (Washington: CQ Press, 2015), 181.

32. Richards J. Heuer, Jr., *The Psychology of Intelligence Analysis* (Washington, DC: Center for the Study of Intelligence, Central Intelligence Agency, 1999).

33. Heuer and Pherson, *Structured Analytic*, 4.

34. US Government, "A Tradecraft Primer: Structured Analytical Techniques for Improving Intelligence Analysis," March 2009, 2, www.stat.berkeley.edu/~aldous/157/Papers/Tradecraft%20Primer-apr09.pdf.

35. Pherson Associates, LLC, website, archived by the Wayback Machine, December 2, 2005, https://web.archive.org/web/20061202021235/http://www.pherson.org:80.

36. Stephen Artner, Richard S. Girven, and James B. Bruce, "Assessing the Value of Structured Analytic Techniques in the U.S. Intelligence Community," RAND Corporation, RR-1408-OSD, 2016, 3.

37. Heuer and Pherson, *Structured Analytic Techniques*.

38. Heuer and Pherson, *Structured Analytic Techniques*, 113.

39. Leon Panetta with Jim Newton, *Worthy Fights: A Memoir of Leadership in War and Peace* (New York: Penguin, 2014), 292–293.

40. Panetta, *Worthy Fights*, 294–295. Michael J. Morell, *The Great War of Our Time: The CIA's Fight Against Terrorism from al Qa'ida to ISIS* (New York: Twelve, 2015), 147–148. Bergen, *Manhunt*, 127.

41. Panetta, *Worthy Fights*, 295–297.

42. Morell, *Great War*, 153. Panetta, *Worthy Fights*, 299.

43. Bergen, *Manhunt*, 129.

44. Bergen, *Manhunt*, 134.

45. Panetta, *Worthy Fights*, 308–309. Morell, *Great War*, 156.

46. Morell, *Great War*, 158–161.

47. Bergen, *Manhunt*, 191.

48. Bergen *Manhunt*, 191–193.

49. Bergen *Manhunt*, 193–194.

50. Bergen, *Manhunt*, 193–194. Morell and James Brennan have written broadly similar accounts of the Red Team. See Morell, *Great War*, 160, and James Brennan, *Undaunted: My Fight Against America's Enemies at Home and Abroad* (New York: Celadon Books, 2006), 238.

51. Bergen, *Manhunt*, 196.

52. Draft description of the "Intel Puzzle Project," in Storer's possession, December 19, 2013.

53. Nada Bakos, "'ZDT' Gets the CIA Wrong: And Not Just in Its Torture Scenes. A Former Operative Weighs in on the Year's Most Controversial Movie," *Salon*, January 18, 2013, www.salon.com/2013/01/18/zd30_gets_the_cia_wrong.

54. Anna Slafer email to Cynthia Storer, January 10, 2014.

55. Morell, *Great War*.

56. Jacqueline Eyl (Director of Youth Education, International Spy Museum) in discussion with Mark Stout and Sarah-Jane Corke, August 12, 2022.

57. Jacqueline Eyl email to Cynthia Storer, September 22, 2022.

58. Morell, *Great War*, 159.

59. Bergen, *Manhunt*, 128–129.

60. Eyl to Stout and Corke, August 12, 2022.

61. Eyl to Stout and Corke, August 12, 2022.

# Counter-disinformation and the Tools of the Intelligence Trade: An Historical Perspective

Gill Bennett

*We often think of covert action as involving violence. The US-UK operation to overthrow Iranian prime minister Mohammad Mosaddegh in 1953 or the recent Russian assassinations of regime enemies spring to mind. However, disinformation is often a more powerful covert tactic. For instance, the United States and many European countries have recently become alert to Russian disinformation operations that seek to sow discord among Russia's rivals. But what can be done to counter disinformation campaigns? In a chapter of applied history, Gill Bennett, the former chief historian of the United Kingdom's Foreign and Commonwealth Office, provides some answers.—The Editors*

The incidence and effects of disinformation have become the subject of constant analysis and redefinition in the twenty-first century. Although the dissemination of false information intended to deceive is by no means a modern phenomenon, its use has multiplied and been weaponized in the digital age. But disinformation is just a part—the offensive element—of information management operations, a tool of statecraft that can be traced back to ancient times. Counter-disinformation, the defensive element, has always been significant but is now increasingly important for both states and citizens. This chapter argues that history, combined with the tools of the intelligence analyst, offers useful lessons in identifying disinformation and building resilience to it. It includes two British case studies: the mismanagement of the Zinoviev Letter, a classic piece of 1920s disinformation; and the Foreign Office's Information Research Department, a counter-disinformation initiative launched in the early Cold War.

In considering how to develop an effective counter-disinformation strategy, it is unhelpful to get hung up on questions of definition, particularly since the range of terms employed is so wide and usage varies in different parts of the world including in civilian versus military contexts.[1] In this chapter, I use the term "disinformation" to mean the offensive component of a suite of information management operations. This includes the dissemination of information that might be misleading or false by a state, government, or interest group to project a particular narrative, promote particular interests to the disadvantage of competitors, and influence opinions or events through disruption or deception. The defensive component, counter-disinformation, includes the identification of such activities, tracing their origin and building the capacity to control or mitigate their effects.

There are, however, some points of definition that are helpful to explore, as they show how perception—in particular whether we are using information in our own interests or are on the receiving end of it—makes a difference. For example, one common definition is that disinformation is information disseminated intentionally to deceive, even if the information may seem truthful, relevant, and based on objective fact. This seems straightforward, but the connotations are entirely negative. Yet in some cases, particularly during wartime, such use of disinformation may be celebrated as a key component of success. The success of the Normandy landings in June 1944 owed much to deception operations by both the Allied High Command (Operation Fortitude) and the Soviets (Operation Bagration).[2] Successful use of disinformation in these operations, combined with the disinformation fed to the Germans by double agents in the British intelligence agency MI5's Double Cross program, meant that in May 1944 the Germans did not know how many forces they would be facing on either the Eastern or Western Front or when and where they would attack.[3] A more recent example was Operation Desert Deception, implemented in the Gulf War (1990–1991), when disinformation was used to persuade the Iraqis that Coalition forces would not attack through the desert.[4]

Of course, many strategies are employed in war that might not be approved (or practicable) in peace. Some may argue also that military deception is not the same thing as a digital campaign designed to influence elections or disrupt order or to spread conspiracy theories or false narratives on social media. They are clearly different in form and medium. But all such operations represent the management of information and its use as a strategic tool, whether for military, political, or social purposes. It is indisputable that in the twenty-first century, as the intelligence expert David Omand writes, "subversion and sedition are now digital."[5] But their purpose, as tools of disinformation, remains the same.

Another area where the definition is disputed is in relation to propaganda. In her book *Anticipating Surprise*, the former Defense Intelligence Agency analyst Cynthia Grabo defines "disinformation" as propaganda based on falsehood, whereas propaganda based on fact is public diplomacy.[6] This definition is problematic, not least because it invokes the presence of

Figures 12.1 and 12.2: During the late 1950s, the best German jazz magazine was *Schlagzeug*. It was actually a product of the CIA, which recognized that jazz was implicitly subversive of communism. In addition, each issue contained one or two more directly subversive articles designed to undermine the communist government in East Germany. However, most of its readers were in West Germany, and few copies made it into communist East Germany. Gift of Thomas Rid.

a benevolent authority that knows what is best for the audience. The line between telling people the facts, and what you want them to believe, may be crossed easily into the realm of disinformation. Distinguishing between false propaganda and public diplomacy can also be deceptive, as an example offered by Grabo shows. In 1965–1966, the North Vietnamese authorities issued a barrage of statements calling for large-scale enlistment in the armed forces and the recruitment of women into the workforce to free up men for military service. The American intelligence community took this to be disinformation—false propaganda—whereas in fact it was the official line put out by the North Vietnamese—that they had no troops in the South and no intention to recruit—that was false.[7]

Clearly, disinformation can be defined in many ways and encompasses a wide range of information management tools including deception, propaganda, and the intentional and accidental manipulation of factual material. It is more important to understand this than to split hairs over points of interpretation. Recognizing disinformation and protecting ourselves against it is a bigger problem than defining it. History can help.

Offensive information management operations are nothing new, even if the means of dissemination have been transformed by digital technology. Plato argued in the fifth century BCE that a ruler is entitled to deceive the populace in the interests of their own safety and the security of the state. Thucydides suggested that a man with good advice to give has to lie to be believed.[8] Both were talking about disinformation justified by a worthy purpose, rather like administering a sort of state medicine, as Karl Popper commented.[9] In Plato's case, one aim was to encourage patriotism—and obedience—by tapping into people's willingness to believe in some sort of mythical golden age when things were different and better. This is a recognizable aim of those engaged in information management throughout history; for example, by Adolf Hitler (encouraging the Nazi doctrine of an Aryan supremacy undermined and poisoned by Jews) and more recently by al-Qaeda and Daesh (pure Islam under attack from infidel Crusaders). In Popper's view, disinformation of this kind, in a Platonic context, is even more powerful and wholesome if those in authority themselves believe it. Yet Greek philosophers also believed that political authority rested upon citizens being able to think and to judge for themselves.

While rulers may use disinformation with good intent, its use can also be pernicious, undermining public trust in authority and alienating citizens from the political system; encouraging the idea of truth as a subjective concept so that any narrative proves acceptable; fostering intolerance and extreme views; or pressuring decision makers into premature or unwise moves. Using disinformation in this way also serves to bolster the stability of authoritarian regimes. Historically, autocratic regimes have proved themselves generally more effective in this respect than liberal democracies, which have fewer control mechanisms at their disposal. It is no coincidence that countries like China, Iran, North Korea, and Russia are identified frequently as possible sources of offensive information management operations.

Modern liberal democracies may seem particularly vulnerable to disruption because of their technological freedom and belief in the importance of freedom of expression. In an information space where anyone is free to post, like, share, or disagree strongly with any given material, a narrative that is false (whether by accident or by design) can reach millions of people in seconds. One scholar has argued that while Western liberal states are vulnerable to "a complex chimera of untamable technology, neoliberal backlash, modern empowerment chic[,] and cyber-enhanced egomania," autocratic regimes are vulnerable to the "existential fear of embarrassment."[10] There is little evidence, however, that purveyors of disinformation are concerned about detection or are embarrassed by challenges to their authority. Indeed, such challenges may provide those responsible with proof that they are under attack by "foreign influences," a useful tool with domestic audiences. One of the reasons that Russian disinformation operations have appeared egregious is that Russian authorities give the impression of not caring whether or not they are detected and attributed to them.

There is no doubt that Russia is skilled in information management, both offensive and defensive. It is indeed possible to make a case that the spectrum of Russian information management operations has remained unbroken, or at least little changed, since the 1917 Bolshevik Revolution, and the two historical case studies in this chapter relate in part to Russian activities. But it is misleading to focus on one country, particularly as the use of proxies and multiple agencies is prevalent. Russia is by no means the only, or necessarily the most prolific, source of disinformation, even if it may be the most frequently identified. As of 2019, more than 70 states could be identified as engaged in political disinformation campaigns.[11] This may have been a conservative estimate, and the number has almost certainly increased since then; the most pervasive information management operations may yet be undetected. For example, Chinese operations, both domestic and foreign, remain underexamined.[12]

While increasing efforts and ingenuity are being put into detecting disinformation, much less effort is being devoted to measuring its impact. Evidence of disinformation during an election campaign does not necessarily mean it influenced the result, as arguments concerning 2016's US

Figure 12.3: Map forged by British intelligence purporting to show Nazi German plans for expanding into South America. The United Kingdom secretly passed it to the US government as part of its effort to persuade the United States to enter World War II. President Franklin Roosevelt denounced these (phony) German plans in an October 1941 speech.

presidential election and UK referendum on membership of the European Union have illustrated. Many information campaigns, particularly those employing social media, are targeted not at a specific outcome but at destabilization and disruption for their own sake. If the intended result is tension and division, it is difficult to determine how much of that may be ascribed to information management. The Cold War Czech defector Ladislav Bittman has stated that the lack of any reliable means of measuring the impact of Soviet disinformation was an intentional element of its employment.[13] Evidence of the incidence of disinformation mounts daily; its effect is far less accurately measurable.

None of this is intended to downplay the potentially pernicious effects of disinformation, particularly when disseminated globally with malicious intent through social media. But motivation and intent are important qualifiers, and one person's disinformation may be another's public education. There is a tendency to interpret disinformation entirely as something "bad" done to us, while our own use of information, however equivocal, is "good." There are parallels with espionage, which may be perceived as bad when we are spied on but good if our spies are successful. Understanding motivation can help with detecting disinformation and with reducing its impact.

A great deal of work is currently being done, particularly through technological means, on detecting, fact-checking, and (where possible) neutralizing offensive information attacks. It is increasingly possible for technically sophisticated governments and organizations to detect such attacks and discover their sources. But the flexibility and speed of communications, and the skills of those involved in information management operations, mean that however comprehensive the regulatory framework, however clever the algorithmic analysis, disinformation is impossible to eliminate completely. It follows that we need to develop a defensive approach that protects and mitigates damage as far as possible. This is where history can help in conjunction with tools already employed in the world of intelligence analysis.

Just as intelligence analysts assessing a piece of information subject it to a number of tests before deciding on its authenticity and relevance, a similar methodology can be applied to information. Techniques potentially useful in detecting and countering disinformation include: (1) interrogating the source, checking where information came from, whether it fits with other information from the same source, and whether similar information can be found from an independent source; (2) if the source is identified, considering the possible motives of those putting out the information—even if an opponent's motives appear to be based on falsehoods or are unacceptable, it is both important and useful to understand them; (3) avoiding bias and mirror-imaging, guarding against accepting information as genuine because it supports what we already believe or feel; (4) assessing the nature of the threat, including accepting a level of shared risk, because disinformation cannot be eliminated;[14] (5) willingness to collaborate with others in identifying and, if possible, mitigating risk; and (6) understanding the kind of damage that could result if information is compromised and disinformation permitted to dominate the public space.

These recommendations also tie in with an approach used by the military: when faced with a threat, separate capability from intent, working out who has the motivation to spread the disinformation and who has both the ability and capacity to do it. This helps to assess the level of risk, since "capability + intent = threat" and "threat combined with vulnerability = risk." These formulas may seem stark and more applicable to the armed forces than to policymakers, but they have a wider civilian application. Knowing who might want to use disinformation against us, and who has the capacity to do so, helps to identify a possible threat—and the more we can protect ourselves against disinformation, the more we can reduce the risks.

The two examples that follow show how the British government (1) mismanaged a case of disinformation in the 1920s by failing to follow sound principles and best practice; and (2) in the late 1940s tried to use those principles and practice to put in place an effective system to counter disinformation. The first episode remains controversial and politically divisive in Britain, and popular suspicion of the activities of the intelligence, media, and political establishments—not just in Britain but also far more widely—has persisted and at times been shown to be justified. It might also be argued that modern technology and communications serve to facilitate the replication on a global scale of the tactics employed so many years ago. Rather, the significance and contemporary relevance of the 1920s example lies in what it reveals about the difficulty of uncovering the source of disinformation and measuring its effect in a situation where allegiances and motives are complex and interconnected.

In the second example, from the late 1940s, it is interesting to note that, as more archival material reaches the public domain, less attention seems to be paid by scholars to effectiveness than to whether the government should have been engaging in such activities in the first place. This risks underplaying the political context and confusing information management activities with more direct, even kinetic action. During what we now call the "Cold War," the ideological element of the East–West conflict meant that information played a particularly significant role even though the threat of armed conflict was very real. It is instructive to differentiate that period from a contemporary context in which ideology may be much less significant but the distinction between the use of information and of weapons is arguably even more blurred. In both examples, there are counter-disinformation lessons to be learned, although subsequent developments might suggest that governments, public authorities, and commentators have failed to learn from the successes and failures exposed in these examples.

The Zinoviev Letter of 1924 was a classic case of disinformation in which a document that was initially authenticated, then suspected of being a forgery, had wide and enduring political consequences. A letter supposedly written in September 1924 by Grigori Zinoviev, head of the Comintern, the Bolshevik propaganda organization, to the British Communist Party, encouraging the British working class to greater revolutionary effort, reached the government through its overseas intelligence organization, the Secret Intelligence Service (SIS). The letter, of which no original was ever discovered, was almost certainly a forgery, as a series of later official investigations has shown.[15] In early October 1924, however, the text reached London in a telegram sent to SIS headquarters from its station in Riga, Latvia, and the SIS authenticated it and circulated it to the Foreign Office and its usual customers. The text was leaked to the right-wing press and used to discredit the left during the general election campaign that followed the resignation of the first British Labour government. The letter caused outrage in political and military circles because it seemed to show the Soviet Union interfering in British political affairs, inciting strikes, and encouraging the military to mutiny.

From the start, British intelligence authorities failed to employ, in their scrutiny of the letter, any of the tools of the intelligence trade that might have identified it as disinformation. Because the letter was received from a Moscow-based agent who had supplied useful reports in the past, and its contents appeared similar to other Comintern messages, SIS passed it on to the Foreign Office without any rigorous interrogation of the source. Because its content conformed to intelligence officers' view of Soviet tactics, they assumed it was genuine and failed to separate capability from intent. They knew the Bolshevik propaganda machine could disseminate material throughout Europe and to all parts of the British Empire very quickly, not least by employing the wireless networks of state intelligence organizations; it had been doing so since 1917. Global dissemination was a feature of Russian information management activities long before the internet. But they failed to consider why the Russians would send such an inflammatory document at a time when they were hoping for approval of a British loan and when intelligence indicated they had suspended aggressive propaganda activities temporarily. SIS claimed—wrongly—to know the identity of everyone who had handled the letter and boasted that the possibility of its being duped was "entirely excluded."[16] The intelligence authorities also ignored the vulnerabilities indicated by the leak of the letter and its manipulation for political purposes.

Questions were asked almost immediately in political and intelligence circles about the authenticity of the Zinoviev Letter, whether it was forged, and who might have forged it. In addition, the government came under criticism for the way it was used. But by the time the authorities began to investigate properly, the damage was done. During the election campaign, the right-wing press stirred up the public with stories of a "Red Scare." Although Labour would have lost the election even absent the letter, the episode humiliated the outgoing government and enraged party members. They suspected it had been concocted deliberately by the Establishment (the "deep state" today) to damage their electoral prospects: whether the Establishment included the Conservative Party, the intelligence agencies, the civil service, the right-wing press, or a combination of all these was unclear.

As a piece of disinformation the Zinoviev Letter was very effective, although the question of who was responsible for it and why it was employed has proved very difficult to answer. A wide spectrum of interests—from the British Conservative Party to the Bolsheviks, from émigré White Russians to the German Interior Ministry, from former Tsarist military officers to disaffected maverick spies—may all have played a part in the affair for their own personal, political, or professional reasons. Whatever the truth, the Soviet disinformation machine capitalized for years on the confusion caused, disseminating a variety of reports of people confessing to having forged the letter and blaming global capitalism for the damage done to Russia's reputation. And in British politics there has never been a decade in which the Zinoviev Letter has not been invoked as proof of right-wing conspiracy and Establishment cover-up.[17]

The second historical example dates from what is now seen as the early Cold War. Between 1941 and 1945, the Soviet Union was a key ally of the United Kingdom and the United States, and the British government initially hoped that postwar relations might be workmanlike and collaborative, if not warm. But by 1947 the flood of hostile Soviet propaganda—"active measures," in their terminology—aimed at British interests on a global scale and intended to encourage the spread of communism constituted a disinformation campaign too pernicious to ignore. This led British Foreign Secretary Ernest Bevin to authorize the creation of a new Foreign Office department whose purpose was specifically counter-disinformation.

During the period of its existence (1948–1977), the Foreign Office's Information Research Department (IRD) disseminated information on a global scale to counter the procommunist propaganda of the Soviet bloc. Although the IRD was an openly avowed component of the Foreign Office, its close association with British intelligence and the semi-clandestine nature of some of its activities (employing forgery as well as bona fide publications) have meant that details of its information management operations have emerged only recently, and while thousands of files have

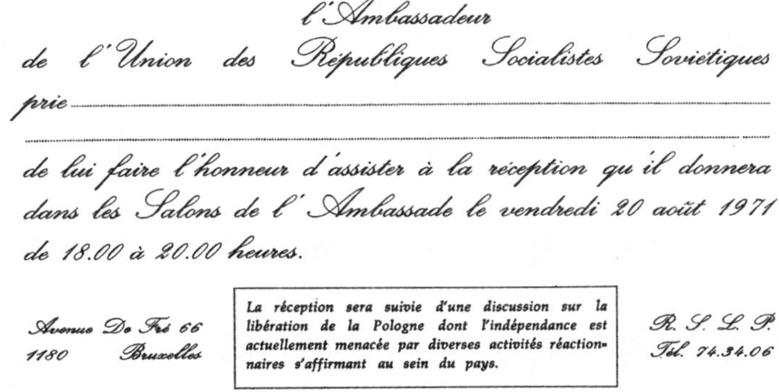

A l'occasion du 3ème Anniversaire de la Libération de la Tchécoslovaquie,

l'Ambassadeur
de l'Union des Républiques Socialistes Soviétiques
prie ..........

de lui faire l'honneur d'assister à la réception qu'il donnera dans les Salons de l'Ambassade le vendredi 20 août 1971 de 18.00 à 20.00 heures.

Avenue De Fré 66
1180 Bruxelles

La réception sera suivie d'une discussion sur la libération de la Pologne dont l'indépendance est actuellement menacée par diverses activités réactionnaires s'affirmant au sein du pays.

R. S. L. P.
Tél. 74.34.06

Figure 12.4: CIA-produced invitation to a nonexistent 1971 reception at the Soviet embassy in Brussels to observe the third anniversary of the "liberation of Czechoslovakia"—actually the date on which the Soviet army had crushed Czechoslovakia's attempt to create "socialism with a human face." The goal was to embarrass the Soviet government in front of the Brussels diplomatic community. From the Collection of H. Keith Melton and Karen Melton at the International Spy Museum.

now been declassified there is much documentation still to emerge.[18] For the purposes of this chapter, however, it is interesting to consider how the techniques of intelligence analysis can be detected within the arguments employed for the establishment of the IRD in 1948 and for its initial operations.

The British government, and the Foreign Office in particular, had been engaged in intensive analysis and assessment of Soviet activities and motivations since the end of World War II in 1945. Opinions were divided, and anti-Soviet hostility hardened as Eastern Europe came under communist control in the ensuing years. Nevertheless, some ministers and officials did try to assess the motivation behind aggressive Soviet information operations and its more direct forms of action. They recognized that the Soviet Union, like the United States and United Kingdom, considered that its contribution to the Allied victory had been decisive and that its vast expenditures of financial and human capital had been neither acknowledged nor rewarded sufficiently in postwar negotiations and settlement. Stalin and his colleagues were not only resentful; they felt threatened by what they saw as an Anglo-American promotion of an exclusive capitalism. That capitalist system could, if unchecked, infringe on Soviets' sovereignty and deny them access to the resources they needed to rebuild the country's economy and play the role of a great power in the postwar world.

The Soviet view of the United States as the embodiment of Western imperialism supported by Britain, whose bourgeoisie was fighting for self-preservation, produced, in the view of Frank Roberts, the British minister in Moscow, a policy of "constant offensive-defensive." In September 1946, Roberts offered some possible interpretations of Soviet uncooperative behavior and aggressive propaganda, which was causing, he said, "bewilderment" in a number of countries. He argued in particular that "a foreign policy of bluff and prestige is needed to distract the attention of the Soviet people and of foreign countries from Soviet post-war weakness" and that the Soviet Union could "get the necessary effort out of her people to overcome her internal problems [only] by persuading them that are surrounded by a hostile world."[19] Both motives can be discerned clearly behind the Soviet information operations employed throughout the Cold War—and indeed behind Russian operations since then.

Soviet attitudes were further hardened by US initiatives such as the Truman Doctrine and the Marshall Plan in 1947.[20] The Russians saw both as threats to the integrity of the Soviet sphere of influence and as a Western propaganda coup; they regarded any such initiatives as offensive information operations aimed at the Soviet Union. The Soviet response was the formation of the Communist Information Bureau (Cominform) in October 1947, an avowed declaration of ideological warfare against the United States and United Kingdom, who were both accused falsely of strengthening imperialism and strangling democracy. The Cominform would warn its audience of the treacherous policies of "right-wing socialists" (a dig at the British Labour government) and urge them to stand firm against Western imperialism, championing instead the egalitarian socialist and democratic ideals of communist societies. This was interpreted in the Foreign Office as marking the end of what might loosely be termed the "Popular Front" phase (whereby Soviet influence was exercised partly through the communist parties of individual countries) and a new phase, termed "Communism versus the Rest."[21]

British Foreign Secretary Ernest Bevin, despite his firm opposition to communism, understood the Soviet viewpoint. Bevin's stance was pragmatic, recognizing that, on a range of issues including shared control of a divided Germany, it was necessary to do business with the Russians. He understood also that parts of the wider Labour Party were more favorably inclined toward the Soviet Union than to the United States and that the image of "Uncle Joe" Stalin as a staunch wartime ally still resonated with the British public. Until the end of 1947, Bevin resisted Foreign Office advice to authorize a more aggressive response to communist offensive information operations. But the collapse of the Council of Foreign Ministers meeting at the end of the year, and evidence of continuing Soviet aggression (including intelligence from defectors), brought a change of heart. Following a range of proposals put forward by the Foreign Office and by the Secret Intelligence Service,[22] the Cabinet in early 1948 approved plans for a new Foreign Office department charged with offensive and defensive information management activities against the Soviet bloc. This was to become the Information Research Department.

Bevin's rationale for launching what was in effect a British counter-disinformation campaign is a good example of the "capacity + intent = threat" equation introduced above. In a paper titled "Future Foreign Publicity," taken by the Cabinet on January 8, 1948, Bevin stated that, as Russia and its communist allies threatened the "whole fabric of Western civilization," it was necessary to "mobilize spiritual forces, as well as material and political," in defense. In his view, the thrust of British counter-disinformation activities should be aimed at the broad mass of workers and peasants in Europe and the Middle East, at governments who were under Soviet pressure, and at potential defectors. Bevin took care to differentiate the position of Britain and Europe from that of the United States:

> It is for us, as Europeans and as a Social Democratic Government, *and not the Americans*, to give the lead in spiritual, moral and political sphere to all the democratic elements in Western Europe which are anti-Communist and, at the same time, genuinely progressive and reformist, believing in freedom, planning and social justice—what one might call the Third Force.[23]

Hitherto, Bevin said, the government had limited its defense against Soviet propaganda to explaining and endorsing government policy, advocating the British way of life, and publicizing its social-democratic policies. Now it was necessary to move on to the offensive:

> If we are to give a moral lead to the forces of anti-Communism in Europe and Asia, we must . . . not leave the initiative to the enemy, but make them defend themselves. . . . We can no longer submit passively to the Communist offensive, we must attack and expose Communism

> and offer something far better. What we have to offer in contrast to totalitarian Communism and *laissez-faire* capitalism, are the vital and progressive ideas of British Social Democracy and Western European civilization.[24]

In other words, Bevin had identified the threat and the vulnerability of Western civilization that it exposed: threat + vulnerability = risk. Information management was only one part of his strategy, together with seeking mutual security arrangements within Europe guaranteed by the United States, including the formation of the North Atlantic Treaty Organization (NATO). But those charged with setting up the IRD and launching its early work clearly interpreted it as a counter-disinformation operation, defensive in orientation, referring in early planning documents to the Political Warfare Executive that had operated during World War II, employing both overt and covert means of disseminating information with the aim of subverting enemy morale and encouraging resistance.[25] The Berlin Crisis in the summer of 1948, and the ensuing Anglo-American airlift operations, made the establishment of a counter-disinformation organization even more pressing. Bevin's articulation of the objectives and potential audience for the IRD's work demonstrates an understanding of how a narrative should be formulated, targeted, and disseminated to counter effectively the Soviet bloc's disinformation campaign.

These two brief historical examples illustrate that the techniques of intelligence analysis—the tools of the trade identified above—can help with the detection of, and protection against, disinformation. In addition, it suggests some useful guiding principles to facilitate effective counter-disinformation. Two are particularly important.

The first guiding principle: *Communicate your own narrative confidently and, as far as possible, tell the truth*. This principle formed a central theme in General Sir Robert Thompson's classic text on counterinsurgency, based on his experiences in Malaya and Vietnam in the 1950s and 1960s, embodying the hearts-and-minds model that continues to resonate.[26] Thompson drew a distinction between what he called "information work" directed against insurgents themselves and that directed at the general population. The first was intended to reduce the will of the enemy to fight and to encourage surrender; the second was to rally the people to the government's cause. Thompson insisted that for information to be persuasive it must be credible. Understatement, factual information (based on good intelligence), and accurate targeting were the most effective tools in information operations. Facts, of course, were not sufficient by themselves: information

Figure 12.5: Soviet cartoon from *Pravda* in 1986. A US military officer and a scientist exchange money for a vial of AIDS, shown as small swastikas. In 1992, under pressure from the United States, Russia admitted that the KGB had been behind the lies to discredit the United States as having created the AIDS virus as a biological weapon. Published in United States Department of State, *Soviet Influence Activities: A Report on Active Measures and Propaganda, 1986–87,* August 1987.

must also address, and respect the sensibilities of, the target audience and be backed up by concrete deeds.[27] Nor should the information disseminated give too rosy a picture of the situation: "Truth made to sound too glowing is no longer believed." Thompson also stressed the importance of timing, since too often the public received an explanation of an event only long afterward.

The second guiding principle: *Get the timing right*. Judging the right time to put out information can involve complex calculations. In his memoir, the journalist Francis Williams (later British Prime Minister Clement Attlee's press secretary) gave an account of his political warfare activities with Lord Mountbatten's Combined Operations Headquarters during World War II. When commando raids were being mounted on the European coast, the planners had to decide how much to tell the public about them and when. When larger raids had gone well, the authorities generally wanted to get the news out to boost morale; sometimes, however, they wanted them to pass unnoticed. But these operations were very secret, and radio silence had to be maintained until the ships were safely back in home waters. The first news of any raid was therefore likely to be broadcast by the Germans in a distorted and misleading account. A procedure was developed for raiding parties to send a coded signal indicating complete or partial success or failure as they were reembarking for home. Williams drafted communiqués for each eventuality, together with fuller guidance for editors indicating what propaganda line the enemy was likely to take and "how this might be handled in order to keep the public informed in a balanced way until the raiders, sometimes accompanied by one or two war correspondents whose stories were pooled, returned." As soon as the signal was received, Williams issued the appropriate communiqué and guidance before getting the full story from the returning troops. As a result, Williams wrote, "we took the propaganda advantage away from the Germans again and again."[28] A good example of preemptive counter-disinformation: communicating a clear narrative, carefully timed.

Another illustration of the importance of timing comes from the NATO air campaign in Kosovo in 1999. NATO had its own communications specialists and press officers. However, the Serbian leader Slobodan Milošević, who controlled his country's media, had a level of control over information management that NATO's 19 members, who had to reach an agreement on press statements, could not match. The result was that it was the Serbian narrative—portraying Serbian attacks on Kosovo as self-defense against NATO air strikes—that tended to be broadcast first rather than reports of Serbian atrocities against Kosovar Albanians or footage of the thousands of refugees on the Macedonian border. If a NATO air strike hit a building, Serbian broadcasters immediately inflated the number of civilian casualties before NATO had time to issue its own narrative. As Prime Minister Tony Blair remarked to President Bill Clinton in March 1999, "if Milosevic had a BBC to deal with, he would not be getting such an easy ride."[29]

As a result, Blair asked communications director Alastair Campbell to work on a counter-disinformation strategy to neutralize the Serbian media machine, setting it, as Campbell noted, "in the context of a battle between a dictator and democracies" because Milošević "had all the levers at his disposal." This could have had a negative effect on NATO's military decision-making, too. Campbell wrote in his diary on April 8, 1999, that it was "all about communication now. Militarily, NATO is overwhelmingly more powerful than Belgrade. But Milosevic has total control of his media and our media is vulnerable to their output. So, we can lose the public opinion battle and if we lose hands down in some of the NATO countries, we have a problem sustaining this."[30]

This episode is an interesting example not only of competing narratives and the power of disinformation but also of the necessity in any joint venture of close collaboration in a proactive information management strategy. This is especially true when structures designed to operate in peace suddenly must gear up for war. As Campbell put it: "[A]s democracies we had inbuilt disadvantages against the Serb lie machine and we had to be clear, imaginative, flexible, cleverer than his people."[31]

Information management operations, both offensive and defensive, have become vastly more sophisticated. Today information management is endemic to a world in which rapid technological development, including the proliferation of social media, means that people are bombarded constantly with information that is cheap to create and easy to disseminate. The speed of communications—combined with international and political instability and a range of other factors including climate change, proliferation of nuclear weapons, and religious intolerance—mean we operate in an environment where disinformation can flourish and be used by a range of actors as a tool of policy. It is right to adopt cutting-edge technologies, study the psychology of disinformation, and devise protection strategies in cyberspace and to take all other feasible precautions against it. But everyone can make efforts to be more discriminating about the information they receive and be more careful about the information they pass on to others. As David Omand says in *How Spies Think*, we should all think more like intelligence analysts do.[32]

Disinformation remains impossible to eliminate. It may not just be difficult to identify; it can pass unnoticed, including when the purveyors of it are our own governments or organizations. And even though the present is a different environment, we can learn from the past, from the mistakes made as well as from the effective steps that were taken. We are not doomed to lose the struggle against disinformation. History can help us win it.

Figure 12.6: British banknote forged by Nazi Germany in Operation Bernhard during World War II. The primary goal was to fuel inflation in the United Kingdom, but German intelligence also used forged bills such as this one to pay agents and informants.

## Further Reading

Galeotti, Mark. *Russian Political War: Moving Beyond the Hybrid*. London: Routledge, 2019.

Hoffman, Frank. *Conflict in the Twenty-First Century: The Rise of Hybrid Warfare*. Potomac Institute, 2000.

Kennedy, Greg, and Christopher Tuck, eds. *British Propaganda and Wars of Empire: Influencing Friend and Foe, 1900–2010*. Ashgate, UK: Routledge, 2014.

Omand, David. *How Spies Think: Ten Lessons in Intelligence*. London: Penguin Random House, 2020.

Rid, Thomas. *Active Measures: The Secret History of Disinformation and Political Warfare*. New York: Profile Books, 2020.

## Notes

1. There is a rich and constantly expanding literature on information operations for those seeking detailed discussion. Thomas Rid provides a comprehensive and authoritative survey. See Thomas Rid, *Active Measures: The Secret History of Disinformation and Political Warfare* (New York: Profile Books, 2020).

2. Fortitude was part of a deception strategy intended to make the German High

Command believe that the main Allied invasion of Europe in 1944 would take place not in Normandy but the Pas de Calais. A parallel deception operation by the Soviet High Command, Bagration, was intended to persuade the Germans that an attack on their forces in Soviet territory would come from the south rather than the north. Antony Beevor, *D-Day and the Battle for Normandy* (London: Penguin, 2012); Richard Overy, *Russia's War* (London: Penguin, 2010).

3. See Michael Howard, *Strategic Deception* (London: HMSO, 1990).

4. "Operation Desert Deception," a report by Lieutenant Colonel Daniel L. Breitenbach, US Army, June 1991 (Newport, RI: Naval War College, 1991).

5. This phrase constitutes Lesson 10 in David Omand, *How Spies Think: Ten Lessons in Intelligence* (London: Penguin, 2020).

6. Cynthia Grabo, *Anticipating Surprise: Analysis for Strategic Warning* (University Press of America, 2004).

7. Grabo, *Anticipating Surprise*, 90–92.

8. Numerous examples in this vein can be found in the Socratic dialogues in Plato's *The Republic*, Book III: "[I]t pertains to the guardians of the city, and to them alone, to tell falsehoods, to deceive either enemies or citizens for the city's welfare." Plato's *The Republic*, Book III (London: Everyman's Library edition, Penguin Random House, 1992), 389. Thucydides, *History of the Peloponnesian War* (London: Penguin Classics, 1972), Book Three, "The Mytilene Debate," 212–245.

9. In his exploration of the roots of totalitarianism, the noted social and political philosopher Karl Popper (1902–1994) commented extensively on ancient Greek thinkers. K. R. Popper, *The Open Society and its Enemies, Volume 1: The Spell of Plato* (London: Routledge & Kegan Paul, 1986 ed.), 139.

10. Joel Rogers de Waal, "The West Should Weaponise Embarrassment in the New Information Wars," April 26, 2019, *RUSI*, https://rusi.org/commentary/west-should-weaponise-embarrassment-new-information-wars.

11. David Alba and Adam Satariano, "At Least 70 Countries Have Had Disinformation Campaigns, Study Finds," *New York Times*, September 26, 2019, www.nytimes.com/2019/09/26/technology/government-disinformation-cyber-troops.html.

12. See Clayton Cheney, "China's Digital Silk Road: Strategic Technological Competition and Exporting Political Illiberalism," *Council on Foreign Relations*, September 26, 2019, www.cfr.org/blog/chinas-digital-silk-road-strategic-technological-competition-and-exporting-political. See also Nigel Inkster, *China's Cyber Power* (London: International Institute for Strategic Studies, 2016).

13. Rid, *Active Measures*, 430. Bittman defected in 1968 and in 1972 published *The Deception Game*, based on his career in the intelligence discipline of disinformation.

14. In his earlier book, Omand wrote that it was important for the public to understand that, since it was impossible for governments to prevent all terrorist attacks, there must be an acceptance of shared risk: "[S]ince there is no absolute security to be had at an acceptable financial or moral cost in this world, at every stage a balance must be maintained within the framework of human rights based on the time-honoured principles of proportionality and necessity" The same rationale is applicable to disinformation. David Omand, *Securing the State* (London: Hurst & Co., 2010), 19.

15. Gill Bennett, *The Zinoviev Letter: The Conspiracy That Never Dies* (Oxford: Oxford University Press, 2018).

16. Bennett, *The Zinoviev Letter*, 95–98.

17. Bennett, *The Zinoviev Letter*, introduction.

18. A great deal of IRD documentation is now open at the National Archives (TNA), in classes FO 1110 and FCO 95 and 168.

19. Moscow telegram No. 2875 to the FO, 4 September 1946, printed in *Documents on British Policy Overseas (DBPO)*, Series I, vol. 11: *European Recovery and the Search for Western Security* (London: Routledge, 2017), No. 9.

20. Both these initiatives are documented fully in *DBPO, European Recovery and the Search for Western Security*.

21. Note of November 7, 1947, for the Russia Committee, *DBPO, European Recovery and the Search for Western Security*, printed as No. 190.

22. These proposals can be followed in FO 1093/375, TNA.

23. Memorandum by Bevin for the Cabinet, CP(48)8, 4 January 1948, printed in *DBPO*, Series I, vol. 10, *The Brussels and North Atlantic Treaties, 1947–1949* (London: Routledge, 2015), No. 8 (emphasis added); the Cabinet discussion on 8 January is printed as No. 11.

24. *DBPO*, Series I, vol. 10, *The Brussels and North Atlantic Treaties, 1947–1949* (London: Routledge, 2015), No. 8.

25. See documents in FO 1110/104, TNA.

26. Sir Robert Thompson, *Defeating Communist Insurgency* (London: Chatto & Windus, 1966).

27. This element is explored in detail in Kumar Ramakrishna, *Emergency Propaganda: The Winning of Malayan Hearts and Minds, 1948–1958* (London: Routledge, 2002).

28. Francis Williams, *Nothing So Strange: An Autobiography* (London: Cassell, 1970), 185–186.

29. Alastair Campbell and Bill Hagerty, eds., *The Alastair Campbell Diaries, Volume 2: Power and the People* (London: Hutchinson, 2011), 695.

30. Alastair Campbell and Bill Hagerty, eds., *The Alastair Campbell Diaries*, 710; page 711ff gives a detailed account of information management operations in relation to the Kosovo campaign.

31. Campbell and Hagerty, eds., *The Alastair Campbell Diaries*, 740.

32. Omand, *How Spies Think*.

# Gray Reflections in the Mirror: The Hanssen Case and American Counterintelligence

John F. Fox Jr.

*The International Spy Museum contains a number of exhibitions that highlight the truism that one country's hero is another country's traitor. One of those cases involves FBI agent Robert Hanssen, who spied for the Soviet Union and Russia. Here, the FBI historian John Fox examines the efforts by which the FBI and the CIA came to identify the traitor in their midst.—The Editors*

James Angleton, the Central Intelligence Agency's legendary and controversial head counterintelligence chief, gifted us with a most striking metaphor for the world of intelligence to describe the Soviet KGB's use of deception in its intelligence work: the "wilderness of mirrors." Since then, the mirrored wilderness has come to be a metaphor not only for intelligence itself but also for counterintelligence and, more specifically, Angleton's approach to counterintelligence.[1] It stands as both a recognition of counterintelligence's complexity and a criticism of its practice. Angleton borrowed the image from the T. S. Eliot poem "Gerontion," a reflection on old age and mortality brought on by the devastation of World War I. In the poem, an "old man in a dry month" reflects:

> In a wilderness of mirrors. What will the spider do
> Suspend its operations, will the weevil
> Delay? . . .

With Eliot's image in mind, let us consider the revelation that Federal Bureau of Investigations Special Agent Robert Phillip Hanssen was a long-standing mole in the Bureau and what it tells us about the art of counterintelligence.

In considering the Hanssen case in light of Elliot's metaphor, we need to keep in mind several things. Clearly the "weevils" are Soviet/Russian moles—Aldrich Ames, Edward Lee Howard, and especially Robert Hanssen—along with their case officers. The "wilderness" is the entirety of the field in which the weevils seek their food. And the spiders? In the US political system, there are many—US intelligence community counterintelligence officers—especially in the FBI and CIA; national security officers throughout the executive branch; congressional oversight committee members; and even the US media. In extending this metaphor, I argue that too often the spiders spend their time trying to strengthen their webs through security fixes and similar strategies, whereas the successful efforts against the weevils were active counterintelligence measures aimed at compromising and penetrating the adversary's webs.

Robert Phillip Hanssen joined the FBI in 1975 and soon began to sell information to the GRU (Glavnoye razvedyvatel'noye upravleniye, or Main Intelligence Directorate of the General Staff), the Soviet military intelligence service. He stopped spying after a year or so, but in 1985 he renewed contact with the Soviet Union, selling secrets now to the KGB (Komitet gosudarstvennoy bezopasnosti, or Committee for State Security), the Soviet intelligence and security service. Hanssen immediately betrayed three Soviet nationals who had been providing information to the United States: Boris Yuzhin, Sergei Motorin, and Valeriy Martynov.[2] He subsequently betrayed many more people working with American intelligence in the Soviet Union and is reported to have compromised billions of dollars in US technical intelligence collections programs as well.[3] At the same time, Aldrich Ames, a counterintelligence officer in the CIA, and at least one other US citizen were betraying this country in the same way. The FBI and CIA began a long-lasting hunt for these moles, who at the time were unknown.

In 1991, as the Soviet Union was about to collapse, Hanssen again broke off his spying activities. Although Ames was identified as a spy soon after, Hanssen was not. Instead, in 1999 he again resumed his espionage, this time for the Russian Federation through its SVR (Sluzhba vneshney razvedki, or Foreign Intelligence Service). And it was over the following October that the FBI finally identified Hanssen as a threat. The Bureau had received material from KGB files about the mole they hunted. It included a cache of documents, an audio recording of an early phone conversation between the mole and his handler, and a fingerprint found on materials the mole had used to enclose documents for one of his earlier drops. A Russian source had sold these things to the Bureau for a significant amount of money, reportedly $7 million.[4] Hanssen was quickly matched to the print, the recording, and the rest of the material that was acquired by the FBI. He was a spy.

Now that Hanssen was identified as the mole, the Bureau turned to gathering the evidence needed to prosecute him. It placed him in a position where he would compromise himself and it began an intense, but

Figure 13.1: Sham award given to FBI Special Agent Robert Hanssen on January 12, 2001, ostensibly for his work with an interagency group. The FBI had already identified Hanssen as a Russia spy and used the award to allay suspicion he may have had at being reassigned back to headquarters—where he could be more easily watched. He was arrested on February 18. From the Collection of H. Keith and Karen Melton at the International Spy Museum.

short, period of surveillance. On Sunday afternoon, a little before 3 p.m. on February 18, 2001, Robert Hanssen hid a package of classified material wrapped in plastic garbage bags under a bridge in Foxstone Park, not far from his northern Virginia residence. As he returned to his car, a well-armed team of FBI agents swooped in and arrested him. Hanssen is said to have asked, "What took you so long?"

Judicial proceedings quickly followed, and Hanssen subsequently pled guilty to multiple charges of espionage and was sentenced to multiple life sentences. He remains incarcerated at ADX Florence, the federal Supermax prison in Colorado.[5] FBI Director Louis Freeh announced that Hanssen's identification and arrest were "counterintelligence at its very best."[6]

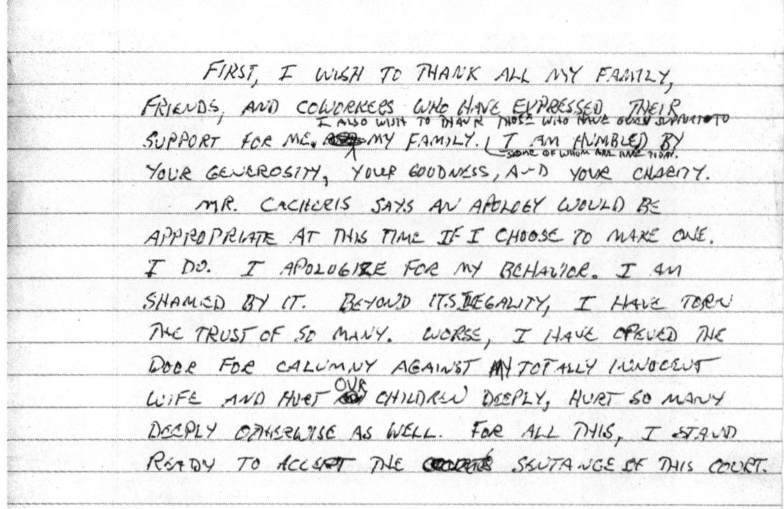

FIRST, I WISH TO THANK ALL MY FAMILY,
FRIENDS, AND COWORKERS WHO HAVE EXPRESSED THEIR
I ALSO WISH TO THANK THOSE WHO HAVE BEEN SUPPORTIVE TO
SUPPORT FOR ME. MY FAMILY. I AM HUMBLED BY
SOME OF WHOM ARE HERE TODAY.
YOUR GENEROSITY, YOUR GOODNESS, AND YOUR CHARITY.
MR. CACHERIS SAYS AN APOLOGY WOULD BE
APPROPRIATE AT THIS TIME IF I CHOOSE TO MAKE ONE.
I DO. I APOLOGIZE FOR MY BEHAVIOR. I AM
SHAMED BY IT. BEYOND ITS ILLEGALITY, I HAVE TORN
THE TRUST OF SO MANY. WORSE, I HAVE OPENED THE
DOOR FOR CALUMNY AGAINST MY TOTALLY INNOCENT
WIFE AND HURT OUR CHILDREN DEEPLY, HURT SO MANY
DEEPLY OTHERWISE AS WELL. FOR ALL THIS, I STAND
READY TO ACCEPT THE SENTENCE OF THIS COURT.

Figure 13.2: Letter of apology written by Robert Hanssen, FBI special agent and Russian spy. He read it aloud to the judge at his sentencing in May 2002. From the Collection of H. Keith and Karen Melton at the International Spy Museum.

Others were less sanguine in their assessment. Studies, reports, congressional oversight, and a slew of articles, books, and movies all followed, dissecting aspects of the case and the long-term counterintelligence failure it represented.

Some of these "spiders," as Angleton described them, concentrated on possible signals from Hanssen's early life as signals were missed. This is misguided. If some spiders start with Hanssen's pre-espionage biography without the benefit of hindsight, they would be hard-pressed to see a future spy. He was well educated, came from a police family, and had been a police officer himself. His letters of recommendations were also strong. The FBI's initial background investigation failed to find concerns in Hanssen's character and personality, but it was not for lack of trying. The retired FBI agent Mike Rochford, a principal investigator on this and related matters, made it clear that at least some people questioned about Hanssen's early adult life had knowledge that they had not shared with the FBI agents who interviewed them during Hanssen's initial screening and instead provided glowing recommendations. According to Rochford, one former college acquaintance of Hanssen's told the media, post-arrest, of Hanssen boasting at parties that he was going to be the greatest spy in the world. Rochford later conceded that he wished this had been brought up the first time the Bureau talked to Hanssen's college associates. However,

Figure 13.3: FBI Special Agent Robert Hanssen at home before he became infamous. From the Collection of H. Keith and Karen Melton at the International Spy Museum.

given the length of time, the changing knowledge of what Hanssen became versus what he was, and the outlandishness of the statement, it is hard to think that Hanssen's schoolmates or the FBI agents conducting his vetting would have taken such a tale seriously. In short, there was no smoking gun to preclude trusting Hanssen.[7]

Nor does current knowledge of Hanssen's early family life suggest that a more accurate psychological profiling would have predicted his future. In the aftermath of Hanssen's arrest, a combination of debriefings intelligence professionals, investigative reporters, and several psychologists who were granted greater or lesser contact with Hanssen, and those around him, developed significant details about Hanssen's personality, many that were then shared with various media figures. Although some stories of Hanssen's youth and school days present troubling aspects of Hanssen's early family life, especially the mental and physical abuse he suffered from

Figure 13.4: The Walther PPK pistol that the FBI special agent and Russian spy Robert Hanssen sometimes carried as his personal weapon. Why did he choose the favored sidearm of James Bond? From the Collection of H. Keith Melton and Karen Melton at the International Spy Museum.

his father, we do not know how this affected his professional life; nor can we say that such experience is predictive of future betrayals. More was shared about Hanssen's sex life and fantasies than many would want to know; but ultimately the apparent contradictions of his life are a mystery. On one hand he was an anticommunist and apparently devout Catholic family man, and on the other he led a second career of espionage for Moscow and had a combination of dysfunctional personal and relationship issues that blended together to present a contradictory picture. In the words of a psychological evaluation done as part of a damage assessment, Hanssen's personality contained a "mix of psychopathic, narcissistic, and dependent features."[8]

Could this have helped the US government identify Hanssen as a mole prior to 2000? Dr. David Charney, a noted expert in the field, has observed that "spies are not born; they are made." He also tells us that Hanssen's traits and pre-FBI experiences are found in many police officers and intelligence agents and do not predict performance or loyalty.[9] In this case, little suggests that the FBI could have identified a future spy like Hanssen before he became a federal agent. That does not mean screening is useless. A good background check can weed out all sorts of threats—Kim Philby and Anna Montes come to mind—but the lack of disqualifiers in Hanssen's background warns us that we will still face weevils in our webs. Perhaps comprehensive psychological services and screening throughout a federal employee's career would be possible and help avoid the drift from unhappy employee to spy, but exigencies of privacy, cost, and other factors suggest this was not a feasible option during Hanssen's career. Furthermore, the short period between Hanssen's joining the Bureau and his initial spying suggests a limited time frame in which such services may have had an impact on Hanssen's path to espionage.

As screening would not have revealed Hanssen as a potential spy, when might he have been caught after his betrayals began? Given the nature of Hanssen's first approach to the GRU and subsequent espionage from 1979 to 1981, the Bureau would have been very unlikely to have identified him without a lucky break. Soon after his transfer to the FBI's New York office, Hanssen contacted a known Soviet intelligence officer and developed a plan to sell secrets. He immediately betrayed Dmitri Polyakov, the FBI/CIA source in the GRU known as TOPHAT/BOURBON, and continued to periodically sell secrets over two years. However, Soviet authorities did not arrest TOPHAT, and he appears to have retired without issue. As a result, there was no evidence at the time that he had been compromised.[10] In 1985, Aldrich Ames exposed TOPHAT/BOURBON again, and this time, within a few months, he was arrested, imprisoned, and eventually executed.[11] Polyakov's final fate was now considered one sign among many that a mole might be at work.[12]

Hanssen's second period of espionage, from 1985 to 1991, left clear clues that a mole was active within the United States Intelligence Community (USIC). Nineteen eighty-five, the year Hanssen resumed spying, was called the "Year of the Spy" by the press. Through that summer, US counterespionage successes had been piling up. Yet by the fall signs of deeper counterintelligence failures were obvious. The CIA (and to a lesser extent the FBI) started to notice lost assets as the euphoria of the Year of the Spy gave way to internal concerns. The wider context, we now know, included several spies other than Hanssen, especially Aldrich Ames and the renegade CIA officer Edward Lee Howard. After the December 1986 arrest of a Marine Corps security guard working at the US embassy in Moscow, Sergeant Clayton Lonetree, he was also considered as a possible source for the losses. Lonetree, though, was ruled out after a couple months. By the end of the 1980s, the American intelligence community's losses had continued to accumulate, costing the lives of more than a dozen people who had willingly worked against the Soviet Union. Billions of dollars were also wasted when several technical intelligence programs were compromised. The losses also threatened relations with key allies whose assets had disappeared and might be chalked up to the American compromises. The overlapping espionage work of Ames, Hanssen, and Howard posed

Figure 13.5: Coffee mug used by members of the CIA's Aldrich Ames Damage Assessment Team. An American eagle grasps a dead mole in its beak. From the Collection of H. Keith and Karen Melton at the International Spy Museum.

serious issues for US intelligence as it tried to unravel its losses and was a boon to Soviet intelligence—especially because by that time only Howard's betrayal was known.

At the CIA, the counterintelligence analyst Jeanne Vertefeuille headed the Special Task Force (STF) for the counterintelligence staff. The STF, considering the losses of human and technical sources, began by considering whether the Soviets had broken into the CIA's communications networks. With no evidence that this had occurred, they next stage considered failed tradecraft practices. Suspicion of this reason, it was later learned, was stoked by Soviet disinformation aimed at protecting Ames and Hanssen, both of whom remained active until the fall of the Soviet Union in 1991.[13] In reviewing Ames's case after his 1994 arrest, the US Senate Select Committee on Intelligence noted three paths this disinformation took: spreading rumors within the KGB that Howard was responsible for the losses; deceiving CIA officers so that it appeared that the Agency's compromised sources were still free and alive; and using at least one false defector to pass disinformation to the CIA about the compromises.[14] Although such deception muddied the mole hunt, the STF did not lose sight of the possibility that there was a mole within the agency.

Meanwhile, the FBI's mole-hunt group (code-named "ANLACE") was more focused, having been set up specifically to consider the losses of Sergei Motorin and Valeriy Martynov, two FBI sources who had been compromised.[15] Its mole hunt was referred to as "GRAY SUIT."[16] The Department of Justice's Inspector General, though, noted that ANLACE had its own problems: there were too many potential subjects with access to the information about the lost human sources. The Inspector General noted that, in the FBI's Washington field office alone, 250 people knew of the two double agents; the length of the access list would have increased even more if Headquarters and former New York agents assigned elsewhere or retired were added to it. After considering traditional motivations for espionage such as money in the life of each candidate on the list, the STF came up empty. So the FBI focused on the mole being outside of the Bureau (i.e., at the CIA), although the Inspector General would later note that the ANLACE group "knew very little" about the CIA's issues.[17]

Although the FBI and CIA task forces met periodically and interacted by other means almost daily, barriers between the two agencies negated the positives of cooperation. CIA analyst Sandy Grimes of the STF (headed by Vertefeuille) noted that a lack of common space, differing focuses, and the withholding of information and conclusions all contributed to this separation. Grimes and Vertefeuille's responses, as described in their book *Circle of Treason*, also illustrate the cultural divide between the FBI and the CIA, specifically the differences among agents and analysts within the Bureau and across the intelligence community. On one hand, the respect Grimes and Vertefeuille had for several analysts on the Bureau side is clear; on the other in *Circle of Treason*, a memoir about the Ames mole hunt, Grimes and Vertefeuille clearly state their frustration and lack of understanding of the agent-driven culture within the Bureau. Grimes's reaction to the way FBI agents interviewing Ames sought to develop rapport also suggests a lack of understanding of how the FBI works. This proved a hindrance in the two task forces working cooperatively.[18]

As the separate investigations continued without bearing fruit, Congress got wind of them and began noting the friction between and within the agencies over the hunts. The House Permanent Select Committee on Intelligence and Senate Select Committee on Intelligence each held hearings on the perennial issue of cooperation in counterintelligence. Congress said that the nation's counterintelligence effort had "serious flaws" and was "poorly organized, staffed, trained, and equipped to deal with continuing counterintelligence challenges." In March 1988, the CIA reorganized its counterintelligence staff into the Counterintelligence Center, embedded within the Directorate of Operations, in response to these sharply critical assessments.[19] Grimes and Vertefeuille suggest that this reform had the baneful effect of suggesting that only the Directorate of Operations at CIA had counterintelligence concerns. Furthermore, Grimes noted, the FBI declined to send a representative to the Counterintelligence Center despite a signed memorandum of understanding on cooperation under which counterintelligence matters were to be brought to FBI quickly.[20]

Such criticism was not entirely fair. By 1991, at least two FBI personnel were working with the STF, helping to narrow down a list of 190 CIA officers with access to information connected to the lost sources. The next year, when CIA analysts Grimes and Dan Payne connected the meetings of Ames and Chuvakin, the Soviet official Ames was supposedly recruiting when he volunteered to spy, with large deposits in Ames's bank accounts, the FBI began to build the evidentiary basis to make a criminal case against Ames.[21] Perhaps the Special Investigations Unit (the STF reconstituted under the Counterintelligence Center) would have liked the Bureau to move faster, as Grimes suggested, but methodically building evidence in a case, finalizing FISA warrants, and wrapping up other practices are critical to successful prosecutions. Furthermore, Grimes does not account for the back-and-forth the FBI engaged in with Justice Department attorneys, who would have to bring the matter to court. Checking, double-checking, and interacting with the lawyers across the street from FBI Headquarters is necessary and time-consuming.[22]

In the wake of the arrest of Aldrich Ames, the Senate Select Committee began reviewing the handling of Ames as a suspect and considering legislative action. Senator Dennis DeConcini, the committee chair, noted that four bills had been put forward to address perceived weaknesses in the intelligence community's failed counterintelligence. Senator William Cohen noted that the proposed bills included recommendations that had been proposed in the wake of the Walker case almost ten years earlier. Cohen suggested that those proposed reforms, which gave the FBI better access to financial and other records in these types of cases, might have prevented Ames from continuing his espionage into the 1990s if enacted 10 years earlier. Testifying at the hearing, FBI Director Freeh noted that, starting in 1991, the FBI and CIA had developed a high degree of cooperation. He also added, not realizing the irony, that "any moles who are still in place must be unmasked."[23] The reforms that Cohen supported were included in the markup of the Intelligence Authorization Act of 1996 and became law.[24]

The CIA and the Inspector General's office also considered the implications of Ames's spying. Inspector General Michael Bromwich reported to the public in 1997 that the central issue in Ames's successful betrayals was communication. At the FBI, senior managers lacked knowledge of and experience in counterintelligence work in general and mole hunts in particular, while lower-level employees had not communicated the severity of the losses and what they meant. Senior managers needed to be briefed more regularly and more accurately. Further, USIC agencies needed to communicate with each other about their losses so that common threads could be identified and followed effectively. Bromwich also noted the weakness in the FBI's handling of analytic material. The Bureau, he concluded, needed a "policy mandating an evaluation of [analytic intelligence] reports to determine whether the conclusions [were] valid and whether any further action [was] warranted."[25] It would take the 9/11 attacks for the FBI to make serious efforts to remedy its approach to intelligence analysis.

The CIA's own inspector general had additional recommendations and conclusions. That office noted an overall neglect of counterintelligence at the Agency and a failure to let policymakers know that sources had been compromised and that reporting based on them could be tainted. In turn, the it recommended significant leadership changes at the CIA, the creation of the CIA National Counterintelligence Center (though headed by an FBI appointee), increased counterintelligence training and activity, new guidelines, and new policies to recruit quality personnel. Together, it was a strong indictment of the Agency, and the CIA director took quick action to address the recommendations.[26]

The unresolved mole hunts continued as Ames's betrayals, even when added to those of Howard and Lonetree, did not explain all the losses the USIC had tallied. Anomalies like the FBI's failed investigation of US Foreign Service officer Felix Bloch in 1990 and the arrest of an old FBI source named Chernov around the same time were counterintelligence failures that were not clearly linked to the earlier losses around the mid-1980s.[27] Despite the various criticisms noted above, both agencies had high points in their broader counterintelligence work, and both agencies continued to work together on an operation begun in the late 1980s (BUCKLURE in the Bureau and RAKETEER in the Agency). The operation consisted of aggressive pitches to known Russian and former Soviet intelligence officials backed up by a guaranteed reward of at least $1 million for cooperation.[28]

Clearly, both the CIA and FBI thought there was another mole who was active at least until 1990, and both thought it was likely to be another penetration of the CIA. The FBI had abandoned ANLACE and adopted a new approach, PLAYACTOR. The PLAYACTOR team sought to create an extensive graphic timeline of the mole hunt.[29] When the CIA case officer Harold James Nicholson was arrested in November 1996 and the FBI Supervisory Special Agent Earl Edwin Pitts was arrested the next month, both accused of spying for Russia, the Bureau spent time considering both as possible suspects for the mole. Neither had the access necessary to be considered as a candidate for the GRAY SUIT penetrations. By 1998, the Bureau's tallying of losses and diagramming of data had led it to focus on a set of five dozen or so items known about the mole.[30] Key entries on this matrix included, among other items, access to reports on weekly Counterintelligence Center meetings, knowledge of the Bloch investigation, and knowledge of the identities of CIA sources in Moscow. As most of the losses had been of CIA sources, Rochford noted, both Bureau and Agency investigators thought the penetration was from the CIA.[31]

This focus on the CIA, and the FBI's criteria list, led the Bureau to focus on one specific CIA officer, a counterintelligence veteran and expert on illegal agents named Brian Kelley. His profile, apparently, fit enough of Rochford's data points that the Bureau was convinced it had its mole. The Bureau called him "GRAY DECEIVER." Having identified a concrete target, the amorphous hunt for GRAY SUIT transformed into an attempt to trick GRAY DECEIVER into compromising himself. With warrants in hand, FBI surveillance began. The Bureau watched him "go to shopping malls and stores that were visited at the same time by Russian intelligence agents." Media sources (after Hanssen's arrest) also noted that a surreptitious entry by the FBI at the subject's house found a map of Nottoway Park, where Kelley jogged; Hanssen, it was later learned, had also filled dead drops there. For an unknown reason, this was considered further proof of Kelley's betrayal.[32] However, when the suspect was polygraphed, he passed. He was also approached under a false-flag operation, which he rejected. Eventually, family and friends were sharply questioned, and he was ostracized at work. For Rochford's team, Kelley's intelligence access, especially his knowledge of the Bloch case, only confirmed a potential fit as the GRAY SUIT mole, and so the Bureau overwhelmingly focused on Kelley for two-plus years.[33]

Finally, in August 1999 the CIA suspended the suspect and revoked his clearances. Kelley was in bureaucratic limbo for almost two more years, by which time Hanssen had been arrested and Kelley exonerated. FBI agent Rochford later noted how wrong he was to focus on Kelley. The Bureau officially stated: "We've acknowledged and expressed regret over the impact of the investigation on this person directly to his attorney."[34] The CIA eventually awarded Kelley the Distinguished Career Intelligence Medal, but in the eyes of many such recognition did not make up for the difficulties he was put through. The nation learned of Kelley's identity first in David Wise's book *Spy* in early 2003, and again, officially, in February 2003, when Kelley was interviewed by *60 Minutes*. The public airing of Kelley's story was part of the federal atonement for what it had put him through and possibly some sibling payback from the CIA to the FBI. "[The Bureau's investigation] was so far over the top," according to Kelley in an interview with a *Hartford Courant* reporter. "This investigation is a mirror of the dysfunctionality in the FBI. It highlights their ineptitude," he continued, with understandable bitterness.[35] Kelley retired from the CIA in 2007 and passed away in September 2011.

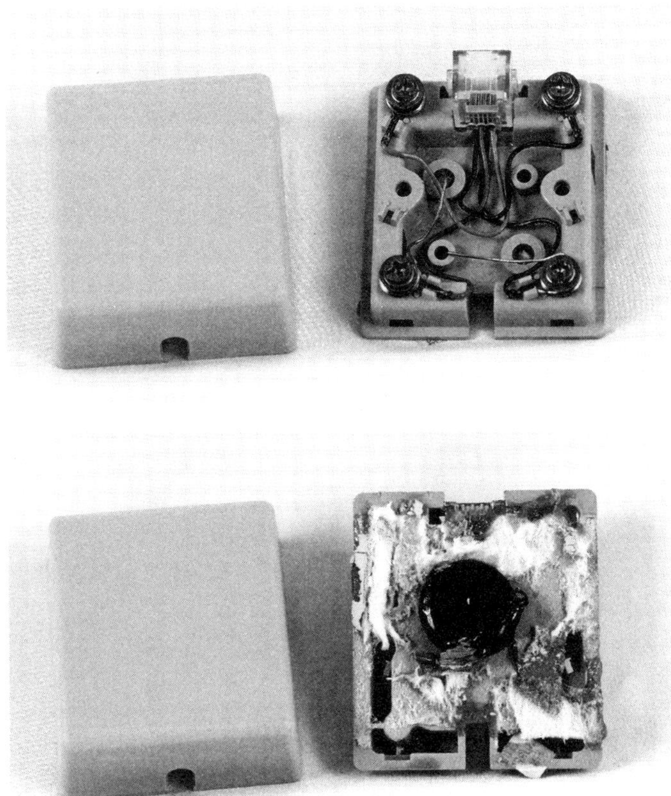

Figures 13.6 and 13.7: Front and back of listening device used by the FBI to bug CIA counterintelligence officer Brian Kelley. Searching for a high-level Russian penetration of the US intelligence community, the FBI initially focused its attention on Kelley and put this bug on the phone jack in his home study. The real spy was actually FBI Special Agent Robert Hanssen. From the Collection of H. Keith and Karen Melton at the International Spy Museum.

Hanssen, meanwhile, had taken the interest in GRAY DECEIVER as a sign to resume espionage work, this time for the SVR. He began mining FBI computer systems and other sources to gather intelligence. While Hanssen was resuming his spy career, Supervisory Special Agent Rochford continued to think Kelley was the likely mole. Like a good intelligence agent, though, he also continued to pitch Russian sources to unearth more and different evidence. By the spring of 2000, Rochford, according to media reports, had identified a taker for an inflated BUCKLURE reward in exchange for a cache of material on a Soviet/Russian mole in the USIC. By October it was in the FBI's hands. The documents provided clearly showed that Kelley could not have been the source.[36] Instead, Robert Philip Hanssen was identified as a spy. Pegged by the fingerprint and the voice recording mentioned earlier, and subsequently confirmed by the detailed investigative work that the Bureau does so well, the FBI built a case by which Hanssen could be convicted; the FBI had found the mole in its ranks.

As Hanssen was to turn 57 in April 2001, reaching the age of mandatory retirement for federal law enforcement officials, the Bureau had to act fast.[37] Over the next month and a half it put together an elaborate plan to catch Hanssen in the act of betraying his oath. First the Bureau had to gather the evidence necessary for a FISA warrant affidavit. Then it instituted extensive surveillance on Hanssen at work, at home, and in between. Lastly, Hanssen was offered a plum promotion to Headquarters, ostensibly to help plan the upgrade of FBI information technology systems and to enhance the Bureau's widespread data needs. For Hanssen it was a plum too good to pass up. He quickly accepted a promotion to return to Headquarters to lead up what was to be a team dedicated to securing FBI computer systems. A Bureau surveillance specialist named Eric O'Neill was assigned as the first member of this team and tasked with monitoring and reporting on Gray Day, as Hanssen was now known. By now Hanssen had begun to suspect that the spiders were spinning their web with him in their sights. His last, plaintive message to his Russian handlers said he feared that something "had woken the sleeping tiger."[38] When he filled what would be his last dead drop on that Sunday afternoon, Hanssen was arrested. The weevil was trapped. The time from his identification to his arrest was approximately four and a half months.[39]

As the impact of Hanssen's arrest shook the webs of US counterintelligence, the spiders were quite active, much like after Ames's arrest. The CIA "quietly reinstated" Kelley, who had been under suspension for 21 months and under suspicion for at least two years.[40] FBI Director Robert Mueller asked the former FBI and CIA director William Webster to independently review the matter. Congress asked to be heard. Details of the FBI's GRAY DECEIVER investigation began to leak; considering that the leaks were coming from on-the-record interviews with Kelley and Rochford and others, both the FBI and the CIA must have acquiesced if not enabled their people to discuss the issues. More about the overall losses, investigations, and responses, of course, came out over the next couple of years, even as the nation's focus shifted to counterterrorism after 9/11 and concerns about intelligence failures related to Iraqi WMD.

The Hanssen case, and questions related to the mole hunts of the 1980s and 1990s that preceded it, did not disappear. The inspectors general reports, William Webster's independent study, and the congressional intelligence committees' oversight all emerged over the next several years. Their focus tended to be security: the FBI relationship to intelligence analysis had already been subsumed under the wider 9/11 investigations as the Bureau enacted extensive reforms in the area.[41] The clear message that came out of Webster's report, Justice's inspector general report, and the Senate Select Committee hearings was that FBI security needed to be improved. And good measures were taken in light of the constructive criticism, especially with regard to enhanced finance reporting measures and increased use of polygraphs. Neither was a cure by itself, of course, but the reforms were not simply security placebos, either. "Recognizing that we cannot eliminate espionage efforts against us," Webster wrote, "[this commission] . . . has attempted to recommend changes in FBI security programs that will minimize the harm that those who betray us can do to our national security and minimize the time between their defection and detection."[42] Congressional proclamations, intelligence community statements, and FBI reforms all embraced this security mindset. In short, the spiders who called for increased security continued to stare into the wilderness of mirrors hoping to improve their ability catch a glimpse of the prey falling into their web.

Given that the American intelligence community—and especially the FBI—had missed Hanssen's weevil ways, and those of Ames and others, until the crops it cultivated (its sources and programs) had been consumed, increasing the security of its webs seems inadequate. Instead, the Hanssen case offers lessons about the nature of counterintelligence, and specifically US counterintelligence practice, that should be considered.

First, counterintelligence is not the flipside of intelligence or a synonym for "security" or "counterespionage." What worked in resolving the 1985 (and surrounding) losses of intelligence were active counterintelligence efforts to understand and penetrate the adversary, not mirror-gazing and tightening security. Good analysis and investigation caught Ames; BUCKLURE/RAKETEER, or something similar, explicitly set up the FBI's ability to build a case and arrest Hanssen. Analysis and actively targeting hostile intelligence services is the heart of counterintelligence. As weevils do not delay, they must be actively sought and eradicated.

Second, the spiders were often distracted from focusing on the weevils. Changing events, bureaucratic shuffles, enemy disinformation, and other matters made impacts on the American intelligence community's ability to focus on the evidence it had and to seek new evidence. Admirably, both the CIA task force and Mike Rochford's crew kept their eyes open for the mole they knew was still in their fields. And yet both sides also closed off angles of vision by focusing too exclusively on one subject, assuming that the job was done after one weevil was discovered or not addressing and compensating for the inherent differences between two agencies with quite different, though interrelated, missions. These matters were not the work of security reform and did not appear to be on the agenda of Congress, the public, or all too often the agencies themselves.

A last lesson that should be drawn from these mole hunts is that trapping weevils can cause our fellow spider's pain. A consideration of the lesson of James Angleton's pursuit of the moles he feared were supporting a Soviet master plan were not considered as Brian Kelley fell under suspicion from the Bureau and the Agency. And yet the spiders genuinely thought they had found a weevil. In the end, they caught one because they continued to be open to other possibilities. Finding ways to minimize the impact of a mole hunt on those touched by the investigation is imperative, but the solutions are unclear. The spiders must make sure that avenues of investigation are not closed off, morale is minimally damaged, and most important that the innocent are not ensnared as we cast our vision beyond our own dim, gray reflections. The Hanssen case, like all penetrations, was a counterintelligence failure, not simply a security failure.

Figure 13.8: Lead film canister used by the CIA to transport unprocessed film passed by Soviet military intelligence officer Oleg Penkovsky through diplomatic channels to CIA Headquarters. The lead blocked any attempt by the Soviets to use irradiation to see or destroy the contents of this box inside a diplomatic pouch. From the Collection of H. Keith Melton and Karen Melton at the International Spy Museum.

## Further Reading

Bearden, Milton, and James Risen. *The Main Enemy: The Inside Story of the CIA's Final Showdown with the KGB*. New York: Ballantine Books, 2003.

Grimes, Sandra, and Jean Vertefeuille. *Circle of Treason: A CIA Account of Traitor Aldrich Ames and the Men He Betrayed*. Annapolis: Naval Institute Press, 2012.

O'Neill, Eric. *Gray Day: My Undercover Mission to Expose America's First Cyber Spy*. New York: Crown Publishers, 2019.

Pluta, Stephan (FBI Special Agent). "An Affidavit in Support of a Criminal Complaint, Arrest Warrant, and Search Warrants." N.d. (c. February 2001). www.fbi.gov/file-repository/hanssen-affidavit.pdf.

Russo, Gus, and Eric Dezenhall. *Best of Enemies: The Last Great Spy Story of the Cold War*. New York: Twelve, 2018.

Wise, David. *Spy: The Inside Story of How the FBI's Robert Hanssen Betrayed America*. New York: Random House, 2003.

## Notes

All information in this paper is from publicly available sources. The facts are all derived from public source material and have not been confirmed against nonpublic material. The analysis and conclusions are the author's and do not represent an official position of the US government or the Federal Bureau of Investigation.

1. Most explicitly, consider the title of David Martin's *Wilderness of Mirrors: Intrigue, Deception, and the Secrets That Destroyed Two of the Cold War's Most Important Agents* (New York: Skyhorse Publishing, 2018), in which Angleton is one of the two protagonists.

2. Eric O'Neill, *Gray Day: My Undercover Mission to Expose America's First Cyber Spy* (New York: Crown Publishers, 2019), 175.

3. The first public recitation of Hanssen's betrayals appeared in FBI Supervisory Special Agent Stephan Pluta's affidavit in support of an arrest warrant for Hanssen from February 2001 (see further reading section at end of chapter text), www.fbi.gov/file-repository/hanssen-affidavit.pdf/view. A more complete official listing is in the 2002 Webster Report (Commission for Review of FBI Security Programs), "A Review of FBI Security Programs," March 2002, https://irp.fas.org/agency/doj/fbi/websterreport.html, accessed 8/25/2021. What is not known is a general timeline of Hanssen's betrayals.

4. David Wise, read by Kevin Pariseu, *The Seven Million Dollar Spy* (United States: Audible Studios, 2019). Wise died before publishing arrangements for this book were completed, hence the audiobook version is the only version available at this time.

5. O'Neill, *Gray Day*, 249.

6. Richard Cohen, "Who Failed at the FBI?" *Washington Post*, 12/27/2001, www.washingtonpost.com/archive/opinions/2001/12/27/who-failed-at-the-fbi/08447fa4-aae0-4360-9e18-7e54f8fc7d64.

7. See the interview of FBI Supervisory Special Agent (Ret) Mike Rochford hosted at the International Spy Museum, 10/23/2013, with the National Law Enforcement Officers Memorial Foundation: "Witness to History: The Investigation of Robert Hanssen," www.youtube.com/watch?v=-IQAhYeHdE8.

8. Ursula M. Wilder "The Psychology of Espionage," *Studies in Intelligence* 61, no. 2, www.cia.gov/library/center-for-the-study-of-intelligence/csi-publications/csi-studies/studies/vol-61-no-2/pdfs/psychology-of-espionage.pdf.

9. David Charney, "What Makes Traitors Tick," Slide 27, www.slideserve.com/gwyn/by-david-l-charney-m-d-noir-for-usa-psychiatrist-specializing-in-the-mind-of-the-spy, accessed December 15, 2020.

10. Milton Bearden and James Risen, *The Main Enemy: The Inside Story of the CIA's Final Showdown with the KGB* (New York: Ballantine Books, 2003), 125–126.

11. David Wise, *Spy: The Inside Story of How the FBI's Robert Hanssen Betrayed America* (New York: Random House Trade Paperback Edition, 2003), 23–24; Bearden and Risen, *Main Enemy*, 125.

12. Bearden and Risen, *Main Enemy*, 153.

13. Sandra Grimes and Jeanne Vertefeuille, *Circle of Treason: A CIA Account of Traitor Aldrich Ames and the Men He Betrayed* (Annapolis: Naval Institute Press, 2012), 107.

14. Senate Select Intelligence Committee, "An Assessment of the Aldrich H. Ames Espionage Case and Its Implications for U.S. Intelligence," Report, S. Prt. 103–91, 103d Congress, 2nd Session, 11/1/1994, 29.

15. Grimes and Vertefeuille, *Circle of Treason*, 108.

16. O'Neil, *Gray Day*, 96.

17. Department of Justice, Office of Inspector General, *A Review of the FBI's Performance in Uncovering the Espionage Activities of Aldrich Hazen Ames, Executive Summary*, April 1997, https://web.archive.org/web/20151006161856/https://oig.justice.gov/special/9704.htm, 5.

18. See Grimes's remarks in "Spy Hunters-The Women Who Caught Aldrich Ames," delivered at the International Spy Museum, Washington, DC, September 18, 2013, www.youtube.com/watch?v=MKLcKm9hKtk, accessed December 15, 2020. Grimes and Vertefeuille, *Circle of Treason*, 107 and following.

19. CIA, "Counterintelligence at CIA: A Brief History," www.cia.gov/news-information/featured-story-archive/2018-featured-story-archive/counterintelligence-at-cia-a-brief-history.html, accessed October 7, 2019.

20. Grimes and Vertefeuille, *Circle of Treason*, 112.

21. Grimes and Vertefeuille, *Circle of Treason*, 205.

22. Grimes and Vertefeuille, *Circle of Treason*, 145.

23. Senate Select Committee on Intelligence, "Chapter 4: Counterintelligence," *Special Report, Committee Activities of the Select Committee on Intelligence*, SR 104-4, 1995, 15–17, www.intelligence.senate.gov/publications/special-report-committee-activities-select-committee-intelligence-january-4-1993, accessed August 25, 2021.

24. Senate Select Committee on Intelligence, "Special Report, Committee Activities of the SSCI," January 4, 1993 to December 1, 1994, www.intelligence.senate.gov/sites/default/files/publications/CRPT-104srpt4.pdf, 5, accessed December 15, 2020.

25. Bromwich, 1997, "A Review of the FBI's Performance in Uncovering the Espionage Activities of Aldrich Hazen Ames: Unclassified Executive Summary," at https://irp.fas.org/agency/doj/oig/amesxsm1.htm.

26. CIA, "DCI Statement on Ames Damage Assessment, Press Release," *Press Release*, 10/31/1995, www.cia.gov/news-information/press-releases-statements/press-release-archive-1995/ps103195.html.

27. Grimes and Vertefeuille, *Circle of Treason*, 114, 206.

28. Grimes and Vertefeuille, *Circle of Treason*, 108.

29. Grimes and Vertefeuille, *Circle of Treason*, 114.

30. Ronald Kessler, "How the FBI Mishandled the Brian Kelley Spy Case," 9/20/2011, Newsmax.com, at www.newsmax.com/ronaldkessler/kessler-fbi-kelley-spy September 9, 2011id/411700.

31. Kessler, "How the FBI Mishandled the Brian Kelley Spy Case."

32. James Risen and David Johnson, "Before Hanssen Arrest, FBI Suspected Another," *Chicago Tribune*, August 12, 2001, http://articles.chicagotribune.com/news/0108120319_1_cia-officer-robert-hanssen-fbi. See also Wise, *Spy*, 204–205; O'Neill, *Gray Day*, 205–206.

33. Kessler, "How the FBI Mishandled the Brian Kelley Spy Case."

34. Wise, *Spy*, 215.

35. Liz Halloran, "Falsely Accused: CIA Agent's Tale," *Chicago Tribune*, December 11, 2002, www.chicagotribune.com/news/ct-xpm-2002-12-11-0212110137-story.html.

36. Kessler, "How the FBI Mishandled the Brian Kelley Spy Case."

37. Gus Russo and Eric Dezenhall, *Best of Enemies: The Last Great Spy Story of the Cold War* (New York: Twelve, 2018), 222–225; Wise, *Seven Million Dollar Spy*.

38. Stephan Pluta (FBI Special Agent), "An Affidavit in Support of a Criminal Complaint, Arrest Warrant, and Search Warrants," n.d. (c. February 2001). www.fbi.gov/file-repository/hanssen-affidavit.pdf.FBI, accessed December 9, 2020.

39. This sequence of events is compiled based on references in O'Neill, *Gray Day*.

40. Risen and Johnson, "Before Hanssen Arrest."

41. See, for example, FBI Director Robert Mueller's testimony to the House Permanent Select Committee on Intelligence, October 6, 2011, https://archives.fbi.gov/archives/news/testimony/the-state-of-intelligence-reform-10-years-after-911.

42. Commission for the Review of FBI Security Programs, "A Review of FBI Security Programs," US Department of Justice, March 31, 2002, www.cbsnews.com/htdocs/pdf/webster_report.pdf, 18.

# "Walk It Out the Door on a Flash Drive": Counterintelligence and the Delisle Spy Case

**Wesley Wark**

*Because of Canada's place in the international system, its intelligence services have traditionally been more defense-oriented than those of the United States. The International Spy Museum describes one important case broken by the Canadian services: the "Toronto 18," who planned a series of terrorist attacks in Ontario in 2006. Here Wesley Wark explains the significance of a more recent case that rocked Canada: the Jeffery Delisle espionage case.—The Editors*

Defensive efforts to protect national security secrets and to counter foreign spies typically operate as the unloved poor cousin to better-resourced intelligence collection on domestic and foreign targets.[1] But rising concerns about insider threats, heightened levels of foreign espionage, foreign interference targeting democratic processes, and the digital enabling that underpins it all have swung the pendulum of attention back to the counterintelligence mission.

The Canadian Security Intelligence Service (CSIS), Canada's main domestic spy agency, with duties akin to the US Federal Bureau of Investigation and British MI5, is alert to this shift in the threat environment. The director of CSIS, David Vigneault, in a rare public speech delivered in February 2021, specifically noted the dangers posed by insider threats and offered an alarming picture of the range of actors that it might entail:

> Employees, former employees, students, professors, contractors, business associates, or any individual with inside knowledge of—or access to—an organization's systems can be targeted by hostile intelligence services to wittingly or unwittingly steal sensitive information. An insider acting at the behest of a threat actor can compromise a system and cause damage or open a backdoor to allow access from across the street or across the ocean. They can steal information outright and walk it out the door on a flash drive.[2]

Walking sensitive information on a flash drive "out the door" was a poignant reference to the case of Jeffrey Delisle, the most damaging example of an insider threat to have impacted Canada since the depths of the Cold War. It serves as a cautionary tale for all counterintelligence efforts.

The Delisle story is an exemplar of security failures and the challenges of counterintelligence.[3] It also represented the first prosecution for security offenses undertaken in Canada since the passage of the post-9/11 Security of Information Act. The Delisle case is a near-perfect illustration of the harm that can be done by an insider penetrating sensitive national security databases in the interest of a foreign power—in this case the GRU, Russia's military intelligence agency. Thanks to court records, it's a rare case whose details can be explored.

Jeffrey Delisle was a junior officer, a sublieutenant, in the Canadian armed forces who had spent his entire service career since the late 1990s in military intelligence. At the time of his arrest in January 2012, he was serving as a threat analyst for the Canadian navy, operating from HMCS Trinity, an intelligence fusion center in Halifax. Delisle had a top-secret clearance and access to all the main classified databases available to the Canadian security and intelligence community. He had an apparently unblemished record and had received good performance ratings. He was described by the then-director of CSIS, Richard Fadden, as "a relatively quiet guy; he did not make a big fuss. . . . He did not do anything obvious that would lead either us or National Defence [Headquarters] to believe that he was a traitor. He sort of chugged along."[4] Of course, Fadden's characterization should raise some eyebrows, as spies generally do not make a fuss. "Invisible men," ordinary-seeming people who make no great surface impression, can make extraordinary spies, as John le Carré often suggested in his spy fiction, notably in the figure of George Smiley.

Jeffrey Delisle, Canada's "invisible man," not only had access to state secrets; he also kept his own. He had serious personal and mental health problems, many revolving around a failed marriage. He had an addiction to online gaming, something that contributed to his failed marriage. He was a quintessential loner who feared for his personal and professional future. His family life was falling apart, and his career in the armed forces was going nowhere because of a diabetic condition that prevented him from being posted on operations.

In July 2007, something broke in Delisle. He made an impromptu decision to offer to spy for the Russians.[5] He was working at the time at National Defence Headquarters in Ottawa. He presented himself to the nearby Russian embassy, dressed in civilian clothes and probably wearing his trademark hoodie to avoid camera surveillance. He offered himself as a "walk-in" agent (a volunteer spy). GRU officials based in the embassy interviewed him in a secure room, took steps to establish his bona fides, and then provided Delisle with a communications protocol, a process for paying him by electronic transfers monthly, and even an exfiltration plan if needed. Once activated, Delisle proceeded to supply the Russians with intelligence, what he called his "data dumps," extracted primarily from Five Eyes signals intelligence (SIGINT) reporting, for the four-year duration of his espionage career. Delisle may have been a very junior officer, but his access had nothing to do with his rank and was extensive. Intelligence drawn from Canada's intelligence partners in the Five Eyes, a long-established network linking Canada with the United States, Britain, Australia, and New Zealand, represents the crown jewel of sensitive information available to Canada. Delisle knew that and proceeded to plunder that resource.

The Delisle story has embedded within it multiple counterintelligence issues, ranging from the manner of his detection to the lessons that were learned. The first thing that stands out about the Delisle case is that he was not caught by any Canadian counterintelligence efforts. Rather, Canada was tipped off about his spying by the Federal Bureau of Investigation.[6] Controversy surrounds the Canadian response to this because the FBI initially went to the Canadian Security Intelligence Service with intelligence about Delisle's espionage. According to media reporting, CSIS officials were called to Washington to discuss the case, which was unearthed through US intelligence knowledge of payments made to Delisle by a Russian intelligence official using the pseudonym "Mary Larkin," who was previously linked to a US spy ring.[7] CSIS then mounted its own counterintelligence investigation, which may have included warranted surveillance of Delisle, but was unwilling to pass its files to the Royal Canadian Mounted Police (RCMP) for fear that CSIS sources and methods might be exposed in court.[8] When US concern mounted over apparent Canadian inaction, the FBI went directly to the RCMP with information about Delisle.[9] The period between initial CSIS knowledge and the subsequent FBI approach to the RCMP was several months.

In a memorandum to the public safety minister, written when CSIS got wind of imminent media reporting on the Delisle case, the interim director of CSIS, Michel Coulombe, argued that "CSIS cooperation and 'de-confliction' with the RCMP, in this case, was considered by all involved to have been appropriate and necessary, in the circumstances."[10] Although the language seems clear, what exactly he meant remains shrouded in secrecy. The reference to "all involved" clearly did not include the FBI. According to the FBI's agent in charge, Frank Figliuzzi, the Bureau's frustration

Figure 14.1: Canadian Security Intelligence Service challenge coin. The CSIS investigates espionage in Canada but has no arrest authorities; those reside within the Royal Canadian Mounted Police. From the Collection of H. Keith and Karen Melton at the International Spy Museum.

with the slow-rolling effort by the Canadians grew to a boiling point and led FBI Director Robert Mueller to call his Canadian counterparts and even to consider a plan to lure Delisle to the United States. In the end, Figliuzzi penned a letter to the RCMP, which he hand-delivered to the Mounties in Ottawa, and briefed them on the case. The date on the letter was December 2, 2011.[11]

The question this raises is a perennial one for Canada, involving the state of cooperation between the RCMP and CSIS, with the Mounties responsible for national security law enforcement and investigations and CSIS for counterintelligence. It would appear to be a classic intelligence-to-evidence problem, which centers on concerns about the exposure of CSIS's investigations in court proceedings and the need for a parallel and separate RCMP investigation of a case to evidentiary standards.[12] The manner of Delisle's detection, while suggesting the value of Canada's close security cooperation with the United States, also raised concerns about Canada's own counterintelligence capabilities.

Following Figliuzzi's briefing, the RCMP began its own investigation, building a profile about Delisle and engaging in a laborious search warrant approval process. The RCMP then mounted a crash surveillance of Delisle over the Christmas holidays in December 2011 (never an ideal time for an emergency response). The surveillance included monitoring Delisle's electronic communications. This allowed the RCMP to covertly track and record exchanges between Delisle and his Russian handlers, including the attempted provision by Delisle of some sensitive CSIS documents, which the Mounties ensured did not reach the GRU. This was a last-ditch effort to ensure that the Canadian authorities would have some evidence of Delisle's spying that could support an arrest and be presented in court. The risk was a discovery by either Delisle or the GRU of the RCMP's lurking presence—but fortunately the RCMP electronic surveillance effort remained hidden. Delisle was taken into custody after armed RCMP officers surrounded him in the driveway of his Halifax home on January 13, 2012, and charged with two counts under the Security of Information Act as well as a breach of trust charge under the Criminal Code.

What happened next further illustrates how counterintelligence and law enforcement objectives do not always align. After his arrest, Delisle was interrogated by a veteran RCMP officer, Jimmy Moffat. An officer renowned within the RCMP for his interrogative skills, Moffat was brought into the case after the RCMP had canvassed its organization to find someone who had recent experience and knowledge about Russian espionage. There was none to be had; the last major spy case involving a Russian mole operating inside Canadian intelligence was decades old.

Moffat's interrogation of Delisle lasted a little over three hours. As an interrogation it was psychologically brilliant, breaking down all of Delisle's barriers and cover stories. It was also a complete success in legal terms in eliciting a full confession from Delisle that could be presented in court.[13] However, as a counterintelligence interrogation it was a dismal failure.[14] Moffat elicited only scant details from Delisle about what intelligence he had passed to the Russians. In fact, Moffat showed very little interest in probing exactly what secrets Delisle had betrayed, and he may have been hamstrung by his lack of knowledge of either Canadian military intelligence or Russian espionage practices. From his interrogator's perspective, he needed to know only enough to serve the purpose of securing a conviction. A confession was key. Digging any deeper risked potential exposure of Canadian secrets at trial.

During the interrogation, Delisle revealed two very unusual facets of the case. One was the rationale he offered for his spying. He told Moffat that he had commenced his espionage career because he wanted to commit "professional suicide." His domestic life was a total mess following his wife's affair and their subsequent divorce. Delisle was not a man with any emotional depth or defenses, but he also found himself incapable of committing the literal suicide that he had contemplated, largely because of the fear of its consequences for his children, to whom he was deeply devoted. Spying for the Russians was his escape from a tormented life. Thus, Delisle did not fit any of the classic "MICE" motives for treason (money, ideology, corruption, and ego).[15] Unlike many of history's greatest spies, he also expected to be caught and thus had no intention of using his exfiltration plan. In his interrogation, he asked officials why it had taken so long to unearth him.

The other unusual thing the case revealed was that Delisle, as a spy for the Russians, was essentially self-tasking. The GRU tasking was loose and generally not aligned with Delisle's access to secrets. Delisle decided that what he could provide, without much prompting from the Russians, was signals intelligence reporting, mostly drawn from voluminous intercept material from the US National Security Agency shared with the Canadians and stored on databases to which Delisle had access. Delisle claimed to be very puzzled by the Russians' lack of interest in the technical side of Canadian SIGINT, a fact giving rise to speculation that the GRU did not fully trust this walk-in, with his uncertain motivation, or—a grim thought—had even better sources and did not pay all that much attention to running Delisle, or that the Ottawa *rezidentura* was incompetent. However, we will never get an answer to this puzzle unless we are treated to a future memoir by a GRU defector with knowledge of the case—and we should not hold our breath about the chances of one appearing.

If the Delisle interrogation suggested that law enforcement and counterintelligence needs could diverge, there are other elements of the story indicating how the exercise of counterintelligence was less than robust. One mystery is that no effort was made to play Delisle back to the Russians as a controlled agent. Such operations can be tricky and delicate, but there were aspects of the Delisle case that suggested tantalizing opportunities if they had been seized. One key was that the Canadian authorities had access to Delisle's communication pipeline to the GRU and knew his reporting schedule. This would have allowed them to attempt to seamlessly continue the message traffic from Delisle, now operating unbeknownst to the GRU, as a Canada-controlled agent. Another situational advantage was that Delisle had always avoided face-to-face meetings with GRU officers, adding to the chances that a standoff playback might have succeeded. Would Delisle have agreed to such a plan in return for more lenient treatment and sentencing? Who can say? Would Delisle have been a good candidate, psychologically, for being played back? Would the Russians have bitten? Could Canada have mounted a successful operation, lacking experience with such things, but presumably drawing on Five Eyes assistance? There is simply no way to know. However, what this lack of effort at double-crossing may suggest is that the Delisle case came as a shock to a system that in 2012 had paid relatively little attention to counterintelligence and had little experience dealing with insider spies caught in the act.

Another testament to the lack of a strong counterintelligence effort during that period was the government's failure to extend a plea deal to him. A plea bargain might have allowed the gaps left by his interrogation to be filled if Delisle agreed to terms that traded a lenient sentence for details on the intelligence he had passed to the Russians.[16] But no plea bargain was forthcoming and Delisle was eventually sentenced to 20 years in jail (minus time served). The puzzle over the absence of a plea deal is that Canadian authorities had no alternative way of finding out the details of Delisle's betrayal. There was no system in place that allowed for a forensic accounting of Delisle's computer access to sensitive databases over the course of his four-year spying career. Delisle had used USBs to transfer information from sensitive to nonsensitive computer systems at his workstation so that they could be brought home and transferred to his personal computer and onward from there as data dumps for the Russians. When Moffat asked hopefully about the whereabouts of the USBs, he was told that they had been overwritten for use on his kids' Xbox game consoles.[17]

The impulse to extract a pound of flesh, rather than obtain valuable counterintelligence information, through either a double-cross operation or a plea bargain, appeared to have prevailed. Many in the Canadian military were furious over Delisle's betrayal of trust and the military code of conduct. There seems to have been no appetite for a lighter sentence, even though there were aspects of Delisle's case that might have warranted it, including the fact that Delisle had on occasion tried to walk away from his Russian spy connection, only to find anonymous brown envelopes in his mail containing surveillance photos of his children. The calculation may even have been that a full accounting of the secrets that Delisle had spilled to the Russians might have made matters worse in terms of Canada's ongoing intelligence relations with its Five Eyes partners, especially the United States, whose SIGINT reporting made up the bulk of Delisle's pilfered secrets. Better in some ways not to know the worst and get on with damage control.

A strong counterintelligence system (a "safeguarding" system in the parlance of the National Security and Intelligence Review Agency [NSIRA]) depends on both preemptive and protective capabilities. Preemptive capabilities involve knowing an adversary's foreign intelligence systems and their operations and being able to deter, preempt, or disrupt espionage efforts. Such capabilities were missing in action in the Delisle case. But they were also not backstopped by any strong protective shield including security measures. The Delisle case was an example of a cascading security failure in which almost every layer of Canadian security defenses was found wanting. Delisle's personal and monetary problems never rose to the surface of the military's attention.[18] The absence of any security spotlight on Delisle as a person was matched by lax physical and IT security at his workplace. There is no record that Delisle was ever searched during his entrance to or exit from his station, including at HMCS Trinity. HMCS Trinity possessed antiquated computer systems, including computers that still used floppy disks in 2011 and allowed for easy transfer of data from classified to nonclassified computer systems. There was no tracking capability for logins and logoffs on the highly classified databases that Delisle could access. Nothing in his work habits aroused any suspicion among his fellow officers. Perhaps worst of all, Delisle's top-secret security clearance was allowed to lapse without affecting his access to sensitive systems. NSIRA commented: "Had proper clearance renewal standards been followed, his loyalty to Canada would have been assessed and other vulnerabilities scrutinized."[19]

Counterintelligence failures on the scale of Delisle's case are typically riddled with missed opportunities. If lax security clearance processes were one such missed chance for Canadian authorities to identify their suspect, another was presented by an incident when Delisle was subjected to a secondary examination by an official of the Canadian Border Services Agency (CBSA) at the Halifax airport following his return from an alleged brief holiday in Brazil on September 22, 2011. The Brazil trip was the first and only time that he had agreed to an in-person meeting with a Russian intelligence officer since offering his services in the summer of 2007.

Although we cannot be certain, it may be that CBSA was alerted to Delisle's travel by CSIS and that his name was placed on a watchlist. The CBSA official was suspicious about Delisle's tale of taking a holiday to gamble in casinos and was attentive to the amount of money that Delisle, a junior Canadian armed forces officer, was carrying. He also noticed that Delisle, despite being on a supposed holiday junket, was still Canadian-pale rather than sporting any Brazilian tan. Some incriminating (in retrospect) material was seized from Delisle, including pocket litter receipts and scribbled notes regarding his email dropbox account with the GRU, the significance of which appears not to have been understood at the time.[20] Once out of secondary examination and free to go about his business, Delisle must have felt some relief, though his GRU handlers suggested he might lay off and go quiet for a while—advice that Delisle ignored. The RCMP was not alerted at the time about the results of the CBSA examination, and Delisle's arrest took place only three months later, following the FBI's direct tipoff. It wasn't until the RCMP began its crash investigation in December that it unearthed the CBSA report on Delisle's trip to Brazil and recognized its significance.

In the aftermath of Delisle's confession, Canadian officials were forced to confront the stark reality that their counterintelligence and safeguarding practices had failed. They were also forced to confront serious concerns over Canada's worthiness as an ally, expressed most strongly by the United States. The Americans were so concerned with the way the Delisle case was handled that they presented an unprecedented ultimatum: either

Figure 14.2: KGB portable electric drill with a pressure gauge for drilling microphone holes. After Jeffrey Delisle's espionage for Russia was discovered, Canadian authorities tore down the building he worked in to locate any possible bugs. From the Collection of H. Keith and Karen Melton at the International Spy Museum.

Canada took steps to fix its security problems, or it would face a drastic reduction of intelligence-sharing.

There was no option for Canadian officials but to make urgent fixes, not all of which are publicly known. HMCS Trinity was torn down and rebuilt to locate any possible bugs left behind by Delisle and to upgrade and harden the computer systems. Major changes were made to security protocols around access to highly classified databases. The most visible change was that made to security screening practices, with the introduction of a completely revamped system, the 2014 Standard on Security Screening, which among other things introduced something that Delisle had never been exposed to: a mandatory polygraph for officials regularly working in a top-secret information environment.[21] The new security screening standard also stipulated a program for aftercare, a euphemism for a protocol that tried to fill the gap between periodic security clearance renewals with an ongoing process of scrutiny of new information about officials with security clearances.[22] The fixes must have been satisfactory, as Canada remains a member of Five Eyes.

While much of the post-Delisle effort was focused on improving security procedures, the question must be asked whether the broader Canadian

Figure 14.3: Russian model revealing how the Soviet KGB bugged the US embassy in Moscow in the 1980s. It is based on information passed by the KGB chief Vadim Bakatin to US Ambassador Robert Strauss in the last days of the Soviet Union. In response, the United States partially demolished and rebuilt its embassy. Canada feared similar problems with its Trinity building and had it destroyed. From the Collection of H. Keith and Karen Melton at the International Spy Museum.

approach to counterintelligence has truly changed in the years since. In some ways, it has. There are emerging strengths in the Canadian system, especially regarding enhanced cybersecurity and new powers provided to Canada's signals agency, the Communications Security Establishment. There is much greater sensitivity to foreign interference, including foreign espionage. There is also increasing attention being paid to economic security issues, which will require enhanced counterintelligence capabilities. But how far the pendulum has swung to counterintelligence and away from a dominant, post-9/11 counterterrorism mission remains unclear.

The reality may be that it will take more than one spectacular counterintelligence failure to truly move the needle. If such is the case, Delisle has now been joined by two more cases of Canadians charged under the Security of Information Act. One involved an arrest in 2013, hard on the heels of Delisle's sentencing, of a civilian contractor, Qing Quentin Huang, for allegedly trying to pass classified information about Canada's naval shipbuilding program to Chinese embassy officials. In a stunning judicial decision, the Huang case has been stayed owing to trial delays, and he is now a free man.[23] A second, more spectacular case, involving the betrayal of sensitive intelligence to international organized crime groups by a senior RCMP officer, Cameron Ortis, came to light with his arrest on September 12, 2019. The commencement of the Ortis trial was delayed until October 2023.[24] He was subsequently tried by jury and found guilty on all counts. The conviction is currently on appeal. Both the Huang and Ortis cases have added to an awakened concern about insider threats.

More momentum for change will result from the work of Canada's National Security and Intelligence Review Agency. The review body, which is responsible for reporting on CSIS and other security and intelligence agencies, announced in its first annual report, for the year 2019, its intention to devote considerable future resources to monitoring and reporting on safeguarding practices. NSIRA's working definition of "safeguarding" is "the protection of people, information and other government assets within the national security and intelligence portfolio," which certainly lends itself to both security and counterintelligence reviews.[25] The Delisle case was very much on the minds of NSIRA as it announced its future review plans, not least for the ways it illuminated the consequences of counterintelligence and security failures. The consequences that NSIRA enumerated included higher risks for intelligence operations, damage to sources, and reputational risks to Canada.[26]

Ongoing and new prosecutions for offenses under the Canadian official secrets legislation (the Security of Information Act) will inevitably bring attention to security and counterintelligence problems and lead to additional pressures for change. But they are also double-edged swords. A key element in secrecy law as a criminal sanction is that it is meant to act as a deterrent. The fervent wish, of course, is that the law never needs to be used to punish offenders. When legal deterrence fails, however, the landscape shifts. If a need emerges to bring down the hammer of the Security of Information Act, it means that a significant act of espionage has occurred—a leak, an act of treason, a mole uncovered. However, prosecution under the act is tricky. There are evidentiary standards to meet in court, disclosure obligations to defendants, inevitable media scrutiny, and international attention from allies and foes. There are risks: unveiling sensitive information and political embarrassment. There is a lot at stake, because losing a secrecy act case would be a nightmare. In the Delisle case the government got lucky: Delisle's confession, secured by Jimmy Moffat, and his subsequent decision to plead guilty spared the government a lengthy open trial. Such luck may not be repeated in the future.

Information brought to light by future review reports and court proceedings may prove the most significant vehicle for change in ensuring that Canada has a more robust counterintelligence system. The Delisle case was where it all began. Getting to the bottom of what went wrong in the Delisle case and fully capturing its lessons, many of which remain hidden in the world of official secrets, would be an excellent starting point. In the depths of the failures surrounding the Delisle case, there are lessons not only for Canada but also for Canada's allies. No one has immunity these days in the face of the insider threat. The best defense is a combination of a strong security culture and a counterintelligence capacity that knows its adversaries and operates on equal terms in resources, talent, and attention, alongside the intelligence collectors and assessors. Let the pendulum swing.

Figure 14.4: KGB Bagulnik device, used to create microdots and "soft film" using cellophane wrappers from cigarette packages and household chemicals. Microdots were a common method for clandestine communication during much of the twentieth century. From the Collection of H. Keith and Karen Melton at the International Spy Museum.

## Further Reading

Andrew, Christopher, and Vasili Mitrokhin. *The Mitrokhin Archive: The Mitrokhin Archive and the Secret History of the KGB*. New York: Basic Books, 1999.

Mahar, Donald H. *Shattered Illusions: KGB Cold War Espionage in Canada*. Lanham, MD: Rowman & Littlefield, 2017.

Molinaro, Dennis G., ed. *The Bridge in the Parks: The Five Eyes and Cold War Counter-Intelligence*. Toronto: University of Toronto Press, 2021.

Wark, Wesley. "Russia, Secrets, Spies, Sold." *Literary Review of Canada* 21, no. 3 (April 2013): 18–19. https://reviewcanada.ca/magazine/2013/04/spy-russians-secrets-sold.

Whitaker, Reg, Gregory S. Kealey, and Andrew Parnaby. *Secret Service: Political Policing in Canada from the Fenians to Fortress America*. Toronto: University of Toronto Press, 2021.

## Notes

1. Frederick L. Wettering, "Counterintelligence: The Broken Triad," in *Secret Intelligence: A Reader* (2nd ed.), ed. Christopher Andrew, Richard J. Aldrich, and Wesley Wark (London: Routledge, 2020), 319–345.

2. Wettering, "Counterintelligence: The Broken Triad."

3. For an overview of the Delisle case, see Wesley Wark, "Russia, Secrets, Spies, Sold," *Literary Review of Canada*, April 2013, https://reviewcanada.ca/magazine/2013/04/spy-russians-secrets-sold. The author served as an expert witness before the Superior Court of Nova Scotia in the sentencing hearings for Delisle. For an account of the sentencing hearings, see CBC, "Damage Done by Navy Spy Disputed by Lawyers," January 31, 2013, www.cbc.ca/news/canada/nova-scotia/damage-done-by-navy-spy-disputed-by-lawyers-1.1372325.

4. Richard Fadden testimony, Senate committee on National Security and Defence, February 11, 2013, https://sencanada.ca/en/Content/Sen/Committee/411/SECD/12ev-49950-e; further details on Delisle's character are contained in Nova Scotia, Department of Justice, Correctional Services, "Pre-Sentence Report," Queen vs. Jeffrey Paul Delisle, December 28, 2012. Copy in possession of the author.

5. Key details about Delisle's spying activities are contained in the official "Agreed Statement of Facts," Her Majesty the Queen v. Jeffrey Paul Delisle, Provincial Court of Nova Scotia. Copy in possession of the author.

6. "Agreed Statement of Facts." The FBI letter to the RCMP was dated December 2, 2011. The author was FBI Assistant Director Frank Figliuzzi.

7. The initial approach to CSIS was uncovered by the Canadian Press journalists Jim Bronskill and Murray Brewster, "CSIS Knew of Navy Spy's Activity, Left RCMP in the Dark," CBC News, May 26, 2013, www.cbc.ca/news/canada/nova-scotia/csis-knew-of-navy-spy-s-activity-left-rcmp-in-the-dark-1.1312803.

8. Jim Bronskill and Murray Brewster, "CSIS Knew of Navy Spy's Activity, Left RCMP in the Dark."

9. Bronskill and Brewster, "CSIS Knew."

10. CSIS, Memorandum to the Minister, TS, "Delisle Case—Media Reporting on

CSIS and U.S., Involvement," May 21, 2013, redacted copy obtained through Access to Information. In possession of the author.

11. Frank Figliuzzi, *The FBI Way* (New York: HarperCollins, 2021), 231–233.

12. Craig Forcese, "Threading the Needle: Structural Reform and Canada's Intelligence-to-Evidence Dilemma," Draft Working Paper, July 2018.
https://papers.ssrn.com/sol3/papers.cfm?abstract_id=3214750.

13. Transcript of the RCMP interrogation of Jeffrey Paul Delisle, RCMP Case # 2011-3421, January 13, 2021, time-stamped 19:37:17 to 22:57:48. Copy in possession of the author.

14. The analysis in this section is based on the RCMP interrogation transcript. Transcript of the RCMP interrogation of Jeffrey Paul Delisle, RCMP Case # 2011–3421, January 13, 2021.

15. On MICE, see Randy Burkett, "An Alternative Framework for Agent Recruitment: From MICE to RASCLS," *Studies in Intelligence* 57, no. 1 (March 2013): 7–17, https://cyberwar.nl/d/fromCIA.gov/Burkett-MICE%20to%20RASCALS.pdf.

16. A plea bargain featured in the case of the US handling of the Walker family spy ring, John Prados, "The John Walker Spy Ring and the U.S. Navy's Biggest Betrayal," *United States Naval Institute*, September 2, 2014, https://news.usni.org/2014/09/02/john-walker-spy-ring-u-s-navys-biggest-betrayal.

17. RCMP interrogation of Delisle, January 13, 2013.

18. Delisle's supervising officer at HMCS Trinity was interviewed by the RCMP on January 14, 2012. He was aware of Delisle's trips to Brazil and Cuba but had no suspicions about him. "RCMP transcript of interview with JF." Copy in possession of the author.

19. National Security and Intelligence Review Agency, *2019 Annual Report*, www.nsira-ossnr.gc.ca/html/2018–2019/index-eng.html.

20. Some details of the CBSA examination of Delisle, based on a report dated September 23, 2011, are contained in "Agreed Statement of Facts."

21. Treasury Board Secretariat (2014) Standard on Security Screening, www.tbs-sct.gc.ca/pol/doc-eng.aspx?id=28115.

22. The Pentagon has announced a similar system for its personnel, which would include something not contemplated in the Canadian practice, i.e., routine scanning of social media posts that might reveal extremist or unlawful activities. Patrick Tucker, "Pentagon Begins 'Continuous Vetting' of All Troops for Insider Threats, Extremism; Social Media May Come Next," *Defence One*, October 5, 2021, www.defenseone.com/technology/2021/10/pentagon-begins-continuous-vetting-all-troops-insider-threats-extremism-social-media-may-come-next/185876.

23. Ontario, Superior Court of Justice, R. v. Huang, ONSC 8372 (CanLII), 2022-10-04, www.canlii.org/en/on/onsc/doc/2021/2021onsc8372/2021onsc8372.html.

24. Canadian Press, "Trial of Alleged RCMP Secret Leaker Delayed a Year After He Gets New Lawyer," September 1, 2022, www.ctvnews.ca/canada/trial-of-alleged-rcmp-secret-leaker-delayed-a-year-after-he-gets-new-lawyer-1.6051257.

25. National Security and Intelligence Review Agency, *2019 Annual Report*, www.nsira-ossnr.gc.ca/html/2018-2019/index-eng.html.

26. National Security and Intelligence Review Agency, *2019 Annual Report*.

# Northern Ireland, 1971: Torture, Accountability, and Sir Dick White

Tony Craig

*In recent decades, the United States used harsh methods—what some people characterize as torture—against suspected terrorist detainees. This caused fierce debate in the country, a debate that the International Spy Museum addresses. Of course, the United States is not the only country to have used detention and even torture in battling terrorists. In this chapter, Tony Craig reminds us of the United Kingdom's experience in this regard while fighting the Irish Republican Army during "The Troubles."*
*—The Editors*

The British army was deployed to Northern Ireland in August 1969 following a period of sustained rioting on the streets. In response, Irish republican paramilitary groups slowly grew and began to target what they interpreted as a concrete manifestation of continued British imperial power in Ireland. For its part, the newly formed Provisional Irish Republican Army (officially the Irish Republican Army, or IRA) targeted the British army and wider security forces murdering a number of police and soldiers in the first months of 1971. By early spring, what had previously been a tense situation had turned into a near insurgency.

In March 1971, Britain's Intelligence Coordinator, Sir Dick White, a former head of both MI5 and MI6, was tasked by the British Cabinet Office's Joint Intelligence Committee (JIC) to report on the improvement of security intelligence in Northern Ireland. White's report, now partially declassified, shows that his opinion was pivotal in securing British government support for the introduction of internment, without trial, for Irish republican paramilitary suspects; it also determined the use of controversial interrogation methods ("interrogation in depth" or the "five techniques") that were applied to a select minority of internees. During interrogation, those selected were hooded, forced to stand against a wall in a stress position between interrogation sessions, subjected to white noise, deprived of sleep, and fed only bread and water for an unlimited amount of time.[1]

Today, it is agreed that the introduction of internment was a disaster. However, this chapter further argues that White's centrality to the interrogation in depth policy raises wider questions regarding the accountability of intelligence consultants. An after-the-fact revision of the official record also highlights problems with the use of state archives to investigate controversial state actions, especially when the people involved in planning policy are also those who offer the first assessments of such policies in the official records. This chapter will show how White incorporated interrogation in depth methods into an already controversial plan to introduce internment without trial for Irish republican suspects in 1971. Further, White then successfully deflected blame for the wider escalation of retaliatory violence that the controversy interrogation in depth had caused.

After Dick White's report, the British government authorized internment in a bid to halt the deteriorating security situation in Northern Ireland, and by August 1971 it was widely considered to be the "only . . . unused major weapon in the government's anti-terrorism arsenal."[2] The use of that weapon began with Operation Demetrius on the morning of August 9, when the British army raided addresses throughout Northern Ireland, taking 342 men into custody.[3] British authorities had used internment against Irish Republicans in 1922–1924, 1939–1945, and 1956–1961. What was different this time was the application of controversial "secondary" interrogation techniques at army-run "special" interrogation centers that were part of a side operation to Demetrius, Operation Calaba. The five techniques were designed to maximize the intelligence flow from a selection of prisoners to turn the tables on the IRA, and they were first mentioned in White's March 1971 report. The results of their use, however, were explosive once news emerged that the government was using what many viewed as torture. These accusations fueled a violent backlash for the rest of 1971. This backlash combined with popular anti-internment protests throughout Ireland and around the world. According to the historians Paul Arthur and Keith Jeffery, internment "turned out to be an unmitigated disaster . . . followed by an increase in the level of unrest." Whereas from January to August 1971 30 people had been killed in the violence, from August to December there were 143 deaths.[4]

Although the interrogation of 14 internees using interrogation in depth methods substantially prolonged the backlash against internment, public blame was consistently placed at the feet of Northern Ireland's prime minister, Brian Faulkner, because he was the one who had requested internment and signed the orders.[5] However, when Faulkner approved internment, he was not aware that new and brutal forms of interrogation would be used. His later admission of culpability was limited to internment itself and therefore does not make him responsible for the subsequent backlash in its entirety.[6] This is true especially when it comes to that part of the backlash sustained by the drip of allegations regarding interrogation in depth methods and how these were then embellished with other lurid accounts that were far less easily verified.[7]

In fact, if one looks more deeply at the origin of Operation Calaba, in particular at the actions of Sir Dick White and Brian Stewart, a senior MI6 officer serving with the JIC, one sees little if any interaction with the Northern Ireland government. It therefore becomes clear that Sir Dick White made his March 1971 recommendation to employ interrogation techniques used by the army in overseas counterinsurgency operations without input from Northern Ireland's government. This chapter looks at the system of decision-making that allowed Calaba (an intelligence operation) to become a part of the internment policy (a security operation) without the knowledge or approval of the Northern Ireland government. Finally, it discusses the problems with using historical records that judge policies when those records were written by the people who created the policies in the first place.

The historian Eunan O'Halpin was the first to identify the role of the JIC (and of Dick White) in the planning of Operation Calaba, specifically the approval of the five techniques of secondary interrogation that the British army had developed during a series of postwar colonial counterinsurgencies in Palestine, Kenya, Malaya, Nigeria, British Guiana, Brunei, Aden, and Oman.[8] Codified by the JIC in 1965, these techniques were justified by the perception of their success when used on persons who had information and "[from] which it was operationally necessary to obtain as rapidly as possible in the interest of saving lives, while at the same time providing detainees with the necessary security for their own persons and identities."[9] In 1967, the JIC confirmed the use of the techniques with the addition of medical supervision of detainees.[10] And while "this fine tuning [by adding medical supervision] may have been sufficient to salve the consciences of the army's interrogators in Northern Ireland in 1971 . . . [the techniques] provoked a firestorm of criticism" when used.[11]

The title of White's biography, *The Perfect English Spy*, gives a taste of the high regard in which White was held within the intelligence community.[12] He had been MI5's first university graduate, played a pivotal role in the establishment of the Double-Cross System that ran a vast network of fictitious Nazi agents in Britain during World War II to deceive the Germans, and led MI5 through troubled times in the 1950s when numerous Soviet spy scandals erupted. Later, he led MI6 for 12 years following the embarrassing Buster Crabb incident, when a Royal Navy diver was lost while secretly inspecting the hull of a Soviet cruiser at Portsmouth Dockyard, before retiring in 1968. Shortly thereafter, however, he took the newly established part-time position of Intelligence Coordinator, a senior

Figure 15.1: Eric Holt-Wilson, deputy director of Britain's MI5 (1912–1940), who oversaw the service's World War I operations, including in Ireland. From a privately published book of caricatures of MI5 personnel, circa 1920. When Irish Republicans proclaimed an armed rebellion against British rule in 1916, MI5 had to divert resources away from the war. From the Collection of H. Keith and Karen Melton at the International Spy Museum.

post in the Cabinet Office liaising between the intelligence community and the British government. By 1971, White was not only a veteran of the JIC but also recognized as possessing both "a vast and unrivaled experience of intelligence matters" and the ability to get his opinions heard throughout the British government, even if he was "rather worn out."[13]

White's March 1971 report (now declassified with redactions) reveals flaws in the architecture of intelligence management in Northern Ireland that allowed for imperial practices to be used without allowing feedback to or from Northern Ireland's own institutions. This issue arose because of the way both Britain's army, and elements of the civil service, had deployed to Northern Ireland following the disturbances in 1969, which allowed White to become far more influential than he ought to have been. He made arguments, for instance, referring to his understanding of the way the Special Branch of the Royal Ulster Constabulary (RUC) felt, which were not verified or fed back once policies were formulated. The network of British security officials within which White operated included the army but did not include the local police or representatives of Northern Ireland's (state) government. Consequently, mistakes that should have been obvious continued to be made by "a decent and intelligent man but one out of touch with contemporary opinion about acceptable treatment of un-convicted suspects in the United Kingdom."[14]

Suspicion of the Northern Ireland government *and* the RUC permeated

Figure 15.2: MI5's 1924 New Year's card. The Irish Free State had been founded a year previously as part of the British Commonwealth. Britain's MI5 had liaised with the Irish police and continued to operate in Northern Ireland. From the Collection of H. Keith and Karen Melton at the International Spy Museum.

Britain's military, intelligence, and diplomatic personnel starting from their initial deployment to Northern Ireland in 1969. This lack of trust stemmed from a belief that mismanagement by the local regime had led to disorder there and so a certain degree of professional distance needed to be maintained. In April 1969, the JIC was asked to consult with the Home Office "on the means for obtaining information other than through the Northern Ireland official sources" by sending an officer from MI5 who would become part of what the JIC chairman, Sir Edward Peck, described as a "slightly better intelligence service on Northern Ireland."[15] In August 1969, when the British army deployed to Northern Ireland at the request of its government, the British government gave the army responsibility for security operations and authority over all security forces including the RUC.[16] As was common practice in colonial conflicts, the Northern Ireland government had input on security policy through daily meetings of the local Joint Security Committee, but, importantly, it no longer had control over operations.

The lack of trust also extended to intelligence matters, and London even withheld the terms of reference of the newly created post of Director of Intelligence for Northern Ireland from the Northern Ireland government. On August 29, 1969, Peck, the JIC chairman, told the deputy chief of the Defence Staff (Intelligence): "I should be against communicating any formal terms of reference to the Northern Ireland authorities. Surely it would be enough for the [General Officer Commanding] to introduce his Director of

Intelligence stating vaguely that he is responsible to him for coordinating intelligence in Northern Ireland and will ensure liaison with the Northern Irish authorities." Peck reasoned that, should the Northern Ireland government see the detail of the new Director of Intelligence's terms of reference, "the Ulstermen [i.e., the local government] might well be [left] wondering what the Director of Intelligence did with all the other intelligence he got when they found out they were not getting it."[17] The implication of course was that Northern Ireland's government was not an equal partner in establishing a program of reform there because its Unionist government (largely Protestant, conservative, and pro-British) would oppose it.

In November, a new top-secret classification, code-named "Perimeter," was created specifically to exclude Northern Ireland officials and ministers from JIC and British cabinet-level papers that related to intelligence in Northern Ireland.[18] The idea was to allow British officials to discuss matters freely and securely. This exclusion, however, damaged relations with Northern Ireland's civil service, some of whom felt belittled in hindsight. One remarked, for instance, "that August 1969 mark[ed] the effective end of 'Stormont' as an autonomous regional government."[19] The fundamental drawback, however, lay in the effect this had on the quality of British decision-making because of the exclusion of potentially valuable opinions from Northern Ireland officials. John Oliver, a senior parliamentary official, later noted the emerging problem of aloofness among British officials as they steadily withdrew from direct contact and gradually built systems of contacts with politicians rather than civil servants. He noted that "[w]e could have learned from them and could have benefited greatly from having them work with us."[20]As a result, "muddles abounded, time was wasted. Blunders were perpetrated."[21] The problem Oliver described would become most acute as the IRA reemerged in 1970 and 1971.

Before Dick White arrived in Northern Ireland, the province (and the RUC) had already endured numerous troubleshooters, consultants, and short-term liaison officers who had often reported back negatively on what they had seen. General Sir Geoffrey Baker (Britain's Chief of the General Staff) reported, for example, that the RUC Special Branch was "behind the times, poorly led and administered."[22] Following Baker's report, a series of short-term military and intelligence liaison officers were sent to support, observe, and report back to London on the Northern Ireland police; some of these visitors were well received, others decidedly not.[23] Ultimately Hunt's report in October 1969 recommended enormous changes to the force and the appointment—over the heads of the RUC and Northern Ireland's government—of Sir Arthur Young, another outsider, as Chief Constable.[24]

The appointment of a Director of Intelligence responsible to the General

Officer Commanding in Northern Ireland was only partially successful in gaining the partnership of the RUC Special Branch in this early period, and the JIC noted tardy reporting on numerous occasions throughout the autumn and winter of 1969, which undoubtedly meant he was not getting enough information to report with any certainty to the JIC.[25] By 1970 it was clear that a problem existed, and in January the JIC dispatched the MI5 director general, Martin Furnival Jones, to investigate.[26] In June, however, reports and assessments were still arriving late in what the JIC described as a "complex but unsatisfactory situation."[27] Even the replacement Director of Intelligence, David Eastwood, failed to help matters; what should have been weekly assessments were late twice in October 1970 alone.[28]

Following a request from Home Secretary Reginald Maudling in February, Sir Dick White was sent to Northern Ireland by the prime minister to thoroughly review the intelligence arrangements in Northern Ireland.[29] Maudling chose White because of his "thorough knowledge of the organization and co-ordination of security and intelligence work," concluding that "he is so obviously the best man."[30] An atmosphere of limited cooperation and increasing distrust on one side and aloofness on the other greeted White when the JIC asked him in 1971 for his suggestions on how to improve security intelligence in Northern Ireland. Assisting White was JIC Secretary Brian Stewart, a Normandy veteran who had later served in a civilian role in Malaya. Stewart brought a keen appreciation of the British military mind and the value of police–army cooperation, especially regarding intelligence in counterinsurgency.[31]

White had less hands-on experience in counterinsurgency than Stewart, and his only experience of internment came in 1939 when he approved of it for German nationals living in Britain.[32] However, White was an advocate of gathering intelligence from secondary interrogation and from Camp 020 and the London Cage during the war, then to Bad Nenndorf shortly thereafter, and he had a mixed record in managing those who ran interrogation centers. In Camp 020—a British interrogation center for captured German agents—though physical violence was not used, death threats and psychological attacks were used during the interrogation process. As the historian Simona Tobia has observed, "violence was banned [at Camp 020], but for technical rather than ethical reasons."[33] Though not outside the ethical mores of the time, there was evidence of maltreatment and poor conditions in the London Cage (an interrogation center where torture *was* used during the war); frostbite, malnutrition, and physical injuries were reported in Bad Nenndorf in occupied Germany, where Nazi officers and later suspected Soviet agents were interrogated and where, when members of staff were charged for their cruelty, Dick White testified for the defense.[34]

On his return from Northern Ireland, White reported his findings directly to the JIC, now under pressure to provide evidence of improved intelligence arrangements.[35] That White's report (drafted by Stewart) so accurately reflects future discussions and later policy decisions means there can be no doubt of this document's importance.[36] What White concluded is, however, hard to determine. A face-value reading of White's report could emphasize his claim that "there was not an intelligence crisis in Northern Ireland."[37] However, the fact that White was only the most recent in a series of visitors sent to investigate problems associated with the RUC Special Branch suggests the opposite conclusion. Reading the report this way, White was determined to make the point that, even if there was no "crisis," the RUC Special Branch was tired of visitors making recommendations for change. In fact, there was now "acute sensitivity to outside interference" as it was in "a highly sensitive state," a result of being the "object over the last two years of close scrutiny and heavy criticism."[38] White's emphasis on the delicacy of the RUC Special Branch's relationship with other military and civil intelligence agencies reflected his discussions with some very weary officers in the Special Branch, some of whom had even mentioned resignation should reinforcements from Scotland Yard or MI5 be imposed on them.[39] White went on to point out that the critical deficiencies he had seen were often related to "systemic processing and collation work," bureaucratic work that limited the time available for cooperation with other British sources.[40] Crucially, however, White warned the JIC that Britain remained reliant on the RUC Special Branch for "80–90% of all secret intelligence available" on Northern Ireland and that "the intelligence situation is thus largely governed by its level of competence and willingness to co-operate."[41] In his conclusions, White pointed to the potential benefit of leaving the RUC Special Branch alone for the moment; anticipating the disruption that imposing direct rule from London might cause, he also noted that "it will be imperative to carry the Northern Ireland police with us and retain every bit of their co-operation. This will be achieved if at that moment their morale and confidence are high, and they see themselves as equal partners with us."[42]

One further recommendation, redacted from the declassified version of White's report, appears in related papers elsewhere. This was that, once the intelligence was in a state that would enable an internment swoop, and "after a lull in its expectation, an internment policy could be expected to yield considerable intelligence dividends."[43] White therefore recommended that "the fullest intelligence support . . . for any detention center; the staff and technical aids . . . be earmarked now and all necessary arrangements [be] synchronized with other physical preparations for detention to ensure the maximum intelligence dividend."[44]

White was not the first to suggest the introduction of internment in Northern Ireland. The topic had been the subject of public discussion there for some months, and Northern Ireland Prime Minister Chichester Clark had publicly declared that he would introduce the measure if his security advisers recommended it. In Whitehall, the British government had already "authorized the putting in hand of a contingency *study* (rather than a contingency *plan*)" that looked at how large numbers of internees could be accommodated by an already overcrowded and insecure prison system.[45] What made White's contribution unique was its emphasis on how an interrogation policy might create an intelligence dividend, with all its intrinsic rewards. White was not, however, concerned about the ramifications such a policy would have on public opinion in Northern Ireland or elsewhere. He had conducted his research solely within the security forces, and there is no evidence that he considered any such wider implications or consulted with those who might have considered them.

Furthermore, White's report effectively tied the hands of the JIC, MI5, and even the British army when discussing the effectiveness of the RUC Special Branch. By emphasizing the importance and the fragility of the RUC Special Branch, White made it clear that no one could afford to upset its officials and that the Special Branch could not be made to report back to the JIC. This problem of a nonreporting RUC Special Branch could not be solved with more visitors, White argued, and coercion risked the branch's collapse. White's report furnished a set of arguments: internment should be introduced to help strengthen Special Branch confidence; the army's secondary interrogation methods would be used on a number of detainees; and the Northern Ireland government (because of Perimeter) would not be made aware that Operation Calaba would occur in conjunction with Operation Demetrius.

The first direct result of White's report was the training, within weeks, of a group of at least ten RUC interrogators at the Joint Services Interrogation Wing (JSIW) at Ashford, Kent, in the five techniques, which was approved by the JIC for use in counterinsurgencies. Physical preparations were then made for a special interrogation center in Northern Ireland at Royal Air Force Station Ballykelly, far from the main internment holding centers in the province. The first 12 internees were interrogated there between August 11 and 17, 1971, with two further internees being subjected to the same treatment between October 11 and 18. These prisoners were

Figure 15.3: A cosh, a weapon similar to a blackjack, circa 1920s, from a US FBI special agent who served during the Bureau's early years. FBI Director J. Edgar Hoover denounced the use of the "third degree" in the 1930s and promoted applying "scientific" principles to criminal investigations. From the Collection of H. Keith and Karen Melton at the International Spy Museum.

interrogated by a team of 20 Special Branch officers alongside 12 JSIW advisers.[46] They were subjected to all five techniques and were beaten when they did not comply, often collapsing from exhaustion before being seen by a doctor. Over both instances of less than a week, prisoners were subjected to periods of stress-position wall-standing that ranged in duration from nine to 49 hours.[47] When the interrogations finished, prisoners were released to the internment camps, where, through visits, accounts of their handling began to appear in the press; once "this trickle became a flood," the real effects of implementing such a policy became clear.[48] The anticipated increase in violence was given fuel, increasing the levels of support for the IRA in Ireland and across the world and increasing the duration of the backlash.

Internment widened the conflict, polarized community relations, and inflamed nationalist opinion in Northern Ireland's rural towns.[49] In the Republic of Ireland, opposition to internment was as vociferous as it was predictable, and the Irish government, having warned against the effects of internment, was immediately forced to take a harder line in its dealings with the British.[50] Leading figures in the ascendant Irish republican paramilitary group, the Provisional IRA, and its political wing Sinn Féin (including Daithí Ó Conaill and Ruairí Ó Brádaigh) resigned from their regular jobs and went full-time in order to cope with the surge. Internment, and anti-British sentiment, amplified by stories of the "Hooded Men,'" became a cause célèbre for a time, as evidenced when the anti-internment song "Men Behind the Wire" by The Barleycorn spent six weeks at number-one on the Irish pop charts from early January 1972, only to be replaced by Paul McCartney's "Give Ireland Back to the Irish."[51] In the United States, Senator Edward Kennedy, brother of the late President John F. Kennedy, cosponsored a resolution in Congress calling for the withdrawal of troops from Northern Ireland and compared the situation to America's involvement in Vietnam.[52] The events inspired two national television documentaries; along with numerous television reports and countless letters from concerned citizens to the British embassy, these evidenced the effect of the policy on Irish Americans.[53] And while the British government tried to restore faith in its internment policy by launching inquiries in 1971 and 1972 into the treatment of these prisoners and banned the use of the techniques altogether, the damage was done.

Despite the expanding international controversy, the archival record largely defended the five techniques in terms of a perceived "operational dividend" that was not sustained by reality. The Ministry of Defence indicated that intelligence about the IRA included details of planned operations, order of battle, and locations of arms caches and safehouses. According to one report, the techniques had resulted in "over 40 outstanding major incidents [being] cleared from Police records."[54] The Ministry of Defence also claimed that by January 1972 "something like three-quarters of the arms and explosives found since 9 August are directly or indirectly attributable to interrogation in depth."[55] However, the historian Samantha Newbery notes that these findings leave significant questions unanswered, as they do not comment on the extent to which this intelligence was new or whether it might have been obtained by other, less controversial means.[56]

More apparent is the positive effect that the internment policy had on army morale and confidence, itself a double-edged sword. That the army felt it was now winning the war of attrition after August 1971 is sustained by its own internal communications, if not by the incident statistics, which showed that the IRA were becoming more rather than less active.[57] For British soldiers on tour in Northern Ireland like "Mick of 1 Para," those days were idyllic. It was why he had joined the Parachute Regiment: "We had a legitimate fight almost every day and every night. We had as much beer as we could take, and we had all the women we could handle. It was absolutely brilliant. A soldier's dream."[58] The opportunity to participate more actively in the conflict may have given the troops a better sense of purpose. However, it did nothing to shorten or ameliorate the conflict. While there was certainly an intelligence benefit to the use (and the threat of use) of interrogation in depth, and the army could tell itself whatever stories it liked, the conflict had actually gotten worse, and both wings of the IRA were strengthening in numbers, support, and finances faster than they were being seized by the security forces.[59]

The public outcry that led to the Compton and Parker inquiries resulted in a significant amount of back-tracking on the utility of the five techniques in softening up subjects prior to interrogation. White and Stewart began justifying their use with arguments that they were being used to protect those being interrogated. Brian Stewart produced documentation in October 1971 that justified hooding, wall-standing, and white noise for "prevent[ing] individuals from seeing and being seen in the interests of their own and of general security;" "secur[ing] discipline in transit;" and "prevent[ing] prisoners overhearing or being overheard." They insisted, therefore, that although the five techniques were useful in "softening up the detainees" this was not their main purpose.[60] Even colleagues, however, were skeptical of this defense. "I do not believe that this approach would be credible," one noted.[61] In November 1971, White recommended that hooding, wall-standing, and white noise should be used only to protect the secrecy of the location, to shield the identities of those being interrogated, and to protect guards.[62] In hindsight, this appears to be an attempt to brush over a policy that deviated from accepted practice in a modern democracy. It also omits the primary purpose of these methods, which White had made clear back in March: the gathering of intelligence. With official inquiries looming, Dick White formally retired for a second time in 1972, with the controversy surrounding these interrogation methods far from resolved.[63]

Ultimately, the blame for the Calaba debacle fell on its implementors rather than its instigators. White himself noted how MI5's David Eastwood, Director of Intelligence for Northern Ireland, who was forced to implement White's plan, bore the brunt of criticism once the use of these interrogation methods became widely known. Eastwood had loyally followed White's March recommendations and had not diverted from them, even when some in the army had questioned the wisdom of handing over such an "exceptionally sensitive" operation to the RUC.[64]

Following the surge in violence and support for the IRA, internment and the torture allegations caused Eastwood to become exhausted under the pressure of his office. After his final visit to Northern Ireland in November 1971, White asked Cabinet Secretary Burke Trend to have MI5 find Eastwood a capable deputy and then have the embattled Director of Intelligence take a lengthy period of leave.[65] That White had been Trend's schoolmaster in the 1930s is crucial to understanding the effect of this. Interpreted this way, one can see the power White had not only over the introduction of internment but also on its subsequent handling and the apportionment of blame for the public reception.

Even the official inquiries portrayed internment as a disaster that was compounded by the methods that had originally been approved for use in colonial counterinsurgencies. However, Lord Gardiner's minority report of the Parker Inquiry into allegations of torture laid the blame for the fiasco on long-retired faceless colonial officials rather than White or Stewart. It argued: "The blame for this sorry story . . . must lie with those who, many years ago decided that in emergency conditions in Colonial-type situations we should abandon our legal, well-tried and highly successful wartime interrogation methods and replace them by procedures which were secret, illegal, not morally justifiable and alien."[66] The proposition in Gardiner's minority report stemmed from Brian Stewart's ultimately successful campaign beginning in September 1971, which argued that the JIC rather than the chain of command should be blamed. The JIC, after all, in its 1965 Directive on Military Interrogation in Internal Security Operations Overseas, had maintained that hooding, wall-standing, and white noise were essential to gather intelligence and to prevent suspects from identifying each other and their location.[67] Despite Stewart's efforts, many historians have focused blame on the politicians who enacted the policy or nameless subordinates who overstepped their marks to protect their managers, their agencies, or the government more generally.[68] This follows closely the line represented in the archives, where from Bad Nenndorf in occupied Germany to Fort Morbut in Aden and from the London Cage to Hola Camp, Kenya, blame has variously been spread among errant interrogators, lack of training, oversight issues, and/or overwork instead of those who actually crafted and advocated for the policy.

Shifting the blame, however, had wider implications. Despite the British government's line that the United Kingdom was not a country that did such things, the journalist Ian Cobain alleged in his book *Cruel Britannia: A Secret History of British Torture* (2012) that Britain since World War II had regularly employed torture as a means of gathering intelligence.[69] Cobain illustrated his argument with a number of examples in which White had been involved. In a 2013 review, however, the historian Calder Walton meticulously punched holes in Cobain's hypothesis, questioning his uses of evidence, definitions, and arguments. Walton outlined the areas where Cobain requires his readers to hold back on immediate judgment and rely on the cumulative weight of circumstantial evidence to create a stronger narrative. Walton instead argues for a "cock-up, not conspiracy" explanation.[70] Indeed, this is a well-tested way of examining and explaining allegations that are not supported by documentary evidence.

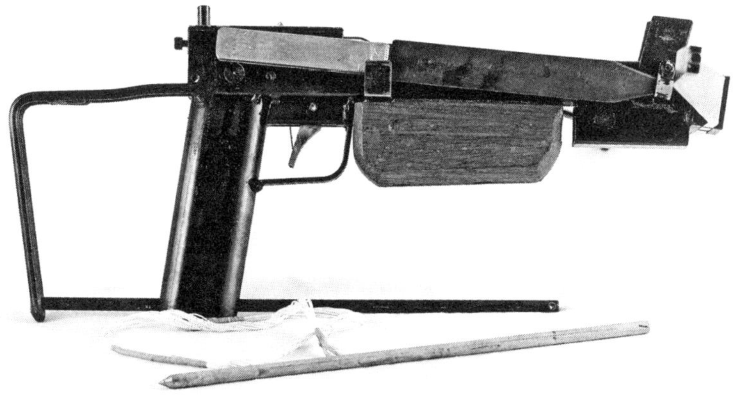

Figure 15.4: UK Special Air Service crossbow, circa 1970s. Originally intended as combat weapons, crossbows were mostly used to silence troublesome dogs. The SAS played a major role in the Troubles in Northern Ireland, conducting reconnaissance and combat missions. From the Collection of H. Keith and Karen Melton at the International Spy Museum.

However, an overreliance on official documentary sources can have its own perils. As Walton argues, "a series of failures, from the London Cage to the horrors of Bad Nenndorf, do not add up to a policy." Nevertheless, blaming underlings (interrogators and site managers) rather than those involved in planning policy is far less sustainable when one finds that there are individuals personally complicit on more than one occasion.[71] The methodical way in which planners and policymakers are shielded from blame is surely demonstrative, if not a policy, of torture, then it is surely a culture of deflection and even coverup. More important, policymakers, perhaps by using their control over what becomes the public record and the documents that historians will use as evidence, can preemptively defend themselves once the record is opened to scrutiny. Indeed, evidence of manipulation of the official record at the end of empire has appeared in recent years regarding places other than Ireland.[72] This should not only help us illuminate what British intelligence was doing; it should enlighten us about *why* documents now in the archives were written the way they were in the first place. Evidence of attempted manipulation in Northern Ireland, where records are comparatively complete, allows us to infer that similar manipulation was practiced in places where the records have since been destroyed. Thus, there is surely room for reappraisal once systemic bias is identified. In Dick White's case, there is compelling evidence to furnish arguments of both a cockup *and* a conspiracy.

Historians of intelligence need to be aware of their own biases toward official sources and may be less inclined than others to point out problematic correlations that they might prefer to write off as outliers. Dick White had experience enough to understand the problems associated with the five techniques, yet he still advised—from a position of authority and experience—that they be introduced and even suggested how to do so. Aware of the risks and against voices of dissent, he ensured that his policy advice reached the people who implemented it. At that level, because those who design policy overlap with those who create the public records, a certain immunity can emerge. Whether this comes from self-interest or from the wider policy risk of full disclosure, historians who use archival materials from intelligence services and governments more generally can benefit from being warier.

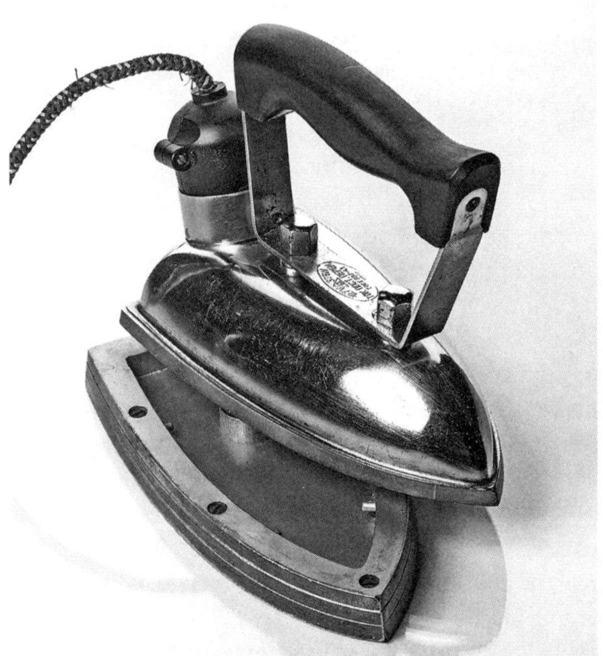

Figure 15.5: Iron used as a concealment device by a spy in West Berlin working for the East German Stasi during the 1960s. In an emergency, the iron could be plugged in to incinerate papers or film hidden inside. From the Collection of H. Keith and Karen Melton at the International Spy Museum.

## Further Reading

Cobain, Ian. *Cruel Britannia: A Secret History of Torture*. London: Portobello, 2013.

Drohan, Brian. *Brutality in an Age of Human Rights: Activism and Counterinsurgency at the End of the British Empire*. Ithaca: Cornell University Press, 2018.

McCleery, Martin. *Operation Demetrius and Its Aftermath: A New History of the Use of Internment without Trial in Northern Ireland, 1971–75*. Manchester, UK: Manchester University Press, 2015.

Newbery, Samantha. *Interrogation, Intelligence and Security: Controversial British techniques 1963–2003*. Manchester, UK: Manchester University Press, 2015.

## Notes

1. In this case, "detainees were exposed to the 'five techniques' over periods ranging from two and a half to almost eight days each." Samantha Newbery, *Interrogation, Intelligence and Security: Controversial British techniques, 1963–2003* (Manchester: Manchester University Press, 2015), 68.

2. Brian Faulkner and John Houston, *Memoirs of a Statesman* (London: Weidenfeld & Nicolson, 1978), 116.

3. Newbery, *Interrogation*, 64.

4. Paul Arthur and Keith Jeffery, *Northern Ireland Since 1968* (Oxford: Basil Blackwell, 1988), 12.

5. Hubert Parker et al., *Report of the Committee of Privy Counsellors Appointed to Consider Authorised Procedures for the Interrogation of Persons Suspected of Terrorism*, Command Paper Cmnd 4901 (London: HMSO, 1972), 2.

6. Faulkner, *Memoirs*, 116.

7. Amnesty International and the *Sunday Times* were describing internee experiences of the five techniques from October 1971. "Torture in Northern Ireland is Charged" *New York Times*, October 18, 1971. In addition, stories of internees being forced to run gauntlets over broken glass, enduring beatings, and being forced to crawl on all fours were being dismissed by the army as methods that were used "for the purposes of speed and security" on "potential gunmen—dangerous men to be handled accordingly.'" Some additional detainees reported being blindfolded, placed in a helicopter, then told they were to be dumped at sea before being thrown from the helicopter just a few feet off the ground, were more difficult to defend but were also not a part of the approved interrogation in depth procedures. "Army Ruse Led to Charges," *Daily Telegraph*, August 30, 1971, and "Internment Explained: When Was It Introduced and Why?" *Irish Times*, August 9, 2019, www.irishtimes.com/news/politics/internment-explained-when-was-it-introduced-and-why-1.3981598.

8. Newbery, *Interrogation*, 15–17.

9. Edmund Compton, *Enquiry into Allegations Against the Security Forces of Physical Brutality in Northern Ireland Arising Out of the Events of 9 August 1971* (London: HMSO, 1971), para. 52, cited in Thomas Hennessey, *The Evolution of the Troubles* (Dublin: Irish Academic Press, 2007), 156.

10. Eunan O'Halpin, "'A Poor Thing but Our Own': The Joint Intelligence Committee and Ireland, 1965–72," *Intelligence and National Security* 23, no. 5 (2008): 671.

11. O'Halpin, "'A Poor Thing but Our Own,'" 671–672.

12. Tom Bower, *Perfect English Spy: Sir Dick White and the Secret War, 1935–1990* (London: Mandarin, 1996).

13. Rory Cormac, *Confronting the Colonies: British Intelligence and Counterinsurgency* (London: C. Hurst and Co., 2013), 162, and Eunan O'Halpin, "The British Joint Intelligence Committee and Ireland, 1965–1972," *Institute for International Integration Studies (IISS)*, Discussion Paper No. 211, March 2007, 9.

14. O'Halpin, "'A Poor Thing but Our Own,'" 672.

15. Cabinet Office Committee Misc. 244, 1st Meeting at Home Office, Sir Phillip Allen (Home Office PUS & Chair), 21 April 1969, Section G, The National Archives of the UK (TNA), CAB 130/422. Followed by Sir Edward Peck (Chairman of the JIC) to Sir Andrew Gilchrist, 5 August 1969, TNA, FCO 33/764.

16. David Charters, "'Have A Go': British Army/MI5 Agent-running Operations in Northern Ireland, 1970–72," *Intelligence and National Security* 28, no. 2 (2013): 205.

17. Peck to North, 29 August 1969, TNA, CJ 3/99.

18. Confidential Annex #5, JIC(A) Minutes, 47th Meeting 20 November 1969, TNA, CAB 185/9.

19. Robert Ramsey, *Ringside Seats: An Insider's View on the Crisis in Northern Ireland* (Dublin: Irish Academic Press, 2009), 57.

20. John A. Oliver, *Working at Stormont* (Dublin: Institute of Public Administration, 1978), 99.

21. Oliver, *Working at Stormont*, 105.

22. CGS Report to MOD (A), May 19, 1969; this note was used in Prime Minister Harold Wilson's brief for his meeting with Northern Ireland Prime Minister James Chichester-Clark on May 21, 1969, TNA, CAB 164/575.

23. An MI5 security liaison officer and a military liaison officer removed themselves from RUC Headquarters in June 1969 following an incident that had caused a "modest amount of friction" with the RUC. Neil Cairncross (Home Office) to Phillip Allen (Home Office), TNA, CJ 3/55.

24. Baron Hunt, *Report of The Advisory Committee on Police in Northern Ireland* (Belfast: Her Majesty's Stationery Office, October 1969).

25. JIC(A)(69) 36th, 40th, 42nd 43rd, and 44th meeting minutes; receipt of the first fortnightly assessment by the Director of Intelligence was noted on October 30, 1969, more than ten weeks after deployment, TNA, CAB 185/9. Secretarial Support from MI5 was eventually sent on the orders of the Cabinet Secretary (Burke Trend) on 6 November, JIC(A)(69) 45th meeting minutes, TNA, CAB 185/9.

26. JIC(A)(70) 2nd meeting minutes, January 8, 1970, TNA, CAB 185/3.

27. JIC(A)(70) 24th meeting minutes, June 25, 1970, TNA, CAB 185/3.

28. JIC(A)(70) 38th and 39th meeting minutes, October 1 and 8, 1970, TNA, CAB 185/4.

29. Newbery, *Interrogation*, 73.

30. Maudling to Edward Heath (Prime Minister), February 26, 1971, TNA, PREM 15/475.

31. Eunan O'Halpin, "The Value and Limits of Experience in the Early Years of the Northern Ireland Troubles, 1969–1972," in *Learning from the Secret Past: Cases in British Intelligence History*, ed. Robert Dover and Michael Goodman (Washington, DC: Georgetown University Press, 2011), 193.

32. "The policy was distasteful and unsuccessful, but I did not oppose it." Tom

Bower, *Perfect English Spy: Sir Dick White and the Secret War 1935–1990* (London: Mandarin, 1996), 40.

33. Simona Tobia, "'A Brutally Tough Place for Brutally Tough People.'" *History Today* 64, no. 1 (January 2014).

34. Ian Cobain, "The Secrets of the London Cage," *The Guardian*, November 12, 2005, www.theguardian.com/uk/2005/nov/12/secondworldwar.world; and The Security Service (MI5), Bad Nenndorf, www.mi5.gov.uk/bad-nenndorf, n.d., accessed October 25, 2024.

35. JIC(A) 9th and 13th meeting minutes, March 4 and 25, 1971, TNA, CAB 185/6.

36. Newbery, *Interrogation*, 74.

37. JIC(A)71 13th meeting minutes, March 25, 1971, TNA, CAB 185/6.

38. Report by the Intelligence Coordinator on the state of Intelligence in Northern Ireland, March 1971, TNA, DEFE 35/204, and JIC(A)71, 13th meeting minutes, March 25, 1971, TNA, CAB 185/6.

39. Report by the Intelligence Coordinator on the state of Intelligence in Northern Ireland, March 1971, TNA, DEFE 35/204.

40. Report by the Intelligence Coordinator, March 1971, TNA, DEFE 35/204.

41. Report by the Intelligence Coordinator, March 1971, TNA, DEFE 35/204.

42. Report by the Intelligence Coordinator, March 1971, TNA, DEFE 35/204.

43. Excerpt from Dick White's report of Northern Ireland Intelligence Arrangements, March 22, 1971, Annex B, in Stewart (JIC) to Hockaday (MoD), TNA, CAB 163/171.

44. Excerpt from Dick White's report of Northern Ireland Intelligence Arrangements, March 22, 1971, Annex B, in Stewart (JIC) to Hockaday (MoD), TNA, CAB 163/171.

45. Home Office Memo, "Internment in Northern Ireland," c.12 February 1971, TNA, PREM 15/475 (emphasis in original).

46. Huw Bennett, "Detention and Interrogation in Northern Ireland, 1969–75," in *Prisoners in War*, ed. S. Scheipers (Oxford: Oxford University Press, 2010), 192.

47. It has been argued that the position in which the hooded detainees were forced to stand did not constitute a "stress position." However, the "detainees' testimony that it was severe enough to be a stress position is persuasive." Newbery, *Interrogation*, 69.

48. Faulkner, *Memoirs*, 124.

49. Martin McCleery, *Operation Demetrius and Its Aftermath: A New History of the Use of Internment Without Trial in Northern Ireland, 1971–75* (Manchester: Manchester University Press, 2015), 128–165.

50. Dermot Keogh, *Jack Lynch: A Biography* (Dublin: Gill and Macmillan, 2008), 312–313.

51. Anthony Craig, *Crisis of Confidence: Anglo Irish Relations in the Early Troubles, 1966–1974* (Dublin: Irish Academic Press, 2010), 106.

52. Andrew Sanders, "Senator Edward Kennedy and the 'Ulster Troubles': Irish and Irish-American Politics, 1965–2009" *Historical Journal of Massachusetts* 39, nos. 1 and 2 (Summer 2011): 217. John Dumbrell, "The United States and the Northern Irish Conflict, 1969–94: From Indifference to Intervention." *Irish Studies in International Affairs* 6 (1995): 115.

53. Andrew Sanders, "Congressional Hearings on Northern Ireland and the 'Special Relationship,' 1971–1981." *Diplomacy & Statecraft* 27, no. 1 (2016): 122–123.

54. "Intelligence Gained from Interrogations in Northern Ireland," unsigned

[MoD], November 1971, TNA, DEFE 13/958. Reproduced in Samantha Newbery et al., "Interrogation, Intelligence and the Issue of Human Rights." *Intelligence and National Security* 24, no. 5 (2009): 635.

55. Hennessey *Evolution*, 220, citing Stephens to Moore, 21 January 1972, TNA, DEFE 23/160.

56. Newbery, *Interrogation*, 117.

57. Hennessey, *Evolution*, 220–225.

58. Peter Taylor, *Brits: The War Against the IRA* (London: Bloomsbury, 2002), 77.

59. Hennessey, *Evolution*, 220–225.

60. Richard Aldrich, "'A Skeleton in Our Cupboard': British Interrogation Procedures in Northern Ireland," in *Learning from the Secret Past: Cases in British Intelligence History*, ed. Robert Dover and Michael Goodman (Washington, DC: Georgetown University Press, 2011), 169–170.

61. AUS(GS) to PUS, Northern Ireland—Interrogation, 23 October 1971, TNA, DEFE 24/968.

62. White, Prisoner Handling in Interrogation Centres in Northern Ireland, November 4, 1971, TNA, CAB 163/171.

63. White's biographer makes no mention of his visits to Northern Ireland and notes only that his assessments were increasingly dismissed and that in 1972 "White quietly slipped out of Whitehall." Bower, *Perfect English Spy*, 364 and 371. "'Hooded Men': PSNI 'Wrong Not to Investigate Torture claims," *BBC News*, December 15, 2021, www.bbc.co.uk/news/uk-northern-ireland-59667405.

64. Brigadier General-Staff (Intelligence) JMH Lewis had even urged the Director of Intelligence to "strongly advise" the RUC that it follow the JIC's directives on interrogation laid down in 1965 "to provide at least some cover to reduce the inevitable recrimination." Lewis to Director of Intelligence, August 6, 1971, TNA, DEFE 24/744.

65. Sir Dick White to Sir Burke Trend, November 15, 1971, TNA, CAB 163/172.

66. Note how even in the minority report the accepted axiom is that wartime interrogation was free of suspicion. Lord Gardiner, January 31, 1972, Minority Report of Parker et al., *Report Interrogation of Persons*, Cmnd 4901 (London: HMSO, 1972).

67. Stewart (JIC) to Home Office (PJ Woodfield (PUS), September 9, 1971, TNA, CAB 163/171, citing JIC, February 17, 1965.

68. Paul Bew, *Ireland: The Politics of Enmity, 1789–2006* (Oxford: Oxford University Press), 502–503, and Newbery, *Interrogation*, 85–86.

69. Ian Cobain, *Cruel Britannia: A Secret History of Torture* (London: Portobello, 2013).

70. Calder Walton, "Cruel Britannia," Letter to the editor, *Times Literary Supplement*, March 1, 2013.

71. Calder Walton, "British Ways with Torture?" Review of *Cruel Britannia: A Secret History of Torture*, by Ian Cobain, *Times Literary Supplement*, February 13, 2013.

72. David M. Anderson, "Mau Mau in the High Court and the 'Lost' British Empire Archives: Colonial Conspiracy or Bureaucratic Bungle?" *Journal of Imperial and Commonwealth History* 39, no. 5 (2011): 699–716.

# Conclusion: The Importance of Intelligence History

**Mark Stout and Sarah-Jane Corke**

Tom Clancy's 1989 thriller *Clear and Present Danger* recounts the story of Central Intelligence Agency officer Jack Ryan's heroic takedown of a fictional Colombian drug lord named Ernesto Escobedo. In 1993, Colombian special forces, supported by United States Army intelligence personnel, including signals intelligence specialists, tracked down and killed the real-life Colombian cocaine kingpin Pablo Escobar.[1] Rumor has it that on Escobar's bedside table the day of his death was a copy of *Clear and Present Danger* with the passages about electronic surveillance highlighted.[2] It is unclear whether this rumor is actually true. However, it is obviously plausible, and that alone shows the power of spy fiction. In addition, of course, spy stories can make hearts pound and keep us up until three in the morning, as President Ronald Reagan found out reading Clancy's first Jack Ryan novel, *The Hunt for Red October*.[3]

However, as chapters in this volume demonstrate, there are remarkable real-life spy stories that don't need fictionalization. We can be fascinated to learn how real scientists, mathematicians, and engineers solve difficult problems to collect technical intelligence. As a former intelligence analyst myself, I'd like to think that it can be engrossing to learn how analysts make sense of the masses of data they receive from collectors.

Stories from the world of intelligence are not just good for entertainment, however. They can actually be good for citizens. Intelligence is an important and necessary function of government. However, used improperly it can also be a threat to the population. For these reasons, citizens of democratic states should understand the topic. They should know what their governments are doing in their name and what kind of security threats—including intelligence threats like espionage and subversion—their governments must guard against and the role that intelligence plays in that process.

But where do people get their understanding of intelligence? For better or worse, spy fiction is one source, and this conclusion discusses its upsides and downsides. Also, real stories about intelligence come to us in multiple ways. Journalism about present-day intelligence activities is a vital one but unfortunately limited. Intelligence history is another, and it reaches citizens and government officials alike through many routes. Among these are podcasts and documentary films. This discussion, however, will focus primarily on written history—books and articles in magazines and journals—and on museums. It will also describe how intelligence history is important to intelligence practitioners and how it comes to them in similar ways.

Unsurprisingly, many people's basic understanding of intelligence comes from fiction. Certainly, some spy fiction created by outsiders can provide genuine insights into intelligence while being entertaining. The 1970s British television show *The Sandbaggers*, for instance, has much to teach about intelligence. Its first episode closes with a valuable line from the protagonist, an MI6 officer: "Our battles aren't fought at the end of a parachute. They're won and lost in drab, dreary corridors in Westminster."[4] By the same token, the 2006 German film *The Lives of Others* is a riveting and broadly realistic portrayal of the consequences of pervasive domestic surveillance in a nondemocratic state, East Germany in the 1980s. (It is also a rare example of spy fiction that focuses on technical collection, not actual espionage.) A third example is Robert Harris's deeply researched novel *An Officer and a Spy*, about the Dreyfus Affair in turn-of-the-century France, one of the most searing events in all intelligence history. That book is a horrifying lesson in the effects on counterespionage of politicization and prejudice.

Spy fiction created or influenced by intelligence practitioners may be more likely to teach useful lessons about intelligence. Perhaps most notable, the novels of the former British intelligence officer John le Carré are rightly renowned. As Wesley Wark, a contributor to this volume, noted elsewhere of le Carré: "[W]ith secrecy still the reigning ethic in the great game of spying, the best spy novels can give us some insights into what makes espionage tick—its people, its organizations, its methods and its outcomes (for good or ill)."[5] Another example is the novel *The Damascus Station*, written by David McCloskey, a former CIA officer. That book provides good insights into espionage tradecraft and the issues that can arise in conducting espionage operations against dictatorial and violent targets. A more tenuous example is the 1992 Tom Clancy film *Patriot Games*. Harrison Ford, who played CIA analyst Jack Ryan, and some of his colleagues visited CIA headquarters prior to making the film. The same group (minus Ford) also visited the National Photographic Interpretation Center, the primary component of the CIA that at that time analyzed satellite imagery.[6] Perhaps not coincidentally, the film contains a few scenes that portray the work of analysts, including imagery analysts, reasonably well. It even subtly hints at some of the moral qualms that can afflict counterterrorism analysts.

All that said, a great deal of spy fiction is divorced from reality and often mixed with a liberal dose of propaganda. Jack Ryan, for instance, is a flag-waving avatar of the military-industrial complex and the American intelligence community.[7] Chapter 3 in this volume, Jonathan Best's contribution about Ronald Seth's spy fiction for teenage boys in the era when the British Empire was in visible decline, provides another good example. Best argues that Seth's work "showcased the superiority of Britain's secret service and challenged the notions of declining British national strength during the 1950s. Seth's fiction, with all the trademarks of the romantic spy genre that glamorized spying, can be viewed as a means of influencing teenage boys in the 1950s to become future Brian Grants protecting British interests at home and abroad."

Undeniably, the foremost example of spy fiction is James Bond, whose creator, Ian Fleming, served in a responsible position in British naval intelligence during World War II. Insider knowledge did not stop him from writing a series of immensely popular spy novels that are unadulterated escapist fantasy. In fact, the Bond books and movies convey much the same message as Seth's fiction but for an adult readership.

Bond has cast a long shadow. Trevor McCrisken and Christopher Moran of the University of Warwick have written that "with intelligence services historically unable and unwilling to open up about their operations, . . . [James] Bond—unclassified and accessible—has functioned as an important site through which the public has come to perceive intelligence, plus the threats faced by intelligence communities."[8] It was this very thought that some years ago motivated the International Spy Museum to put on a temporary exhibition focused on Bond villains and through them addressed the fears of Bond viewers and the real-world threats that Western intelligence has faced over the past 60-plus years. Remarkably, in chapter 2 of this volume Jonathan Nashel demonstrates that the outlandish fictional Bond also influenced the real CIA. Daniel Lomas and Stephen Ward have pointed to other pernicious effects of James Bond fiction. For instance, they argued that the dominance of Bond in the imagination of the British public and journalists deformed the public debate about important intelligence legislation in 2021, diverting it from important issues to trivial ones such as whether British intelligence was being given a double 0–style license to kill, which it most certainly was not.[9]

In the same vein, the former head of Britain's MI5, Dame Stella Rimington, once commented in a video that was part of the Bond villain temporary exhibition at the International Spy Museum that "the James Bond films have probably caused British intelligence to be best known throughout the world of any intelligence services but the worry, I suppose, is that people think that they go around shooting people which, of course, they don't."[10] Dame Stella's concerns are well-founded. A 2013 survey showed that 27 percent of British people thought that British intelligence was allowed to kill people in other countries with no questions asked from other parts of the British government. Twenty percent even thought that British intelligence was allowed to kill people in Britain with no questions asked.[11]

Similar problems exist in the United States, where Bond is also wildly popular. The Stanford University political scientist Amy Zegart found in surveys conducted in 2012 and 2013 that "the more frequently American viewers watched spy-themed TV shows and movies, the more likely they were to support aggressive counterterrorism tactics" such as torture. She also found that the public knew very little about the National Security Agency (NSA), the US signals and cyber intelligence agency. In her words, this meant that, after Edward Snowden's leaks in 2013, "the biggest crisis in NSA history was unfolding against a backdrop of widespread public misperception and ignorance." Nevertheless, "the more that people watched spy-themed television shows and movies, the more they liked the NSA, the more they approved of NSA's telephone—and internet-collection programs, and the more they believed that the NSA was telling them the truth about its surveillance activities."[12]

Of course, nobody argues that people should not consume spy fiction. Personally, we love James Bond and John le Carré's George Smiley, and *The Damascus Station* is gripping, but it is vital to be able to differentiate between the fantasy and the reality found in spy fiction, often on adjacent pages. In addition, nonfiction works about intelligence need to be accessible and fill the knowledge gap so that spy fiction can function primarily as entertainment. Recall that we made this binary explicit in the introduction, only to show the way it has broken down, often through former intelligence officers writing great fiction.

One source of nonfiction information about intelligence is journalism, which is often called the "first draft of history." Journalism, particularly of the investigative type, is an indispensable source of nonfiction information about present-day intelligence issues. Unfortunately, such operations and analysis are invariably shrouded in secrecy. This means that journalists are able to report only on a small fraction of what is important—most frequently failures and scandals. And as hard as investigative journalism about intelligence is in the United States, it can be even harder in other democratic countries such as Canada and the United Kingdom, which have much stricter secrecy laws. Secrecy, of course, does not just prevent stories

Figure 16.1: Sign carried at a protest against NSA domestic surveillance in Washington, DC, in 2013 in the wake of Edward Snowden's revelations.

from being written; it also increases the likelihood of errors in reporting, even by the best journalists. For instance, Seymour Hersh's reporting that the CIA overthrew the government of Chile's president, Salvador Allende, in 1973 was incorrect yet implanted itself into the public consciousness across the Americas. (The CIA opposed Allende's government, but the coup was not controlled by the Agency and came as a surprise, a useful lesson that intelligence agencies are not all-powerful and that people on the ground retain agency.)[13]

This is where history comes in. Written historical works (such as this book) and museums can tell stories about intelligence activities of the past that are no longer hidden behind the veil of secrecy. These stories can give invaluable context to help us understand the secret intelligence activities of today. For instance, they can describe the bounds of what is possible and not possible for intelligence to accomplish. Similarly, knowledge of past successes and failures can help us understand why intelligence agencies make the choices they do today. Intelligence history can also describe the beginnings of programs and activities that continue to the present day. It can illustrate the ethical and legal considerations that do—or perhaps do not—factor into intelligence activities. Likewise, it can help us understand the nature of some of the threats that our countries face including espionage, subversion, and terrorism.

Historians are constantly asking new questions about the past, reexamining existing records, and searching for new records to help answer questions. Intelligence historians are eager for newly declassified documents that can, among other things, allow the correction of errors in our historical understanding of events. For instance, for many years American schoolchildren, including one of the editors of this volume (Stout), were taught that the world's first electronic digital computer was the American ENIAC. However, as David Schaefer notes in this volume (see chapter 8), the first such computer was the British Colossus, used at Bletchley Park during World War II. We were not taught that, however, because the British government kept the fact of Colossus's existence secret until the mid-1970s when it allowed a trickle of information to come out before finally deciding to be more forthcoming in the early 1980s. Similarly, as Stephen Budiansky has observed, "probably the greatest distortion that secrecy [about World War II codebreaking] caused was to make a number of allied commanders look like intuitive military geniuses for their uncanny ability to anticipate the enemy's plans—when in fact it was SIGINT that really deserved the credit."[14] Intelligence history also allowed the resolution of a painful question that for decades was the subject of often vitriolic debate between left and right in the United States: whether the American diplomat Alger Hiss had been a spy for the Soviet Union during the 1930s and 1940s. With the NSA's 1995 declassification and the examination by historians of the once extremely sensitive VENONA decrypts, reinforced in 2001 by documents brought out of Russia by a former KGB officer, it became clear that Hiss had been guilty.[15]

The era of substantial declassification of intelligence records started in the United Kingdom during the 1970s, and scholarly intelligence history has flourished since the end of the Cold War. So, too, has high-quality, popular intelligence history, such as the books of Ben Macintyre and Liza Mundy.[16] This volume, of course, aims to be scholarly *and* popular using examples of how an understanding of history can help citizens formulate views on intelligence. For instance, many Americans criticized the United States Intelligence Community because the hunt for Osama bin Laden took ten years, a tale recounted in chapter 11. They might have had a different perspective if they knew that it took Israeli intelligence about 15 years to find Adolph Eichmann, the leading architect of the Holocaust. Emil Draitser's chapter 5, on Dmitri Bystrolyotov, the Romeo spy who sexually manipulated women in service to Joseph Stalin, can cause us to reflect on what ethical standards should apply to the conduct of espionage. Likewise, the British government's mishandling of the Zinoviev Letter, which Gill Bennett in chapter 12 describes as a "classic piece of 1920s disinformation," might hold lessons for us during an era when hostile intelligence services are bombarding Western countries with forgeries, fake news, and similar disinformation measures. The British experience using torture against Irish Republican Army suspects in the 1970s, detailed in Tony Craig's contribution (chapter 15), might also have served as a cautionary tale for Americans during the Global War on Terrorism. John Fox's account of the Robert

Hanssen spy case (chapter 13) and Wesley Wark's discussion of the Jeffrey Delisle spy case (chapter 14) recount shortcomings in counterintelligence in the United States and Canada. Those two chapters also include recommendations for how intelligence agencies can improve, recommendations that might be of real use to counterintelligence officers. On a related note, at least four chapters in this book—those on Mata Hari, Dmitri Bystrolyotov, Robert Hanssen, and Jeffrey Delisle—invite us to ponder the question of why people spy. A traditional answer is encapsulated in the acronym "MICE" (money, ideology, compromise, ego), but is this tidy formulation adequate to cover the variety of human experiences?[17] And if not, then what might that imply about the often fraught topic of who should receive security clearances?

Intelligence history can be especially important in countries that have recently undergone political transitions from authoritarianism to democracy. And this is where museums come in: they are frequently purveyors of history. They take history and make it tangible—something you can see, touch, and explore in ways beyond the written word. Museum exhibitions can also arguably have a profound effect on a larger slice of the public than all but a tiny handful of books or articles. Sometimes museums can also serve as a bulwark for democracy by illustrating the cruelties of past authoritarian regimes and their intelligence and security services. For instance, in Tallinn, Estonia—formerly part of the Soviet Union—one can visit the KGB Prison Cells, a branch of the Vabamu Museum of Occupations and Freedom, which describes its mission as encouraging "visitors to reflect on recent history, feel the fragile nature of freedom, and stand up for liberty and justice."[18] In what used to be East Berlin, the former headquarters of the infamous Stasi is now a museum. Also in the former East Berlin is the Berlin–Hohenschönhausen Memorial, once a Stasi prison for political prisoners undergoing interrogation or awaiting trial. The museum's mission is described in part as "encouraging a critical awareness of the methods and consequences of political persecution and suppression in the communist dictatorship."[19] Tour guides, many of them former inmates, describe how the Stasi used psychological pressure rather than physical torture to break prisoners. Another example is the House of Terror Museum in Budapest. It resides in the building that was the headquarters of the Hungarian fascist Arrow Cross party during World War II and then became the headquarters of the ÁVH, the Hungarian communist counterpart to the Soviet KGB and the East German Stasi.[20] A booklet sold at the museum notes that, "for too many decades, we have passed by this building with downcast eyes, with hurried steps, knowing, sensing that its walls were hiding monstrous crimes, a sea of suffering. . . . [Now it] has become a shrine, an homage to the victims. The House of Terror Museum is proof that the sacrifice for freedom is not futile."[21]

The most prominent intelligence museum, however, is the International Spy Museum in Washington, DC. It took only seven years for it to welcome its five-millionth visitor. In 2020, at the height of the COVID-19 pandemic, its programming was entirely virtual and reached almost four million people.[22] The museum highlights a great number of intelligence stories from the past, some of which are presented using interactive exhibitions, that deal with how intelligence is collected, how it is analyzed, and hopefully used by policymakers. It also has exhibitions on counterintelligence, counterterrorism, and covert action. One multimedia exhibition explains how intelligence was important to George Washington during the Revolutionary War, suggesting that intelligence history is a deeply embedded part of American history. (Indeed, stories that highlight the use of intelligence can be found throughout history and around the world.[23])

The final section of the museum challenges visitors to appreciate the often neglected role of women in intelligence and to grapple with past intelligence failures and ethical issues such as leaking and whistleblowing and domestic surveillance. Less visibly, an important function of the International Spy Museum has been to provide expertise to journalists and documentary filmmakers. Indeed, good journalists on the intelligence beat will often call on intelligence historians, whether at the International Spy Museum or elsewhere, to help them think their way through a story or even to quote or invite on the air. Several of the contributors to this volume have done just that.

So intelligence history is important to regular citizens, but it is equally important to intelligence practitioners. This is why the CIA, from its earliest days, had an in-house history effort.[24] The pioneering intelligence analyst Sherman Kent encapsulated the importance of this endeavor, noting how "problems of the [CIA's] first five years are likely still to be, in one form or another, the problems of the next one hundred."[25] In other words, Kent and CIA historians over the years have believed that intelligence agencies, if they are to be efficient and effective, must learn from history. The CIA is far from alone in this realization. Many other American intelligence agencies have historians or history staffs, among them the Defense Intelligence Agency, the National Security Agency, the National Reconnaissance Office, and the FBI. Other US government agencies that contain intelligence organizations, such as the Department of State and the US Army, also have robust history efforts that often produce intelligence histories or histories that include discussions of intelligence.

The CIA historian Nicholas Dujmovic, writing in 2011, by which time the CIA's History Staff was well-resourced and serving a wide variety of customers in the Agency, described the importance of history in the CIA. He wrote that in-house historians at CIA depend heavily on the work of outside intelligence historians.[26] At the same time, CIA historians did research to enable public outreach and to contribute to the work of outside scholars. However, Dujmovic maintained that the most important reason for the Agency to do history was to allow it to learn from its past, including successes and failures. This allowed it to improve its work and better "appreciate the reasons for public criticism [and] distrust."[27] He provided several examples but writes that, "in perhaps the best example of influence, CIA historians were asked to review the record over several decades of a particular type of intelligence operation; our conclusions about what practices worked, in what situations, have been used in high level decisions on whether to pursue this type of operation in a particular place."[28] Dujmovic may have been referring to the question of whether the CIA should help arm Syrian rebels. In 2014, *New Yorker* magazine quoted President Barack Obama as saying how "very early in this process, I actually asked the C.I.A. to analyze examples of America financing and supplying arms to an insurgency in a country that actually worked out well. And they couldn't come up with much."[29]

Probably many other intelligence services in democratic countries would agree that intelligence history is useful to conducting their work. They certainly seem to have invested in historical efforts. In Europe, the German Federal Intelligence Service (the Bundesnachrichtendienst, or BND) and the United Kingdom's Government Communications Headquarters have a staff historian and employed academics to write authorized histories.[30] Norway seems to have pioneered the practice of commissioning outside scholars to write authorized histories in the 1990s with a history of the Norwegian Intelligence Service and another of Norway's security surveillance and counterespionage efforts.[31] Britain's MI5, MI6, and Joint Intelligence Committee and Australia's Security Intelligence Organization have followed suit.[32]

Government intelligence museums also exist to help agencies carry out their missions. Intelligence agencies use them to promulgate historical lessons to employees and to inculcate values and a sense of heritage and pride. Some probably also use them to help recruiting efforts.[33] And intelligence agencies often use museums to burnish their image and to persuade the public of the importance of their work, even if the examples they give are in the past, not the present day. Public support gives intelligence agencies what Daniel Lomas and Stephen Ward have called a "license to operate."[34] Two of the government intelligence museums in the Washington area illustrate this while varying in their accessibility to the public. The CIA has a well-known museum inside its headquarters building in McLean, Virginia, but it is not physically accessible to the public.[35] The CIA museum's primary audience is CIA officers. It is in part celebratory, but it also focuses on prominent failures such as the Bay of Pigs and the Iraqi WMD debacle. In 2023, Robert Byer, the museum's director, told PBS that "we need to make sure our officers don't forget the lessons of the past because if so, they are just going to repeat them."[36] At the same time, the museum's website notes that "although the CIA Museum is not open to the public . . . we can do the next best thing and open our virtual doors to you."[37] Visitors can thus view the museum's artifacts online.

If the CIA museum faces both in and out, the NSA museum faces both out and in. It resides in a former motel immediately outside the agency's fence line in Maryland. It is, in the words of its website, "NSA's gateway to the public and educates visitors about the role of cryptology in shaping history."[38] That museum, the National Cryptologic Museum, offers tours to the public and new NSA employees, giving a sense of the history and heritage of the agency and of the broad sweep of American codebreaking and code-making more generally. The museum also includes a library open to the public, with major holdings of books and papers relating to cryptology.[39] It may be worth noting that the executive director of the National Cryptologic Museum is a former historian and curator at the International Spy Museum.

The United Kingdom also has government-affiliated intelligence museums but, given the country's stricter approach to secrecy, they are less public than their American counterparts and little is known about some of them. For instance, there are hints that MI6 has a museum, but if one exists it is not accessible to the public.[40] MI5 at least admits to having a museum in the basement of its headquarters building in London, and it uses the museum to provide material for its social media presence. However, as with the CIA museum, outsiders cannot visit it.[41]

The BND's visitor center in Berlin also reflects its country's political culture, one that strives to learn negative lessons from the intelligence systems of Nazi Germany and postwar East Germany. Accordingly, the service has a visitor center in Berlin open to the public and a web presence. The visitor center is eager to describe how the BND is democratically accountable. Its website states that, "during your 90-minute stay on site or in our virtual room, our colleague will explain the working methods and control mechanisms of the BND to you in a lecture."[42] It goes on to say that "we are aware of the special responsibility that intelligence services bear. That is why it is so important that our work and the use of intelligence resources are democratically controlled."[43]

Intelligence agencies understand that history is important to their ability to do their work well, so they tend to pay enduring attention to it. They also understand that history can help them maintain their standing and legitimacy in the eyes of the public. The public's attention to intelligence has tended to wax and wane over time. However, since 2001 intelligence has been prominently and persistently in the public eye in the United States and many other places. Even when they are exercising their right to protest particular actions of intelligence agencies, most citizens of democratic countries understand that those agencies help their government to better serve the people. They also understand that intelligence work done poorly can waste lives and money, cause political embarrassment, and even become a menace to the people. As citizens of democracies, their opinions and preferences shape government policies and actions. This means that intelligence history and the channels through which it can be learned, including museums, are important to a free and open society.

## Notes

We owe thanks to Vincent Houghton, Gregory Elder, and Daniel Lomas for providing useful information and insights that helped us write this conclusion.

1. Mark Bowden, *Killing Pablo: The Hunt for the World's Greatest Outlaw* (New York: Atlantic Monthly Press, 2001), 72–78.

2. Chris Fite-Wassilak, "Into the Ryanverse: Tom Clancy's Tom Clancy," *The Quietus*, February 12, 2022, https://thequietus.com/articles/31120-tom-clancy-jack-ryan-military-entertainment-complex; Martin Plimmer and Brian King, *Beyond Coincidence: Amazing Stories of Coincidence and the Mystery Behind Them* (New York: Thomas Dunne Books/St. Martin's Griffin, 2007), 150–51.

3. Benjamin Griffin, *Reagan's War Stories: A Cold War Presidency* (Annapolis: Naval Institute Press, 2022), 87–88, 90.

4. "First Principles," *The Sandbaggers*, Yorkshire Television, September 18, 1978.

5. Wesley Wark, "Wark: In Praise of John Le Carre, Master of the Spy Novel," *Ottawa Citizen*, September 22, 2017, https://ottawacitizen.com/opinion/columnists/wark-in-praise-of-john-le-carre-master-of-the-spy-novel.

6. Tom Secker, "CIA Documents on Assisting Patriot Games," *Spy Culture* (blog), August 29, 2015, www.spyculture.com/cia-documents-on-patriot-games.

7. Walter Hixson, "'Red Storm Rising': Tom Clancy Novels and the Cult of National Security," *Diplomatic History* 17, no. 4 (1993): 605–613.

8. Trevor McCrisken and Christopher Moran, "James Bond, Ian Fleming and Intelligence: Breaking Down the Boundary Between the 'Real' and the 'Imagined,'" *Intel-*

*ligence and National Security*, May 9, 2018, 806, https://doi.org/10.1080/02684527.2018.1468648.

9. Daniel W. B. Lomas and Stephen Ward, "Public Perceptions of UK Intelligence: Still in the Dark?," *RUSI Journal* 167, no. 2 (February 23, 2022): 11, https://doi.org/10.1080/03071847.2022.2090426.

10. *Casino Royale Bond Assessment—Stella Rimington*, International Spy Museum, video, 2014, www.youtube.com/watch?v=gE9lu23LT1Y.

11. Joel Rogers de Waal, "Public Opinion and the Intelligence Services," *YouGov UK* (blog), October 11, 2013, https://yougov.co.uk/politics/articles/7520-british-attitudes-intelligence-services?redirect_from=%2Ftopics%2Fpolitics%2Farticles-reports%2F2013%2F10%2F11%2Fbritish-attitudes-intelligence-services.

12. Amy Zegart, "How Fake Spies Ruin Real Intelligence," *Atlantic*, January 9, 2022, https://web.archive.org/web/20220119202214, www.theatlantic.com/international/archive/2022/01/how-fake-spies-ruin-real-intelligence/621187.

13. Kristian Gustafson, *Hostile Intent: U.S. Covert Operations in Chile, 1964–1974* (Washington, DC: Potomac Books, 2007), introduction.

14. Stephen Budiansky, "What's the Use of Cryptologic History?," *Intelligencer: Journal of U.S. Intelligence Studies* 18, no. 3 (Summer/Fall 2011): 29–30.

15. John Earl Haynes, Harvey E. Klehr, and Alexander Vassiliev, *Spies: The Rise and Fall of the KGB in America* (New Haven: Yale University Press, 2009), 18–27.

16. See, e.g., Ben Macintyre, *The Spy and the Traitor: The Greatest Espionage Story of the Cold War* (London: Viking, 2018); Ben Macintyre, *A Spy Among Friends: Kim Philby and the Great Betrayal*, 1st Broadway paperback ed. (New York: Broadway Books, 2014); Liza Mundy, *Code Girls: The Untold Story of the American Women Code Breakers of World War II* (New York: Hachette Books, 2018); Liza Mundy, *The Sisterhood: The Secret History of Women at the CIA* (New York: Crown, 2023).

17. Randy Burkett, "An Alternative Framework for Agent Recruitment: From MICE to RASCLS," *Studies in Intelligence* 57, no. 1 (2013): 7–17.

18. Vabamu, "About Us," https://vabamu.ee/en/about-us, accessed January 13, 2024.

19. Stiftung HSH, "About Us," www.stiftung-hsh.de/about-us, accessed January 13, 2024.

20. Gellért Rajcsányi, "Never Forget: 20 Years of Remembrance in the Museum of Terror," *Hungarian Conservative*, March 12, 2022, www.hungarianconservative.com/articles/current/never-forget-20-years-of-remembrance-in-the-museum-of-terror.

21. Mária Schmidt, ed., *Terror Háza, Andrássy Út 60.* (*House of Terror, Andrássy Út 60*) (Budapest: Public Endowment for Research in Central and East-European History and Society, 2003), 5.

22. "Spy Museum Celebrates 20th Anniversary by Looking Back at 20 Milestones," *International Spy Museum* (blog), July 19, 2022, www.spymuseum.org/press/press-archive/2022-press-releases/spy-museum-celebrates-20th-ann.

23. Christopher Andrew, *The Secret World: A History of Intelligence* (New Haven: Yale University Press, 2018).

24. Gerald Haines, "The CIA's Own Effort to Understand and Document Its Past: A Brief History of the CIA History Program, 1950–1995," *Intelligence and National Security* 12, no. 1 (January 1997): 201–223, https://doi.org/10.1080/02684529708432406.

25. Haines, "The CIA's Own," 205.

26. Nicholas Dujmovic, "Getting CIA History Right: The Informal Partnership be-

tween Agency Historians and Outside Scholars," *Intelligence and National Security* 26, nos. 2–3 (April 2011): 239–240, https://doi.org/10.1080/02684527.2011.559143.

27. Dujmovic, "Getting CIA History Right," 228.

28. Dujmovic, "Getting CIA History Right," 238.

29. David Remnick, "Going the Distance," *New Yorker*, January 19, 2014; Mark Mazzetti, "C.I.A. Study Says Arming Rebels Seldom Works," *New York Times*, October 15, 2014.

30. John Ferris, *Behind the Enigma: The Authorized History of GCHQ, Britain's Secret Cyber-Intelligence Agency* (New York: Bloomsbury, 2020).

31. Olav Riste, *The Norwegian Intelligence Service: 1945–1970*, Cass Series, Studies in Intelligence (London and Portland, OR: Frank Cass, 1999), ix–xi.

32. Christopher M. Andrew, *Defend the Realm: The Authorized History of MI5* (New York: Knopf, 2009); Keith Jeffery, *The Secret History of MI6* (New York: Penguin Press, 2010); Michael S. Goodman, *The Official History of the Joint Intelligence Committee* (London and New York: Routledge, Taylor & Francis Group, 2014); D. M. Horner, ed., *The Spycatchers: The Official History of ASIO, 1949–1963* (Sydney: Allen & Unwin, 2014); D. M. Horner, ed., *The Protest Years: The Official History of ASIO, 1963–1975* (Sydney: Allen & Unwin, 2016); John Charles Blaxland and Rhys Crawley, *The Secret Cold War: The Official History of ASIO, 1975–1989* (Sydney: Allen & Unwin, 2017).

33. Central Intelligence Agency, "Tour Policy," n.d., C06399222, CIA Freedom of Information Act Electronic Reading Room, www.cia.gov/readingroom/document/06399222.

34. Lomas and Ward, "Public Perceptions of UK Intelligence," 10.

35. Central Intelligence Agency, "CIA Museum," www.cia.gov/legacy/museum, accessed June 22, 2023.

36. *A Rare Look Inside the Newly Renovated CIA Museum, PBS News Hour*, 2023, www.youtube.com/watch?v=TTEf4XDXF9Q.

37. Central Intelligence Agency, "CIA Museum."

38. NSA, "National Cryptologic Museum | Cryptologic History," www.nsa.gov/museum, accessed June 22, 2023.

39. "National Cryptologic Museum | Cryptologic History."

40. Macintyre, *The Spy and the Traitor*, 330.

41. "MI5 Reveals 'secret to Successful Spying' in First Instagram Post," Sky News, https://news.sky.com/story/mi5-launches-instagram-account-to-reach-out-in-new-ways-12283358, accessed June 22, 2023; "MI5 on Instragram: 'This Is the Original Door Number for a Room That Served as MI5's Secret London Address,'" February 6, 2023, www.instagram.com/p/CoVFBJdNPNu; MI5, "MI5 on Instagram: 'MI5 Has Used Cameras to Support Our Work to Keep the Country Safe since before World War I. They Were Often Hidden in Unique Places. Take a Look at Some of the Cameras We Have on Display in the Secret MI5 Museum. #MI5 #HistoryatMI5 #KeepingTheCountrySafe #photography #camera,'" Instagram, March 24, 2023, www.instagram.com/reel/CqK0RzVNOLJ.

42. BND, "Unser Besucherzentrum," www.bnd.bund.de/DE/Der_BND/Besucherzentrum/besucherzentrum_node.html, accessed June 22, 2023.

43. BND, "Unser Besucherzentrum."

# About the Editors and Contributors

## Editors

Dr. Sarah-Jane Corke is Associate Professor at the University of New Brunswick. She is the cofounder and past president of the North American Society for Intelligence History, which is now the Society for Intelligence History. Her first book was *US Covert Operations and Cold War Strategy: Truman, the CIA, and Secret Warfare* (2008). Dr. Corke has also published articles in the *Journal of Strategic Studies*, *Intelligence and National Security*, *Journal of Conflict Studies*, *International Journal of Intelligence and Counterintelligence*, and *H-Diplo*. She is currently working on a dual biography of John Paton and Patricia Davies and a history of the Office of the Director of National Intelligence.

Dr. Mark Stout is retired from Johns Hopkins University's Krieger School of Arts & Sciences Advanced Academic Programs in Washington, DC, where he was a senior lecturer and directed the MA program in Global Security Studies from 2013 to 2021. He also directed the postbaccalaureate program in Intelligence from 2014 to 2019. A former intelligence officer, he served in the State Department's Bureau of Intelligence and Research and in the Central Intelligence Agency. From 2010 to 2013 he was the Historian and Curator at the International Spy Museum, and he was the founding president of the North American Society for Intelligence History. His book *World War I and the Foundations of American Intelligence* was published by the University Press of Kansas in 2023.

## Contributors

Dr. Alexis Albion was a Curator at the International Spy Museum, with a focus on Special Exhibits. Since 2014, she served as Lead Curator, responsible for conceptualizing and creating all new content for the museum's move to its current location at L'Enfant Plaza. She then moved on to provide overall content expertise that underlies all museum exhibitions, programs, and public and press inquiries. Dr. Albion served as a Professional

Staff Member for the 9/11 Commission from 2003 to 2004, where she was lead investigator on the CIA and lead writer for key policy sections of the commission's report. Dr. Albion served as Deputy Chief Strategist in the Office of the Coordinator for Counterterrorism at the US Department of State from 2006 to 2008 and as Assistant to the President of the World Bank Group from 2008 to 2012. She has a PhD in International History from Harvard University.

Gill Bennett, MA, OBE, FrHistS, has worked as a historian within the British government for over forty years, advising ministers and officials and publishing official accounts of foreign policy. She is a specialist in the history of secret intelligence, and her publications include studies on decision-making and on the interface of the intelligence world and policymaking.

Dr. Jonathan Best is a historian of modern Britain and Europe who has researched British and European intelligence studies, the history of British spy fiction, and British political history. He undertook his PhD at Queen's University Belfast under the supervision of Professor Keith Jeffery and Dr. Paul Corthorn, and he completed it in 2018. He has explored the reflective relationship between the British spy novel and British secret services from the late Victorian era until the Cold War.

Dr. Tony Craig is Associate Professor in Modern History at Staffordshire University, United Kingdom. His research focuses primarily on the contemporary security history of Britain and Ireland, with a particular interest in the role of intelligence in counterterrorism, parallel diplomacy, and propaganda.

Dr. Emil Draitser is Professor Emeritus of Russian at Hunter College of the City University of New York. He is the award-winning author of 17 volumes of scholarly and artistic prose, including *Stalin's Romeo Spy: The Remarkable Rise and Fall of the KGB's Most Daring Operative*; *Techniques of Satire*; *Shush! Growing Up Jewish Under Stalin*; and, most recently, *Laughing All the Way to Freedom: Americanization of a Russian Émigré*. His scholarly articles have appeared in the *Journal of Intelligence History*, *Studies in Comparative Communism*, *Gulag Studies*, *Slavic and East European Journal*, and other publications.

Dr. John F. Fox Jr. has been the FBI Historian since 2003. His articles have appeared in a number of journals, on the FBI's website, and in other venues. He has contributed chapters to several books and coauthored *The FBI: A Centennial History* (2008). Fox has been involved in several cooperative museum projects, including the temporary exhibition on the FBI and the media that was on display at the Newseum from June 2008 until June 2016. He has appeared in many documentaries in the United States and Europe, on C-Span, *CBS Sunday News*, CNN, Netflix, and Turner Classic Movies. He was awarded a PhD in modern American history from the University of New Hampshire in 2001 and an MA in political science from Boston College in 1993.

Dr. James L. Green, NASA's former Chief Scientist, has conducted research into Civil War balloon usage, as a passionate personal interest, for several decades. He served as an adviser on the Intrepid project, an initiative to construct and fly the world's first replica of a Civil War manned balloon at the Genesee Country Village & Museum in Mumford, New York. He also worked with the Civil War Trust by identifying locations of the balloon stations during the Peninsula Campaign for historic preservation and commemoration.

Dr. Jonathan Nashel is Professor of History at Indiana University South Bend. His writings include *Edward Lansdale's Cold War* (2005) and articles on the Vietnam War and the CIA. His current project, "'Darkness Visible': A Cultural History of the CIA," is a monograph-length work that examines how and why the CIA was ever-present in the lives of presidents and ordinary citizens since its formation in 1947. It contrasts the CIA's staid bureaucratic history with a multitude of imagined and fantastic narratives that dominate our understanding of the Agency.

Jack O'Connor directs and teaches in the Master of Science in Geospatial Intelligence program at Johns Hopkins University's Krieger School of Arts & Sciences Advanced Academic Programs. Previously, he spent nearly all his 31-year government career in geospatial intelligence and imagery analysis. During this time, he supported, managed, led, studied, and taught geospatial intelligence in CIA and Defense Department organizations. After retiring from the National Geospatial-Intelligence Agency, he wrote a cultural history of an important National Geospatial-Intelligence Agency predecessor organization, *NPIC: Seeing the Secrets, Growing the Leaders* (2015), and an explanation of the newest "int," *A Short Introduction to Geospatial Intelligence* (2023). A recipient of the Galileo Prize from the Office of the Director of National Intelligence and the National Intelligence Medal of Achievement, his current research involves the history and future of geospatial intelligence.

Amanda A. Ohlke is Director of Adult Education at the International Spy Museum. As a key member of the Spy Museum's creative team since 2004, she has worked on a many exhibitions and programs on topics ranging from Mata Hari to Civil War espionage to intelligence experts' perspectives on current events.

David Schaefer is Lecturer in the National Security College at the Australian National University. He was previously a Postdoctoral Research Fellow in the Department of War Studies at King's College London, where he worked as part of the King's Centre for the Study of Intelligence. He has a professional background in track 1.5/2 diplomacy.

David Sherman retired in 2017 after having served for 32 years at the National Security Agency. He also held positions on the staffs of the National Security Council and National Economic Council and represented the NSA at the Office of the Secretary of Defense and the Joint Chiefs of Staff. He was Dean of Academic Programs and Visiting Professor at the National War College from 2007 to 2010. Prior joining the government, he was a member of the Adjunct Faculty at Cornell University, where he taught for four years.

Anna Slafer served as Vice President of Exhibitions & Programs at the International Spy Museum's inception in 2002, establishing and managing the Exhibitions, Curatorial, Education, and Collections divisions. She oversaw the creation of the exhibitions for the new location at L'Enfant Plaza, which opened in May 2019, winning awards for label copy, films, and digital interactives. In 2023 she became the museum's Senior Creative Strategist, spearheading development of new national and international projects to expand the museum's brand and reach. In 2024 she left SPY to start her own business, Anna Slafer Creative, serving as a consultant to museums around the world. Prior to her work at SPY her career included a number of pioneering positions and projects, including serving as the founding Director of Education at the National Building Museum, codeveloper/manager of the first *Hands on History Room* at the Smithsonian Institution's National Museum of American History, and developer of *Rolling Rainforest*, an immersive mobile exhibition. Ms. Slafer has coauthored three award-winning educational publications, including the book *Why*

*Design?* Her work has appeared in professional journals such as the *Journal of Museum Education* and *Exhibitionist*. She is an Adjunct Lecturer with Johns Hopkins University's Master of Arts program in Museum Studies. She holds a BA in Geography/Conservation and Analysis of Ecosystems from UCLA and an MAT in Museum Education from George Washington University.

Cindy Storer is a former CIA analyst who spent the majority of her 20-year career at the Agency studying terrorism and related topics. After leaving the CIA in 2007, she contributed to intelligence- and terrorism-related education and training at the federal, state, and university levels. Currently, she is Adjunct Lecturer for Johns Hopkins University and the University of Texas at El Paso.

Dr. Wesley Wark is Senior Fellow at the Centre for International Governance Innovation. He has served as an adviser to successive Canadian governments on national security and intelligence matters and was appointed as an expert witness at the sentencing hearing for Jeffery Delisle. He is working on a book on spy leaks.

Dr. Silke Zoller is Assistant Professor of History at Kennesaw State University. Her research focuses on international security collaboration against terrorism and political violence in the second half of the twentieth century. Silke earned a PhD in History from Temple University in 2018 and previously held postdoctoral fellowships at the Clements Center for National Security at the University of Texas at Austin and at the John Sloan Dickey Center for International Understanding at Dartmouth College.

# Photo Credits

**Grayscale Images**

© Arcaid Images, 3368-40-1, Niall Clutton
Figure 0.2

© The Richard Avedon Foundation
Figure 2.7

Jonathan Best
Figures 3.1, 3.2

Getty Images
Figure 2.6

Ivan Harbour/RSHP
Figure 0.3

Sam Kittner for the International Spy Museum
Figures 0.1, 0.5

© Tina Krohn
Figures 9.4, 11.4

© Robert Lautman Photography, National Building Museum
Figure 0.4

Nic Lehoux, Courtesy of Rogers Stirk Harbour + Partners (RSHP)
Figure 0.6

Library of Congress
Figures 6.1, 6.2, 6.4

George C. Marshall Foundation, Lexington, Virginia
Figure 9.1

Seeley G. Mudd Manuscript Library at Princeton University
Figures 2.4, 2.5

National Archives and Records Administration
Figure 6.3

National Geospatial-Intelligence Agency
Figures 7.3, 7.4, 7.5

National Security Agency
Figures 9.2, 9.3

Emily Rens for the International Spy Museum
Figure 3.3

Franklin D. Roosevelt Presidential Library and Museum
Figure 12.3

Rogers Stirk Harbour + Partners (RSHP)
Figure 0.5

© Erik Sharar
Figures 8.1, 8.2, 8.3, 8.5, 15.5

Dan Treado for the International Spy Museum
Figures 1.1, 1.2, 1.3, 1.4, 1.5, 1.6, 1.7, 2.1, 2.2, 2.3, 2.8, 2.9, 3.4, 3.5, 4.1, 4.2, 4.3, 4.4, 4.5, 5.1, 5.2, 5.3, 5.4, 5.5, 6.5, 6.6, 6.7, 6.8, 7.1, 7.2, 7.6, 7.7, 8.4, 9.5, 10.1, 10.2, 10.3, 10.4, 10.5, 10.6, 11.1, 11.2, 11.3, 12.1, 12.2, 12.4, 12.6, 13.1, 13.2, 13.3, 13.4, 13.5, 13.6, 13.7, 13.8, 14.1, 14.2, 14.3, 14.4, 15.1, 15.2, 15.3, 15.4, 16.1

**Color Plates**

© Arcaid Images, 12357-250-1, Richard Bryant
Plate 2

© Arcaid Images, 11217-70-1, Richard Bryant
Plate 3

© Arcaid Images, 11645-70-1, Richard Bryant
Plate 4

Jonathan Best
Plates 23, 24

© 2002 Handshouse Studio, Inc.
Plate 6

Interspectral
Plate 69

Sam Kittner for the International Spy Museum
Plates 5, 109

© Tina Krohn
Plates 33, 55

Gordon Lau Photography
Plate 1

Nic Lehoux, Courtesy of Rogers Stirk Harbour + Partners (RSHP)
Plate 14

RodneyBailey.com
Plates 28, 92

D. A. Peterson Photography for the International Spy Museum
Plate 83

Ronald Reagan Library
Plate 104

© Erik Sharar
Plates 22, 28, 67, 71, 72, 75, 97, 125

Dan Treado for the International Spy Museum
Plates 9, 12, 13, 14, 15, 16, 17, 18, 19, 20, 21, 25, 26, 27, 29, 30, 31, 32, 34, 35, 36, 37, 38, 39, 40, 41, 42, 43, 44, 45, 46, 47, 52, 58, 59, 70, 76, 93, 94, 95, 96, 98, 99, 100, 101, 102, 103, 105, 106, 107, 110, 111, 112, 113, 114, 115, 116, 117, 118, 119, 120, 121, 122, 123, 124, 125, 126, 127, 128, 129, 130, 131, 132

© Albert Vecerka/Esto
Plates 7, 8, 10, 11, 68, 84, 85, 108

# Index

Italicized numbers indicate pages with grayscale figures.
Numbers preceded by "P" indicate color plate number.